D0216101

10-18-73

SOCIETY FOR NEW TESTAMENT STUDIES
MONOGRAPH SERIES

GENERAL EDITOR
MATTHEW BLACK, D.D., F.B.A.

ASSOCIATE EDITOR
R. McL. WILSON

21

PRE-EXISTENCE, WISDOM, AND
THE SON OF MAN

PRE-EXISTENCE, WISDOM, AND THE SON OF MAN

A STUDY OF THE IDEA OF PRE-EXISTENCE IN THE NEW TESTAMENT

BY

R. G. HAMERTON-KELLY

Professor of the New Testament
McCormick Theological Seminary, Chicago

CAMBRIDGE
AT THE UNIVERSITY PRESS
1973

Published by the Syndics of the Cambridge University Press
Bentley House, 200 Euston Road, London NW1 2DB
American Branch: 32 East 57th Street, New York, N.Y. 10022

Library of Congress Catalogue Card Number: 72–78890

ISBN: 0 521 08629 9

Printed in Great Britain
at the University Printing House, Cambridge
(Brooke Crutchley, University Printer)

For Rosemary, Ruth and Paul

1774196

CONTENTS

CONTENTS

PREFACE

The rationale of this endeavor is explained in the Introduction, and so a brief preface will be an opportunity to record some remarks of a more personal nature.

One's debts to teachers and colleagues are always great, but especially so in the case of the first book. My chief debt is to W. D. Davies, who guided my doctoral studies at Union Theological Seminary, in New York City, with great sensitivity and devotion, and who has been a source of encouragement and sound counsel to me ever since. During those years I also profited from the advice of John Knox and J. Louis Martyn, and, in the field of Old Testament, from James Muilenburg and Samuel Terrien. The foundation of my interest in Biblical Studies was laid by Leslie Hewson of Rhodes University in the Republic of South Africa, and nurtured by C. F. D. Moule, Hugh Montefiore and Ernst Bammel at Cambridge University. To all these men I owe more than can be expressed.

Most of this work was written in the stimulating atmosphere of Claremont, California. My colleagues and students in the Humanities at Scripps College provided the indispensable atmosphere of lively scholarship and broad humanistic interest, in which theology can live and breathe as a vital human concern. Colleagues and graduate students in the Institute for Antiquity and Christianity and at the Claremont Graduate School taught me the real meaning of the phrase 'a community of scholars'. To all these I express my gratitude.

Thanks are also due to the enlightened administration of Scripps College, who by manifold considerations made scholarly research by the faculty a part of normal academic existence; to the Ford Foundation which provided a summer stipend for this work, and to the administration of McCormick Theological Seminary for generous support in matters of typing and duplicating. To Dr R. McL. Wilson I express my thanks for careful and considerate editing.

More than all of these I owe my wife the sustaining encouragement and support without which nothing would have been accomplished. She also typed the manuscript.

With so rich a background of support and help my one regret is that the finished work is not more worthy of those who have contributed to it.

R. G. HAMERTON-KELLY

Easter 1971

ABBREVIATIONS

A. and P.	*The Apocrypha and Pseudepigrapha of the Old Testament,* ed. R. H. Charles (2 vols., Oxford, 1913)
Ab.T.A.N.T.	*Abhandlungen zur Theologie des Alten und Neuen Testaments*
Arb.L.G.H.	*Arbeiten zur Literatur und Geschichte des hellenistischen Judentums*
B.A.	*The Biblical Archaeologist*
B.A.S.O.R.	*The Bulletin of the American School of Oriental Research*
B.H.T.	*Beiträge zur historischen Theologie*
B.J.R.L.	*The Bulletin of the John Rylands Library*
C.B.Q.	*Catholic Biblical Quarterly*
C.H.	*Corpus Hermeticum – texts from Hermès Trismégiste,* ed. A. D. Nock and A. J. Festugière (Paris, 1960)
C.N.T.	*Commentaire du Nouveau Testament*
Ephem. Theol. Lov.	*Ephemerides Theologicae Lovanienses*
Ev.T.	*Evangelische Theologie*
F.R.L.A.N.T.	*Forschungen zur Religion und Literatur des Alten und Neuen Testaments*
H.N.T.	*Handbuch zum Neuen Testament*
H.-S.	Edgar Hennecke, *New Testament Apocrypha,* ed. W. Schneemelcher, E.T. ed. R. McL. Wilson (2 vols., Philadelphia, 1963 and 1965)
H.T.R.	*Harvard Theological Review*
I.D.B.	*Interpreter's Dictionary of the Bible*
I.Z.B.G.	*Internationale Zeitschriftenschau für Bibelwissenschaft und Grenzgebiete*
J.A.A.R.	*Journal of the American Academy of Religion*
J.B.L.	*Journal of Biblical Literature*
J.N.E.S.	*Journal of Near Eastern Studies*
J.T.S.	*Journal of Theological Studies*
L.N.T.	Walter Bauer, *Lexicon of the New Testament*
N.T.D.	*Das neue Testament Deutsch*
N.T.S.	*New Testament Studies*
Nov. Test.	*Novum Testamentum*
O.U.D.	*Oxford Universal Dictionary*

Philo's treatises are cited according to the abbreviations in F. H. Colson, *Philo,* Loeb Classical Library (12 vols., London, 1962), 10, xxxv–xxxvi

R.B.	*Revue Biblique*
R.G.G.	*Die Religion in Geschichte und Gegenwart* (Tübingen, 1913, 1930, 1961)
R.H.P.R.	*Revue d'Histoire et de Philosophie Religieuses*
R.S.P.T.	*Revue des Sciences Philosophiques et Théologiques*
S.B.T.	*Studies in Biblical Theology*
S.-B.	Hermann L. Strack and Paul Billerbeck, *Kommentar zum Neuen Testament aus Talmud und Midrash* (6 vols., Munich, 1926–56)
S.N.T.S.	*Studiorum Novi Testamenti Societas*
T.D.N.T.	*Theological Dictionary of the New Testament*, Kittel and Friedrich, trans. G. W. Bromiley
T.W.N.T.	*Theologisches Wörterbuch zum Neuen Testament* (German original ed. of the preceding)
Th.L.Z.	*Theologische Literaturzeitung*
T.H.N.T.	*Theologischer Handkommentar zum Neuen Testament*
Th.Stud.u.Krit.	*Theologische Studien und Kritiken*
T.Z.	*Theologische Zeitschrift*, Basel
V.T.	*Vetus Testamentum*
W.M.A.N.T.	*Wissenschaftliche Monographien zum Alten und Neuen Testament*
W.U.N.T.	*Wissenschaftliche Untersuchungen zum Neuen Testament*
Z.K.G.	*Zeitschrift für Kirchengeschichte*
Z.K.T.	*Zeitschrift für katholische Theologie*
Z.N.W.	*Zeitschrift für die neutestamentliche Wissenschaft und die Kunde der älteren Kirche*
Z.R.G.G.	*Zeitschrift für Religion und Geistesgeschichte*
Z.T.K.	*Zeitschrift für Theologie und Kirche*

INTRODUCTION

The precise subject of this book is not immediately evident from the title. In contemporary usage, 'pre-existence' signifies the idea that the individual soul existed before its life on earth. The idea is expressed in the various doctrines of pre-existence and metempsychosis, from Plato and the philosophies of the East, to Gnosticism and occultism, both ancient and modern. Our concern in this work is not limited to the pre-existence of the individual soul; it encompasses any person or thing thought of as existing before its own manifestation or before the creation of the world.

At the outset we are faced with a peculiar difficulty. It is not possible to define the term 'pre-existence' *a priori*. All that can be said *a priori* is that 'pre-existence' means 'existence before...'. The meaning of the term must be established *a posteriori* for every context in which it is used. Where the meaning of a term under consideration is not self-evident, one must proceed by proposing a hypothetical or working definition and refining it as the discussion develops. We shall follow this method.

Our difficulty arises from this need for a hypothetical or working definition. Such a definition should be based only on the texts; but, since the term itself never occurs in the texts, its distinctive content is not apparent from a preliminary survey. Our only recourse is to the work of scholars who have used the term before us.

Adolf Harnack[1] used 'pre-existence' to signify a theory held by 'the Ancient Jews and by all the ancient Semitic nations' that everything of real value which, at some time, appears on earth, exists in heaven perpetually.[2] This heavenly existence was of two kinds: most frequently the valuable entities were thought

---

[1] *Lehrbuch der Dogmengeschichte*, 2nd ed. (Freiburg i. B. 1888) I, 710–11.

[2] This emphasis on 'real value' probably derives from A. Ritschl's influence on Harnack. Pre-existence is not a metaphysical term but an axiological one. Cf. Heitmüller, *R.G.G.* IV (Tübingen, 1913) col. 1712: 'die Ueberzeugung von dem ewigen Wert und der schlechthinigen Gewissheit wichtiger religiöser Güter fand ihre Ausprägung in dem Glauben dass diese Güter vor aller Welt bei Gott vorhanden seien, um dann zu ihrer Zeit in die Erscheinung zu treten'.

to exist in God's knowledge, as part of his plan for the world; less frequently the entities were thought to exist in heaven, independently and in their own right.[1] The former type of pre-existence Harnack calls 'ideal'; the ideal entities are just as real as those existing in their own right. We suggest that the latter type of pre-existence be called 'actual'. We shall therefore use the terms 'ideal pre-existence' and 'actual pre-existence', regarding the entities in both types as equally 'real'.

Harnack's use of 'real' in connection with existence in the mind of God needs some explanation. Apparently he understands the texts to teach that there is a difference between the mind of God and the mind of man, so that, whereas in the mind of man things can exist only as ideas, in the mind of God they can and do exist with such a greater degree of reality than the ideas in a human mind that they can be said to have 'real' existence.[2] We are aware that there are many philosophical 'loose ends' in this brief statement, but Harnack can plead the exigencies of the texts themselves. One cannot be more precise than the evidence. Therefore, we accept as a working hypothesis the somewhat strange notion that things have real existence, before their manifestation on earth, in the mind of God. The reality of these things should probably be imagined by analogy with real things existing in the world. Some commentators describe this idea by means of the accurately paradoxical phrase 'ideal pre-existence'.[3]

We may, at this point, distinguish the meaning of 'ideal pre-existence' from that of 'predestination'[4] or 'fore-knowledge'. It would seem that 'ideal pre-existence' and predestination are

---

[1] E.g. Ex. 25: 9, 40, 26: 30, 27: 8; Num. 8: 4.

[2] Harnack, *Dogmengeschichte* I, 710.

[3] E.g. H. L. Strack and P. Billerbeck, *Kommentar zum Neuen Testament aus Talmud und Midrasch* (6 vols., Munich, 1926–61), II, 334–5 (cited henceforth as S.-B.), on 'Die ideelle Präexistenz des Messias in der Gedankenwelt oder in dem Weltplan Gottes...'. The term 'ideal pre-existence' goes back to A. Ritschl, who, in his dislike for the classical doctrine of the 'substantial' divinity of Christ spoke of the '"ideale" Präexistenz Jesu Christi im Ratschluss Gottes'; quoted from P. Althaus, *R.G.G.*[3] v, (Tübingen, 1961) col. 492.

[4] For a definition of predestination see: Paul Volz, *Die Eschatologie der jüdischen Gemeinde im neutestamentlichen Zeitalter*, 2nd ed. (Tübingen, 1934), p. 109; G. E. Mendenhall, *The Interpreter's Dictionary of the Bible, ad loc.*; R. Otto, *The Idea of the Holy* (London, 1959), p. 105.

the same thing. Both terms seem to describe the pre-existence of entities in God's mind. Harnack does not clearly distinguish 'ideal pre-existence' and predestination, therefore we venture to suggest a distinction of our own.

Entities – that is, persons or things – can be said to exist, but events are usually said to 'happen'. Therefore, only entities can be pre-existent. For events that are planned and known beforehand, 'pre-existence' is not an accurate description. The precise word for describing such events is predestination (or foreknowledge, or foreordination). We therefore suggest that 'ideal pre-existence' be used to describe *entities* which pre-exist in the mind or plan of God, and 'predestination' for *events that are known and planned* by him beforehand. We shall not be concerned with predestination in this work.

Therefore, if we follow Harnack, we must consider all texts which tell of God's planning things beforehand, and all which tell of entities existing in heaven.

Since Harnack, there has been no serious attempt, as far as we know, to delineate the structures or trace the history of the idea of pre-existence in the Biblical traditions. This does not mean that scholars have not used the term, especially in discussions of Christology; but it does mean that there has been a singular lack of clarity in their usage. We shall therefore consider the way in which selected representatives of modern scholarship have referred to or used the idea of pre-existence; but before we do that, some further discussion of Harnack's treatment is in order. This will lead us conveniently into the modern discussion.

Harnack's implication that 'value' was the impulse which led the ancient people to attribute pre-existence to certain objects, raises the question of the possible motive for this idea. Since most of the objects which were pre-existent were religious objects, it seems not unlikely that value had something to do with the development of the idea of pre-existence; but was it the only agent in the development of this idea? Harnack assumes that 'value' is the essence of the religious attitude; but this assumption does not seem to be entirely justified.

Mowinckel[1] is more judicious when he allows, in addition to the expression of value, that pre-existence probably also ex-

---

[1] S. Mowinckel, *R.G.G.*[2] (Tübingen, 1930), IV, col. 1384.

3   1-2

pressed the divinity or ultimacy of an entity in a 'substantial' sense (as in the case of Wisdom and 'Son of Man'), as well as the need for speculation and rational clarification (as in the case of the pre-existence of souls), on the part of the promulgators of the idea.

Fred B. Craddock,[1] in a somewhat cursory study, carries the discussion of the motives which gave rise to the idea of pre-existence so far that one may suspect that he sometimes has gone beyond the evidence. His intention is declaredly hermeneutical; he attempts to discover the 'meaning' or 'function' that the idea had for those who used it in the Biblical tradition, hoping thereby to recover some meaning for today. It is assumed that every time the category occurs it answers some felt human need. For instance, in apocalyptic circles it speaks to a sense of hopelessness about the course of history by pointing to a trans-historical ground of hope, or, in opposition to a 'gnosticizing' denial of the value of this world, in favor of a transcendent world, pre-existence also affirms that value by linking this world and the transcendent world. This, although Craddock does not perceive it, is precisely the reverse of the function that, he claims, pre-existence performs in apocalyptic. Instead of leading one from this world to the other, it brings one from the other into this. Thirdly, in answer to the Church's need to understand the continuity between itself and the people of the Old Testament, pre-existence binds the two testaments by means of the idea of the pre-existent Word who spoke in the prophets and was incarnate in Jesus.

What we miss in Craddock's work is a careful analysis of the structures and history of the idea of pre-existence, on which the judgements about its function are based. He does, in passing, distinguish various structures of the idea; for example, he refers to 'precreation' as distinct from 'preincarnation';[2] but there is no sustained attention to the phenomenology of the idea. Neither is there much consideration of the way in which the structure of the idea changed from one layer of the tradition to the other. His concentration on the function of the idea tends to overshadow his treatment of its history and changing form. But

---

[1] Fred B. Craddock, *The Pre-existence of Christ in the New Testament* (Nashville and New York, 1968), *passim*. See the review of this work by Robin Scroggs, in *J.A.A.R.* 37 (1969), 170–3.   [2] *Ibid.*, p. 113.

this is all consonant with his intention, which is somewhat anti-historical. He expresses dissatisfaction with 'the method of study which attempts to illuminate ideas by tracing them back to their sources.' He writes:

It is quite evident that it is not sufficient to ask of a passage that reflects the idea of pre-existence, What is its source? Even if the source were known, the same questions must be asked of the source that are asked of the text: What is the function of the idea of pre-existence within the context where it is found? How is pre-existence conceived in each particular affirmation?[1]

We have attempted to answer Craddock's last question, 'How is pre-existence conceived in each particular affirmation?' and we have tried to do so for all the layers in the New Testament tradition. We have not asked about the function of the idea, because we have not, as he has, conceived ours to be a direct attempt at interpretation. Craddock may be right in his claim that the 'function' of an idea illuminates its meaning, but that is a claim which presupposes a great deal about the nature of ancient and modern processes of understanding, and we simply have not been able to investigate the philosophic justification for such a method. Rather, we have followed the established procedure of historical and phenomenological analysis, in the confidence that this method still yields understanding.

Despite our criticism, we welcome Craddock's book as an important contribution to a neglected area in Protestant scholarship. Our own contribution, in addition to differing in method and intention, also differs in scope. Whereas he is concerned with the pre-existence of Christ only, we are concerned with the idea of pre-existence in itself, whatever person or thing it is attributed to. We hope that our contribution will take its place along with his work, and help to illuminate an important aspect of Biblical theology.

Recent attempts to define pre-existence agree that it involves and presupposes a whole view of reality. Beth,[2] writing in 1930, emphasized that it presupposes the existence of a world of reality not perceptible by the senses. He includes the Platonic world of ideas among the pre-existent entities. Ratschow,[3] in

---

[1] *Ibid.*, p. 27.
[2] *R.G.G.*[2] (Tübingen, 1930), IV, cols. 1382–3.
[3] *R.G.G.*[3] (Tübingen, 1961), V, cols. 490–1.

1961, maintains that pre-existence can be spoken of only within a context of discourse in which 'existence' is clearly defined as a time-bound category. Where there is no clear understanding of existence as temporal, and as distinct from a non-temporal essence, there can be no idea of pre-existence. It would appear, therefore, that pre-existence belongs in the realm of discourse which is concerned with the world of reality other than the sense-perceptible world, namely, in the realm of metaphysical discourse.

Contemporary Protestant Biblical scholarship, however, seems, on the continent at least, to interpret pre-existence in such a way as to minimize its reference to a metaphysical realm. The idea occurs exclusively in the discussion of Christology, and it is understood as describing an element in the experience of salvation.

R. Bultmann, for example, writes: 'To the extent that the statements about Christ's pre-existence and incarnation are of a mythological nature, they neither have the character of direct challenge, nor are they expressions of the faith that is surrender of "boasting". Yet in context within the proclamation they express a decisive fact: the origin and significance of Jesus' person and his fate are not within earthly occurrence, but God was acting in them and this action of his took place "when the fulness of time was come" (Gal. 4: 4).'[1]

The soteriological emphasis of this passage from Bultmann is clear. Pre-existence expresses the dimension of transcendence in the experience of responding to the Christian proclamation. Bultmann's view does not deal seriously with Christ as the mediator of creation. It seems arbitrary to assume, as he does, that the idea of pre-existence intends only to illuminate salvation, and not to say anything important about creation. It seems to be important for the theology of Paul, which is under consideration here, that the same power operative in the redemption was operative in the creation as well – and this seems to be a significant thing to say about the creation. We detect in this formulation of Bultmann's the influence of continental dogmatic theology, which, as Norman Pittenger reminds us,[2] tends to

[1] R. Bultmann, *Theology of the New Testament*, trans. Kendrick Grobel (2 vols., New York, 1951), I, 304–5.

[2] W. Norman Pittenger, *The Word Incarnate* (New York, 1959), p. 131. He writes, 'It appears to me that the line of thought which would suggest some

6

treat Christ as an alien intruder into a world with which he has no ontological connection.

The idea of Christ as one who 'breaks in' is even more dramatically stated by one of Bultmann's followers, Hans Conzelmann. He writes: 'That Jesus is not of worldly origin, but nevertheless is "born of a woman", means that salvation does not develop out of the world, say as the meaning and goal of world history. It is not a possibility immanent in the world, but *breaks in from outside* [our italics] and thus remains God's salvation. *Pre-existence thus means that salvation is founded on God's miraculous act* [our italics]; the word means the actualization of the prevenient salvation event and this describes the objective priority of God's act to my faith.'[1]

For these two commentators, therefore, pre-existence in Paul's theology describes an element in the historical experience of believing response to the proclamation. It designates the transcendent source of that experience, but it does not communicate anything about that source in its own essence. Since the language describing the pre-existent Christ is mythological, it is interpreted, according to Bultmann's well-known existentialist method, as an objective and therefore misleading presentation of subjective experience. As myth, it presents the existential phenomena of lived existence in this world, as a happening in another world.

It is not our purpose to discuss the general validity of this existentialist translation of myth. We shall be concerned, rather, to observe the history and structures of the 'myth' of pre-existence, and to leave it to the reader to decide whether, as far as can be judged, all forms of the idea are patient of the interpretation Bultmann suggests, or whether some other interest (we do not say 'function'!) is not served by the myth.

catastrophic intrusion, some entirely unprecedented down-thrust without parallel in any degree, makes nonsense both of the actual picture of Jesus in the gospels and of the experience of men in finding God in Jesus as their human Brother. At the same time it introduces a view of the relation of God and his world which I find both essentially unbiblical and thoroughly incredible in the light of our best knowledge.' See also pp. 132–45, where Pittenger expounds and criticizes Emil Brunner's Christology for precisely this view of the incarnation.

[1] Hans Conzelmann, *An Outline of the Theology of the New Testament* (New York, 1969), p. 201.

Oscar Cullmann proposes a view of the pre-existence of Christ that is similar in an essential respect to Bultmann's. The pre-existence of Christ in the New Testament does not

indicate unity in essence or nature between God and Christ, but rather a unity in the work of revelation, in the *function* of the pre-existent one.[1]

This seems to mean that the pre-existence of Christ is an element in the historical phenomenon of Jesus; some intuition, or aura, of his transcendence. Cullmann does allow that John 1:1 indicates some interest in the 'unity in essence or nature' between Christ and God, but this is peripheral, according to him, and is not developed.[2] Attacked by Roman Catholics[3] as advocating a Sabellian interpretation of the New Testament Christology by denying the essential and separate person of the Son, Cullmann insists that the 'function is personal in the incarnate Christ and in the pre-existent Christ',[4] but still refuses to allow that the New Testament has any interest in the nature of Christ in himself, apart from his soteriological function.

Although this accusation levelled against Cullmann is not entirely fair to the point of view expressed in the *Christology of the New Testament*, it is true that Cullmann leaves himself open to such attack. His point is valid, that the New Testament speaks of Christ on the basis of the experience of his work as Saviour, but he emphasizes it so much that one easily misses the few statements to the effect that Christ performs this work because of what he is in himself.[5] We have attempted to pay attention to the New Testament statements about the transcendent nature

---

[1] Oscar Cullmann, *The Christology of the New Testament*, trans. S. C. Guthrie and C. A. M. Hall (Philadelphia, 1959), p. 247. See the judicious discussion of Cullmann's 'functional' interpretation by R. H. Fuller, *The Foundations of New Testament Christology* (New York, 1965), pp. 247–50.

[2] Cullmann, *Christology*, pp. 248–9; cf. Conzelmann, *Outline*, pp. 343–44.

[3] E.g. L. Malevez, 'Functional Christology in the New Testament', *Theology Digest*, x (1962), 77–83.

[4] O. Cullmann, 'Functional Christology: A Reply', *ibid.*, p. 216.

[5] E.g. 'According to the witness of the whole Gospel tradition, the "Son of God" title as applied to Jesus expresses the historical and qualitative uniqueness of his relation to his Father.' (*Christology*, p. 275.) 'Like his consciousness of being Son of Man, Jesus' consciousness of being Son of God refers both to his person and to his work: his work of salvation and revelation shows that the Father and the Son are one.' (*Ibid.*, p. 290.)

of Christ, to see how they answer the question, Who is this that does these things? In this way the true balance of emphasis in the Christology of the New Testament may, we hope, be perceived.

Roman Catholic scholarship continues to take the view that the testimonies to Christ's pre-existence in the New Testament express his unity with God in essence.[1] It sees the mythological statements about Christ's pre-existence as a primitive, but nevertheless real, attempt to talk about the transcendent aspect of Christ's person.[2] The metaphysics of being, essence and existence, to which Catholic scholarship, for the most part, still subscribes, might be regarded as an alternative – and earlier – attempt at demythologizing, to the existentialist interpretation of Bultmann.

All the examples of the use of the term 'pre-existence' so far have come from the Christological discussion. The term is, however, also used in the discussion of Jewish apocalyptic. The idea that the things to be revealed in the eschaton already exist in heaven has been called a commonplace of apocalyptic thought.[3] Albert Schweitzer, in his great book on Paul, interpreted the apostle's thought consistently in the categories of Jewish apocalyptic. He concludes as follows:

The Pauline mysticism is therefore nothing else than the doctrine of the making manifest in consequence of the death and resurrection of Jesus, of the pre-existent Church (the community of God).[4]

The apocalyptic idea of pre-existence was often expressed by means of the term 'mystery' (μυστήριον) which referred to the

---

[1] E.g. Malevez, 'Functional Christology'; A. Grillmeier, 'The Figure of Christ in Catholic Theology Today', in *Theology Today*, vol. I, *Renewal in Dogma*, trans. P. White and R. H. Kelly (Milwaukee, 1965), pp. 66–108. An older, but still important treatment, of many of the texts discussed in this work of ours is J. Lebreton, *Histoire du Dogme de la Trinité des Origines au Concile de Nicée* (2 vols., Paris, 1927), I. Lebreton shows the Catholic interest in 'substantial' pre-existence and its importance for the doctrine of the Trinity.

[2] Mircea Eliade, *The Myth of the Eternal Return*, trans. W. R. Trask (New York, 1954), believes that mythology is a primitive form of ontology.

[3] By Norman Perrin, *Rediscovering the Teaching of Jesus* (New York, 1967), p. 171, and Morna D. Hooker, *The Son of Man in Mark* (Montreal, 1967), pp. 42–3, cf. pp. 25 and 29.

[4] Albert Schweitzer, *The Mysticism of Paul the Apostle*, trans. W. Montgomery (London, 1931), p. 116.

hidden pre-existent things. In connection with this term, and on the basis of the apocalyptic scheme entailing pre-existence in general, recent Catholic scholarship has delineated a doctrine of the pre-existence of the Church in the New Testament.[1] We hope to show that this is, indeed, an important form of the idea of pre-existence in the New Testament, although we have reservations about the methodology of the Catholic scholarship we have consulted.

Erik Sjöberg[2] attempted a consistent interpretation of the Messianic witness of the gospels, from the self-understanding of Jesus to the most obviously interpretative layers of the Johannine tradition, in terms of the apocalyptic idea of the hidden, pre-existent Son of Man. Beginning with the phenomenon of the 'Messianic secret' in Mark, he argues that there is a consistent understanding in all the major layers of the Synoptic tradition of Jesus as the hidden, pre-existent Son of Man, revealed only to 'those who have ears to hear'. The parables are mysterious presentations of Jesus' dignity, solved only by a few; the miracles, likewise, are misunderstood by most, but seen by the few as revelations of Jesus' pre-existent nature. There is much in Sjöberg's book that is illuminating, chiefly because it has been neglected by most recent scholarship, but there is also much that seems to us forced and untenable. A most telling point made against Sjöberg, by H. E. Tödt,[3] is that there is no precedent in the apocalyptic Son of Man traditions for the concealment of that heavenly figure on earth, and that it is doubtful procedure to use the idea of concealment in heaven to explain the rejection of Jesus as the concealment of the Son of Man on earth. A more general criticism that might be made is that Sjöberg overestimates the clarity of profile and the extent of influence of the figure of the Son of Man in Jesus' time. Furthermore, Sjöberg's zeal for his apocalyptic scheme in the gospels causes him to overlook other possible influences. His interpreta-

[1] E.g. M. J. Le Guillou, O.P., *Christ and Church, A Theology of the Mystery*, trans. C. E. Schaldenbrand (New York, 1966); L. Cerfaux, *The Church in the Theology of St. Paul*, trans. G. Webb and A. Walker (New York, 1959).

[2] Erik Sjöberg, *Der verborgene Menschensohn in den Evangelien*, Acta Reg. Societatis Humaniorum Litterarum Lundensis, LIII (Lund, 1955).

[3] H. E. Tödt, *The Son of Man in the Synoptic Tradition*, trans. Dorothea Barton (Philadelphia, 1965), pp. 297–302.

tion of Matt. 11: 19 par. Luke 7: 34–5[1] is seriously awry, because he has neglected the presence of a 'Wisdom' tradition in
this text, and in Q as a whole.

Nevertheless, Sjöberg's insistence that Jesus' use of the term
'Son of Man' does entail the idea of pre-existence, and, accordingly, reveals something important about his self-conscious-
ness, is a valid emphasis.[2] Our investigations will suggest that
Sjöberg is essentially right at this point, and that H. E. Tödt,
who stridently and repeatedly denies that the idea of pre-
existence is present in any layer of the Synoptic Son of Man
tradition, cannot be followed on this point. However, the idea
of the hidden, pre-existent Son of Man seems to us a much
smaller element in the total picture of Jesus in the gospels than
Sjöberg claims, and many of the features he attributes to
apocalyptic influence most probably derive from a 'Wisdom'
tradition. The matter is more complicated than he suggests.

On the basis of the foregoing, we may propose the following
preliminary definition of pre-existence. *'Pre-existence' is a
mythological term which signifies that an entity had a real existence
before its manifestation on earth, either in the mind of God or in heaven.*

This definition, based inductively on the actual use made of
the term in modern scholarship, covers the heart of the idea; but
we must also consider the *a priori* logically possible forms it
might take. On this definition the entity is said to *pre*-exist
because it exists with God *before* its *own* manifestation. But there
could be entities which were thought to have existed before the
manifestation of anything at all, that is, before the creation of
the world. (The Logos of the Gospel of John is an actual
example of this type.) There are also entities which could have
been thought to have existed before creation but whose manifestation on earth was never expected. (The Throne of God in the
Rabbinic tradition is an actual instance of this type.) A working
definition must, therefore, include at least four types of 'existence before...': (1) one in which an entity exists before its own

---

[1] *Verborgene Menschensohn*, p. 181. However, H. E. Tödt's strident denials
of any hint of pre-existence in this text, in the course of his criticism of Sjöberg, are not, in our opinion, accurate either (*Son of Man*, p. 301).

[2] *Verborgene Menschensohn*, pp. 243–4. He does, however, acknowledge that
the idea of pre-existence has faded into the background because of the emphasis in the teaching of Jesus and the gospel traditions on the end of things.

manifestation but not before the creation; (2) another in which an entity exists before its own manifestation and before the creation; (3) a third in which an entity exists before the creation but is not necessarily manifested at all; (4) and a fourth in which things simply exist in heaven, without reference to creation or manifestation. We shall see whether these logically entailed forms are also actually present in the texts.

Our definition assumes a doctrine of creation according to which this world began to be at a point in time, and that it is possible to use such phrases as 'before Creation'. It also assumes an image of time as a line with a beginning. It is well known that early Judaism held such a doctrine of creation and the point needs no proving here.[1] It is well established also that it included, amongst others, such a view of time.[2]

With these working definitions in mind, we turn to the Biblical texts. We trust they will enable us to recognize what we are looking for when we see it. We have tried to proceed inductively, simply allowing the texts in all their variety to speak for themselves; but, of course, as the need for a working hypothesis shows, such totally free induction is not possible to human

[1] See G. E. Wright, 'Schöpfung im Alten Testament' in *R.G.G.*[3] *ad loc.* J. Bonsirven, *Le Judaïsme Palestinien au temps de Jésus-Christ: Sa Théologie,* 2nd ed. (2 vols., Paris, 1934), I, 162 ff.

[2] There has been considerable debate about the Biblical and early Jewish image of time. One side of the debate is represented by: O. Cullmann, *Christ and Time: The Primitive Christian Conception of Time and History,* rev. ed., with a new introductory chapter (London, 1962); G. Delling, *Das Zeitverständnis des Neuen Testaments* (Gütersloh, 1940). They emphasize the linear image of time which they claim is the antithesis of any Platonizing interpretation of Biblical time and eternity. The other side is represented by J. Marsh, *The Fulness of Time* (New York, 1962); and T. Boman, *Hebrew Thought Compared with Greek* (Philadelphia, 1960). They emphasize the non-linear nature of Biblical time and its similarity to Platonic ideas of time and eternity.

J. Barr, *Biblical Words for Time* (London, 1962), criticizes the methodology of these works, and shows that most of the debate springs from the misunderstanding of the evidence.

W. Eichrodt, 'Heilserfahrung und Zeitverständnis im Alten Testament', in *Theologische Zeitschrift,* XII (1956), 103–25, and N. H. Snaith, 'Time in the Old Testament' in *Promise and Fulfilment,* ed. F. F. Bruce (Edinburgh, 1963), pp. 175–86, give accounts of the Biblical idea of time which transcend the differences between the views represented by Cullmann and Marsh respectively, and show that the linear image of time is well attested.

beings. Therefore, as the working hypothesis changes into a definite thesis in the course of the investigation, so it begins to function, for the subsequent study, as a source of deduced judgements. We hope, however, that this has not led us to torture the evidence, but rather has resulted in that intimate embrace of theory and fact which is genuine understanding.

A final note on our method seems in order: as we have already said, we have attempted to ascertain the history and structures of the idea, rather than its 'function' or meaning. In order to do this we have simply followed the texts in the approximate order of their occurrence, and attempted to see what emerged from them by way of induction. We have in general tried to avoid systematic arrangement of the material because, it seems to us, such arrangement too often pre-determines the results of the investigation. Therefore, although in the New Testament pre-existence features in Christology and Ecclesiology, we have not arranged our discussion under those headings.

Furthermore, we have, as far as possible, avoided basing any analysis on single words, not even on the so-called 'Christological titles'. An analysis based on 'words' tends, in our opinion, to lift the concept under discussion out of the actual written contexts in which it occurs, and to treat it as if it existed timelessly, in a world in which there is a changeless correlation between word and concept.[1] We have chosen the less tidy, but we hope more honest, way of trying to understand the idea within the tradition in which it occurs, and then to trace its path from one layer of tradition to another. What we have sacrificed in elegance of presentation, has been offered to accuracy of argument. Our comfort is that lived history is seldom elegant.

---

[1] On this subject see J. Barr, *Biblical Words for Time*, and *The Semantics of Biblical Literature* (Oxford, 1961).

PRE-EXISTENCE IN EARLY JUDAISM

The idea that certain things pre-exist in the mind of God or in heaven has a long history in the Biblical and early Jewish traditions. Knowledge of this history is essential for an understanding of the idea of pre-existence in the New Testament. Our first task, therefore, is to summarize the relevant material in these traditions. We have set out elsewhere the discussion on which this summary is based.[1]

In the pre-exilic religion of Israel the theology of 'promise and fulfilment' entailed the idea that the things promised pre-existed in God's mind. While the incident of Abraham's bargaining with God for Sodom and Gomorrah in Gen. 18: 17–33 shows that the details of God's purpose are contingent on man's response, the ultimate goal of that purpose, to judge the cities, remains unalterable. In the Balaam oracles the prophet Balaam is said to have seen the future Israel (Num. 24: 16–17).[2] He cannot curse Israel, because God has blessed him (Num. 23: 8, 18) and already Israel exists in God's mind in that state of blessedness. Balaam saw this blessed Israel of the future in God's mind. The status of this object of Balaam's vision is very elusive; but the suggestion that Israel pre-exists in God's mind is present. In any case, a pattern of thinking is evident which is the basis for the later development of this idea.

In Deuteronomy the 'name' of God is the agency through which God is present in the temple (Deut. 12: 21, 14: 24). Although the idea of God's revealing himself by his name is present elsewhere in the Old Testament (Ex. 20: 24, 23: 21, Is. 30: 27), 'the assumption of a constant and almost material presence of the name at the shrine' is new. The 'name' in

---

[1] R. G. Hamerton-Kelly, *The Idea of Pre-Existence in Early Judaism, A Study in the Background of New Testament Theology*, unpublished dissertation, University Microfilms (Ann Arbor, Michigan, 1966), Order number 66–11,546.

[2] W. F. Albright, 'The Oracles of Balaam', *J.B.L.* 63 (1944), 207–33. H.-W. Kuhn, *Enderwartung und gegenwärtiges Heil: Untersuchungen zu der Gemeindeliedern von Qumran, S.U.N.T.* 4 (Göttingen, 1966), pp. 11, 170.

Deuteronomy is a definite conception with a definite function, unlike the idea of the 'name' in other Old Testament sources, and according to von Rad, 'it verges closely upon a hypostasis'.[1] This is an important foreshadowing of the later idea of pre-existent hypostases.

The visions of the prophets (Is. 6, Jer. 1, Ezek. 1) anticipate the flowering in apocalyptic thought of the conception of the heavenly world which contains the pre-existent things, and which the chosen seers are able to visit. In the Psalms there are further references to the heavenly world (Ps. 139: 8, 103: 19) as well as a suggestion that there is a corresponding relation between things in heaven and things on earth (Ps. 11: 3-4, cf. Jer. 25: 30).

Another point of interest in the Psalms is the celebration of the future kingship of God as if it were an accomplished fact. This occurs in the 'enthronement psalms', as they are called by Mowinckel (Pss. 47, 93, 95, 96, 97 and 81).[2] Mowinckel discerns in these psalms a 'sacramental moment' which is also the epiphany of Yahweh and 'the experience of an all-embracing "now" that includes the future – "the eternal now"'.[3] The future victory of God is a present reality in this experience, and the same pattern of thought as in the Balaam oracles is thereby evident.

By means of three ideas, therefore, – the presence of the future, the 'name' as a quasi-hypostasis, and the heavenly world – the religion of Israel provided points of contact for the later ideas of pre-existence in Judaism.

After the exile Palestinian Judaism produced three major traditions – the priestly, the apocalyptic, and the 'wisdom'. Each of these developed at least one of the ideas mentioned above. The priestly tradition used the idea of the heavenly world; apocalyptic thought combined with the heavenly world the idea of the presence of the future; and the wisdom tradition developed the idea of the hypostasis. We shall consider each one in turn.

[1] G. von Rad, *Studies in Deuteronomy*, trans. D. Stalker (London, 1953), pp. 37-44.
[2] S. Mowinckel, *The Psalms in Israel's Worship*, trans. D. R. Ap-Thomas (2 vols., New York and Nashville, 1962), I, pp. 106 ff.
[3] *Ibid.*, p. 187.

The P source is essentially an account of the revealing of eternal ordinances.[1] It reaches a climax in the account of the revelation of the tabernacle at Sinai (Ex. 25–31). The tabernacle is a heavenly entity, which God reveals to Moses on the mountain. Moses is commanded to construct a copy of the heavenly model (Ex. 25: 9, 40, 26: 30, 27: 8, cf. Num. 8: 4, I Chron. 28: 11–19, Ez. 43: 10–12).[2] The idea of the shrine as a heavenly entity probably came from a Canaanite sanctuary which was taken over, along with its cultic ideology, by the Israelites during the conquest. The idea was developed by the priests of Jerusalem probably under the influence of the Tyrian builders of Solomon's temple.[3] The idea, therefore, is an old one in the religion of Israel; it is only in the post-exilic P source, however, that the idea becomes a controlling one in a particular tradition.

The eschatological hope of the prophets came together with the priestly idea of heavenly entities to form the ground-plan of apocalyptic thought. Ezekiel and his circle were the catalysts for this reaction.[4] In the eschatological hope the future could be treated as if it were present. When this idea of the present future is combined with the idea of heavenly entities, the result is that the entities to be revealed in the future pre-exist now in heaven. This is the fundamental structure of apocalyptic thought.

The most important pre-existent entity in the apocalyptic literature is the Son of Man (I En. 46: 1–3, 48: 1–7). The objection made by T. W. Manson that the Son of Man did not pre-exist, but only his name,[5] has been convincingly answered in subsequent scholarship.[6] The Son of Man came into being

---

[1] C. R. North, *The Old Testament Interpretation of History* (London, 1946), pp. 110–11; M. Noth, *Überlieferungsgeschichtliche Studien*, 2nd ed. (Tübingen, 1957), p. 209.

[2] Harnack, *Dogmengeschichte*, I, p. 711; M. Noth, *Das zweite Buch Moses: Exodus, A.T.D.* 5 (Göttingen, 1959), pp. 162–3.

[3] These conclusions are based on, but not attributable to: K. Koch, *Die Priesterschrift von Exodus 25 bis Leviticus 16* (Göttingen, 1959); Menahem Haran, 'Shiloh and Jerusalem: The Origin of the Priestly Tradition in the Pentateuch', *J.B.L.* 81 (1962), 14–24.

[4] R. G. Hamerton-Kelly, 'The Temple and the Origins of Jewish Apocalyptic', *V.T.* 20 (1970), 1–15.

[5] 'The Son of Man in Daniel, Enoch and the Gospels', in *Studies in the Gospels and Epistles*, ed. M. Black (Philadelphia, 1962), p. 136.

[6] E.g. J. A. Emerton, 'The Origin of the Son of Man Imagery', *J.T.S.*, N.S. 9 (1958), 225–6; H. L. Jansen, *Die Henochgestalt* (Oslo, 1939), pp. 86–7;

before the creation (I En. 48: 6) and now exists in heaven, waiting to be revealed in the last times. The explicit statement that he existed before the world is an important new element in the idea of pre-existence in apocalypticism. The relationship of the pre-existent entities to creation was not originally a concern in apocalypticism. It thought only of their pre-existence before the end.

Another variation of the idea in apocalypticism is present in II Bar. 4: 2–7. The temple and the city of Jerusalem were already built when God made paradise, and were visible to Adam. After Adam's sin, however, they were removed to heaven, along with paradise, and are being kept there. It is not stated explicitly that the heavenly Jerusalem will be revealed in the end, but that may be inferred from the wider teaching about the New Jerusalem (e.g. IV Ezra 7: 26, 8: 52, Rev. 3: 12, 21: 2). These entities exist before their manifestation in the eschaton, but not before creation. They pre-exist in their own right, outside the mind of God. We have called this idea 'actual' pre-existence.

There is also in apocalypticism the idea of things pre-existing in the mind of God. The idea that everything takes place according to God's plan is central to the apocalyptic outlook (I En. 9: 3, 39: 11, Ass. Mos. 1: 12–14, 12: 4). The whole creation exists in the mind of God before it takes place (1 Q.S. 3: 15–17, 1 Q.H. 1: 19–20). This idea is similar to Philo's concept of the noetic world, which we shall consider shortly, and provides an important point of contact between apocalypticism and Jewish platonism. We have called this idea 'ideal' pre-existence, as Harnack suggested.

The contents of God's plan is called 'the mystery' or 'mysteries' (1 Q.M. 14: 4, Dan. 2: 19, 28–9), and the knowledge given the seer is a revealing of mysteries.[1] These mysteries are sometimes thought of as written on heavenly tablets (I En. 81: 1–3, 93: 2, 103: 2–3). The idea of the plan of God written on heavenly tablets, could have contributed to the development of the later rabbinic idea of the (written) Torah as the pre-existent

M. Black, 'The Son of Man in Recent Research and Debate', *B.J.R.L.* 45 (1963), 305–18.

[1] R. E. Brown, 'The Pre-Christian Semitic Concept of "Mystery"', *C.B.Q.* 20 (1958), 417–43; G. Bornkamm, *T.D.N.T.* 4, 802–27.

instrument or plan of creation (e.g. Ber. Rabb. 1 : 1); however, the main contributor to that development was the Wisdom tradition.

In the apocalyptic texts, therefore, actual and ideal pre-existence are present. There is also a twofold relation between the pre-existent entities and the creation. Some exist before the creation (the Son of Man), some subsequent to creation (the heavenly Jerusalem). The Son of Man pre-exists both creation and his eschatological manifestation; the heavenly Jerusalem only pre-exists its manifestation. We must decide, in due course, how these types of pre-existence should be classified; but only after we have considered all the evidence.

It is well known that the figure of Wisdom was a pre-existent (before the creation), personified being in early Judaism.[1] In Job 28 Wisdom is an uncreated, independent entity, which God used as the regulative principle in creation. Wisdom is not a person; it is fully subordinated to God's will. The four verbs in verse 27 describe God's appropriation of Wisdom for his purpose of creation: He 'saw it', 'declared' or 'probed' it, 'established' it and 'searched it out'. Wisdom, therefore, was something independent which God confronted when he began to create.

In Prov. 8: 22–30, Wisdom is personified and, again, takes part in the activity of creation. Verses 24–6 probably reflect the influence of the myth of the creation of the first man, and suggest that in the process of Wisdom's personification that myth played a part.[2] However, the influence of a foreign goddess, rival to Yahweh, probably played the major part in shaping the figure of personified Wisdom. Ashtarte[3] and Isis have both been suggested, and most recent scholarship seems to favor the latter.[4]

---

[1] H. Ringgren, *Word and Wisdom* (Lund, 1947). There is a useful presentation of the Wisdom myth in all its stages in Felix Christ, *Jesus Sophia, Ab. T. A.N.T.* 57 (Zürich, 1970), pp. 156–63, in five tables.

[2] W. Schencke, *Die Chokma (Sophia) in der jüdischen Hypostasen-Spekulation* (Kristiania, 1913), pp. 17 ff; B. Gemser, *Spruche Salomos* (Tübingen, 1963), pp. 47–8.

[3] G. Boström, *Proverbiastudien* (Lund, 1935); O. S. Rankin, *Israel's Wisdom Literature* (Edinburgh, 1936), pp. 229–30; H. Ringgren, *Word and Wisdom*, pp. 134, 138.

[4] C. Kayatz, *Studien zu Proverbien 1–9*, *W.M.A.N.T.* 22 (Neukirchen/Vlyn, 1966); B. L. Mack, *Logos und Sophia*, unpublished dissertation, Göttingen, 1967; H. Conzelmann, 'Die Mutter der Weisheit', *Zeit und Geschichte*, ed. E. Dinkler and H. Thyen (Tübingen, 1964), pp. 225–34.

In Sir. 24: 1–29 the same figure appears, but this time she seeks a dwelling among men, and is commanded by God to dwell with the people of Israel (verse 7). She is then identified as the Torah (verse 22). Another version of this form of the myth occurs in I Enoch 42, where, unable to find any dwelling among men, Wisdom returns rejected to heaven. In the Palestinian Wisdom traditions,[1] therefore, Wisdom pre-existed, actually, before the creation.

This Wisdom tradition was developed further by the rabbis and the hellenistic Jews respectively. Amongst the rabbis Wisdom was identified with the Torah. That this identification was made by the Tannaim can be seen from Aboth 3: 14, which is attributed to R. Akiba (d. 137): 'Beloved (of God) are Israel, for to them was given the desirable instrument; (but) still greater was the love since it was made known to them that to them was given the desirable instrument wherewith the universe was created.'[2] Altogether there were seven pre-existent things in the opinion of the Tannaim – Torah, repentance, Eden, Gehenna, the throne of glory, the Temple, and the name of the Messiah (Pes. 54a, Ned. 39b).[3] These all have actual pre-existence, we may assume, since, later, when the influence of Platonism makes it necessary to distinguish actual and ideal pre-existence the rabbis do so explicitly (Ber. Rabb. 1: 4).

While amongst the Tannaim Wisdom became Torah, amongst the Alexandrian Jews she became Logos. This is evident to us in the writings of Philo (Leg. All. I, 65; II, 86; Quod Det. 116–19; Quaes. Gen. IV. 97, etc.).[4] Philo transforms Wisdom thereby from an actual to an ideal entity. The Logos is the container of the κόσμος νοητός which is a world of ideas (Op. 20, Quaes. Gen. IV, 48). Although the noetic world is said to be 'older than' the world of sense perception (Quod Deus 31–2), that is merely metaphorical, since the noetic world is not subject to time in any way. The proper understanding of the relationship between the noetic and the sense-perceptible worlds is as model to copy (Op. 16).

---

[1] See further 11 Q. Ps.ª xvii, I Bar. 3: 9–4: 4; IV Ezra 5; II Bar. 48.

[2] P. Blackman, *Misnayoth* (6 vols., New York, 1965), IV, pp. 512–13.

[3] See also *S.-B.* II, 353–7.

[4] H. Wolfson, *Philo* (2 vols., Cambridge, Mass., 1962), I, pp. 253–82; E. R. Goodenough, *By Light, Light, The Mystic Gospel of Hellenistic Judaism* (New Haven, 1935), p. 23.

This Platonic interpretation is probably Philo's own. There were, however, other more 'literal' interpretations of the world beyond sense-perception prevalent in the Hellenistic synagogues, and some of them are present in Philo's works. E. R. Goodenough[1] and J. Pascher[2] believe that they can detect a 'light mysticism' in Philo, in texts like Quaes. Ex. II, 62–8, which included the notion of a pleroma of seven heavenly beings. Pascher is more inclined to understand these mythologically, as actual heavenly entities, than Goodenough. If, as is likely, one or another of the traditions in Philo's synagogue understood these entities to be actual, the same alternative ideas of pre-existence as are present in the apocalyptic tradition would be present in the Hellenistic synagogues – actual and ideal pre-existence. In any case, however, the dominant type of pre-existence in Philo is 'ideal'.

There are, therefore, four distinctions that have to be made in the idea of pre-existence, on the basis of the evidence from early Judaism: 'ideal' and 'actual', 'before creation' and 'before manifestation'. 'Ideal' and 'actual' distinguish respectively pre-existent entities which exist within or alongside the mind of God. We suggest that 'protological' and 'eschatological' be used respectively of entities which pre-exist creation on the one hand, and their own manifestation, on the other.

[1] *By Light, Light.*

[2] G. Pascher, *Der Königsweg zu Wiedergeburt und Vergottung bei Philon von Alexandreia, St. z. Ges. u. Kul. d. Alt.*, vii/3–4 (Paderborn, 1931).

CHAPTER 2

PRE-EXISTENCE IN THE SYNOPTIC TRADITION

In the Synoptic tradition the idea of pre-existence is always implied, never discussed explicitly. The two elements in the tradition which seem to imply pre-existence most clearly are the themes of Wisdom and the Son of Man. We shall therefore concentrate our attention on these themes as they occur in the different layers of the tradition.

I. Q

Before we take up the concepts of Wisdom and the Son of Man, certain preliminary considerations about the nature of Q as a whole will ease the way of understanding.

W. D. Davies has shown, by careful argument, that Q is dominated by a sense of eschatological crisis.[1] Its teaching was preserved and handed down not in catechetical channels but rather,

The Church had preserved a tradition of the ethical teaching of Jesus which it regarded as *in itself part of the crisis wrought in his coming*. To put it yet more forcibly, *this teaching itself helped to constitute that crisis*...[it] was preserved not merely as catechetically useful, and not only as radical demand, but as revelatory: it illumines the nature and meaning of the coming of the Kingdom as demand, which is the concomitant of the coming of the Kingdom as grace.[2]

Such an understanding of ethical material could take place only as a result of:

the moral enthusiasm of the earliest Christians, the 'first fine careless rapture' of a community which confronted and dared the impossible...[3]

---

[1] W. D. Davies, *The Setting of the Sermon on the Mount* (Cambridge, 1964), pp. 366–8. There is a good review of the opinions about Q in modern scholarship in H. E. Tödt, *The Son of Man in the Synoptic Tradition* (Philadelphia, 1965), pp. 234–6.

[2] Davies, *Sermon on the Mount*, p. 384.   [3] *Ibid.*

The crisis of the old order and the inauguration of the new are achieved by the coming of Jesus and so are focused in the figure of Jesus himself.[1] Q, therefore, presents the person of Jesus as the one who, by means of his teaching, brings the present world to judgement and inaugurates the new. The community which produced Q was one in which eschatological hope and moral enthusiasm ran high.

Bultmann, on the other hand, draws attention to the similarity in form between many of the sayings of the Lord in Q and the Meshalim of the Wisdom-tradition.[2] He describes Jesus, from the point of view of these sayings, as a 'Wisdom-teacher'. The similarity between these 'words of the Lord' and proverbs from the Wisdom tradition, coupled with the evidence of Luke 7: 18–35 and 11: 31 and 49ff., led Bultmann to the idea that a Wisdom myth lay behind the understanding of Jesus expressed in these sayings, and in the prologue to the gospel of John.[3]

J. M. Robinson has recently attempted to identify a genre of religious literature, corresponding to Q, which may be called the 'Wise-words' genre.[4] Several examples, such as the gospel of Thomas and the Pirke Aboth, are extant.[5] He believes he has identified a genre of literature about Jesus unlike the gospels of the canon,[6] which lacked any reference to the passion, and re-

[1] *Ibid.*, p. 382.

[2] *Die Geschichte der synoptischen Tradition* (Göttingen, 1961), pp. 73ff.; cf. J. M. Robinson, ' ΛΟΓΟΙ ΣΟΦΩΝ: Zur Gattung der Spruchquelle Q', in *Zeit und Geschichte*, p. 78. Cf. G. Quispel, 'The Gospel of Thomas and the "Gospel of the Hebrews"', *N.T.S.* 12 (1965–6), 371–82.

[3] Robinson, 'Spruchquelle', R. Bultmann, 'Die religionsgeschichtliche Hintergrund des Prologs zum Johannes-Evangelium', *Eucharisterion*, *F.R.L.A.N.T.*, Neue Folge 19 (2 vols., Göttingen, 1923), II, 3–26.

[4] The German equivalent to our term 'genre' or 'type' is 'Gattung'. Robinson suggests that we all use this terminology to refer to collections of material, and reserve the word 'form' for the individual units within a genre. He follows Conzelmann in this, and precise discourse must follow him ('Spruchquelle', p. 77 n. 3).

[5] *Ibid.* The *Pirke Aboth* does not, however, present itself as the work of one figure in the same way as the Gospel of Thomas. See W. D. Davies, 'Reflexions on Tradition: The Aboth Revisited', in *Christian History and Interpretation*, Studies presented to John Knox, ed. W. R. Farmer, C. F. D. Moule and R. R. Niebuhr (Cambridge, 1967), pp. 127–59.

[6] Cf. H. Köster, 'One Jesus and Four Primitive Gospels', *H.T.R.* 61 (1968), 203–47, who argues that there were four types of 'gospel' about Jesus in the earliest church. (See pp. 90–91 below.)

ferred very little, if at all, to the physical activity of Jesus. Jesus' words are his deeds.

Elsewhere, Robinson has spoken of Q as 'a book of the acts of Spirit Sophia'.[1] He suggests, somewhat tentatively, that this might have been the sort of tradition about Jesus that the Corinthian opponents of Paul, in I Cor. 1–4, had known, and which influenced the development of their Christology.[2] Q, as Robinson sees it, begins with the 'Word of God' coming upon John (Luke 3: 2),[3] whose teaching is presented immediately thereafter; then the 'Spirit' descends on Jesus (Luke 3: 22) and his teaching is presented. The relationship between John and Jesus, and their mutual rejection by Israel, is discussed (Luke 7: 18–33) and they are both identified as 'children of Sophia' (Luke 7: 35). Like their master, the disciples have no home (Luke 9: 57–60), and they are on a mission (Luke 10). The 'finger of God' which is at work in Jesus' exorcisms (Luke 11: 20) is the Spirit which aids the disciple when he suffers persecution (Luke 12: 12);[4] it is given in response to prayer (Luke 11: 13). The wisdom of Solomon and the preaching of Jonah are comparable to the power operating in Jesus (Luke 11: 49). If this power is the Spirit (= Wisdom) present in Jesus, then the blasphemy against the Spirit would be the single most serious sin, from Q's point of view (Luke 12: 10). Thus Robinson argues that Q understands Jesus as the manifestor of the power of the Spirit, which, in turn, has been identified with Wisdom.[5]

There is a significant agreement between Davies and Robin-

---

[1] 'Basic Shifts in German Theology', *Interpretation* 16 (1962), 76–97, 83.

[2] A close examination of I Cor. 1–4, however, shows that the understanding of the heretical Christology in I Cor. 1–4, which Robinson inherits from U. Wilckens' *Weisheit und Torheit*, *B.H.T.*[26] (Tübingen, 1959), is not beyond doubt. See pp. 112 – 23 below.

[3] The inspiring of the prophets with the 'Word of God' was traditionally the work of the Spirit in Early Judaism; cf. C. K. Barrett, *The Holy Spirit and the Gospel Tradition* (London, 1958), pp. 108–9.

[4] In the Old Testament 'Priestly' tradition, 'Spirit of God' and 'Finger of God' were interchangeable terms. Cf. R. G. Hamerton-Kelly, 'A Note on Matt. 12: 28 par. Luke 11: 20', *N.T.S.* 11 (1964–5), 67–9.

[5] On the identification of Spirit with Wisdom in early Judaism, and on the whole subject of Wisdom in the Synoptic tradition, see M. Jack Suggs, *Wisdom, Christology and Law in Matthew's Gospel* (Cambridge, Mass., 1970), especially p. 54. He cites Is. 11: 2, I Enoch 49: 3, Wisd. 1: 6–7, 7: 22, 9: 17 as examples of this identification; cf. Felix Christ, *Jesus Sophia*.

son on the nature of Q: it is not a catechetical source; rather, its interest is Christological. Q expresses a lofty understanding of the person of Christ; Davies believes that it identifies his person and teaching as the eschatological hinge of the ages, the judgement upon the old and the inauguration of the new; Robinson prefers to emphasize the elements in Q which suggest that Jesus' person was interpreted in terms of the Wisdom myth.[1] A reconsideration of the text in the light of these two positions shows that both the eschatological note and the Wisdom myth are important in Q's Christology.

At the outset it is useful to recall two aspects of the Wisdom mythology which are of special importance for the synoptic tradition: (i) the saving activity of Wisdom[2] and (ii) the relationship between Wisdom and the primal man. Then we shall go on to examine (iii) the role of the Wisdom myth in Q.

Prov. 1: 20–30 presents Wisdom as a street preacher:

Wisdom cries aloud in the street;
   in the markets she raises her voice...
How long, O simple ones, will you love being simple?
Give heed to my reproof;
   behold, I will pour out my thoughts on you;
I will make my words known to you.
Because I have called and you refused to listen,
I have stretched out my hand and no one has heeded,
   and you have ignored my counsel
   and would have none of my reproof,
I also will laugh at your calamity;
I will mock when panic strikes you
   when panic strikes you like a storm...
Then they will call upon me, but I will not answer;
   they will seek me diligently but will not find me...[3]

The appeal of Wisdom is apparently made in the face of some impending disaster, since she warns those who reject her that they cannot expect any aid from her 'when panic strikes like a storm'. The chief elements in this passage are: (a) pre-existent

---

[1] He follows Bultmann's basic orientation, first set forth in 'Die religionsgeschichtliche Hintergrund'. See also Suggs, *Wisdom, Christology and Law*, pp. 5–29, on Q. He supports Robinson's view.

[2] Cf. Bultmann, 'Die religionsgeschichtliche Hintergrund', pp. 6–11.

[3] R.S.V. translation. Cf. Bultmann, *ibid.*, pp. 9–10. See also Suggs, *Wisdom, Christology and Law*, pp. 39–42, on Wisdom's saving activity.

Wisdom comes to man offering him herself; (b) men reject her; (c) rejection of Wisdom means that men must face an impending catastrophe without aid; it is implied that acceptance of Wisdom would have saved men in the coming evil. There is a certain similarity between the structure of the ideas here, and those in Luke 12: 8–9 (par. Matt. 10: 32–3).

And I tell you, every one who acknowledges me before men, the Son of Man [Matt. has 'I' instead of 'Son of Man'] also will acknowledge before the angels of God; but he who denies me before men will be denied [Matt. has 'I also will deny'] before the angels of God.

Because men reject Wisdom when she offers her aid before the catastrophe, she will reject their pleas for aid after the catastrophe has begun; those men who deny the Son of Man in this world he will deny in the final judgement.[1] It would be premature to say that there is an eschatological view expressed in Prov. 1: 20–32, but to a reader with thoughts of the imminent end on his mind, like an early Christian, it would read like an account of how pre-existent Wisdom came as a street preacher to warn men of impending doom, was rejected, and now waits to vindicate herself in the eschatological judgement.

Sirach 24: 7ff. portrays the role of Wisdom in the history of salvation:

> With all these [i.e. the creation] I sought a resting place,
> And [said], In whose inheritance shall I lodge?
> Then the creator of all things gave me a commandment,
> And he that created me fixed my dwelling place [for me],
> And he said: Let thy dwelling place be in Jacob,
> And in Israel take up thine inheritance... (24: 7–8)

The implication in this passage is that Wisdom could find no place to dwell in all creation, excepting Israel; the creation rejected her. In Israel she took up her abode, and she is identified with Torah (verse 23). Enthroned on Zion she invites all men:

> Come unto me ye that desire me,
> And be ye filled with my produce. (24: 9)[2]

---

[1] Bultmann, *Geschichte*, p. 117, classifies Luke 12: 8 par. Matt. 10: 32ff. as a 'threat'. As such it belongs with the prophetic literature; but the similarity in content with Prov. 1: 20ff. shows that it belongs to a tradition in which 'prophecy' and 'Wisdom' are both at home. Cf. Jer. 7: 1–17, 17: 19–27, 22: 1–5, 25: 1–13, B. L. Mack, 'Logos und Sophia', p. 38.

[2] Cf. Prov. 9: 4, Matt. 11: 28ff.

and she is mentioned in connection with the primal man and the last man:

> The first man knew her not perfectly,
> So also the last will not trace her out.   (24: 28)

Bultmann calls Sir. 24: 1–11 a 'self-revelation' of Wisdom; he sees the same 'form' in I Baruch 3: 9 – 4: 4, which tells of Wisdom being rejected by men (3: 11–13), but calling them to repent and accept (3: 9, 4: 2). The theme of the rejection of Wisdom is explicit in I Enoch 42: 1–2, where she returns to heaven, having failed to find an earthly dwelling place.

Wisd. Sol. 7: 27–8 tells how Wisdom, in her saving activity, finds temporary lodging in various special men.

She is but one, yet can do everything; herself unchanging, she makes all things anew; age after age she enters into holy souls, and makes them God's friends and prophets, for nothing is acceptable to God but the man who makes his home with wisdom.

In Wisd. Sol. 1: 4–7, Wisdom is identified with the Spirit of God, and Wisd. 10: 1ff. is largely an account of Wisdom's saving activity through pivotal historical figures from Adam to Moses. One may compare Wisd. 7: 27–8 with the following statement from the 'gospel of the Hebrews' as Jerome preserves it in his commentary on Isaiah (IV, on Is. 11: 2).

And it came to pass when the Lord was come up out of the water, the whole fount of the Holy Spirit descended upon him and rested upon him [cf. Is. 11: 2, 62: 1] and said to him: My Son, in all the prophets I was waiting for thee that thou shouldest come and I might rest in thee [cf. Sir. 24: 7]. For thou art my rest [cf. Ps. 132: 14]; thou art my first-begotten Son [cf. Ps. 2: 7, Luke 3: 22d, Mk. 1: 11, Exod. 4: 22, Jer. 31: 9, Col. 1: 15, Hebr. 1: 6] that reignest for ever [cf. Ps. 89: 29ff., Luke 1: 33].[1]

In all of these texts Wisdom comes to seek a dwelling place among men, in order to bestow her gifts; she is rejected by most men; but some accept her (cf. John 1: 11–13). In the text from the 'gospel of the Hebrews', Wisdom is identified with the Holy

---

[1] Text in *Edgar Hennecke, New Testament Apocrypha*, ed. W. Schneemelcher, E.T. ed. R. McL. Wilson (2 vols., Philadelphia, 1963) (cited H.-S.). For a similar concept in Philo see E. R. Goodenough, *By Light, Light*, and in particular, Philo, *De Abrahamo*.

Spirit (cf. Wisd. 1: 4–7), with which Jesus is endowed, and this Spirit–Sophia is precisely what Robinson, on internal grounds, sees as the dominant Christological endowment in Q.

Sir. 24: 28 suggests that there was some connection between Wisdom and the primal man. The author denies a relationship between the two; this suggests that he is aware of a view which either identified them, or related them very closely. There are clear traces of such a view in the tradition.[1] In Sir. 17: 1–14, there is a passage which suggests that wisdom is a natural endowment of created man.[2] In Job 15: 8 the primal man is pictured in the council of the gods before the world was made, listening as Wisdom came to speech from the divine mouths. In Prov. 8: 24–6, fragments of the 'man' myth occur in a passage dealing with pre-existent Wisdom – like the man of Job 15: 8, Wisdom is said to have been 'brought forth before the hills'. I Enoch 42: 1–2 occurs in the context of passages concerning the Son of Man, and there is much talk of his wisdom.[3]

However, there is no clear evidence in pre-Christian Judaism that Wisdom was ever identified with the Son of Man, as one 'person' is identified with another. W. D. Davies has shown that the well-known passages in I Enoch 48: 1–7, 49: 2–3 (etc.) do not identify the two figures.[4] Nevertheless these passages, together with the other evidence we have seen, show that the Son of Man is the possessor of 'divine wisdom' in the highest degree. He is *the* wise man. We must recognize a frequent association of the figures of Wisdom and the Son of Man. How Q

---

[1] See p. 19 above.

[2] B. L. Mack, 'Logos und Sophia', pp. 15–17.

[3] Cf. J. Muilenburg, 'The Son of Man in Daniel and the Ethiopic Apocalypse of Enoch', *J.B.L.* 79 (1960), 197–209. A. Feuillet, 'Le Fils de l'Homme de Daniel et la tradition biblique' (suite) *R.B.* 60 (1953), 321–46, and the criticism of this position by J. Coppens, 'Le messianisme sapiential et les origines littéraires du Fils de l'Homme daniélique', *Wisdom in Israel and the Ancient Near East*, Suppl. to *V.T.* 3 (Leiden, 1955) pp. 33–41. Suggs, *Wisdom, Christology and Law*, pp. 48–55, accepts the evidence of a close association between Wisdom and the Son of Man, although he does not seem to believe that the two figures were ever identified.

[4] W. D. Davies, *Paul and Rabbinic Judaism, Some Rabbinic Elements in Pauline Theology*, 2 (London, 1955), pp. 158–62, carefully denies H. Windisch's thesis ['Die Weisheit und die paulinische Christologie' in *Untersuchungen zum Neuen Testament* (Leipzig, 1912), pp. 220ff.] that Wisdom and the Messiah were identified in pre-Christian Judaism.

understands this association and what it means for his Christology, must now be considered.

(a) *Luke 9: 58, par. Matt. 8: 20*

Foxes have holes, and the birds of the air have nests; but the Son of Man has nowhere to lay his head.

Bultmann suggests that this was originally an old Wisdom saying which the tradition changed into a saying of Jesus.[1] Its form is clearly aphoristic, and one could hear traces of the theme of Wisdom's rejection and homelessness (Sir. 24: 7, I Enoch 42), if one reads it against the background of the Wisdom tradition.

It is difficult, at this point in the exposition, to explain the precise meaning of this saying. It brings together the theme of homelessness on earth and the name of the 'Son of Man'.[2] We shall, therefore, note the hint of a possible identification of the Son of Man with Wisdom here, by means of the attribute of homelessness, common to both. In the myth Wisdom is homeless on earth; in this saying the Son of Man is homeless. May we draw the conclusion that the Son of Man in this saying is to be identified with Wisdom?

At this point such a conclusion would be premature. We must consider more evidence.

(b) *Luke 7: 33–5 par. Matt. 11: 18–19*

For John the Baptist has come eating no bread and drinking no wine; and you say, 'He has a demon'. The Son of Man has come eating and drinking, and you say, 'Behold, a glutton and a drunkard, a friend of tax collectors and sinners!' Yet wisdom is justified by all her children.

[1] *Geschichte*, pp. 27–8. Cf. Philo, Abr. 31: 'A Sophos has no house or kinsfolk or country, save virtues and virtuous actions'. We take the second clause to be Philo's own moralizing interpretation of a tradition represented by the first clause.

[2] Bultmann, *ibid.*, p. 27 n. 3, argues that 'Son of Man' is in this case an erroneous substitute for 'man-in-general', as compared to the animals. Whatever it may have meant originally, Q understood 'Son of Man' in this saying to be a title of Jesus with a special meaning. Tödt, p. 133, argues that the element of homelessness intends to express the 'all-embracing claim' of discipleship and not to illustrate the humiliation of the Son of Man. We disagree; the reference to discipleship seems to be a secondary application of a primarily Christological statement.

This is Luke's version; Matthew differs only inconsequentially, excepting in the last sentence. The last sentence in Luke reads: καὶ ἐδικαιώθη ἡ σοφία ἀπὸ πάντων τῶν τέκνων αὐτῆς (7: 35); while that in Matt. reads: καὶ ἐδικαιώθη ἡ σοφία ἀπὸ τῶν ἔργων αὐτῆς (11: 19). Suggs[1] regards the Lukan version as the original Q form. His reasons, set out in a note, seem persuasive.

There is an obvious allusion in this text to the activity of Wisdom in the history of salvation through the prophets and wise men.[2] We are faced with the question whether Jesus and John, as two 'prophets' in the series by which Wisdom manifested herself in history,[3] are on the same level of importance, or whether Jesus is accorded any precedence in Q. Suggs understands both John and Jesus to be envoys of Wisdom, and although the attribution of the title 'Son of Man' to Jesus

subordinates John to Jesus, we may not assume that for Q the title takes Jesus out of the line of Wisdom's children. He like John before him, like the prophets before John, is sent by Wisdom – the heavenly revealer who retains her priority even over the Son of Man. Jesus and John stand as the eschatological envoys of Wisdom. Their position in relation to the eschaton gives them special status: John is Elijah, Jesus is the Son of Man. They, like the emissaries who preceded them, are rejected. It would thus appear that this section of Q has been so constructed as to find its summation in the concluding logion, in which – as Bultmann argued long ago – the phrase 'children of wisdom' designates the Baptist and Jesus as envoys of Wisdom, as prophets.[4]

This is a very helpful summary of the teaching of this pericope. While Jesus is distinguished as the final envoy of Wisdom by the title 'Son of Man', he remains, with John, an envoy of Wisdom. He is not identified with pre-existent Wisdom herself. However, although John is given a high position in Q – as one of Wisdom's prophets – Jesus is even higher; he is the one in whom, to use the words of the 'gospel of the Hebrews', Wisdom found her 'rest'.

In this saying, therefore, the theme of the rejection of Jesus by

---

[1] Suggs, *Wisdom, Christology and Law*, p. 33 and especially p. 35 n. 9.
[2] *Ibid.*, pp. 33–48.
[3] *Ibid.*, pp. 21–4, 33–6, 39–44.   [4] *Ibid.*, pp. 54–5.

this world is associated with the title 'Son of Man' and the tradition of the rejection of Wisdom's envoys.[1]

(c) *Luke 11: 49–51 par. Matt. 23: 34–6*

Therefore also the Wisdom of God said, 'I will send them prophets and apostles, some of whom they will kill and persecute', that the blood of all the prophets, shed from the foundation of the world, may be required of this generation, from the blood of Abel to the blood of Zechariah, who perished between the altar and the sanctuary. Yes, I tell you, it shall be required of this generation.

Matthew omits the opening statement, 'Therefore also the Wisdom of God said...' and by so doing makes Jesus the speaker. If, as is generally assumed, the Lukan version of Q is nearer the original than the Matthean, the question is whether Matthew has simply made explicit what Q was able to assume, namely, that the 'Wisdom of God' is Jesus, or whether in identifying Jesus with Wisdom he is taking a new step.[2] Suggs has reviewed the possible interpretations of this passage quite conveniently.[3] The use of the aorist εἶπεν (Luke 11: 49), rather than the present, excludes the possibility that Q intends this as a direct word of Jesus, who is identified as the divine 'Wisdom'.[4] Wisdom said this in the past, and Jesus is 'repeating', as it were, what Wisdom said. Most probably this is an oracle spoken by personified Wisdom in some pre-Christian tradition.[5] It also seems that Wisdom spoke this oracle before the foundation of the world, as a declaration and a prophecy about the nature of her revelation to men and the fate of her messengers. This is evident from the future tenses of the verbs.[6]

In its present form the saying is a warning or threat to the contemporary generation, that the long history of the rejection

---

[1] Cf. Wisd. 2, where the wise man is portrayed in terms of the 'suffering servant' of Is. 53. M. J. Suggs, 'Wisdom of Solomon 2: 10–5: A Homily based on the Fourth Servant Song', *J.B.L.* 76 (1957), 26–33. For a discussion of the theme of the rejection of the prophets in the other traditions of Judaism besides the Wisdom tradition, see O. H. Steck, *Israel und das gewaltsame Geschick der Propheten, W.M.A.N.T.* 23 (Neukirchen, 1967).

[2] Bultmann, *Geschichte*, p. 119. He believes the saying is a citation from a lost document, and was originally spoken by Wisdom.

[3] Suggs, *Wisdom, Christology and Law*, pp. 13–29, especially pp. 17–20.

[4] *Ibid.*, p. 18.   [5] *Ibid.*, p. 19–20.

[6] *Ibid.*, p. 21.

of God's prophets is about to come to an end, in the present actualization of the retribution incurred by all previous generations. The prophets who have perpetually been rejected are Wisdom's – those whom she made 'friends of God and prophets' (Wisd. 7: 24). Now she announces the end and the judgement.

We find together in this text the themes of personified Wisdom, the chain of prophets, their rejection by men, and the eschatological judgement. The title 'Son of Man' is missing. Instead there is the note of eschatological judgement. The Son of Man in I Enoch is predominantly associated with the eschatological judgement. We can only conjecture that the idea of the Son of Man may be implied in this reference to judgement. Jesus does not, in this saying, seem to be identified with Wisdom, but he is the last, judgement-bringing prophet in Wisdom's line, the one who announces that this generation will be required to answer for the blood of the prophets. Matthew, however, by his alteration of the introduction to make it an 'I' saying of Jesus, and his alteration of the tenses from future to present, clearly identifies Jesus and pre-existent Wisdom.

(d) *Luke 13: 34–5 par. Matt. 23: 37–9*

O Jerusalem, Jerusalem, killing the prophets and stoning those who are sent to you! How often would I have gathered your children together as a hen gathers her brood under her wings, and you would not! Behold, your house is forsaken! And I tell you, you will not see me until you say, 'Blessed is he who comes in the name of the Lord.'

Bultmann argues that the order in Matthew, where this saying occurs immediately after the one we have just left, represents Q's order.[1] One cannot be certain; but the fact that the two sayings occur together in Matthew shows that some part of the early tradition – either Q or Matthew – understood the present saying to be part of the Wisdom tradition. Bultmann is probably right in regarding it as a fragment of the words of pre-existent Wisdom, like those in Matt. 23: 34–6.[1] It continues the threat against 'this generation'. Wisdom is about to withdraw

---

[1] *Geschichte*, pp. 120–1.

[2] *Ibid.* Also, Suggs, *Wisdom, Christology and Law*, p. 67. Suggs believes that Q presented it as a saying of pre-existent Wisdom, but that he did not identify Christ with that Wisdom.

altogether from the world, rejected by men; she will return when the Messiah comes (Matt. 23: 39, Luke 13: 35). Her withdrawal seems to be the judgement;[1] it leaves Jerusalem 'forsaken and desolate'. Once again the question whether Jesus is identified with Wisdom in this saying is relatively easily answered for the Matthean layer of the tradition. In view of the step taken by Matthew in the preceding pericope, the answer is affirmative. For the Q layer things are more difficult: Luke puts the saying on the lips of Jesus, and, therefore, portrays him as personified Wisdom. Suggs would have us believe that 'Luke, of course, improperly attributes it to Jesus',[2] but this is not as much a matter of course as he believes. Why would Luke, who has no interest in identifying Jesus with Wisdom, as far as one can tell from the rest of his work, have made the identification here? One possible answer is that this is what he found in Q, that Q had Jesus speaking the lament of pre-existent Wisdom. This is not more than a possibility, however; the Lukan attribution of this saying to Jesus at this point could serve Luke's own literary interest.

(e) *Luke 11: 29–32 par. Matt. 12: 38–42*

This is an evil generation; it seeks a sign. And no sign shall be given it excepting the sign of Jonah. For as Jonah was a sign to the Ninevites so shall the Son of Man be to this generation. The queen of the south will arise in the judgement with the men of this generation and condemn them. For she came from the ends of the earth to hear the wisdom of Solomon, and, behold, a greater than Solomon is here. The men of Nineveh shall arise in the judgement with this generation and shall condemn it, because they repented at the preaching of Jonah, and, behold, a greater than Jonah is here.

This is an extraordinarily difficult passage to interpret. Tödt suggests that the Son of Man saying might be a riddle.[3] As the passage stands, it seems that the second saying – about the queen of the south and Jonah – explains the first. In answer to the question, What is the sign of Jonah? Q explains that it is his preaching of repentance to the Ninevites.[4] The logic of the

---

[1] That means that the return is not for judgement but for salvation, as the joyous, 'Blessed be he that cometh in the name of the Lord' suggests.

[2] Suggs, *ibid.*, p. 67 n. 15. [3] Tödt, p. 53.

[4] Matthew's explanation in 12: 40 is secondary, having developed later in

33

argument is: Sign of Jonah = Preaching of Jonah; Sign of the Son of Man = preaching of Jesus.[1] It seems that one should complete the syllogism and conclude: the Son of Man = Jesus. The preaching of Jesus is the Sign of the Son of Man understood, by comparison with Jonah's preaching, as a call to repentance. In the preaching of Jesus the Son of Man calls men to repent. Therefore Jesus is the Son of Man on earth.[2]

Tödt, however, rightly emphasizes that the Son of Man is spoken of in the future tense, 'so shall...' He believes that this makes it impossible to regard the Son of Man in this saying as one already acting in the present.[3] He explains the 'sign of the Son of Man' as both the teaching of Jesus in the present, and the future judgement of the Son of Man, which 'will make this generation repent...but this acknowledgement will come too late'.[4] This interpretation fails to explain why the proclamation of the eschatological judge – the future Son of Man – should be compared to the prophetic preaching of repentance; especially if, as Tödt agrees, that repentance would be too late.

We prefer to see the Son of Man in this saying as Jesus, in his function as a preacher of repentance. He is greater than Jonah because in his preaching men encounter the summons of the eschatological judge. On their response to the Son of Man now depends their status in the judgement. The future judgement takes place in the present, in the preaching of Jesus.[5] On this view, the future tense (ἔσται) referring to the Son of Man should

the tradition; thus E. Schweizer, 'Der Menschensohn', *Z.N.W.* 50 (1959), 200. In the same way we must regard the reference to 'the Sign of the Son of Man' in Matt. 24: 30 as the product of Matthew's own apocalyptic tradition. The understanding of the sign as Jesus' preaching of repentance, present in Q, is more primitive than either.

[1] So also Tödt, p. 53.

[2] So also Schweizer, 'Menschensohn'.

[3] Tödt, p. 53 n. 4.   [4] *Ibid.*, p. 53.

[5] Cf. E. Kaesemann, 'Sentences of Holy Law in the New Testament' in *New Testament Questions of Today*, trans. W. J. Montague (Philadelphia, 1969), pp. 66–81. He argues that precisely this present experience of the judgement happened in the prophetic expressions of judgement in the early Church. He writes: 'For while the judgement which they (the prophets) announce applies to the whole world, it is yet addressed most immediately to those who, as members of the Christian community, know themselves to be determined by such a future, and, precisely for that reason, to be standing today "before the face of Christ" as the Judge of all' (p. 68).

be taken in a general sense to refer to the ministry of Jesus; to describe it as still lying ahead of him, both in part of its historical duration, and in the revelation of its significance, as the eschatological call to repentance issued by the Son of Man.

At this point, however, the important thing to recognize is that the Son of Man on earth is described as greater than Solomon and Jonah. The messages of these two ancient divine envoys – wisdom and prophecy respectively – are taken up into and surpassed by the preaching of Jesus. Jesus, as the Son of Man on earth, is the fulfilment of the self-revelation and approach of God to men in the wise men and prophets. He is not, however, identified as pre-existent Wisdom herself; he is, rather, her final envoy.

Suggs argues that in Q Jesus was not identified with preexistent Wisdom; that he was, rather, one of Wisdom's envoys.[1] Does the evidence we have considered confirm this judgement? In (a) (Luke 9: 58 par. Matt. 8: 20) we found the name of the Son of Man linked with Wisdom by means of the theme of homelessness on earth, explicitly attributed to the Son of Man in the text of Q, and part of Wisdom's fate in the Jewish tradition. In the contexts of both gospels the saying is attributed to Jesus, who is identified, thereby, with the Son of Man.

In (b) (Luke 7: 33–5 par. Matt. 11: 18–19), Jesus and John are both presented as rejected envoys of Wisdom. Jesus is not identified with Wisdom, but neither is he on the same level as John, as one amongst the other envoys. He is, rather, the Son of Man.

In (c) (Luke 11: 49–51 par. Matt. 23: 34–6), Matthew identifies the 'Wisdom of God' of Luke 11: 49 with Jesus. Luke, however, probably representing Q most authentically, attributes the saying to another figure than Jesus – the Wisdom of God. This is the clearest indication so far that Jesus was not identified with Wisdom in Q.

In (d) (Luke 13: 34–5, par. Matt. 23: 37–9), the lament over Jerusalem, recognized by many as a saying of pre-existent Wisdom, is attributed to Jesus, both in Matthew and Luke. This

---

[1] *Wisdom, Christology and Law*, p. 97: 'Speculation about Wisdom emanated from circles which tended to see Jesus' significance largely in terms of his function as Sophia's final and finest representative, as the mediator of eschatological and divine revelation.'

2-2

double attribution could go back to Q, and indicate that Q did identify Jesus with Wisdom, but this is uncertain.

In (e) (Luke 11: 31–2 par. Matt. 12: 38–42, cf. Luke 11: 29–30), Jesus seems to be identified with the Son of Man in his capacity as the wise man and prophet greater than Solomon and Jonah respectively.

The evidence therefore seems to confirm Suggs' judgement that Q did not identify Jesus with pre-existent Wisdom. It does, however, regard him as the final envoy of Wisdom, and, in that capacity, it calls him 'Son of Man'. 'Son of Man' therefore seems to be a designation for Jesus as the final, but rejected, envoy of Wisdom.

The idea of the envoys of Wisdom comes from Hellenistic Judaism. D. Georgi[1] has enabled us to understand the rather subtle relationship between Wisdom and her envoys in Wisd. 1–9, which probably reflects the tradition used by Q. According to Georgi, Hellenistic religion typified and even hypostatized certain ways of life. In Wisd. 1–9 the life of the wise man was typified as the life of transcendent Wisdom. The ideal type of wise existence was located in the world of 'Spirit' (Wisd. 1: 13, 16, 2: 23, 5: 23), while in this world the wise man was nameless and humiliated. Thus the unreality of this order of existence was emphasized by comparison with the other world. The life of the wise man in this world was essentially docetic, while reality lay with hypostatized 'wise existence' or Wisdom in another dimension of existence. On this interpretation of the tradition in Wisd. 1–9 one can understand how Q can express the closest association between Jesus and Wisdom without literally identifying the two.

We have already seen how important the term 'Son of Man' is for Q. Now it is necessary to pay close attention to it in order to gain as clear an understanding of its meaning as possible. There is a vast literature on the Son of Man, and we cannot take all of it into consideration in this brief subsection of our argument.[2] We shall, however, attempt to do justice to the dominant opinions on the subject in recent scholarship.

[1] Dieter Georgi, 'Der vorpaulinische Hymnus Phil. 2: 6–11', *Zeit und Geschichte, Dankesgabe an Rudolf Bultmann zum 80 Geburtstag*, Erich Dinkler ed. (Tübingen, 1964), pp. 263–93.

[2] For a recent review of the literature see I. H. Marshall, 'The Synoptic Son of Man Sayings in Recent Discussion', *N.T.S.* 12 (1965–6), 327–51;

An important part of the modern discussion attempts to ascertain how Jesus himself used the term, if indeed, he used it at all. We shall postpone consideration of that question. At present we are concerned to understand what the phrase 'Son of Man' means in the Q layer of the Synoptic tradition. Since, however, a knowledge of the background of the term in Jewish apocalyptic literature is essential for an understanding of its usage at any level of the Synoptic tradition, we shall begin by (i) summarizing that background.[1] Then we shall (ii) examine the relevant texts in Q.

The chief Jewish texts which deal with the Son of Man are: Daniel 7: 13ff., IV Ezra 13 (the Sixth Vision), and The Parables of Enoch (I Enoch 37–71).

There are currently two dominant views concerning the figure of the Son of Man in these texts. On the one hand, German scholarship, as represented, for our purposes, by H. E. Tödt, understands these texts to present

the conception of a transcendent, pre-existent heavenly being, the Son of Man, whose coming to earth as judge would be a major feature of the drama of the end time.[2]

Tödt does allow that there are differences in the three presentations of the Son of Man in the apocalyptic texts under discussion. In Daniel 7 there is only 'the somewhat hazy picture of a heavenly figure with an appearance like that of a human being.'[3] In IV Ezra 13, the figure 'is distinguished both by its content and its form from the visions of the Son of Man in Dan. 7 and in the Similitudes of I Enoch,' although it shares the traits of sovereignty with the other two.[4] The Parables of Enoch show the greatest interest in the person of the Son of Man and give

Ransom Marlow, 'The Son of Man in Recent Journal Literature', *C.B.Q.* 28 (1966), 20–30; Gunter Haufe, 'Das Menschensohn-Problem in der gegenwärtigen wissenschaftlichen Diskussion', *Ev.T.* 26 (1966), pp. 130–41; M. Black, 'The Son of Man Problem in Recent Research and Debate', *B.J.R.L.* 45 (1962–3) 305–18.

[1] Our discussion is based on: Norman Perrin, *Rediscovering the Teaching of Jesus* (New York, 1967), pp. 164–73; Morna D. Hooker, *The Son of Man in Mark* (Montreal, 1967), pp. 11–74; H. E. Tödt, *The Son of Man in the Synoptic Tradition*, pp. 22–9; F. H. Borsch, *The Son of Man in Myth and History* (Philadelphia, 1967).

[2] Perrin, *Rediscovering*, p. 164.   [3] Tödt, p. 24.

[4] *Ibid.*, p. 27.

the clearest presentation of his identity; but the account is so dominated by the author's techniques of 'collecting and compiling' that no coherent and continuous description of his activity is presented. Unlike IV Ezra 13, where such an account does occur, I Enoch gives no description of an 'itinerary' of the Son of Man, comparable to those in the Gnostic myths.[1] Despite these qualifications, however, Tödt assumes that in the background of the New Testament there was a defined idea of the Son of Man, which was shared by many, and which invested that figure with certain relatively stable attributes, such as pre-existence, and the function of the eschatological judge.

Norman Perrin challenges this understanding of the Son of Man in Jewish apocalyptic. He argues that since the only feature that all three presentations of the Son of Man have in common is the apocalyptic commonplace of pre-existence, there is no reason to see an identifiable figure behind the three texts. Therefore, 'it would be better to speak of an "image", and of the varied use of "Son of Man" imagery in Jewish apocalyptic.'[2] According to Perrin, the apocalyptists who wrote IV Ezra and the Parables of Enoch each independently used the seventh chapter of Daniel for his own expository purposes.

What we have, in fact, in Jewish apocalyptic is not a Son of Man conception at all, as Tödt and others assume, but a use of Dan. 7: 13 by subsequent seers, a usage which does not end with apocalyptic, but continues on into the Midrashim.[3]

Perrin is able to show how I Enoch interprets the basic tradition of Enoch's translation to heaven (Gen. 5: 22, 24) by imagery drawn from Ezekiel 1 and Daniel 7 (I Enoch 70–1). Enoch's summons to heaven is presented partly by means of the imagery of Ezekiel's call and vision, and partly by means of the scene in Daniel of the Son of Man coming with the clouds to be enthroned by God. Once the identification of Enoch and the Son of Man has been made, the other characteristic apocalyptic attributes of pre-existence and the functions of reveler and judge, are attached to him.[4] IV Ezra 13 proceeds in a similar

---

[1] *Ibid.*, p. 28.
[2] Perrin, *Rediscovering*, pp. 165–6.   [3] *Ibid.*, p. 166.
[4] See I Enoch 46: 1–47: 4 for the application of Dan. 7 to the 'extended' apocalyptic picture of the Son of Man.

way, according to Perrin, to interpret the tradition about the Messiah in Ps. Sol. 17, in terms of Dan. 7.[1]

The great merit of Perrin's work is to focus attention on the exegetical procedure of the apocalyptists in question, rather than on the 'concept' of the Son of Man. As a result we see that the common element in the 'tradition' – if we may call it a tradition – is not the concept, but the text of Dan. 7. Perrin's approach seems to cohere with what we know from elsewhere about the exegetical nature of the Jewish religious tradition of the period. The 'pesher' commentaries from Qumran bear witness to this tradition.

We may ask, however, whether in using Dan. 7 the exegetical tradition was not governed by certain basic elements in Dan. 7 itself, so that the tradition of interpretation shows some consistency. Perrin points out that Dan. 7, IV Ezra 13 and the Parables of Enoch all attribute pre-existence to the Son of Man. He says that pre-existence is an apocalyptic commonplace, and not necessarily an indication that there existed a prior concept of the pre-existent Son of Man. However, the Son of Man does seem to be pre-existent in Dan. 7, and it would seem that, whether pre-existence is a commonplace or not, Dan. 7 is the immediate cause of the attribution of pre-existence to the 'Men' in IV Ezra and I Enoch. Can one discern any other constant elements in the use of Dan. 7 which might come from the text of that chapter and contribute to a relatively stable group of ideas, if not a fixed concept of the Son of Man?

To answer that question one needs to establish the meaning of Dan. 7 in itself. Perrin accepts the view that Dan. 7 adapts a myth which tells how in the assembly of the gods power is passed from one god named 'Ancient of Days' to another named 'Son of Man'. The myth is present in another form in the texts from Ugarit and Tyre.[2] Daniel interprets the myth by identifying the Son of Man with the 'saints of the most high'. These are the Maccabean martyrs, in Perrin's opinion, whose

---

[1] Perrin, *ibid.*, pp. 166–71.

[2] *Ibid.*, pp. 166–7. He follows L. Rost, 'Zur Deutung des Menschensohnes in Daniel 7' in *Gott und die Götter: Festgabe für Erich Fascher* (Berlin, 1958); and J. Morgenstern, 'The Son of Man of Dan. 7: 13 ff., A New Interpretation', *J.B.L.* 80 (1961), 65–77. See also F. H. Borsch, pp. 140–5.

coming to power is portrayed in the myth, and is understood as a reward for their sufferings. Perrin concludes:

That the figure is 'one like a Son of Man' is probably a pure accident; any other cryptically designated figure would have served his purpose equally well. His purpose was to bring to his readers a message of assurance, of power and glory to be theirs as a reward for their constancy, and nothing more should be read into his use of this Son of Man imagery than that.[1]

Perrin, perhaps, goes too far in denying that the symbol of the Son of Man has any intrinsic meaning in Dan. 7. M. D. Hooker suggests that the Son of Man is a symbol for Adam, and for Israel the true descendants of Adam.[2] The beasts that precede the Son of Man in Dan. 7 recall the chaos monsters, Leviathan and Tiamat, according to Hooker, and the basic form of the drama is determined by the creation mythology of the Ancient Near East. As in Deutero-Isaiah (Is. 51: 9–14) and the Psalms (74: 12–17, 89: 10 (9)ff.), the imagery of the conquest by Yahweh of the chaos-monsters in creation is used to express the redemption and restoration of Israel. The 'Son of Man' symbolizes the King of Israel, representative of the nation as a whole, temporarily dethroned by his enemies, the beasts, but now coming back into power. According to Hooker, the comparison between the 'man' and the beasts suggests Gen. 1: 28, where dominion over the animals is given to Adam. The Son of Man in Dan. 7 represents Adam, the forefather of the truly human race, Israel, having suffered the usurpation of his dominion by the beasts, receiving that dominion back again.[3]

Hooker emphasizes other passages in the Jewish literature of the time which suggest that Israel is the truly human nation, the only real descendants of Adam (e.g. IV Ezra 6: 53–9, 8: 26–30, Sir. 17: 2–4, 11–14, Wisd. 9: 1–4).[4] In this capacity Israel is symbolized by the Son of Man – the true man.[5]

We find Hooker's arguments somewhat contrived, and, although Dan. 7 does recall the mythology of creation, one may ask whether she does not make the references to Adam clearer than in fact they are. Nevertheless, there seems to be significance

---

[1] Perrin, *Rediscovering*, p. 167.
[2] M. D. Hooker, *Son of Man*, pp. 2–17.
[3] *Ibid.*, pp. 17–30.   [4] *Ibid.*, pp. 33–72.
[5] *Ibid.*, pp. 71–2.

in the fact that the one who receives final dominion has the attributes of a man rather than a beast. It does not seem to be the case that 'any other cryptically designated figure would have served as well', as Perrin avers. The enthronement of the 'Man' signifies not only the vindication of the Maccabean martyrs, but also the restoration of the right order in the universe, a work comparable to creation. Since this restoration has the form of the enthronement of the 'Man' over the beasts, one cannot ignore the hints of the dominion once enjoyed by Adam. However, in Dan. 7 the primary intention of the imagery is, as Perrin argues, to express the future vindication of the martyrs.

Therefore, although the Son of Man was not a well-defined figure or 'concept' in Jewish apocalyptic, there was a relatively stable group of ideas associated with the term. The meaning of the term was determined chiefly by the context in which it was used. In Daniel 7 it signified the true Israel; in I Enoch, the exalted and enthroned righteous Enoch, the head of the elect saints, and in IV Ezra the conquering Messiah of Ps. Sol. 17. There are, however, at least two features that are constant in all these applications of the image. One is that he is a man – as contrasted with the beasts – and the other, that he is pre-existent. We suggest that these two ideas probably were in mind wherever, in Jesus' time, the term 'Son of Man' was used.

Most scholars classify the Son of Man sayings as follows: the sayings concerning the coming Son of Man; the sayings concerning the Son of Man on earth; and the sayings concerning the suffering and rising of the Son of Man.[1] We shall observe this classification in our discussion. Unfortunately we cannot treat all sayings with the same attention, but must concentrate on those most important for our purpose. We shall deal with the sayings in order of their occurrence.

(a) *Luke 6: 22 par. Matt. 5: 11* (Son of Man on Earth)

Blessed are you when men hate you, when they reproach you and cast out your name as evil, for the sake of the Son of Man.

Matthew has 'for my sake' instead of 'for the sake of the Son of Man'. The Lukan reference to the Son of Man is probably

---

[1] Tödt, *passim*. See the discussion of this classification in Borsch, pp. 33–45; Hooker, pp. 77–80. It can be misleading if used without care.

original in Q, however.[1] This saying expresses the hostility of men towards the Son of Man on earth, hostility which his followers experience as his representatives. As Tödt says,

here a persecution is spoken of which occurs on account of the Son of Man's activity on earth. He alone exists in the tension over against this generation...Thus, here too, the name Son of Man is used to designate Jesus' acting in a certain way...In this way the name is here a title designating the specific unique authority of the one who bears the title.[2]

The first Son of Man saying in Q therefore tells of his rejection by men. Those who experience this rejection with him are given the eschatological promise: 'Blessed'. The same promise is given in Mark 8: 38, Luke 12: 8ff., and Matt. 19: 28.[3] The saying is probably a creation of the community.[4]

(b) *Luke 7: 34–5 par. Matt. 11: 19* (Son of Man on Earth)

The Son of Man came eating and drinking and you say, 'Behold a glutton and a drunkard, a friend of tax collectors and sinners!' Yet wisdom is justified by all her children.

Tödt interprets this saying as another example of the supreme authority of Jesus, expressed by the use of the title 'Son of Man'. In bestowing table-fellowship on the outcasts he demonstrates this authority. The objection to this generosity creates a situation comparable to that in the controversy dialogues in Mark (e.g. Mark 2: 15–17). The verb 'came' (ἐλήλυθεν) expresses the sovereignty of the Son of Man in his whole mission, according to Tödt, but must not be taken to mean that the sovereignty of the heavenly Son of Man is thereby seen as having come down to earth.[5]

We do not see why the idea of the heavenly Son of Man come down to earth should be so categorically excluded. If the term 'Son of Man' meant anything to Jesus' hearers, or to the Q tradition, the fact that the Son of Man is a heavenly being must have been present to some extent in their understanding. As our

[1] E. Schweizer, 'Der Menschensohn'; Borsch, pp. 328–9; Tödt, p. 123, is less certain, but allows that it might be original with Q.

[2] Tödt, *ibid.*   [3] *Ibid.*, pp. 123–4.

[4] *Ibid.*, p. 123; Schweizer, 'Menschensohn', p. 200.

[5] Tödt, pp. 115–16.

earlier discussion has shown, the rejection of the Son of Man is, for Q, the result, not only of his authority, but also of his being an envoy of Wisdom, whose messengers were traditionally rejected. Be that as it may, authority is a characteristic of the Danielic Son of Man (Dan. 7: 13), and insofar as Jesus exercised authority and, as we shall argue, called himself 'Son of Man', he was probably identified by his hearers with the Danielic figure.

Tödt's view of the history of the tradition (which we shall discuss later) obliges him to regard all sayings concerning the Son of Man on earth, including this one, as formed by the community. Schweizer is also uncertain about the authenticity of this saying as a word of Jesus.[1]

(c) *Luke 9: 58, par. Matt. 8: 20* (Son of Man on earth)

And Jesus said to him, The foxes have holes and the birds of the air have nests, but the Son of Man has nowhere to lay his head.

Dibelius takes this as expressing the contrast between the heavenly dignity of the Son of Man and his earthly obscurity and humiliation.[2] Tödt objects that there is no hint of the concealment of the Son of Man here, or in any of the sayings about the Son of Man on earth. Tödt is mistaken in his denial of any hint of concealment in the sayings, as Luke 12: 10 par., to be discussed below, shows.

We have already seen how the theme of homelessness recalls the Wisdom myth. The use of the term Son of Man here shows that for Q it has a special association with the humiliation of Jesus on earth. True, as Tödt says, there is no explicit reference to concealment here, but when this saying is read along with the other Son of Man sayings in Q, the theme of rejection and humiliation, which is tantamount to concealment of his heavenly dignity, becomes apparent.

Schweizer[3] regards this saying as an authentic word of Jesus, with some plausibility.

---

[1] *Ibid.*, pp. 117–18; Schweizer, *ibid.*
[2] M. Dibelius, *Jesus*, p. 91, quoted by Tödt, p. 121.
[3] Schweizer, 'Menschensohn', p. 199.

(d) *Luke 11: 30 par. Matt. 12: 40* (Son of Man on Earth/Coming Son of Man)

Already discussed above.

(e) *Luke 12: 18 par. Matt. 10: 32* (Son of Man on Earth/Coming Son of Man)

But I say to you, whoever confesses me before men, the Son of Man will also confess him before the angels of God. [Matthew again has 'I' for 'Son of Man'.]

Tödt regards this saying as the bedrock of Jesus' own teaching on the Son of Man, chiefly because of its simplicity and because it distinguishes the Son of Man from Jesus.[1] Kaesemann rejects its authenticity because it has the form of an eschatological judgement saying, which Kaesemann attributes to the early Christian prophets.[2] Schweizer points out that there is no overt reference to the future coming of the Son of Man.[3] The confession before the angels takes place in heaven. The contrast is between the humiliated Jesus and the exalted Son of Man.

We agree with Tödt that it is possibly an authentic saying, but, with Schweizer, do not see any reference to the coming Son of Man. Rather it refers to the future when, in heaven, the Son of Man will confess those who confess Jesus on earth.

We shall return later to this saying, in the discussion of the history of the tradition.

(f) *Luke 12: 10 par. Matt. 12: 32* (Son of Man on Earth)

And everyone who speaks a word against the Son of Man, it will be forgiven him, but to him who blasphemes against the Holy Spirit it will not be forgiven.

This saying probably arose in the post-Easter community and shows that 'Son of Man' was especially a title of the earthly Jesus.[4] If a blasphemy against the risen Lord, revealed by the

---

[1] Tödt, pp. 55–60.

[2] E. Kaesemann, 'Sentences of Holy Law', pp. 66–81; Cf. Perrin, *Rediscovering*, pp. 187–91; cf. Klaus Berger, 'Zu den sogennanten Sätzen heiligen Rechts', *N.T.S.*, 17 (1970–1), 10–40.

[3] E. Schweizer, 'The Son of Man', *J.B.L.* 79 (1960), 120.

[4] Schweizer, 'Menschensohn', p. 200. Tödt, p. 119.

Spirit, is unforgivable, the implication is that there is some mitigating circumstance included in the title 'Son of Man'. It is difficult to see any such circumstance on Tödt's view of the earthly Jesus, as one exercising sovereignty so clearly. Rather, 'Son of Man' must express some sense of the hiddenness of the authority of Jesus on earth. With this meaning it reiterates the point made by the previous saying.

There are two other versions of this saying: Mark 3: 28–9, and Thomas 44. Mark has no reference to the Son of Man, while in Thomas the reference is to 'the Son'. Thomas' version shows signs of a trinitarian formula and so is probably late.

Taylor and Bultmann think that Mark preserves the more original form.[1] In Mark the saying warns against blaspheming the Spirit. Q, or its tradition, added the reference to the Son of Man, suggesting that the Son of Man, as one whose presence on earth was veiled, is a special interest of Q. The fact that Q adds the reference to the Son of Man on earth could be the result of good tradition about Jesus.

In our earlier discussion we saw that 'Spirit' was identified with Wisdom and expressed the divine dignity of Christ in Q. 'Son of Man' seems therefore to express paradoxically the human humility of the pre-existent Christ.

(g) *Luke 12: 40 par. Matt. 24: 44; Luke 17: 23–4 par. Matt. 24: 26–7; Luke 17: 26–7 par. Matt. 24: 37–9 (cf. Luke 17: 28–30, Matt. 10: 23, 19: 28)* (Coming Son of Man)

Tödt regards these sayings as part of the original teaching of Jesus. They all seem to refer to the future coming of the Son of Man, as of some one other than Jesus himself. Although Tödt would have us exclude any hint of pre-existence from these sayings, we cannot do so.

Talk about the 'coming' of the Son of Man implies that there is a place whence he comes and that he already exists in that place. The logic of the language dealing with the coming Son of Man entails the apocalyptic idea of pre-existence.

There are therefore five sayings on the Son of Man on earth: (a), (b), (c), (e) and (f); three sayings on the coming Son of

---

[1] Vincent Taylor, *The Gospel according to St. Mark* (London, 1957), p. 242; Bultmann, *Geschichte*, p. 138.

Man: (g); and one doubtful (d), which we tend to regard as a saying about the Son of Man on earth.[1] There is no reference in Q to the crucifixion and resurrection of the Son of Man, although all of the sayings about the Son of Man on earth mention that he was rejected.

There is some reason to see the group of sayings about the Son of Man on earth as influenced by the Jewish Wisdom myth. Schweizer believes the influence came from the same sources as Wisd. 2–5,[2] which portrays the wise man as persecuted on earth and vindicated after death. In this group of sayings, therefore, 'Son of Man' is a title for the earthly Jesus, Wisdom's final messenger, who is humbled and rejected. Paradoxically, it expresses the pre-existent status of the humble 'man'.

The sayings concerning the 'coming' Son of Man seem to reverse the meaning of the term. In them it is a title for a future being, powerful and glorious, and not for a humiliated divine being. It is not clear whether Jesus and the Son of Man are identified in these sayings; they seem, at first sight, to distinguish the two figures. Since most of these sayings refer to the 'coming' (Luke 12: 8ff. par., 12: 40 par.) or the 'day' (Luke 17: 23–4 par., 17: 26–7 par., 17: 28–30) of the Son of Man, meaning his coming to judge, they seem to imply that the Son of Man has apocalyptic pre-existence. He exists before his manifestation.

In the idea of the envoys of Wisdom, whom Wisdom enters, making them prophets (cf. Wisd. 7: 28), the protological pre-existence of Wisdom is probably assumed. In the sayings about the coming Son of Man eschatological pre-existence is, likewise, present. The interesting question, however, is whether Q regarded the Christ as pre-existent.

In identifying Christ as Wisdom's final envoy, by means, amongst others, of the title 'Son of Man', Q assigns to him a delicately defined position of dignity. On the one hand, he is not protologically pre-existent Wisdom; on the other he is not merely one amongst her many envoys; he is the eschatological messenger. In this capacity he is the Son of Man – a title which

---

[1] Ten sayings in all; Tödt, p. 365, conjecturally includes Matt. 10: 23 and 19: 28 in Q. We, however, shall treat them as part of Matthew's special material. Luke 17: 28–30 we tend to regard as part of Q because of its close similarity to the other Q passages in its immediate context.

[2] Schweizer, 'Menschensohn', p. 205.

probably suggested a heavenly origin for its designee, although in Q it is used in connection with his rejection by men.

The Wisdom tradition in Q would not, by itself, entitle us to say that Christ is pre-existent. On that basis he is the supremely inspired prophet. However, the coupling with this of the Son of Man tradition indicates a possible understanding of Jesus as a heavenly being, not protologically pre-existent like Wisdom or Enoch's Son of Man, but nevertheless pre-existent before his coming as Wisdom's eschatological envoy.

II. MARK

J. M. Robinson has drawn our attention recently to the peculiar nature of the 'historical' narrative in Mark's gospel. He calls it 'eschatological history'.[1] It is not history in the usual sense of a series of events caused by ordinary factors in the horizontal course of human life; neither is it a record of transcendental religious experience. It is a presentation of happenings in this world, as if they were initiated from beyond the world.

Robinson begins by drawing attention to Mark's presentation of the history of Jesus as a narrative of the struggle between God and Satan. Mark presents it as a conflict (a) between the Spirit and Satan (1: 9–12); (b) between the Son of God and the demoniacs (1: 24, 3: 11, 5: 7); and (c) between Jesus and his opponents (2: 1–3: 6 etc.).[2] This scheme may be too neat, and Robinson agrees that it should not be 'pressed'; nevertheless it is a useful point of departure for our discussion. If the gospel presents a trans-historical conflict, does this presentation imply that Jesus is pre-existent? The first thing to notice is the transition in 1: 7–8 from the 'one-dimensional' history of John the Baptist to the 'cosmic' dimension of Jesus' presence in 1: 9–13. Suddenly,

we find the heavens splitting, the spirit descending like a dove, a voice from heaven, God's Son, the Spirit driving him into the wilderness, Satan tempting, with the wild beasts and ministering angels. The disappearance of all humans from the narrative after the act of

[1] *The Problem of History in Mark*, S.B.T. 21 (London, 1957). Cf. Ernest Best, *The Temptation and the Passion: the Markan Soteriology*, S.N.T.S. Monograph 2 (Cambridge, 1965), pp. 18–23, where Robinson's view is criticized.

[2] Robinson, *Problem of History*, pp. 34–5.

baptism is accentuated by the address of the heavenly voice to Jesus rather than to the crowd or John.[1]

One must recognize, however, that if this be true in Mark, it is even more compelling in Q, where an elaborate description of the exchanges between Jesus and Satan, in the wilderness, is given (Matt. 4: 1–11 par. Luke 4: 1–13). This confirms our judgement of Q, that it too sees the presence of Jesus on earth against the background of transcendence; but we return to Mark.

In the synagogue at Capernaum people marvel at his teaching 'for he taught them as one who had authority (ἐξουσία) and not as the scribes' (1: 22); and the authority of his teaching casts out a demon, who recognizes him publicly as 'the Holy One of God' (1: 24). The amazed judgement of the onlookers is interesting in that it identifies the authoritative teaching as the power which exorcizes the demon: 'What is this? A new teaching! With authority he commands even the unclean spirits, and they obey him' (1: 27).[2] The rhetorical questions point to the transcendent dimension of his presence, and link the experience of that dimension to the authoritative nature of his teaching. His language drives even the demons before it! Out of what authority does he speak? The demon gives the answer: he is 'the Holy One of God'.[3]

In 1: 38 Jesus confirms his divine origin when he says that he 'came out' (ἐξῆλθον) for the purpose of preaching in other villages. One may compare this statement with that of the demons in 1: 25: 'Have you *come* to destroy us?' We are left to

---

[1] *Ibid.*, p. 27.

[2] On the textual problems of 1: 27b see Vincent Taylor, *Mark*, p. 176 n. 2. Taylor understands 1: 27 to indicate an astonishment at the fact that Jesus performed an exorcism by the power of his word alone, not by using a magic spell. There might well be an intention behind this passage, to present Jesus as mightier than the magicians, who have to use (borrowed) spells in exorcizing.

[3] This title does not occur in the Synoptic tradition outside of the parallel in Luke 4: 34. Otherwise it occurs in the Johannine tradition (John 6: 69, I John 2: 20, Rev. 3: 7). The title was applied to Aaron (Ps. 105 (106): 16). Taylor (*Mark*, p. 174) says that it is used 'with Messianic significance, as expressing a sense of the presence of a supernatural person'. E. Lohmeyer, *Das Evangelium des Markus*, Meyers Kommentar 1/2 (Göttingen, 1959), p. 37, emphasized its cultic origin and sees in the whole scene the confrontation of the evil spirits by the holy eschatological priest.

ask, 'Came out from whence?' The answer is obvious, as Luke saw, when he paraphrased 'came out' into 'was sent' (Luke 4: 43) – from God.[1] This mysterious divine origin is hinted at in 3: 34–5, where he refuses to recognize human family relationships and declares his true kin to be those who have the same relationship with God as he does.

In 2: 10 the authority of Jesus is emphasized again, and now it is the authority of the Son of Man on earth, about which the people say, 'We never saw anything like this' (2: 12b). As the Son of Man he is Lord of the Sabbath (2: 28), claiming thereby that his authority was greater than the authority of the Law;[2] and, as usual, it is the demons who explain why: 'You are the Son of God' (3: 11, cf. 5: 7). He is the strong man who has entered Satan's house and is plundering his goods (3: 27).

The centre of his teaching is the sovereign activity of God (1: 27) called 'the Kingdom of God' (1: 14–15).[3] The uncomprehending astonishment of the witnesses to his miracles shows that the understanding of the divine nature of that activity remains a secret (4: 11); but soon it will be revealed to all (4: 22). Even the disciples ask, 'What then is this that even the wind and sea obey him?' (4: 41), and his fellow Nazarenes in the synagogue at Nazareth ask, 'Where did this man get all this? What is the *wisdom* given to him? What mighty works are wrought by his hands!' (6: 2).[4]

We may pause here to consider the elements common to the

[1] E. Lohmeyer, p. 43. Taylor, p. 184, regards this interpretation as too 'dogmatic'. He takes the passage to refer to the 'going out' into Galilee in mission.

[2] See Hooker, pp. 81–102. We shall return to these texts. M. Albertz (*Die Botschaft des Neuen Testaments* (1946), cited by H. E. Tödt, p. 128) sees Mark 2: 1–3: 6 as comprising 'controversy dialogues' and all the individual points of controversy to be concerned with the question of the authority of this new teaching.

[3] As recently re-emphasized by Perrin, *Rediscovering*, pp. 54–63.

[4] E. Lohmeyer, p. 111 n. 3, understands this parallel between σοφία and δυνάμεις to correspond to the more usual distinction between λόγος and ἔργον. In Job 12: 13 they are divine attributes. In Ps. Sol. 17: 24–6 both attributes belong to the Messiah. In I Cor. 1: 24, Christ is θεοῦ δύναμιν καὶ θεοῦ σοφίαν. Lohmeyer also refers to Is. 11: 2, but that text does not seem appropriate. This association of Wisdom and mighty works recalls Wisd. 10: 16: (Wisdom) 'entered the soul of the servant of God and he withstood formidable kings with signs and wonders (τέρασι καὶ σημείοις).'

various reactions to Jesus' teaching so far reported by Mark. Hitherto, the three important scenes have been those in the synagogues at Capernaum (1: 22–7) and Nazareth (6: 1–6a), and that following the healing of the paralytic (2: 10–12). The first common feature to notice is (a) that the teaching is identified with Jesus' miraculous activity – it is not the imparting of information, but an activity of exorcism and healing. (b) The second is the astonishment of the onlookers and hearers who ask about the source of all this teaching, indicating that it is altogether new and unparalleled in their experience. (c) The third is that explanations of that source are offered: in 1: 24 the demon explains that Jesus is powerful because he is 'the Holy One of God'; in 2: 10 Jesus explains that he is powerful because he is the Son of Man on earth; and in 6: 2 the Nazarenes explain that his power stems from the wisdom that has been given him.

This threefold explanation of the power of Jesus' words and deeds is important for our understanding of pre-existence. 'Holy one of God' (1: 24), 'Son of Man on earth' (2: 10), and 'the wisdom given to him' (6: 2) are intended to give information about his transcendent nature. In Q, as we have seen, the title 'Son of Man' is applied to Jesus on earth, possibly identifying him as the pre-existent eschatological envoy of Wisdom in a state of humiliation, persecuted and rejected by men. Here in Mark the title 'Son of Man' (2: 10) and the reference to the 'wisdom given him' occur in contexts dealing with the conflict between Jesus and the Jewish authorities, on the one hand (2: 6–11 etc.) and with Jesus' rejection in his own home (6: 3), on the other. We suggest that the myth of Wisdom's messengers exercised some influence on Mark's Christology here. The remaining title 'Holy one of God' is a confession by the demons, who 'knew him' (1: 34), of Jesus' status as a divine being (3: 11–12).[1] We may notice that each of the three appellations is attributed to a different source: the demons call Jesus 'the Holy one of God', the people exclaim 'What is this wisdom?' and Jesus calls himself, 'the Son of Man'.

There seems to be a pattern of question and answer in terms of which Mark expresses his Christology. (b) and (c) above suggest this pattern. It can also be seen in 4: 41, 'What then is this, even the wind and sea obey him?', to which the demoniac

[1] F. C. Grant, *The Interpreter's Bible*, vol. 7, 1951, pp. 661–2.

in 5: 7 answers, 'Jesus, Son of the Most High God!' and in 2: 24, 'Why are they doing what is not lawful on the Sabbath?' to which Jesus himself answers in 2: 27, 'the Son of Man is Lord even of the Sabbath.' The pattern is used in 6: 14–16, where, in answer to Herod's question who Jesus might be, 'some' suggested that John the Baptist might have come back to life, or Elijah, or that a prophet 'like one of the prophets of old' (6: 15) had arisen. Luke understood the last phrase to mean that one of the prophets of old had returned (Luke 9: 8) and he is perhaps not far from the real import of the saying. It would seem that behind this saying lies a myth of a transcendentally grounded series of imperishable agents of God's saving purpose, who might come to earth more than once. This conception is similar to the myth of Wisdom's saving activity in history; and it is surely significant that this passage occurs soon after the attribution of Jesus' authority to the 'wisdom' he received.

Between the scene in the Nazarene synagogue and 'Herod's question' is an account of the sending out of the disciples as missionaries (6: 7–13). The authority of Jesus is transferred to the disciples:

And he called to him the twelve, and began to send them out two by two, and gave them authority over the unclean spirits. (6: 7)

Here we have an appropriation of the 'history' of Jesus by the twelve, understood as representatives of the Christian community. Robinson points out that previous scholarship usually explained the phenomenon of the transference of Jesus' authority in one of two ways: either the cult relived the experiences of Jesus' history in a mystical way, or the 'apologetic pragmatism' required by the Church in its struggle for survival led to basing various customs of the Church's life on incidents in the life of Jesus. Both of these views, according to Robinson, overlook Mark's 'eschatological understanding of history, which sees Jesus and the Church engaged in the same cosmic struggle against the same demonic force of evil.'[1] This judgement is based on the fact that in the Markan apocalypse (ch. 13) events of the Church's life (13: 5ff., 7ff., 11: 12, 13, 21ff.), are presented in the form of a prophecy of Jesus. In this way the Church con-

[1] *Problem of History*, p. 63.

51

fesses its belief that their struggle is Jesus' struggle. Our present text shows how the Church claims Jesus' authority and power for that struggle. There is only one conceptual scheme in the tradition we have examined so far in terms of which such a transference of authority and power can be understood: the Wisdom myth – 'she enters men and makes them friends of God and prophets'.[1]

The mention of wisdom in 6: 2 and the rejection of Jesus by his homeland (πάτρις) (6: 1) suggest that the Wisdom myth is the background of chapter 6. The rejection of Wisdom's envoys is essential to the myth. Mark 6: 1–6a is, in fact, an account of the rejection of Jesus by his own people; and the rejection is summed up in a proverb of popular wisdom:[2] 'A prophet is not without honour, except in his own country, and among his own kin, and in his own house' (6: 4). Mark leaves the rejection without overt explanation; and he 'forecasts' the same fate for the missioning disciples. In Mark 6: 8–12 there is only the briefest hint of acceptance (6: 10), whereas there is explicit instruction about what to do in the case of rejection (6: 11). However, in the concluding verse (6: 13), the disciples do seem to be able to cast out demons, although, if that is what 'mighty work' means, Jesus was prevented from doing so by the unbelief of the Nazareans (6: 5). This suggests some acceptance of the Gospel – the different situation after the resurrection.

Regarded in isolation, the theme of the rejection of Jesus and his disciples does not show that Mark has the Wisdom myth in mind. However, taken with the other hints we have seen (e.g. 6: 2) it might indicate the presence of the myth in Mark.

The next indication of Jesus' supernatural origin occurs in 6: 45–52, where he walks on the sea; it is followed in 6: 53–6 by a summary of his healing activity. Then in 8: 27–9 the

---

[1] Cf. Philo, Gig. 24 ff., on the transference of Moses' power to the seventy elders, and Deut. 34: 19, 'And Joshua the son of Nun was full of the spirit of wisdom for Moses had laid his hands upon him.'

[2] Bultmann, Geschichte, pp. 79 and 107. C. H. Dodd, The Interpretation of the Fourth Gospel (Cambridge, 1960), p. 325, points out that the rejection of the 'divine man' by his homeland is a common feature of such a figure. In view of the presentation of the wise man as a divine man in Philo, this element is not surprising in a Wisdom context in the Synoptic tradition. Cf. Letters of Apollonius, xliv in Philostratus, Life of Apollonius of Tyana, ed. Conybeare, Vol. II, p. 436.

questioning is resumed: Jesus asks his disciples, 'Who do men say that I am?' and the same answer is given as the one which Herod received in 6: 14–16: 'John the Baptist...Elijah...one of the prophets', and Luke again paraphrases 'one of the old prophets has risen' (Luke 9: 19). This suggests that the chain 'John the Baptist, Elijah, one of the prophets' was a relatively established unit of tradition. In 8: 29, however, it is rejected in favour of the simple declaration: 'You are the Christ'. It would seem, therefore, that we have here a rejection of a Christology of Wisdom's envoys in favour of some other. What this other Christology is must now be determined.

The account of the Transfiguration (9: 2–8) tells what this Christology is. The key to its interpretation lies in the preceding (8: 31ff.) and following (9: 12–13) references to the rejection and humiliation of the Son of Man. Lohmeyer entitles the section 9: 2–29 'The Revelation of the Son of Man'.[1] He divides it into three stages: the revelation on the mountain (9: 2–8), on the descent from the mountain (9: 9–13), and at the foot of the mountain (9: 14–29). It includes a revelation of his glory, of his rejection and humiliation and of his redeeming work on earth (the healing miracle of 9: 14–28).

Lohmeyer understands the Transfiguration to be a revelation of Jesus' dignity as the Son of Man in glory.[2] He sees some influence from Daniel 7 on this pericope. He points to Daniel 7: 9 and Rev. 1 and claims that they portray the Son of Man arrayed in white.[3] This is simply not so. In Dan. 7: 9 it is the 'Ancient of Days' who is thus clothed, and in Rev. 1: 13, where the robe of the Son of Man is mentioned, there is no reference to its colour.

An argument can, however, be presented on the basis of Dan. 7: 9 and Rev. 1: 14 to make the same point that Lohmeyer seeks to make. In Rev. 1: 14 an attribute of the 'Ancient of Days' in Dan. 7: 9 – namely his white hair – has been transferred to the Son of Man. In Dan. 7: 9, the white robe is an attribute of the 'Ancient of Days', while in Mark 9: 3 it belongs to the transfigured Jesus. This could mean that in Mark 9: 3, as in Rev. 1:

[1] Lohmeyer, pp. 172–3.
[2] *Ibid.*, pp. 172–81. W. D. Davies, *Sermon on the Mount*, pp. 50–1, accepts this view; cf. H. Baltensweiler, *Die Verklärung Jesu, Historisches Ereignis und synoptische Berichte, Ab. Th. A.N.T.* 33 (Zürich, 1959).
[3] Lohmeyer, *ibid.*, p. 175.

14, an attribute of the 'Ancient of Days' has been applied to Jesus, understood as the Son of Man.

There are two other features of this pericope which suggest that Jesus is being presented as the Son of Man in glory. One is the context in which Mark has placed the pericope. From 8: 31, the first prediction of the Passion of the Son of Man, through 8: 38, the warning that those who are ashamed of the Son of Man in this generation, of them he will be ashamed in the judgement, and 9: 9–12, two more predictions of the passion, to 9: 31, a final passion saying on the Son of Man, the context is evidently concerned with the Son of Man. Its major emphasis is on the suffering which the Son of Man must undergo. However, the Son of Man saying nearest to the beginning of the Transfiguration account is the warning about being ashamed of the Son of Man in this generation (8: 38). It is followed by the saying on 'Some standing here who will not taste death before they have seen the Kingdom of God come in power', and then comes the Transfiguration account. It seems to us that the Transfiguration, in its present position, is intended to reveal who this humble, suffering Son of Man is, for the sake of those who might be tempted to be ashamed of him because of his suffering.

The intervening saying in 9:1 about 'seeing the Kingdom come in power' could, on this view, also refer to the Transfiguration. In Dan. 7: 14 the Son of Man receives ἀρχὴ καὶ ἡ τιμὴ καὶ ἡ βασιλεία.[1] If we accept C. H. Dodd's translation of Mark 9: 1c 'until they have seen that the Kingdom of God has come with power' (ἕως ἂν ἴδωσιν τὴν βασιλείαν τοῦ θεοῦ ἐληλυθυῖαν ἐν δυνάμει) which we are inclined to do,[2] then the kingdom of God – understood as God's sovereign power[3] – could be Jesus himself, revealed in the Transfiguration as the Son of Man of Dan. 7: 13–14. This is precisely how Matthew understood Mark 9: 1, as he shows in Matt. 16: 28: ἕως ἂν ἴδωσιν τὸν υἱὸν ἀνθρώπου ἐρχόμενον ἐν τῇ βασιλείᾳ αὐτοῦ.[4]

---

[1] This is the Θ text. It translates the Aramaic שלטן ויקר ומלכו most accurately. The LXX has a different text, but expresses the same idea. Both Θ, LXX and the Aramaic end verse 14 with the statement that 'his kingdom shall never pass away'. The N.E.B. translates 'Kingdom' as 'sovereignty' in Dan. 7: 14.

[2] For the debate about this translation see Taylor, p. 385.

[3] Thus Perrin, *Rediscovering*, pp. 54–5.

[4] Hooker, p. 125, points out that Origen (Commentary on Matthew,

The other feature of the Transfiguration pericope which suggests the influence of Dan. 7: 13–14 is the reference to the cloud in 9: 7. In Dan. 7: 13 the Son of Man comes 'with the clouds of heaven' to receive his power. Perrin has shown how the feature of the clouds was taken over from Dan. 7: 13 in Mark 13: 26 and 14: 62 as a fixed element in the presentation of the eschatological Son of Man in the early Christian exegetical tradition.[1] Lohmeyer refers also to II Macc. 2: 7, where the clouds are an eschatological sign, as they are in the Christian exegetical appropriation of Dan. 7: 13 in Mark 13: 26 and 14: 62.

It remains for us to explain the significance of the appearance of Elijah and Moses with Jesus. Elijah was an eschatological figure in the Judaism of the time as 9: 11–13 shows (cf. Mal. 4: 4–5). Moses was also an eschatological figure.[2] In Mark 9: 7–8, after Jesus has been declared the beloved Son of God, whose words are to be 'heard', Elijah and Moses disappear and Jesus remains alone. We understand this to signify that Jesus, not Elijah or Moses, is the eschatological figure.

If this analysis is correct, the argument moves through three Christological designations: from 'Christ' in 8: 29, through the 'Son of Man' in 8: 38 and 9: 2–6, to the 'Son of God' in 9: 7.[3] One should notice at this point that in 8: 38 'Son of Man' and 'Son of God' are identified when it is said that the Son of Man

Book 12, 31) reports that certain commentators in the early Church saw the Transfiguration as the fulfilment of the promise to 'see' the Kingdom, or the Son of Man come in power. Hooker argues that in Mark 9: 5 Peter is shown to understand the Transfiguration as the dawning of the eschatological day and the vision of the Son of Man in glory (*ibid.*, p. 125).

[1] Perrin, *Rediscovering*, pp. 173–81.

[2] See the recent presentation of this view by J. L. Martyn, *History and Theology in the Fourth Gospel* (New York, 1968), pp. 91–135; and W. A. Meeks, *The Prophet King, Moses Traditions and the Johannine Christology*, Supplements to Novum Testamentum 14 (Leiden, 1967); also M. Thrall, 'Elijah and Moses in Mark's account of the Transfiguration', *N.T.S.* 16 (1970), 305–17. She sees in the account an attempt to counteract the view that Moses and Elijah were of the same dignity as Jesus (as eschatological figures).

[3] Hooker, p. 125. In 14: 61b–62 the same three titles occur in the order 'Christ', 'Son of God' ('Son of the Blessed One'), 'Son of Man'. Tödt, p. 84, points out that Mark seems to present all three titles as of the same importance, whereas Matthew (26: 64) seems to present 'Son of Man' as preferable to the other two.

will come 'in the glory of *his* Father'. Hooker considers it appropriate that Peter uses the term Messiah (and Rabbi in 9: 5) to express Jesus' dignity in human terms, Jesus himself uses 'Son of Man' and the voice from heaven uses 'my beloved Son', as reported in 1: 11 also. The significant thing to notice, however, is the implied identification of 'Son of Man' and 'Son of God'. As Son of Man and Son of God, Jesus is the eschatological figure.

We have seen how Mark presents Jesus as the one whose history is regulated from 'beyond'; as the one whose mysterious authority over demons causes men to ask about its source; whose own origin is from 'beyond'; whose authority over the Law puts him into conflict with the religious leaders; and causes him to be rejected by his own folk. This combination of authority, conflict and rejection is explained by identifying him as the Son of Man who has been given wisdom. Herod's question about his identity fits into a pattern of question and answer, by which Mark presents Jesus' transcendent dignity. The answer given Herod suggests that Jesus is understood as part of the chain of the envoys of God down through the ages, which recalls the Wisdom tradition. The transference of authority from Jesus to his disciples also recalls this tradition, while the answer given by the disciples to the question at Caesarea Philippi is so similar to the answer given to Herod that one might assume that the myth of the 'chain of God's envoys' was a fixed element in Mark's tradition.

The 'chain' is, however, rejected in favour of Peter's declaration that Jesus is the Christ (8: 29), which, in turn, is immediately interpreted by means of the title 'Son of Man'; who is presented as about to suffer and be rejected, but nevertheless is the eschatological Son of Man who possesses the power of God's sovereignty, and whose word is, therefore, to be heard (9: 7–8). We have, therefore, in Mark, a Christology which uses both the Wisdom myth and the Son of Man, and then relinquishes the former in favour of the latter.

We have already seen how important the Son of Man image is for the Markan Christology. There is no need to repeat the arguments already made. We shall now, therefore, consider the Son of Man sayings as a group, and then discuss selected sayings.

Of the thirteen sayings occurring in Mark, (i) eight (8: 31,

9: 9, 9: 12, 9: 31, 10: 33, 10: 45, 14: 21, 14: 41, of which 8: 31, 9: 31 and 10: 33 are very similar in content and structure)[1] concern the rejection and suffering of the Son of Man; (ii) three concern the future coming of the Son of Man (8: 38, 13: 26, 14: 62) and (iii) two concern the Son of Man on earth (2: 10, 2: 28).

It appears that the characteristic Markan understanding of the Son of Man is of one who must suffer the Passion.[2] There is a clear and specific reference to the Passion in the sayings in group (i). This may be compared to the more general reference to his rejection and homelessness in the Q sayings we have examined. Therefore, the tradition that Mark presents in the 'Passion sayings' seems to identify Jesus with the Son of Man on earth and appeals specifically to the cross and resurrection as the events that certify this identification.

We shall not discuss these sayings individually; but point out certain features that seem to us to imply the idea of the pre-existence of the Son of Man.

(a) The Son of Man is the one who rises from the dead[3] (8: 31, 9: 9, 9: 31, 10: 33). Tödt points out that these sayings use an identifiable formula to express the rising of the Son of Man – μετὰ τρεῖς ἡμέρας...ἀναστῆναι.[4] In 14: 28 and 16: 6, by comparison, the verb used to signify the resurrection is ἐγείρω. We agree with Tödt that the phrase using ἀναστῆναι comes from the pre-Markan tradition, while the other is Mark's own terminology.[5] In 14: 28 and 16: 6, which Hahn calls the

---

[1] Tödt, pp. 152–86, speaks of and analyses a 'train of terms' which s common to these three sayings in particular. The other sayings on the suffering of the Son of Man also partake in differing measure of the 'train of terms'. These terms come from pre-Markan tradition. The simplest form of the saying, distilled from the three predictions under discussion, is, according to Tödt: 'The Son of Man will be delivered to the chief priests and scribes and be killed and will rise in three days' (p. 153).

[2] Note that these sayings all occur after the 'Confession' at Caesarea Philippi in 8: 27ff., and here in two sections, 8: 27 – 10: 52 and 14: 1–42; 8: 27 – 10: 52 is 'systematically' arranged according to the three predictions of the Passion. There seems also be a geographical arrangement: 8: 31 in the north, 9: 31 in Galilee, 10: 33ff. on the road to Jerusalem (Tödt, ibid., p. 145).

[3] Ibid., pp. 180–6.

[4] 9: 9 omits the reference to three days.

[5] Ibid., p. 183.

'Christos tradition', since Jesus is called 'Christos' in these sayings, as opposed to 'Son of Man' in 8: 31 etc., the verb ἐγείρειν is used in the passive. This signifies that the Christ was raised by God. In the 'Son of Man tradition' ἀναστῆναι is used in the active voice to express 'a degree of sovereignty...for the suffering and rising one which is not attempted in the Christos tradition.'[1] It signifies that the Son of Man himself arose in his own power.

The use of the name 'Son of Man' together with a verb which signifies his sovereignty in rising from the dead, suggests that the Son of Man is thought of as someone with power of his own. Tödt is adamant that there is no association here with the idea of the transcendent Son of Man, as set forth in I Enoch, for instance. He rejects the argument of E. Lichtenstein, based in turn on the work of R. Otto, that these sayings allude to the descent and concealment of the pre-existent Son of Man of I Enoch, on the one hand, and to his return to eternity on the other.[2] Tödt's objections to this mode of procedure have some justification, because, as Perrin has helped us to see,[3] there was no common 'concept' of the Son of Man in early Judaism at that time which included detailed characteristics. Rather, we have suggested, the title was the centre of a varying congeries of ideas, of which only the pre-existence and the humanity of the figure were constant.

If, however, Dan. 7: 13ff. played a central role in the early Christian interpretation of the resurrection,[4] and if that tradition was essentially exegetical in nature, as Perrin believes, we may see in the use of ἀναστῆναι an interpretation of the resurrection as the exaltation of the Son of Man to power. On this view,

[1] Ferdinand Hahn in a letter to Tödt, quoted by Tödt, pp. 185–6. Hahn is speaking about 9: 31 particularly, where the killing of the Son of Man is expressed in the passive voice and the rising in the active. This reverses the formula in the 'Christos' sayings, which is 'to die...to be raised'; it becomes 'to be killed...to rise'.

[2] Tödt, p. 183. He refers to E. Lichtenstein, 'Die älteste christliche Glaubensformel', Z.K.G. 63 (1950/51), 1–74, esp. 51ff., and R. Otto, The Kingdom of God and the Son of Man (1938), pp. 194ff.

[3] Perrin, Rediscovering, pp. 164–73.

[4] Perrin, ibid., pp. 173–85. He discusses Mark 13: 26 and 14: 62. He shows how these sayings were composed in an exegetical tradition which, in this case, used Dan. 7: 13ff., Ps. 110: 1 and Zech. 12: 10ff. to provide the various elements.

the coming to power of the Son of Man in Dan. 7: 13 provided the basic impetus for this idea of exaltation. Hosea 6: 2b provided the idea of 'on the third day', which has been altered in the 'Son of Man' tradition – as opposed to the 'Christos' tradition – to 'after three days'. This alteration expresses, as Lichtenstein correctly points out,[1] the idea of a three-day sojourn in the realm of death as opposed to the idea of the eschatological 'day of resurrection' which the phrase 'on the third day' expresses. Lichtenstein calls the Christology expressed by these terms a 'Christology of Exaltation'.[2]

(b) The next emphasis to notice is that the Son of Man suffers, according to the Scriptures (8: 31, 9: 9, 9: 12, 9: 31, 10: 33, 14: 21, 14: 41).

M. D. Hooker points out that in Dan. 7 the Son of Man, identified with the 'saints of the Most High (Dan. 7: 27)' suffers the persecution of the beasts (Dan. 7: 21, 25) before he comes into his power.[3] She finds in this element of Dan. 7 an explanation of the 'necessity' (δεῖ) of the Son of Man's sufferings (8: 31, 9: 12, 10: 45, 14: 21, 14: 41).[4]

Tödt's discussion[5] of the theme of 'necessity' in these sayings is most illuminating. He shows that it expresses the understanding that the Passion took place in accordance with God's will revealed in Scripture,[6] and is not a fixed 'apocalyptic eschatological "must" formula' like the one expressed in LXX Dan. 2: 28. The simplest evidence for this view is that the term δεῖ, essential to the 'formula', occurs only once in the sayings (8: 31). Otherwise the idea of necessity is expressed by the phrase 'it is written' (9: 12, 14: 21); or by the statement that he 'came in order to give his life' (10: 45); or by the phrase 'the hour has come' (14: 41). Tödt goes so far as to say that the 'must' in 8: 31 is to be understood as equivalent to 'it is written' in 9: 12.[7]

If one asks precisely what scriptures this tradition had in view when it expressed the necessity of the suffering of the Son of

---

[1] Cited by Tödt, p. 183. We find Tödt's objections to this argument unconvincing.

[2] *Ibid.*, p. 181.

[3] Hooker, pp. 24–30, 108–9; W. D. Davies, *Paul*, p. 280 n. 1.

[4] Hooker, p. 108.   [5] Tödt, pp. 188–94.

[6] See also Matt. 26: 54, Luke 24: 25–7, 44 *passim.*

[7] Tödt, p. 192.

Man, one has to recognize that Dan. 7 has the strongest claim to attention, simply because of the use of the name 'Son of Man'. In Dan. 7 the Son of Man suffers as the symbol of the Maccabean martyrs – the 'saints of the Most High'. If Jesus was understood under the image of the Son of Man of Dan. 7, his suffering would correspond to the suffering of the Son of Man. Jesus' resurrection is understood in this tradition as the exaltation to power of the Son of Man; it would seem probable therefore that his sufferings and death were understood as the sufferings of the Danielic Son of Man, which in the text – and therefore necessarily, by the logic of an early Christian exegete – precede his exaltation.

We may now attempt to explain the change which the tradition made in Hos. 6: 2b from 'on the third day' to 'after three days', expressing thereby the idea of a three-day sojourn in the realm of death. That realm is the realm of the beasts in Dan. 7, in which the Son of Man temporarily sojourned before his exaltation.

These two elements – the exaltation and the suffering – suggest that Daniel 7 was operative in the tradition that formed the Passion sayings. If this is so, the Son of Man, exalted out of his suffering, is a heavenly being. From the point of view of the post-resurrection tradition he had already been exalted. From the point of view of the sayings themselves the Son of Man is still under the dominion of the 'beasts'.

Does the identification of Jesus with the Son of Man of Dan. 7 imply the pre-existence of Jesus? We wish to postpone discussion of this question for the present. However, at this point one should notice that the Passion and exaltation of the Son of Man were understood to be the fulfilment of scripture. Dan. 7 was understood to have been speaking about Jesus and his experience, before Jesus appeared in history. In some way, not clear to us, the pre-existence of Jesus is implied in this idea of the fulfilment of scripture.

We must also consider the Future, coming Son of Man (8: 38, 13: 26, 14: 62). Perrin has shown to our satisfaction that 13: 26 and 14: 62 are the products of a Christian exegetical activity similar in method to the pesher exegesis of the Qumran commentaries.[1] They testify to an interpretation of the resurrection

---

[1] Perrin, *Rediscovering*, pp. 173–85.

in terms of Dan. 7: 13 (from which the element of the 'clouds' comes, as well as the term 'Son of Man'), Zech. 12: 10ff. (from which the reference to 'seeing' comes) and Ps. 110: 1 (from which comes the reference to being 'at the right hand of God'). Mark 13: 26 and 14: 62 therefore provide more evidence for the identification of Jesus with the Danielic Son of Man, as a result of his resurrection.

8: 38 is central to the discussion about the possible authenticity of some Son of Man sayings as words of Jesus. We shall discuss it when we deal with Luke 12: 8 (pp. 93–6 below).

Finally we consider the two texts which tell of the Son of Man on Earth (2: 10, 2: 28)

(a) But that you may know that the Son of Man has authority to forgive sins on earth – he says to the paralytic. (2: 10)

There is some variation in the textual tradition in the place in which the phrase 'on earth' occurs. It is even omitted altogether in some manuscripts. Other manuscripts have it after 'Son of Man', which is the position adopted by Matt. 9: 6 and Luke 5: 24. The Markan textual tradition that places it in the latter position is probably due to influence from Matt. and Luke,[1] and so it seems likely that the text adopted above is nearest to the Markan autograph.

The Markan version seems to emphasize the authority of the Son of Man to forgive sins, whereas the Matthean and Lukan version seems to emphasize that it is on earth that he forgives sins. This may, however, be hairsplitting, since the claim of the saying is clear in both versions: the Son of Man has authority during his earthly life to forgive sins.

We cannot accept the view that 'Son of Man' is here a mistaken translation of an original reference to man. Such an original saying would be bathetic and blasphemous, as well as incomprehensible within the context of contemporary Judaism.[2] Neither can we go into the debate about the unity of Mark 2: 1–12. Hooker regards it as an essential unity based on the historical event itself. Jesus actually healed a paralytic by proclaiming the forgiveness of his sins, and then defended his action by appealing to his dignity as the Son of Man and his authority to forgive sins.[3] Tödt recounts Albertz's and Bult-

---

[1] Hooker, p. 90.   [2] *Ibid.*, pp. 83–4.   [3] *Ibid., passim.*

mann's opinion that 2: 1–12 is really a 'controversy story', and Dibelius' view that verses 6–10 are an insertion into a paradigm of 'an imaginary conversation proclaiming Jesus' authority to forgive sins'. Tödt himself is content merely to recognize that the saying on the Son of Man belongs to a section which most scholars agree was formed by the community. The identification of Jesus with the Son of Man indicates this, according to Tödt.[1]

The central affirmation of the saying is that Jesus has authority (ἐξουσία) to forgive sins. This claim – unparallelled in contemporary Judaism or the Synoptic tradition – is so extraordinary that it must, in our opinion, go back to the historical Jesus. We have therefore a creative modification of the image of the Son of Man by the historical Jesus himself.[2] The Son of Man became the one who forgives sins.

Tödt is, however, concerned to deny the influence on the Synoptic tradition of the transcendent Son of Man in Jewish apocalyptic. Therefore he points out that there is no hint in the apocalyptic tradition that the Son of Man forgives sins. That is the prerogative of God alone. Since Jesus here claims to forgive sins, Tödt takes it as proven that the Son of Man referred to in this saying could not be the transcendent Son of Man of the apocalyptic tradition. But this is a fallacious argument.

The title 'Son of Man' and the claim to have authority (ἐξουσία) recall Dan. 7: 13. The phrase 'upon earth' suggests a contrast with heaven, and, therefore, that the account in Dan. 7: 13 where the Son of Man acts in heaven is being corrected. The forgiveness of sins has been added as a new element along with this correction of Dan. 7. The 'authority' of the Son of Man, therefore, is the authority of a heavenly figure, defined in this saying as the authority to forgive sins, exercised on earth by Jesus himself.

The 'authority of the Son of Man' expresses a Danielic idea. In Dan. 7 the 'authority' is never defined. Here it is defined as the authority to forgive sins. It seems clear that Jesus claimed

---

[1] Tödt, p. 126. Tödt sees it as the product of the Palestinian tradition, because of its similarity with the Q sayings. Bultmann sees it as the product of the Hellenistic branch of the tradition (*ibid.*, p. 127). We shall return to the question of the history of the tradition.

[2] Cf. Tödt, p. 129.

that authority, and referred to himself, by implication, in exercising that authority, as the Son of Man.

(b) So the Son of Man is Lord even of the Sabbath. (2: 28)

We follow Tödt is regarding 2: 28 as an independent saying which expresses 'a fundamental lordship of the Son of Man over God's holy institution of the Sabbath.'[1] Once again, the authority of Jesus is expressed in conjunction with the title 'Son of Man'.

Tödt points out the similarity between these two sayings (2: 10, 2: 28) and the equivalent group in Q.[2] Both here and there they occur in a context of conflict. Tödt believes that they occur here in Mark – so oddly isolated from Mark's main section on the Son of Man in ch. 8 following – because they came to him embedded in controversy stories. There seems, therefore, to be an association between the Son of Man on earth and conflict, in the early strata of the Synoptic tradition. We suggest that this is good historical tradition coming from the life of Jesus.

The dominant tradition in Mark concerns the suffering and rising Son of Man. The rising is conceived of as an exaltation, which we understand to reflect the influence of Dan. 7 in the exegetical tradition which gave these sayings their present form. The same influence can be seen in the expression of the necessity of the suffering of the Son of Man; the Son of Man in Dan. 7 suffered before he came to his power and since Jesus 'fulfils' that scripture in his own history, he must suffer too.

The 'future Son of Man' sayings clearly show the influence of Dan. 7 and the exegetical nature of the tradition; the 'Son of Man on earth' sayings can be understood in the same way, excepting that in this case Jesus himself probably interpreted the Danielic passage.

We have established, therefore, that Dan. 7 was a powerful influence in the formulation of the Son of Man tradition in Mark. We suggest that the initial impulse for this use of Dan. 7 came from Jesus himself, who implied that he was the Son of

---

[1] *Ibid.*, p. 131.

[2] *Ibid.*, pp. 132–3. Mark, however, pays more attention to the authority of the Son of Man than Q; Q pays more attention to the arguments of the opposition.

Man on earth, exercising the authority of the Danielic figure, understood by Jesus as the authority to forgive sins.

There remain to be discussed some miscellaneous texts from Mark. In 10: 35–45 we find the apocalyptic idea of a pre-existent salvation prepared for the elect. When James and John ask for positions of privilege in Jesus' 'glory', he replies, 'to sit at my right hand or at my left is not mine to grant, but it is for those for whom it has been prepared' (10: 40).

In 10: 45, the phrase 'the Son of Man *came*' implies pre-existence, as it did in 1: 38 earlier.[1]

In 11: 10, the coming pre-existent entity referred to in 10: 40 is named by the crowd when they cry, 'Blessed is the kingdom of our father David that is coming! Hosanna in the highest!' Neither Matthew nor Luke follows this allusion. The idea behind the Markan saying is that the glorious kingdom of David, eternal by God's promise (II Sam. 6: 16ff.), had been removed to heaven because of Israel's sin, but would return to earth, and that return would constitute the Messianic age.

12: 35–7a presents the pre-existence of Christ by means of an exegetical subtlety. Assuming that the Psalms were written by David, and that Psalm 110: 1 refers to Jesus the Messiah, the exegete concludes that David spoke of Jesus in Ps. 110: 1, calling him 'Lord'. The initial intention of this exegesis is to establish the superiority of Jesus over David; in the course of the argument the ideal pre-existence of Jesus the Messiah is assumed.[2] An idea that can be pre-supposed as the basis for further argument is one generally accepted by the readers; the pre-existence of the Messiah could be assumed.[3]

The matter of pre-existence as one of the presuppositions of exegesis is also raised by the enigmatic saying,

For the Son of Man goes as it is written of him, but woe to that man by whom the Son of Man is betrayed. (14: 21, cf. 14: 49)

[1] Tödt, pp. 135–8, regards Mark 10: 45 as a saying about the Son of Man on earth.

[2] Cf. S. Mowinckel, *He That Cometh* (New York and Nashville, 1954), pp. 334, 386–9; B. Lindars, *New Testament Apologetic* (Philadelphia, 1961), pp. 210–11.

[3] Cf. J. Knox, *Christ the Lord* (Chicago, 1945), pp. 94ff., who notes that Paul, too, assumes the idea of pre-existence in texts such as Phil. 2: 6, II Cor. 8: 9, Rom. 15: 3. Cf. Mark 1: 38, 10: 45 (Lindars, *Apologetic*, p. 211 n. 2).

The interpretation of the significance of Jesus in terms of the Old Testament scriptures was a major theological enterprise of the earliest Church.[1] The early Christians understood the Old Testament texts as prophecies of Christ. This understanding implies some form of ideal pre-existence for Christ. The 'prophetic' nature of the scriptures is assumed as a ground for further exegetical argument, and this indicates some connection between the early Christian understanding of exegesis and the understanding prevalent at Qumran. It is an apocalyptic view of exegesis, expressed most succinctly, if somewhat obliquely, in Jesus' description of the apocalypse of chapter 13: 'But take heed; I have told you all things beforehand.' The words of Jesus describe the eschatological events, before they take place.

This brief survey of the gospel shows that the Markan tradition understood Jesus to be transcendent both in time and space – he *was* before he began to be at a point in time, and he *is*, beyond what can be seen and handled of his history in this world.

Before we leave these general considerations, the fact which constitutes the 'Messianic Secret' must be dealt with. Most of the revelations of Jesus' divine dignity are followed by stern commands from him that the information be kept secret (e.g. 1: 34, 3: 12, 8: 30, 9: 9); but there is obviously no serious attempt to maintain secrecy. The situation is one of an 'open secret'. Three significant attempts have been made to explain the phenomenon. Wrede[2] argued that it was a literary device for explaining why Jesus, whose resurrection marked him out as the transcendent Son of God, had not displayed the characteristics of divinity during his historical lifetime. The basic historical tradition about Jesus testified that he was a natural man; the faith of the church based on the resurrection interpreted him as a pre-existent being; the way in which Mark reconciled these two views was to portray the history of a divine being who kept his divinity secret. It has also been suggested that Jesus in fact kept his true identity a secret – although well aware of it himself – in order to prevent a misunderstanding of the nature of his mission, as, for example, a political phenomenon.[3]

[1] Cf. C. H. Dodd, *According to the Scriptures; the Sub-structure of New Testament Theology* (London, 1952).

[2] William Wrede, *Das Messiasgeheimnis in den Evangelien* (Göttingen, 1963); first published 1901, reprinted unchanged.

[3] Taylor, *Mark*, pp. 122–4.

Erik Sjöberg[1] has suggested that the hiddenness of Jesus' identity on earth corresponds to the hiddenness of the Son of Man in apocalyptic texts such as I Enoch. This is an ingenious and plausible suggestion, but it founders on the fact that there is no precedent in apocalyptic for the concealment taking place on earth. One cannot simply transfer the pattern of understanding of the Son of Man in the parables of Enoch to the Jesus portrayed on earth in Mark. The process of inter-action between Jesus and the Son of Man in the history of the synoptic tradition is more complicated than Sjöberg realizes.

The history of the tradition is also more complicated than Wrede realized, but the general contours of his explanation are still the most appropriate to the problem: the Messianic secret is a Markan theological device. H. D. Betz is probably correct when he suggests that it was developed by Mark to reconcile the theology of one of his main sources – a presentation of Jesus as a 'divine man' – with the theology of the passion-kerygma of the Markan church. The 'divine man' source had no theology of the Cross; for it Jesus' divine dignity is manifest in his every deed. For the passion-kerygma his divine dignity was manifest only in the Cross and resurrection. Therefore, the 'divine man' layer of the tradition had to be counteracted. This was done by the overt references to the secrecy of the Messiahship, and by a special interpretation of the miracles.[2] The commands to secrecy are Mark's way of emphasizing that the full revelation of Jesus' person could not take place before the crucifixion and resurrection. This proposal is ingenious and may, indeed, be correct.

The mysterious origin of Jesus is a major theme in Mark. This alone hints at his pre-existence. The myth of Wisdom's Envoys is used, amongst other themes, to express this point, but it is deliberately replaced by the Christology of the Son of Man, revealed in the Transfiguration as the Son of Man of Dan. 7 in his pre-existent glory. The Son of Man is presented as the one who has authority on earth to forgive sins and to act freely on

[1] Erik Sjöberg, *Der verborgene Menschensohn*. See Tödt, pp. 297–302, for a negative critical review of Sjöberg's argument.

[2] H. D. Betz, 'Jesus as Divine Man' in *Jesus and the Historian*, written in honour of Ernest Cadman Colwell, ed. F. Thomas Trotter (Philadelphia, 1968), pp. 114–33, p. 124.

the Sabbath. He is, however, chiefly portrayed as the one who must suffer, die and rise again to exaltation.

We suggest that Mark has taken up and interpreted some of the same traditions as occur in Q. The identification of Jesus in Q as Wisdom's eschatological envoy and the rejected Son of Man is adapted by Mark so as to make Q's point more explicit. Q suggests that Christ, in this twofold capacity, is a heavenly being, occupying a place below Wisdom herself, but above her other envoys. Mark regards the view of Jesus as Wisdom's final messenger as inadequate. He takes it up in order to go beyond it to a Christology of the heavenly Son of Man and Son of God. Thus he makes explicit the view of Jesus as a pre-existent heavenly being. Mark also takes up the theme of Christ's rejection in order to go beyond it, by an overt understanding of the rejection as taking place in the passion.

Mark, therefore, in the traditions of Wisdom and Son of Man, seems to have been aware of the understanding of them in Q – which does not necessarily mean that he knew Q itself – and to have adapted them to his own purposes. In the matter of pre-existence, he makes explicit what is implicit in Q, by developing it further.

III. MATTHEW

M. Jack Suggs[1] has shown to our satisfaction that Matthew identified Christ with Wisdom and Torah, as these entities were understood in the Jewish traditions we have already examined. Since Suggs' work is now available we shall merely summarize the evidence and refer the reader to Suggs' detailed discussion.

In Matt. 23. 34–6 par. Luke 11: 49–51, Matthew identifies Jesus as the 'Wisdom of God' who speaks in Luke's version; and he includes the lament over Jerusalem (Matt. 23: 37–9, par. Luke 13: 34–5) immediately after this saying, thus presenting a continuous discourse which identifies Jesus with Wisdom.[2]

---

[1] *Wisdom, Christology and Law*; cf. F. Christ, *Jesus Sophia*.

[2] Suggs, *Wisdom, Christology and Law*, pp. 63–71. E.g. 'Matthew intends the saying (the Lament) to be understood as a word of incarnate Wisdom whom he sees in Jesus' (p. 67); 'Jesus is Wisdom incarnate' (p. 71). Cf. G. Strecker, *Der Weg der Gerechtigkeit, Untersuchung zur Theologie des Matthäus, F.R.L.A.N.T.* 82 (Göttingen, 1962), p. 113, who understands the Jesus of the lament to be in the place of the Shekinah.

The added importance of the Wisdom tradition for Matthew is attested by his addition of the saying concerning the easy yoke in 11: 28–30.[1] For a long time it was argued that this was part of the extended saying which begins in 11: 25 with 'I thank thee Father, Lord of heaven and earth', and that the whole unit originally belonged to Q. The matrix out of which the saying came, it was argued, was a gnosticizing Wisdom tradition, whose beginning can be seen in Sir. 51, and whose development could be traced in Philo and the Odes of Solomon.[2] W. D. Davies[3] showed that the decisive contours of the passage 11: 25–30 are attested at Qumran, and this checked the speculation about gnostic sources, which had occupied German scholarship up to that point. Nevertheless, we cannot ignore possible Hellenistic elements in the sectarian Judaism by which the saying is influenced. Betz is correct when he writes: 'The pericope belongs within a Hellenistic-Jewish syncretism, the characteristics of which must be carefully examined'.[4]

Matthew's addition to Q in 11: 28–30 presents Christ as Wisdom, who since he invites men to take upon themselves his yoke, is also Torah.[5] The parallels to this addition are Sirach 51: 23ff., 24: 19ff., Prov. 1: 20ff., 8: 1ff.[6] Jesus is identified with pre-existent Wisdom, as the one who is humble and gentle.[7]

From this text (11: 25–30) indicators point to other elements characteristic of Matthew's Christology. If one reads the pericope 11: 25–30 as a whole – the Q section plus Matthew's addition – as Matthew obviously intended it to be read, a counterpart appears in Matt. 28: 18–20. In 11: 25–30 Jesus is the pre-existent Wisdom-figure, in humility praying to the Lord of heaven and earth, and inviting men to come to him, the

---

[1] T. Arvedson, *Das Mysterium Christi, Eine Studie zu Mt. 11: 25–30* (Leipzig and Uppsala, 1937), pp. 209–18, believes that Matthew identifies Jesus here and elsewhere with Wisdom.

[2] H. D. Betz, 'The Logion of the Easy Yoke and of Rest (Matt. 11: 28–30)', *J.B.L.* 86 (1967), 10–24, esp. p. 16.

[3] '"Knowledge" in the Dead Sea Scrolls and Matthew 11: 25–30' in *Christian Origins and Judaism* (London, 1962), pp. 119–44, originally in *H.T.R.* 46 (1953), 113ff.

[4] Betz, 'Easy Yoke', p. 19.

[5] Suggs, *Wisdom, Christology and Law*, pp. 100–8.

[6] R. Bultmann, *Geschichte*, pp. 171ff.; Betz, 'Easy Yoke', p. 17.

[7] Suggs, *Wisdom, Christology and Law*, pp. 99–108.

source of knowledge; in 28: 18–20 he is the one who has all authority in heaven and earth, sending men out to teach the world. To 'teach them whatever I have commanded you' (28: 20) is to teach them what it means to say, with the Messiah, 'I am gentle and lowly of heart' (11: 29). The 'rest' which the humble Jesus promises (11: 29) is the presence of the Risen Lord with his disciples, and this 'presence' implies a special relationship with the Lord at the end of the age, as the account of the last judgement shows (Matt. 25: 31ff.).[1]

The theme of humility is central to the Matthean portrait of Jesus. G. Barth deals with it in conjunction with the theme of the 'presentness of the risen one' in a section entitled 'The Lowliness of Jesus, the βασιλεὺς πραΰς and the presentness of the risen one,' which is, in turn, part of his examination of the relationship between Christ and the Law.[2] In 12: 17–21 Matthew adds the passage Is. 42: 1–4 to a greatly abbreviated version of Mark's summary (3: 7–12) of the mighty deeds of Jesus. The Isaianic text emphasizes the gentleness of God's servant:

He will not wrangle or cry aloud, nor will anyone hear his voice in the streets; he will not break a bruised reed or quench a smoldering wick... (Matt. 12: 19–20)

A similar demonstration of his lowliness occurs in 8: 17, where he is identified as the suffering servant by the citation of Is. 53: 4, and in 21: 4ff., the quotation from Zechariah 9: 9 is changed, by the omission of δίκαιος καὶ σώζων αὐτός after ἔρχεταί σοι (Matthew follows the LXX to this point), so that πραΰς stands at the midpoint, dominating the quotation.[3]

11: 25–30, when read in conjunction with 28: 18–29,[4] expresses the fact that the one who is gentle and lowly is really the one who has all authority in heaven and on earth. Therefore he can invite men to himself and promise them rest. These texts express the contrast between the appearance of the divine as humble at

[1] Betz, 'Easy Yoke', p. 24. In 25: 31ff. the promised 'rest' is the 'kingdom prepared for you from the foundation of the world'.

[2] G. Barth, 'Matthew's Understanding of the Law' in *Tradition and Interpretation in Matthew*, by G. Bornkamm, G. Barth and H. J. Held (Philadelphia, 1963), pp. 125ff.

[3] *Ibid.*, p. 130.

[4] On this pericope see G. Barth, *ibid.*, pp. 131–7, and G. Strecker, *Der Weg der Gerechtigkeit*, pp. 208–14.

one time and exalted at another, and the continuity of the divine nature in both modes of existence. The reference to the 'authority' of the risen Christ in 28: 18 recalls Daniel's picture of the exalted Son of Man who has ἐξουσία, but most especially the Son of Man who has authority on earth (9: 6).[1] In the juxtaposition of 11: 25–30 and 28: 18–29 there is a hint of the Son of Man – associated with Wisdom/Torah – humiliated and exalted.

In 11: 28–30 Jesus places himself in the role of the Law. For Matthew this Jesus is the risen Christ present to his church. In 28: 16–20 the injunction to teach all men the commands of Jesus explicitly replaces the Law with the teaching of Jesus; but it does not separate the teaching from the person; he is present with them. Thus we hear the confession of the church that the risen Jesus is in their midst, and that, as such, he is the locus of the Shekinah. This is stated even less equivocally in 18: 15–20: 'For where two or three are gathered in my name, there am I in the midst of them' (18: 20) and 'whatever you bind on earth shall be bound in heaven, and whatever you loose on earth shall be loosed in heaven' (18: 18). G. Barth summarizes well:

The presence of Jesus in the congregation is here described as analogous to the presence of the Shekinah (cf. Aboth 3. 2); the place of the Torah is taken by the ὄνομα of Jesus; the place of the Shekinah by Jesus himself.[2]

We have, therefore, a complex of Christological ideas which begins with the presence of the exalted Lord in the congregation and goes on to identify him as Wisdom, Torah and Shekinah.[3]

---

[1] Strecker, *ibid.*, p. 127 n. 2.

[2] G. Barth, *Tradition*, p. 135. For an illuminating discussion see W. D. Davies, *Sermon on the Mount*, pp. 221ff., esp. pp. 224–5, where he shows that the conception of the church and its discipline portrayed in 18: 10ff. is very similar to the community of Qumran. The statement in 18: 10 concerning the guardian angels is a commonplace of Judaism, but that they see God is extraordinary (Davies, p. 226). 1 Q.S. 11: 8ff. portrays the community as one which has company with the angels – a heavenly community. Matt. 18: 18 on 'binding and loosing' is more Rabbinic than sectarian, however. Davies concludes: 'We find, therefore, in 18: 15–20 the collocation of sectarian and rabbinic usage' (p. 225).

[3] Cf. A. M. Goldberg, *Untersuchungen über die Vorstellung von der Schekhinah in der frühen rabbinischen Literatur* (Berlin, 1969). According to Goldberg, Shekinah is the name of God in His real presence in Israel and in the world – His 'direct and immediate' presence.

The time of his earthly life is viewed as a time of humiliation for the pre-existent one. We may presume that the idea of the pre-existence of Christ was expressed in the Matthean congregation by means of the Wisdom myth, with special emphasis on the identification of Wisdom with Torah, as witnessed in Sir. 24: 23, I Baruch 4: 1, and the Rabbinic tradition.

There are several miscellaneous texts in Matthew pertinent to the idea of pre-existence. Some suggest that the Kingdom of heaven is a pre-existent place. In 25: 34, the kingdom has been prepared for the elect 'from the foundation of the world'. This rather overt reference to the apocalyptic kingdom prepared and concealed in heaven until the last times enables us to understand other elements in Matthew's references to the Kingdom. In 18: 3 Matthew talks about 'entering' the kingdom, whereas Mark (10: 15) and Luke (18: 17) talk in the first place about 're-ceiving' it (cf. 7: 21, 21: 31, 23: 13). In 19: 28 Matthew has elaborated a saying from Q (Luke 22: 28–30) – which in itself testified to the apocalyptic view of the kingdom as a heavenly 'place' – into one portraying the Son of Man sitting on his throne surrounded by the twelve, each on his own throne.

These sayings convey an idea of the Kingdom as a literally conceived heavenly place, existing before its manifestation, and at least since the foundation of the world.[1]

There is a great emphasis on the coming judgement in Matthew.[2] Only Matthew presents detailed accounts of the last judgement (7: 21ff., 13: 36ff., 25: 31ff.) and these accounts state clearly that Jesus is the judge. In 7: 21–3, for instance, two sayings from Q (Luke 6: 46, 13: 26–7) are edited so as to make it unmistakably clear that Jesus is the one who in the judgement will decide who 'enters' the kingdom and who is excluded. Other apocalyptic traits in Matthew are: the references to angels (2: 13, 18: 10, 26: 56); the idea of warning through dreams (27: 19); and the intensification of the cosmic disruptions and portents which the tradition associated with the death (27: 51–4) and resurrection of Jesus (28: 2 and 4); but the most important apocalyptic trait of all is the doctrine concerning the interpretation of scripture.

---

[1] See Strecker, *Der Weg*, pp. 166–75, for a discussion of other aspects of Matthew's doctrine of the Kingdom.

[2] Cf. G. Barth, *Tradition*, pp. 58–62; Matt. 10: 22, 12: 36, 13: 24–30, 36–43.

Although Krister Stendahl is less certain than he was in 1954 that Matthew's gospel was produced by a 'school' of exegetes, he still insists that the use of the Old Testament in Matthew, particularly with respect to the textual traditions which are followed, is sophisticated and testifies to considerable 'exegetical' ability amongst the members of Matthew's church.[1] We agree with this judgement. Stendahl's demonstration of the 'exegetical' nature of at least one strand of the early Christian tradition has been used by N. Perrin[2] and B. Lindars[3] to illuminate a wide spectrum of sayings in the Synoptic tradition.

Stendahl emphasized those quotations which Matthew introduces with the formula: 'That the word spoken by the prophet might be fulfilled', or some variant of that phrase.[4] He finds these 'formula quotations' to have been produced by a method of exegesis very similar to the 'pesher' exegesis employed at Qumran.[5] He talks of 'a pesher type in Matthew's quoting'.[6]

The basic assumption of pesher exegesis is that the scriptures are prophetic and tell about the eschatological events. The prophets, for instance, wrote under God's inspiration, about the eschatological time (1 Qp Hab. 2: 9, 7: 1). They did not understand the full significance of what they wrote. The 'Teacher of Righteousness' was sent by God to interpret the words of the prophets (1 Qp Hab. 2: 8ff., 7: 4).[7]

We shall consider one of Matthew's 'formula quotations' as an example of 'pesher' exegesis.[8] Matt. 13: 35 is a good example

[1] K. Stendahl, *The School of St. Matthew and its use of the Old Testament*, with a New Introduction by the Author (Philadelphia, 1969) (first published 1954). See especially the new preface, pp. i–xiv. See W. D. Davies, *Sermon on the Mount*, pp. 208–56, for a broader discussion of the possible relationship between Matthew and the Dead Sea sect.

[2] *Rediscovering, passim.*   [3] *Apologetic.*

[4] Stendahl, *School of St. Matthew*, pp. 97–127. The 'formula-sayings' are: 1: 23, 2: 6, 2: 15, 2: 18, 2: 23, 4: 15–16, 8: 17, 12: 18–21, 13: 35, 21: 5, 27: 9–10.

[5] *Ibid.*, pp. 190–202. See also Otto Betz, *Offenbarung und Schriftforschung in der Qumransekte*, *W.U.N.T.* 6 (Tübingen, 1960), p. 79.

[6] Stendahl, p. 201.

[7] Otto Betz, *Offenbarung*, pp. 74–80; W. H. Brownlee, 'Biblical Interpretation among the Sectaries of the Dead Sea Scrolls', *B.A.* 14 (1951), 54–76, especially pp. 60–2, where he sets out thirteen exegetical principles that, he believes, govern the pesher method of interpretation.

[8] Lindars, *Apologetic*, pp. 156–9; W. D. Davies, *Sermon on the Mount*, pp. 234–5; Stendahl, *School*, pp. 116–18.

in itself, and the context in which it occurs – the explanation of the teaching in parables – is especially important for understanding Matthew's theology.[1]

Matthew appends to the Markan summary of Jesus' parabolic teaching in Mark 4: 33–4 the following:

This was to fulfil what was spoken by the prophet: I will open my mouth in parables, I will utter what has been hidden since the foundation of the world (Ps. 78: 2).

Matt. 13: 35	LXX Ps. 78: 2	Hebrew
ἀνοίξω ἐν παραβολαῖς	ἀνοίξω ἐν παραβολαῖς	אפתחה במשל
τὸ στόμα μου,	τὸ στόμα μου,	פי
ἐρεύξομαι κεκρυμμένα	φθέγξομαι προβλή-	אביעה חידות
ἀπὸ καταβολῆς	ματα[2] ἀπ᾽ ἀρχῆς	מני קדם

Matthew has taken over the LXX version of the first part of the verse, but for the second part has given 'an independent rendering of the Hebrew text'.[3] The most notable change in Matthew's version is the translation of חידות (lit. 'riddles' as the Greek versions have it) as κεκρυμμένα ('hidden things'). Lindars points out that this contradicts the meaning of the Psalm, which tells of things handed down – the mighty acts of God – which the Psalmist will *not hide*, but pass on to succeeding generations. The re-interpretation, however, expresses the assumption of pesher exegesis that all the scriptures are prophetic[4] and that the meaning of the text could be understood fully only in the eschatological time, since it referred 'mysteriously' to the eschatological events. Pesher exegesis is precisely the revealing of the 'hidden things' to which the text referred. No one understood Ps. 78 until Jesus came and revealed that he indeed is 'the testimony established in Jacob' and 'the Law appointed in Israel' (Ps. 78: 5, cf. Sir. 24: 23, I Bar. 4: 1).

[1] See Wilhelm Wilkens, 'Die Redaktion des Gleichniskapitels Mark 4 durch Matth.', *T.Z.* 20 (1964), 305–27; J. D. Kingsbury, *The Parables of Jesus in Matt. 13* (Richmond, 1969).

[2] Aquila: αἰνίγματα Symmachus: προβλήματα.

[3] Lindars, *Apologetic*, pp. 156ff.

[4] Cf. Otto Betz, *Offenbarung*, pp. 74–8. Brownlee, 'Biblical Interpretation', pp. 60–2. Note that Matthew introduces the quotation from the Psalm as a word 'spoken by the prophet' (verse 35), cf. 21: 10, 24: 15. K. Stendahl, *School*, pp. 183–202.

What is the meaning of the Psalm for Matthew? It exhorts men to 'set their hope on God' and 'obey his commandments' and not to be 'like their fathers, a stubborn and rebellious generation, a generation whose heart was not steadfast, whose spirit was not faithful to God' (verses 7–8). For every gracious act of God on their behalf, men set up rebellion and sinful resistance. The dialectic between God and his people continues throughout the Psalm, reaching a climax in 'David his servant' (τὸν δοῦλον αὐτοῦ), chosen to be the 'shepherd of Jacob his people' (verses 70–2). Matthew believed that only the Christian scribe could understand this Psalm, because all the saving activity of God was summed up in Jesus, and all the hostility of Israel in his opponents.

The phrase 'What has been hidden since the foundation of the world' (Ps. 78: 2) describes, for Matthew, the plan of salvation as it was conceived in God's mind, and as it has been played out in the sacred history. It is the same idea as Qumran expresses by the term רזים, and Paul by the term μυστήριον.[1] Only the Christian scribe can understand the scriptures aright. It is the same idea of privileged revelation as is expressed in 11 : 25ff.[2] The established scribes and the 'wise' could not understand.

W. D. Davies suggests that Matt. 13: 36ff. should also be connected with 13: 35 in any attempted interpretation. He writes:

The meaning of the parable of the Tares is explained privately and the explanation turns out to be an interpretation of history similar to that granted to the initiates of the Dead Sea Sect, as we have seen. The κεκρυμμένα announced previously in the parables are now expounded. Jesus as Messiah *reveals*: he performs the function ascribed in I Qp H vii. 4ff., as Stendahl points out, to the Teacher of Righteousness.[3]

The exclusive privilege of the Christian scribe to understand the hidden meaning of the scriptures can be seen even more

---

[1] See also R. E. Brown, 'The Pre-Christian Semitic Concept of Mystery', *C.B.Q.* 20 (1958), 417–43; L. Cerfaux, 'La Connaissance des Secrets du Royaume d'après Matt. XIII. 11 et Parallèles', *N.T.S.* 2 (1955–6), 238–49. The idea probably goes back to Daniel 2.

[2] W. D. Davies, '"Knowledge" in the Dead Sea Scrolls', *passim*; *Sermon on the Mount*, p. 214.

[3] *Sermon on the Mount*, pp. 234–5.

clearly by considering Matthew's treatment of the reference to the parabolic teaching in Mark 4: 10–12 (par. Matt. 13: 11).[1]

For to you has been given the mystery (μυστήριον) of the Kingdom of God but for those outside everything is in parables; so that they may indeed see but not perceive, and may indeed hear but not understand; lest they should turn again and be forgiven.

Matthew takes this over, and makes the following changes: (i) 'mystery' becomes the plural 'mysteries'; (ii) after 'mysteries of the Kingdom of heaven' he inserts, 'but to them it has not been given', instead of Mark's 'but for those outside everything is in parables'. Mark leaves at least some possibility that those outside might solve the 'riddle' of the parables and gain knowledge of the mystery; Matthew's statement flatly excludes them (cf. 22: 11–14);'(iii) ἵνα becomes ὅτι (vs. 13) thus expressing that the lack of understanding is a fait accompli; (iv) after that, Matthew inserts a saying (Matt. 13: 12, par. Mark 4: 25, par. Luke 8: 18b) which emphasizes the exclusive privilege of the disciples and threatens those outside with the judgement:

For to him who has will more be given, and he will have abundance; but from him who has not, even what he has will be taken away.

(v) There follows the Markan allusion to Isaiah 6: 9ff.;[2] to which Matthew adds a Q saying, which is determinative for an understanding of Matthew's view of the parabolic teaching:

But blessed are your eyes, for they see, and your ears for they hear. Truly I say to you, many prophets and righteous men longed to see what you see, and did not see it, and to hear what you hear, and did not hear it (Matt. 13: 16–17 par. Luke 10: 23–4).

Here we have the explanation of τὰ κεκρυμμένα in 13: 35! The meaning of the history of God's saving acts (Ps. 78) has been hidden from all until now; those who come to Jesus can understand it, for it reaches eschatological fulfilment in him.

Several important results emerge from these considerations: What begins in Matthew as a statement about the parabolic teaching of Jesus (13: 11) – that only the disciples can under-

---

[1] Cf. Lindars, *Apologetic*, pp. 155–6.

[2] The full quotation of Is. 6: 9–10 in vss. 14–15 is probably an insertion made at a time later than Matthew's own composition (Stendahl, *School*, p. 131; Strecker, *Der Weg*, p. 70 n. 3).

stand it – broadens into a claim that only the Christian exegete can understand the scriptures (13: 16–17). 13: 35 identifies the traditions 'that our fathers have told us...the glorious deeds of the Lord, and his might, and the wonders he has wrought' (Ps. 78: 3–4) with the parabolic teaching of Jesus. More precisely, that teaching fulfils the promise, 'we will not hide them from their children but tell them to the coming generation'. This is nothing less than a claim that the teaching of Jesus expresses the true meaning of the scriptures, and that they are closed to all who do not approach them from the Christian point of view.

This view explains, on the one hand, the authority of Jesus' teaching over previous interpreters of the scriptures, expressed in the sayings, 'You have heard that it was said to the men of old...but I say to you' (5: 21–2, 27, 28, 31–2, 33–4, 38–9, 43–4), and on the other, his solemn assurance, 'Think not that I have come to abolish the law and the prophets; I have come not to abolish them but to fulfil them' (5: 17). The meaning of 'fulfil' here is best taken, as W. D. Davies argues, 'in the light of its total context, to mean "to complete" or "to bring to its destined end".'[1] The first important result is that the Matthean circle identified the parables of Jesus and the scripture as entities of the same kind; revelatory words whose meaning could be understood only by those who realized that Jesus himself is the eschatological fulfiller, and understood that this realization is the key to the revelatory words.

The second important result concerns the idea of pre-existence. Such a view of scripture – and therefore of sacred history – implies the ideal pre-existence of Christ. If Christ is

---

[1] *Sermon on the Mount*, pp. 100–2. See also his explanation of the antitheses, on the basis of D. Daube's judgement: 'the Matthean form is far milder, less revolutionary than one might incline to believe...these declarations "Ye have heard...But I say unto you", are intended to prove Jesus the Law's upholder, not destroyer. The relationship between the two members of the form is not one of pure contrast; the demand that you must not be angry with your brother is not thought of as utterly irreconcilable with the prohibition of killing. On the contrary, wider and deeper though it may be, it is thought of as, in a sense, resulting from and certainly including the old rule; it is *a revelation of a fuller meaning for a new age.* The second member unfolds rather than sweeps away the first.' (D. Daube, *The New Testament and Rabbinic Judaism* (1956), p. 60, cited W. D. Davies, *ibid.*, p. 102.)

the fulfilment of scripture he must have been present – at least as an idea in the mind of God – when the plan of salvation to which the scriptures bear witness was formulated.

A third result is to confirm the influence of Jewish apocalyptic on the theology of Matthew. One of the ways in which it exercised its formative function was by means of pesher exegesis. This 'pesher' exegesis, whose basic assumption was that Jesus fulfils the scriptures and therefore was present in the plan of God – the outworking of which is recorded in the scriptures – was not practised only by Matthew. Matthew merely uses it more explicitly. Lindars[1] and Perrin[2] have shown that it occurs widely in the early tradition. It would seem, therefore, that Matthew gives us a glimpse into a widespread assumption of early Christian theology – that Christ pre-existed in the plan of God.

It remains simply to note the birth narrative in 1: 18–25. Lindars identifies this as a product of the controversy about Jesus' origins,[3] whereas W. D. Davies sees it as a product of the Church's meditation on the mystery of Christ's origin.[4] It is constructed on the pesher citation of Is. 7: 14, which is quoted at verse 23, together with a fragment of Is. 8: 8 and 10 ('which means God with us'). Fragments of Is. 7: 14 occur in verse 18 (ἐν γαστρὶ ἔχουσα) and in verse 21 (τέξεται δὲ υἱόν, καὶ καλέσεις τὸ ὄνομα αὐτοῦ); and the latter part, about the 'naming' of the child, is repeated in verse 25. The Matthean exegetes interpreted Is. 7: 14 to indicate that Jesus was conceived by the Holy Spirit and born of a virgin, which, while it does not say that he existed before he was conceived, does state most clearly that in Jesus 'God is with us'; his presence is a transcendent presence.

Davies[5] suggests that phrases like βίβλος γενέσεως (Matt. 1: 1) which recall Gen. 2: 4a and 5: 1 indicate that Matthew had the narratives of the creation of the world (Gen. 1: 1 – 2: 4) and of Adam (Gen. 5: 1–3) in mind. The role of the Spirit in the creation of the universe is well known in Gen. 1; the conception of Jesus by the Spirit, therefore, indicates that a new creation has come into being. This interpretation would make Jesus the

---

[1] *Apologetic.*   [2] *Rediscovering.*

[3] *Apologetic*, pp. 213–16.

[4] *Sermon on the Mount*, p. 66 and Appendix III, pp. 443–4.

[5] *Ibid.*, pp. 67–73.

new Adam. This view is probably correct, especially since Hellenistic Judaism magnified the role of the Spirit in creation, and Hellenistic thought is where the idea of divine conception would have been at home.[1]

There has been some speculation in scholarly circles that the word ἀνατολή in Matt. 2: 1, 2 and 9 and Luke 1: 78 signifies the pre-existence of the Messiah.[2] The association of light with the advent of important persons is attested. Bentzen suggests that ἀνατολή is equivalent in meaning to ἔξοδοι (= origin) in Micah 5: 2 LXX, which Matt. understands to be a Messianic prophecy (2: 6). Micah 5: 2 says of the Messiah that his 'origin (ἔξοδοι) is from old, from ancient days'. Luke 1: 78 speaks of the Messiah's 'rising', ἀνατολή. Benoit points out that the Messianic usage of ἀνατολή was prepared for by the use of ἀνατέλλειν in 'Messianic' passages, especially Num. 24: 17, the 'Star' passage, and Mal. 4: 2.[3] Davies concludes:

The term ἀνατολή clearly has Messianic nuances, which connect the appearance of the Messianic deliverer with creation itself. Perhaps the term ἐν τῇ ἀνατολῇ in Matt. ii. 3, 9 should not be emptied of such significance.[4]

Luke 1: 78, therefore, suggests that the Messiah is a pre-existent being come to earth; Matt. 2: 1–2 and 9 may also reflect something of this understanding.

A second indication of the presence of the idea of pre-existence in this context is the genealogy (Matt. 1: 2–17, cf. Luke 3: 23–38). The threefold division into groups of fourteen shows that with Jesus a new stage in history begins. This 'grouping' is probably the result of the influence of the apocalyptic idea of 'epochs'. Jesus is presented as the fulfilment of Abraham's line. Therefore Jesus was pre-existent in the mind of God when the plan of the generations was formed. This is the same idea of pre-existence as that implied by the theory of pesher exegesis. Once again we conclude with Davies' summary:

the genealogy, as such, is an impressive witness to Matthew's conviction that the birth of Jesus was no unpremeditated accident but

[1] C. K. Barrett, *Holy Spirit*, pp. 21–4.
[2] W. D. Davies, *Sermon on the Mount*, pp. 445–6.
[3] All this follows W. D. Davies, *ibid.*, pp. 445–6.
[4] *Ibid.*, p. 446.

occurred in the fullness of time and in the providence of God, who overruled the generations to this end, to inaugurate in Jesus a new order, the time of fulfilment.[1]

Following the procedure of Tödt, we shall, in considering the Son of Man, discuss two of Matthew's own formulations first, and then consider selected examples of his treatment of sayings from Mark and Q.

(a) 13: 41-2

The Son of Man will send out his angels, and they will collect everything that causes men to stumble and those who work lawlessness, out of his kingdom, and they will cast these into the blazing furnace.

This saying occurs in the explanation (13: 36–43) of the parable of 'the wheat and the tares' (13: 24–40). The explanation is Matthew's own composition.[2] As proof of the Matthean origin of the passage, Jeremias points, amongst other things, to the peculiar references to the 'angels of the Son of Man' (verse 41) – which occurs elsewhere only in Matt. 16: 27 and 24: 31 – and to the 'kingdom of the Son of Man' (verse 41) – which also occurs elsewhere in the New Testament only in Matthew (Matt. 16: 28).[3]

As Tödt points out, the Son of Man is spoken of in three ways in 13: 36–43.[4] In verse 41 he is the judge of the world; in verse 41b he is, by implication, the possessor of a kingdom; and in verse 37 he is the one who, by his preaching on earth, sows the good seed, which is 'the sons of the kingdom' (13: 38).[5]

The Son of Man as judge is especially emphasized in I Enoch;[6] the theme of the angels of the Son of Man who punish evil-doers is also present in I Enoch.[7] The final separation of the evil-doers from the righteous is portrayed in Matt. 13: 40b–43 in 'lurid apocalyptic colours'.[8] We may, therefore, assume that in these verses Matthew has in mind a Son of Man like the Son of Man

---

[1] *Ibid.*, p. 73. See also M. D. Johnson, *The Purpose of the Biblical Genealogies*, S.N.T.S. Mon. 8 (Cambridge, 1969), pp. 139–228.

[2] J. Jeremias, *The Parables of Jesus* 6 (New York, 1963), pp. 81–5.

[3] *Ibid.*, p. 82.   [4] Tödt, pp. 69–70.

[5] See I Enoch 62: 8, 'And the congregation of the elect and holy shall be sown.'

[6] I Enoch 45: 3, 46: 1ff., 49: 4.   [7] I Enoch 53–4.

[8] Tödt, p. 70.

in I Enoch. This Son of Man is clearly a pre-existent being, who exists before his own manifestation. We cannot decide at this point whether Matthew's Son of Man was (like Enoch's) also thought to be pre-existent before the creation. We do not know whether the Enoch tradition that Matthew was using was the same as that available to us in the extant Ethiopic Enoch. It would be too hazardous to assume that because there is a correspondence between the figures in Matthew and I Enoch in the element of 'judgement', that the other aspects of Enoch's Son of Man – in this case especially pre-existence before the creation – can be transferred to Matthew's figure.

An important feature of this passage is the distinction it makes between the 'kingdom of the Son of Man' and the 'kingdom of their Father' (verse 43). The former is a temporary kingdom that includes both the righteous and the wicked whereas the latter includes only the righteous and seems to be the final permanent kingdom. Tödt is probably right in understanding 'the kingdom of the Son of Man' to be the Church on earth.[1] The Son of Man is, therefore, Lord of the Church.

How is this Lordship to be understood? In verses 41–2 it is exercised as judgement upon the Church, and in verses 37–8 it is the power that calls people into the Church, that sows the good seed. Tödt insists that the Son of Man is not the Lord of the Church in the sense that he rules over it during its existence on earth. Only the calling of the Church into existence and its judgement are in view, since the 'intermediate' stage of the Church existing in history and ruled by the Spirit has not yet developed.[2]

We find Tödt's strictures to be too severe. True, the 'explanation' of the parable of the Tares (13: 36–43) rather changes the point of the original parable – namely, the exhortation to patience[3] – because of its eagerness to portray the judgement. Nevertheless the judgement is still in the future (40b, οὕτως ἔσται ἐν τῇ συντελείᾳ τοῦ αἰῶνος), and the 'kingdom of the Son of Man' does exist for a time between its inception and the judgement, precisely as the Son of Man's kingdom. We may probably see, therefore, the Lordship of the Son of Man over the Church on earth implied in these sayings.

[1] *Ibid.*, p. 71.   [2] *Ibid.*, p. 73.
[3] Jeremias, *Parables*, p. 81; Bultmann, *Geschichte*, p. 203; Tödt, p. 70.

(b) 25: 31

When the Son of Man comes in his glory and all the angels with him, then he will sit on the throne of his glory.

This is probably a stylized introduction by Matthew himself.[1] The only other reference to the Son of Man upon his throne, in the New Testament, is Matt. 19: 28, and in 16: 27 the same association as occurs here, of the Son of Man with the judgement, occurs in the Matthean version of a saying from Mark (8: 38).

There are strikingly similar statements in I Enoch. In 61: 8 we have:

> And the Lord of the Spirits placed the Elect One on
> the throne of glory
> And he shall judge all the works of the holy above
> in heaven,
> And in the balance shall their deeds be weighed.

and in 62: 2,

> And the Lord of Spirits seated him (the Elect One)
> on the throne of his glory,
> And the spirit of righteousness was poured out upon
> him.

When these parallels are considered along with the role of the Son of Man as judge, here and in the previous saying, the correlation between Matthew and I Enoch becomes clearer and more extensive.

There is an interesting phrase in verse 34: 'the kingdom prepared for you from the foundation of the world'. It has a parallel in I Enoch 71: 15:

> He proclaims unto thee peace in the name of the world
> to come;
> For from hence has proceeded peace since the creation
> of the world.

as well as in IV Ezra 8: 52,

> For you Paradise has been opened, the tree of life
> planted, the future age prepared...

[1] Jeremias, *Parables*, p. 206.

There are also less direct passages in I Enoch that express the idea of the place prepared for the righteous. The first thing Enoch sees in his vision is 'the dwelling places of the holy and the resting-places of the righteous' (39: 4), and then 'the dwelling place of the Elect One (= Son of Man) of righteousness and faith' (39: 6a and 7a). In 41: 1–2 there is a passage that describes these places 'of the elect and holy' in the context of a judgement scene:

And after that I saw all the secrets of the heavens, and how the kingdom is divided, and how the actions of men are weighed in the balance. And there I saw the mansions of the elect and the mansions of the holy, and mine eyes saw there all the sinners being driven from thence which deny the name of the Lord of Spirits, and being dragged off...

The kingdom referred to in Matt. 13: 34 is therefore pre-existent.[1] It seems to be the same kind of entity as the 'dwelling places of the elect' referred to in I Enoch. It would also seem to be the 'kingdom of the Father' in the previous passage discussed, rather than the kingdom of the Son of Man (13: 41–3).

The area of similarity between Matthew and I Enoch in these two sayings is great, and there can be no real doubt that for Matthew, as in Enoch, the term 'Son of Man' signifies a pre-existent heavenly being. However, it is clear that pre-existence is never mentioned or treated for its own sake. The chief attribute of Enoch's Son of Man as far as Matthew is concerned is his role as the eschatological judge. It is also obvious that for Matthew the Son of Man in these sayings is Jesus.[2] According to Tödt, the apocalyptic details in these two sayings are not included for their own sake but as part of the exhortation to the disciples.[3] They have a hortatory function only. This seems to be true for the latter passage, chapter 25, but somewhat strained in the former case. In 13: 36–43, the main interest seems to be to explain what will happen in the judgement; there is a definite apocalyptic interest, but no obvious hortatory intention.

Most of Matthew's modifications of sayings from the tradition make the same points as the two original compositions we

---

[1] *Ibid.*: 'The pre-existence of the Kingdom emphasizes the certainty of the promise.'

[2] Tödt, p. 77. [3] *Ibid.*, p. 79.

have just investigated. We wish, therefore, to notice here only the substitution of the 'I' of Jesus for 'Son of Man' in the Q saying (Matt. 10: 32 par. Luke 12: 8), 'Anyone who confesses me before men, *I* will confess him before my father in heaven.' This is similar to the change in another Q saying (Matt. 23: 32–6 par. Luke 11: 49–51) where Matthew omits the phrase 'Therefore also the Wisdom of God said', and so makes Jesus the speaker and thus identifies him as 'the Wisdom of God'.

By omitting the name 'Son of Man' in 10: 32 par. Luke 12: 8, Matthew has avoided making the Son of Man both advocate and judge. In Luke 12: 8 the Son of Man is the advocate for those who acknowledged him before the eschatological judge; in Matthew the Son of Man is the judge.

In summary one may say that Matthew identified Christ with pre-existent Wisdom-Torah; that he added apocalyptic elements to the tradition, expressing the idea of the kingdom as a heavenly place, and he used the 'pesher' method of exegesis, which assumes that Christ pre-existed in the plan of God. He also identified Christ with the Son of Man of the same tradition as that in I Enoch – the eschatological judge. In I Enoch the Son of Man pre-exists the creation, as does Wisdom also, in the Jewish myth. Pre-existence before creation is probably implied by this twofold identification of Jesus with Wisdom and the Enochian Son of Man in Matthew.

IV. LUKE–ACTS

It is easy to be discouraged by the judgements of Conzelmann[1] that 'the idea of pre-existence is completely lacking in Luke's Christology', and 'that the place of Jesus in the course of redemptive history does not depend on any idea of pre-existence';[2] but there is more to the matter than that.

In the first place, Conzelmann assumes that his readers have a single, uniform idea of what pre-existence means; and this is not the case. One may guess that he uses the word as Bultmann does – because of his known connection with Bultmann, and because Bultmann's view is the only one that makes sense in Conzelmann's usage. On this view, pre-existence has meaning

[1] H. Conzelmann, *The Theology of Luke* (New York, 1960), p. 173.
[2] *Ibid.*, p. 185.

only within the myth of the redeemer, where it refers to that stage of his existence which preceded creation and his coming to earth; but there are, as we have seen, other ideas of pre-existence.

In the second place, to say that the place of Jesus in the redemptive history does not depend on the idea of pre-existence does not exclude the possibility that it may entail pre-existence. That possibility is indeed realized in the text of Luke–Acts; and so, although we accept the illuminating discovery of a three-fold organization of salvation-history in Luke–Acts, which we owe to Conzelmann, we shall try to press beyond his strictures on pre-existence.

The most significant element in the theology of Luke–Acts is the simple existence of Acts. Whereas in Matthew and Mark the early congregation could assimilate their own experience to the history of Jesus so perfectly that they could present it in the garb of the history of Jesus, in Luke the distance between Jesus and the Church is such that a separate history of the Church must be written. The historical gap between Jesus and the Church is real in the Lukan consciousness; clock-time cannot be annihilated as it is in Matthew and Mark. Whereas for Matthew and Mark Jesus is a phenomenon of the present, and so his earthly life is presented as the presence of the eternal in time, which can never really become past, for Luke he is a phenomenon of the past-and-the-present. Jesus has gone and is exalted now in heaven; the Holy Spirit and the 'name' represent the presence of Christ in the Church.

Therefore Jesus is present in a twofold way: as the living Lord in Heaven, and as a figure from the past by means of the picture of him presented by tradition.[1]

Within this new view of the phenomenon of Jesus as an historical event the same apocalyptic elements as determined the structure of thought in the other two gospels are present. They are simply rearranged. Apocalyptic thought is especially fond of arranging the sequence of history in 'epochs'. Luke's tri-epochal redemptive history is an apocalyptic history. The development of doctrine may be reconstructed as follows: the resurrection of Christ was experienced as the eschatological

[1] *Ibid.*, p. 186.

event, the end of 'clock-time' as the end of the epochal series; the delay of the parousia led to the realization that the 'time' of Jesus had not been the end of clock-time, but another epoch along that same line, albeit the centre of the line. This means that Luke is really a re-activation of the apocalyptic view of history,[1] in the wake of the delay of the parousia; and with this 'reactivation' the apocalyptic ideas of pre-existence become a possibility.

Quite as much as Matthew, Luke–Acts emphasizes the fulfil-ment of scripture. The scriptures are interpreted from the point of view of certain historical events which are claimed to be the fulfilment of the texts, but, going beyond Matthew, the range of the interpretive events has been extended to include not only Jesus, but the Church also. The history of Jesus and the Church is the fulfilment of the scriptures and of God's promise to Abraham (1: 45, 54–5, 73); it comprises the salvation prepared beforehand by God (2: 31). Luke alone makes Jesus say at his 'inauguration' in Nazareth, 'Today this scripture has been fulfilled in your hearing', after the citation of Is. 61: 1–2 and 58: 6. There is a comparative absence of references to the fulfil-ment of scripture in the body of the ministry in Luke; they begin again with the references to the passion (e.g. 18: 31, 21: 22, 22: 37, 24: 26–7). The fulfilment theme is most prominent, therefore, at the beginning and end of Christ's life, in Luke's gospel. How are we to explain this?

In Acts we have accounts of the apostolic preaching, pro-bably based on early tradition, even though they were com-posed by 'Luke'.[2] They show that the argument that the death and resurrection of Jesus fulfilled God's purpose expressed in scripture is of the essence of that preaching (2: 22ff.). In 2: 25–31 there is an explicit example of the exegesis Luke pre-supposes in these statements about the fulfilment of scripture. In 2: 25–8, Ps. 16: 8–11 is cited. It refers to one who is not allowed to 'see corruption', and this is understood to mean that God promises to deliver the speaker from death. David, the

---

[1] Cf. *ibid.*, p. 97, '...salvation is delayed. Thus the way is open for accepting the old apocalyptic ideas.' Cf. Luke 10: 20.

[2] Thus E. Haenchen, *Die Apostelgeschichte* (Göttingen, 1961), pp. 148–52. Haenchen believes that Luke drew on old units preserved in the liturgical tradition of his Church, which were 'surprisingly stable' (*ibid.*, pp. 148–9).

presumed speaker is dead and buried, as everyone knows, therefore he must have been talking about someone else. That 'someone else' is one who has indeed been delivered from death, namely, Jesus; David, being therefore a prophet, and knowing that God had sworn with an oath to him that he would set one of his descendants on this throne (Ps. 132: 11), 'he foresaw (προϊδών) and spoke of the resurrection of Christ' (2: 30–1).[1] In Acts the references to the fulfilment of scripture are concentrated in and around the kerygmatic speeches.

We have before us the fact that the references to scripture and the plan of God in Luke–Acts are clustered around the beginning and end of Jesus' ministry in the gospel, and in the kerygmatic sections of Acts. This probably reflects pre-Lukan tradition, but Luke does not extend the references to the other parts of the history. The beginning and end of Jesus' ministry are the points at which the idea of his transcendence is most prominent. One of the ways of expressing his transcendence as the kerygmatic passages in Acts show, was the theme of the fulfilment of scripture. This theme implies a plan of God of which Jesus, and the Church (cf. Acts 2: 16–21), were a part, right from the beginning.

The division of history into epochs, and the idea of the fulfilment of scripture seem to imply that the history of Jesus and the Church took place according to a predetermined divine plan.

The sayings on the Son of Man peculiar to Luke[2] do not add to what we already know about the Son of Man. The sole saying outside the gospels occurs in Acts 7: 56. It tells of the presence of the Son of Man at the right hand of God. Stephen sees him in the moment of death and goes to him. The idea is similar to that expressed in Luke 23: 42–3, where Jesus promises the repentant thief a place 'this day' with him in paradise, and in 22: 69, which tells of the Son of Man sitting at the right hand of power.[3] The apocalyptic heavenly world in which the pre-existent things are is present here.[4]

[1] Cf. Acts 3: 18, 24, 4: 25–8, 7: 52–3, 8: 34–5 (9: 22), 10: 43, 13: 16, 13: 46, 15: 15, 17: 2–3.

[2] Luke 6: 22, 12: 8, 17: 22, 18: 8, 19: 10, 21: 36, 22: 22, 48, 24: 7.

[3] Tödt, p. 102. This is the only saying in the Synoptic tradition whose main point is the *sessio ad dextram dei*.

[4] Haenchen, *Apostelgeschichte*, p. 246, writes of 'den Blick in die aller irdischen Polemik unendlich überlegene himmlische Wirklichkeit'. Tödt, p. 98, writes, 'The Son of Man belongs to God's transcendent reign which

This is an example of the Lukan rewriting of eschatology in the light of the delay of the parousia.[1] The death of the individual Christian is marked by a personal revelation of the Son of Man, and an individual admission to the heavenly and future paradise. It is not a proleptic view of a future parousia, but an actual revelation of the Son of Man to an individual. It is the clearest indication outside the Fourth gospel of the heavenly pre-existence of the Son of Man.[2]

Luke, therefore, suggests that God has a plan for history and that things exist as ideas in that plan before their manifestation in history. He also presents the idea of a heavenly world, as a place where things exist before (and after) their manifestation.

V. THE HISTORY AND PHENOMENOLOGY OF THE IDEA OF PRE-EXISTENCE IN THE SYNOPTIC TRADITION

The Synoptic tradition uses three terms which imply the idea of pre-existence: Wisdom, Son of Man and the kingdom. The kingdom as a heavenly place (Matt. 25: 34 etc.), prepared for the elect, is attested chiefly by Matthew. The idea is a well known part of apocalyptic thought and needs no further discussion.[3] We shall, however, bear it in mind as we pursue the history of the other two terms.

The parables, the Lord's prayer and the preaching concerning the Kingdom probably constitute the authentic core of the recoverable teaching of Jesus.[4] None of these items as preached by Jesus displays the idea of pre-existence explicitly, but all testify to the centrality of the experience of transcendence – of the 'grace from beyond' – as the subject of Jesus' teaching. The parables speak in 'this-worldly' terms, of ordinary life unexpectedly broken open by an experience of joy, a display of 'recklessness', or a summons to decision. They portray a

will come with certainty in the future and which already exists now in heaven.'

[1] C. K. Barrett, 'Stephen and the Son of Man' in *Apophoreta, Festschrift für E. Haenchen*, ed. W. Eltester and F. H. Keltter (Berlin, 1964), pp. 32–8, esp. p. 35.

[2] Cf. E. Schweizer, *Menschensohn*, pp. 202–5.

[3] W. D. Davies, *Paul*, pp. 314–19; N. Perrin, *The Kingdom of God in the Teaching of Jesus* (Philadelphia, 1963).

[4] Perrin, *Rediscovering*, p. 47; Jeremias, *Parables, passim.*

creative upsetting of the normal order of things. They say nothing explicitly about God or any world other than this one.

The 'Lord's prayer' does say something explicit about God: that he is 'Abba';[1] and it refers to heaven as the place where God's will is perfectly fulfilled; but in essence it is a prayer that heaven may be established on earth, that is, that God's will be done here as in heaven. It is a prayer for the coming of God's kingdom, understood as the fulfilment of His will.

The preaching concerning the Kingdom proclaims not a place or a state, but an act – God's eschatological saving act, whose essence is the forgiveness of sins.[2] The 'Kingdom' happens in the preaching of Jesus as sinners, hearing his words, know themselves to be near to God, and it dawns upon them that God has drawn near. In the table-fellowship with Jesus, and in renewed health of body and mind produced by that fellowship, the harlots, renegades, paralytics and possessed experience 'grace', the forgiveness of sins and the removal of the distance between man and God.[3]

The relationship between the person of Jesus and this experience of the nearness of God is a problem. Did his hearers actually experience the same revelation of grace and summons to decision in the teaching of Jesus as the hearers of the apostolic preaching experienced? Bultmann's famous dictum that the teaching of Jesus belongs to the prolegomena to Christian theology, rather than to the Christian message itself, expresses the view that they could not have done; Jesus' preaching concerned an unrealized future which did not begin to become available to men before the resurrection and the concomitant proclamation of the kerygma. The so-called 'New Quest',[4] however, shows that Bultmann was probably in error on this matter. There is a continuity of 'language' and experience between the teaching of Jesus and the kerygma.[5] We may accept the emerging scholarly consensus that the witnesses of

[1] Cf. J. Jeremias, *Abba, Studien zur neutestamentlichen Theologie und Zeitgeschichte* (Göttingen, 1966), pp. 15–67.

[2] On the Kingdom as an 'act' see Perrin, *Rediscovering*, pp. 54–63; as a future expectation, *ibid.*, pp. 159–64.

[3] Jeremias, *Parables*, pp. 124–46.

[4] Cf. J. M. Robinson, *The New Quest of the Historical Jesus* (Naperville, 1959); G. Bornkamm, *Jesus of Nazareth* (London and New York, 1960).

[5] See also E. Jüngel, *Paulus und Jesus* (Tübingen, 1964), pp. 278–9.

the historical Jesus could have seen in his actions and heard in his words the same 'Word of God' as men later heard in the kerygma – and some did.[1]

This acceptance, in turn, solves the problem of future and realized eschatology, along the lines suggested by Kümmel.[2] The promised nearness of God in his sovereign grace is a present fact in Jesus; but it is also a future reality. After his rejection and death, the same sovereign grace which men experienced in his historical presence becomes present in the kerygma, which replaces the historical Jesus. The hope that that grace will finally prevail over all mankind is outstanding and looks to the future for fulfilment. In the teaching of Jesus the sovereign act of God's grace – the kingdom of God – is both present and future, realized and outstanding.[3]

While it may be true that one simply cannot conceive of a sane human consciousness which could believe itself to be pre-existent as the Christian tradition understood this idea,[4] it is quite conceivable that a man's words and deeds should be such that others would attribute pre-existence to him. This at least we believe to have been the case with Jesus.[5] The history of the idea of pre-existence in the synoptic tradition begins, we suggest, with the experience of the sovereignly active grace of God in the historical Jesus. Another way of expressing it is to say that pre-existence is implied by realized eschatology and that any history of the idea in this tradition must begin with the element of realized eschatology in the teaching and activity of the historical Jesus.

[1] Cf. J. M. Robinson, 'Jesus' Parables as God Happening', in *Jesus and the Historian*, pp. 134–50, esp. p. 139, where he cites E. Fuchs: 'We must break with the stiff-necked prejudices to the effect that Jesus' parables apply primarily to our relation to God. It seems to me that they apply to our relation to Jesus himself.' (*Th.L.Z.* LXXIX (1954), cols. 345–8). He also cites Jeremias' welcome of Fuch's opinion that there are in the parables 'hidden Christological testimonies to himself' (*Parables*, p. 230 n. 1).

[2] W. G. Kummel, *Promise and Fulfilment, the Eschatological Message of Jesus* (Naperville, 1957).

[3] For a useful review of the discussion concerning the Kingdom of God see N. Perrin, *The Kingdom of God*.

[4] Cf. J. Knox, *The Death of Christ*, pp. 52–77.

[5] On this view, Jesus seems to be a more credible historical figure than he does on Bultmann's view that a miracle – the resurrection – transformed a relatively unremarkable prophet into a transcendent being.

The idea of pre-existence is expressed in the presuppositions of eschatologically determined exegesis and by means of the myths of Wisdom and the Son of Man. We shall now attempt to sketch briefly the history of this exegesis and of both of these myths in the synoptic tradition.

B. Lindars and N. Perrin have shown that new insights into the history of the tradition can be gained by taking seriously C. H. Dodd's observation that the initial theological enterprise of the Church was the exegesis of the scriptures in such a way that it found in them a context within which to understand the history and experience of Jesus and his first followers.[1] With this new method of investigating the tradition goes a new understanding of the Church. The form critics understood the earliest Church chiefly as a cultic community, frequently engaged in missionary proclamation and polemic. Lindars accepts the form critic's position when he argues – as the title of his book 'New Testament Apologetic', indicates – that the chief impulse leading to this early exegetical activity was the need to explain and defend their attachment to Jesus, but he adds another possible *Sitz im Leben* – the exegetical 'school'. Combined with the images of it provided by the form-critics, the new view of the early church as a 'school' of exegesis[2] expands our understanding of the matrix of the tradition.

Another new and fruitful approach to the history of the tradition concerns itself with genres as distinct from forms. H. Köster[3] has suggested that there were four genres in the pre-synoptic stage of the tradition: a 'sayings' genre, such as Q and Thomas,[4] an 'aretalogy' genre such as the series of miracle stories in Mark and John, and those elements throughout the sources which treat Jesus as a divine man; a 'revelation' genre,

---

[1] C. H. Dodd, *According to the Scriptures*; Lindars, *Apologetic*, pp. 14ff.; Perrin, *Rediscovering, passim.*

[2] Stendahl, *School*; cf. H. Conzelmann, 'Paulus und die Weisheit', *N.T.S.* 12 (1965–6), 231–44.

[3] 'One Jesus and Four Primitive Gospels.'

[4] Tödt, pp. 247–53, describes the impulse behind the compilation of Q as the impulse to continue to teach the teaching of Jesus. He writes: 'Of course, this idea upsets the prevailing notion that the earliest and central message was the passion kerygma alone. Instead this idea assumes that there was a community which accepted as its central commission the communication of Jesus' teaching' (*ibid.*, p. 247).

such as the gnostic Apocryphon of John; and the well known 'Passion-Resurrection' genre which finally became the standard, and until recently determined the definition, of a 'gospel'.

The chief theological significance of these, as yet imperfect, theories is to show that the significance of Jesus could be presented without necessarily referring to his death and resurrection. H. D. Betz,[1] for instance, has shown some reason to believe that a pre-synoptic theology of Jesus as a divine man existed apart from the kerygma of his passion and resurrection, and that Luke and John never do come to terms with the passion,[2] while Mark invokes the pall of secrecy – that Jesus' status as a divine man be not revealed until the passion is past and the resurrection here. Thus the Messianic secret is explained as a result of the bringing together of a 'divine man' Christology and the passion-kerygma.[3]

If the situation was really anything like this, then Lindars' claim that all reflection on the theological significance of Jesus – which leads ultimately to the idea of his pre-existence – began with the resurrection, is not true. Q, for instance, presents us with a 'gospel' which contains no account of the passion and resurrection. It expresses the significance of Jesus, we have argued, by means of an eschatological version of the Wisdom myth, and regards his teaching as the saving 'event'. Betz argues that the Johannine 'Signs source' and a proto-Markan 'miracles' source were similar 'passionless' gospels.

All this recent discussion means that two central points of Lindars' scheme have to be modified: apologetic was not the only impulse to develop Christology, and the resurrection was not the only starting point. In a 'school' of exegetes inspired by the same eschatological understanding of exegesis as the covenanters at Qumran, there would have been more positive impulses to unpack the mysteries from the scriptures, at last unlocked by the Messiah, than apologetic alone. Secondly, although the resurrection is the starting point for most Christological reflection, there is some indication that the teaching and activity of the historical Jesus gave rise to such reflection also.

---

[1] 'Jesus as Divine Man', in *Jesus and the Historian*, pp. 114–33.

[2] *Ibid.*, pp. 126–7. They simply treat the cross as the way to exaltation and pass from the earthly lord to the exalted lord.

[3] *Ibid.*, pp. 121–5.

The question we now face is, given that some of the impulse to Christological development came from the teaching of the historical Jesus, and some from the experience of the resurrection, can we ascertain to what extent the traditions about the Son of Man were initiated and/or formed by each of these basic impulses?

The discussion[1] of the authenticity of the Son of Man sayings usually utilizes the threefold classification of those sayings. There seems to be some agreement that the 'Passion' sayings are *vaticinia ex eventu*, and therefore not under discussion when the question of authenticity is being considered. Each of the remaining two groups has its champion. The Bultmannian school of interpretation, represented for our purposes by the admirable study of H. E. Tödt,[2] defends the authenticity of the 'Future' group, while E. Schweizer[3] skillfully argues for the group which presents the Son of Man on earth. Ernst Kaesemann[4] and Philipp Vielhauer[5] deny the authenticity of all three groups, while M. D. Hooker, objecting to the threefold classification as prejudicial to unprejudiced discussion, affirms the authenticity of some sayings in every group.[6]

There are two phenomena that have to be explained if one is to discover the origin of the Son of Man tradition: (a) How the sayings which present the Son of Man and Jesus as different

[1] For a brief but helpful presentation of the state of the debate, see Perrin, *Rediscovering*, pp. 259–60.

[2] Tödt, *passim*.

[3] E. Schweizer, 'Der Menschensohn', 185–209; 'Son of Man', *J.B.L.* 79 (1960), 119–29; 'The Son of Man Again', *N.T.S.* 9 (1963), 256–61; *Lordship and Discipleship*, S.B.T. 21 (London, 1960), *passim*.

[4] Kaesemann, 'Sentences of Holy Law', in *New Testament Questions of Today*, pp. 66–81, 'The Beginnings of Christian Theology; *ibid.*, pp. 82–107; 'On the Subject of Primitive Christian Apocalyptic', *ibid.*, pp. 108–37.

[5] P. Vielhauer, 'Gottesreich und Menschensohn' in *Festschrift für Günther Dehn*, ed. W. Schneemelcher (Neukirchen, 1957), pp. 51–79. 'Jesus und die Menschensohn', *Z.T.K.* 60 (1963), 133–77. 'Ein Weg der neutestamentlichen Theologie? Prüfung der Thesen Ferdinand Hahns', *Ev. T.* 25 (1965), 24–72. Perrin summarizes the position of Kaesemann and Vielhauer as follows: 'they believe that Jesus' message was concerned with the Kingdom and with God drawing near to men in the immediacy of the proclamation of that Kingdom, and that, therefore, Jesus could not also have proclaimed the coming of an eschatological figure other than himself in the future' (*Rediscovering*, p. 186).

[6] Hooker, pp. 77–80, 189–98.

figures could have arisen in a tradition that tended to identify the two; and (b) why, out of eighty occurrences of the term in the New Testament, all references to the Son of Man, except for Acts 7: 56 and the 'figurative' use of the image in Rev. 1: 13ff., occur on the lips of Jesus.[1]

Tödt[2] follows Bultmann in regarding the 'future' sayings as authentic. The basic reason for this is that these sayings generally speak of the Son of Man as some one other than Jesus, and, in a tradition which identified Jesus with the Son of Man, the preservation of such sayings could have been due only to strong tradition attaching them to Jesus. He identifies the following as coming from Jesus himself: Luke 11: 30, 12: 8 par., 12: 40 par., 12: 9 par., 17: 24, 26. There are two major themes associated with these sayings: the threat of judgement and the promise of salvation. Luke 12: 8 epitomises these authentic sayings:

But I say to you, everyone who confesses me before men, the Son of Man will confess him before the angels of God.

It is not dominated by apocalyptic visionary themes, rather it lays a simple and direct claim on the hearer. Therefore, in the teaching of Jesus, the source from which the image of the Son of Man came into the Synoptic tradition, according to Tödt, there is no allusion to the pre-existence of the Son of Man. The farther the tradition moves from the teaching of Jesus, the more traditional apocalyptic features the sayings acquire (e.g. Matt. 19: 28, Mark 8: 38, 13: 26 and 14: 62) and so the probability that the Son of Man was understood as pre-existent, at least in some stages of the tradition, increases. Tödt, however, denies any presence of the idea at any stage of the tradition.

Perrin argues that the original form of Luke 12: 8 – Tödt's touchstone for the teaching of Jesus on the Son of Man – had a passive verb instead of the subject 'Son of Man' and read as follows:

Everyone who acknowledges me before men, he will be acknowledged before the angels of God.

The grounds for this opinion are: the occurrence of the Aramaism ὁμολογεῖν ἐν, and the passive in the corresponding place

---

[1] Schweizer, *Lordship and Discipleship*, pp. 40–1.
[2] Tödt, pp. 64–7.

in verse 9. Such a passive is an Aramaism, and therefore seems appropriate in a saying in which another Aramaism occurs. Thus the original saying was not a Son of Man saying at all. It used a passive to indicate the activity of God.[1] In the tradition this passive verb was interpreted independently by Matthew, who substituted for it the 'I' of Jesus (Matt. 10: 32), and Luke, who substituted 'the Son of Man'.

This interpretation cannot be accepted. There is no good reason for assuming an original that used only the passive verb and no clear subject. The argument from the presence of one Aramaism to the hypothetical presence of a conjectured second Aramaism is unconvincing. The parallel passive verb in 12: 9 is by Perrin's own argument secondary, and although it could reflect a hypothetical original it should be admitted only as corroborative evidence for an original whose existence has been established on other grounds. We therefore see no reason for departing from Tödt's view that it was originally a Son of Man saying. The 'I' in Matthew seems to be Matthew's own adaptation, in order to emphasize Jesus' role as the eschatological judge, in accordance with Matthew's well-recognized theological propensity.

E. Schweizer[2] argues that this saying does not describe the future 'coming' of the Son of Man, but rather his advocacy in heaven of the cause of those who have acknowledged Jesus on earth. The parallel text in Mark 8: 38, where the Son of Man is explicitly said to be the 'coming' one (cf. Mark 13: 26 and 14: 62 etc.), is the result of influence from Jewish apocalyptic sources in the developing tradition.[3] If Schweizer is correct, and we think that he is, the association between Jesus and the Son of Man is closer than it is if the Son of Man 'comes' from elsewhere in the future. It is so close that we tend to see the identification of Jesus and the Son of Man implied in this saying. What the saying then expresses is that Jesus as the Son of Man will acknowledge those who acknowledged him as merely Jesus. It expresses

---

[1] Perrin, *Rediscovering*, pp. 187–91; p. 189: 'This passive was a circumlocution for the activity of God, as is regularly the case in Aramaic. As the tradition developed, there was an increasing Christological emphasis and this led to the ascription to Jesus of the original function of God in the saying.'

[2] 'Der Menschensohn', p. 200.

[3] Schweizer, *ibid.*, p. 188, is not clear on this saying. We follow Tödt, pp. 40–6, and Perrin, *Rediscovering*, p. 186.

the present concealment and future revelation of the dignity of Jesus as the one who pleads in heaven for mankind, the Son of Man. M. D. Hooker summarizes our position as follows:

Jesus speaks of his future activity in terms of the Son of Man because it is then – and only then – that his authority as Son of Man will be generally acknowledged.[1]

This idea has a parallel in Dan. 7, where the Son of Man comes as representative of the 'Saints of the Most High' from obscurity and oppression under the dominion of the beasts into full authority, and in I Enoch 62, where he ascends the throne of judgement.[2]

Luke 12: 8 is, therefore, probably a saying concerning the Son of Man on earth, expressing the present humility and future exaltation of the Son of Man. It is also probably authentic. It coheres with all the sayings from Q (Luke 6: 22, Luke 7: 34 par. Matt. 11: 19, Luke 9: 58 par. Matt. 8: 20, Luke 11: 30 par. Matt. 12: 40, Luke 12: 10 par. Matt. 12: 32) and Mark (2: 10, 2: 28)[3] which speak of the Son of Man on earth. The Q sayings express the humility and rejection of the Son of Man on earth, and hint at his authority, whereas the Markan sayings emphasize his authority on earth. Both groups occur in the context of conflict between the Son of Man and the 'world'. Tödt summarizes as follows:

Since sayings concerning the Son of Man acting on earth occur in Q and in the pre-Markan controversial discourses as well as in Mark 10: 45 and in material peculiar to Matthew and to Luke, we can affirm that their roots must have been widespread in the history of tradition. The fact that they appear also in Q excludes the assumption that it was the Hellenistic community which first produced these sayings.[4]

Schweizer's analysis of the tradition saying by saying leads him to believe that the sayings concerning the Son of Man on earth are from the teaching of Jesus,[5] and the evidence we have considered seems to suggest that he is correct.

---

[1] Hooker, p. 121.   [2] *Ibid.*, pp. 120–1.

[3] Other 'Son of Man on earth' sayings are Matt. 13: 37, Mark 10: 45, Luke 19: 10 (Tödt, pp. 133–8).

[4] Tödt, p. 138.   [5] Schweizer, 'Menschensohn', *passim.*

We conclude therefore that Jesus referred to himself as the Son of Man in contexts in which his authority was challenged, or his person rejected. He implied by the title that he would appear as the heavenly advocate in the future, and then men would see who he really is. Even on earth he was the Son of Man, but rejected and humiliated. It is not difficult to see how the sayings concerning his 'coming' and his 'suffering' grew out of these authentic sayings. They might be said to have been implied in the authentic teaching of Jesus concerning the Son of Man.

We referred earlier to two questions which must be answered if one is to understand the origin of the Son of Man tradition. Our solution answers them as follows: the tradition does not refer to the Son of Man as someone other than Jesus in the sayings concerning his coming; it understands the Son of Man to be Jesus. The reason why the Son of Man sayings, with two exceptions, all occur on the lips of Jesus in the Synoptic tradition, is that Jesus in fact taught about himself as the Son of Man, and this was remembered.

The various layers of the tradition went on to interpret the authentic sayings in terms which were congenial to their own situations. Q interpreted them in terms of the Wisdom myth; Mark in terms of the Old Testament – especially Dan. 7, Zec. 12 and Ps. 110, as well as in terms of the history of the Passion and Resurrection. Matthew applied the Jewish apocalyptic tradition present chiefly in I Enoch to present the Son of Man as the eschatological judge; and Luke used the apocalyptic idea of the heavenly world to present him as the exalted ruler of his church.

The evidence that we have examined suggests that the Jewish Wisdom tradition played a significant part in the Christology of the Synoptics. We shall summarize our discussion and see if any pattern can be discerned in the usage of the Wisdom tradition.

Q identifies Jesus as the eschatological envoy of Wisdom, using the title 'Son of Man' to make the identification, in most, but not all, of the relevant sayings. The sayings in which this identification occurs belong to a primitive layer of tradition, and could reflect the teaching of Jesus.[1] They generally have

[1] *Ibid.*, p. 205.

the form of Wisdom sayings, and could reflect the habit of Jesus of teaching in the style and form of the Wisdom tradition.[1] Matthew identifies Jesus with the figure of Wisdom itself, transforming the Q references and adding sayings of his own. In Mark, we have argued, hints and traces of the Wisdom tradition can be discerned, chiefly in the controversial sections. In Mark, however, the emphasis in these presentations of Jesus in conflict is on the title 'Son of Man' and his authority, rather than on the idea of Jesus as Wisdom's envoy.

It seems, therefore, that in the earliest layers of the tradition, represented by the Q sayings we have examined, Christ was given a position of dignity below pre-existent Wisdom but above her other envoys. He was a pre-existent being, but not protologically pre-existent. 'Son of Man' designates the heavenly dignity of this rejected messenger.

Mark put most of the emphasis on the Son of Man, leaving only hints of the identification with Wisdom's envoy. This was probably due to his interest in the Passion, combined with a growing influence from Jewish apocalyptic. These two factors made the Son of Man, who is portrayed as a suffering figure in Dan. 7, more appropriate than the figure of the rejected envoy of Wisdom, to express the theme of passion and exaltation. The 'passion' sayings concerning the Son of Man probably come from this development in the tradition. The idea of suffering and exaltation was not absent from the Wisdom tradition, however, as Wisd. 2–5 shows, and may have been the point of departure for the Markan re-interpretation.

Matthew, on the other hand, emphasized the identification of Jesus with Wisdom, because of his interest in presenting Jesus as the one who replaces the Torah as the mode of God's presence to men. The Torah had already been identified with Wisdom in the tradition.[2] Matthew interprets the Son of Man chiefly as the eschatological judge, again as an expression of his legal interest. Jesus as the Son of Man judges the Church on the basis of its

---

[1] Bultmann, *Geschichte*, pp. 73–113; G. Bornkamm, *Jesus of Nazareth*, pp. 87–9, 106, 108. Bornkamm points out (p. 88) that Jesus uses appeals to the natural order of life, as the Wisdom literature does, in order to impress upon his hearers the urgency of the Kingdom's coming. This seems to confirm our impression of the connection between the Wisdom tradition and eschatology in the Synoptic tradition, and possibly in the teaching of Jesus.

[2] S.-B. II, 353–7.

obedience to Jesus as the Torah, present in their midst. This identification of Jesus with Wisdom and Torah, and with the Son of Man, was developed and modified further in the Fourth Gospel and in Paul.

The relationship between Wisdom and the Son of Man is rather subtle in the Synoptic tradition. Jesus is the middle term in the identification: Jesus is Wisdom, Jesus is the Son of Man, therefore Wisdom is the Son of Man. This equation seems to hold true at least for Matthew, although we have to recognize that it never occurs as a direct assertion, but has to be constructed out of the texts and contexts. The interest of the tradition is expressed in the structure of this argument. It is concerned with the dignity of Jesus, not with the relationship between Wisdom and the Son of Man. We may ask, however, what elements there were in Jewish tradition which made the application of both these ideas to Jesus, in similar contexts and with similar meanings, an understandable procedure.

We have already seen that there was a tendency in the Palestinian Wisdom tradition to associate Wisdom with the primal man. The Hellenistic-Jewish tradition made the identification between these two directly, by means of the term 'Logos', as we have seen. There is also evidence, admittedly controversial, from Qumran, which suggests that 'Man' (geber גבר) was a Messianic title in Qumran's exegesis, and in that sense was associated with Wisdom terminology. The chief proponents of this view are W. H. Brownlee and Geza Vermes.[1] Brownlee has recently reaffirmed his original argument and added some interesting evidence.[2] He refers to I Q.H. 3: 7–10, the well-known hymn which describes a woman 'who is pregnant with a man [geber]' and says that 'a man [geber] shall be delivered from a birth canal' (1: 9–10). Then he presents the following translation of 1 Q.S. 4: 18–23:

Now God, in the mysteries of his understanding and in his glorious wisdom, has assigned a limited time for the existence of perversity;

---

[1] For a review of the discussion and a renewed affirmation of the Messianic meaning of 'Geber', see Geza Vermes, *Scripture and Tradition in Judaism, Haggadic Studies, S.P.B.* 4 (Leiden, 1961), pp. 56–66. This view was first expressed by W. H. Brownlee in 'The Servant of the Lord in the Qumran Scrolls', II, *B.A.S.O.R.* 135 (1954), 36–8.

[2] W. H. Brownlee, 'Jesus and Qumran' in *Jesus and the Historian*, pp. 52–81, especially pp. 59–64.

and at the season appointed for divine intervention, He will destroy it for ever. At that time, the truth on earth will emerge victorious; for it has become polluted by the ways of wickedness, under the dominion of perversity, until the season of the decreed judgement. *At that time, God will purify by his truth all the deeds of a Man* [geber] *and refine him more than the sons of men, in order to destroy every perverse spirit from the inner parts of his flesh and to cleanse him through the Spirit of Holiness from all wicked practices; and He will sprinkle upon him the Spirit of Truth like the water of purification,* so as to cleanse him from all untrue abominations and from being polluted by the Spirit of Impurity *so that he might give the upright insight into the knowledge of the Most High and into the wisdom of the heavenly beings, in order to make wise the perfect of way*...for God has chosen them to be an eternal covenant, *and all the glory of Adam will be theirs.* There will be no more perversity, all works of fraud being put to shame.[1]

Brownlee's translation has been criticized by Millar Burrows, who does not see any special significance in the references to 'man'.[2] There does not seem to be any way out of the linguistic stalemate, but Vermes[3] has shown that a rather explicit tradition concerning 'the man' as a messianic symbol existed in contemporary Jewish exegesis. He draws attention to the following texts in which the references to *geber* (= 'Man') in the M.T. were understood messianically in the LXX, and/or in the Targums: II Sam. 23: 1, Zech. 13: 7, Num. 24: 17, 24: 7, Jer. 31: 21, Is. 66: 7; *'ish* (= 'man') was understood in that way in the Targum on Zech. 6: 12. He also shows a similar correspondence between other words in 1 Q.H. 3: 7–10 ['zakar' (= 'manchild'), 'crucible', 'wonderful counselor'] and in 1 Q.S. 4: 20–2 ('refine', 'purifying', 'teach' and 'cause to understand') and the Messianic references in the LXX and Targums. In brief, the same words used in the two passages from Qumran are used in those passages which Palestinian and Hellenistic-Jewish exegesis understood as having Messianic meaning. On these grounds it seems probable that Brownlee and Vermes are right in their understanding of these Qumran texts.[4] 'Man' (*geber*) was used as a designation of the Messiah at Qumran.

---

[1] Brownlee's translation, *ibid.*, p. 61.
[2] M. Burrows, *More Light on the Dead Sea Scrolls* (London, 1958), pp. 316ff., 330, 334.
[3] G. Vermes, *Scripture and Tradition*, pp. 56–66.
[4] They are also followed by F. H. Borsch, *The Son of Man*, p. 109 n. 3.

Furthermore, it seems that this 'Man' was thought of as a 'wise man' or 'sage'. In 1 Q.S. 4: 18–28 there are several phrases which could belong to the language of the wisdom tradition. The most obvious one is:

so that he might give the upright insight into the knowledge of the Most High and into the wisdom of the heavenly beings, in order to make wise the perfect of way.

The 'Man' or Messiah is, therefore, a dispenser of heavenly wisdom and knowledge. Brownlee adduces other evidence from Qumran which seems to present the Messiah as a wise man. In 11 Q. Pss.ᵃ David is portrayed as a wise man:

Now David son of Jesse was a sage and a light like the light of the sun, a scholar and full of insight and perfect in all his ways before God and men. And the Lord gave him a spirit of insight and illumination.[1]

In an Aramaic fragment from cave IV a wisdom figure, who might be the Davidic Messiah, is described:

He will know the secrets of all living beings; and all plots against him will come to an end.[2]

Although this evidence is not definite or clear-cut, it does seem to indicate that in Palestine, at approximately the time that Q was being formed,[3] the Messiah was called 'Man' and was understood as a wise man. It is possible that Jesus, in teaching in the style of a sage, and referring to himself as the 'Son of Man', consciously took up this tradition, and by using the term 'Son of Man' – which had certain connotations of transcendence – rather than 'Man', interpreted the tradition to make it express the heavenly nature and pre-existence of the Messiah.

Jesus referred to himself, in his earthly ministry, as the Son of Man. Although the Son of Man was not a defined concept in Judaism at that time, it was, at least, a recognized image, one of whose recurrent components was the idea of pre-existence. In using this self-designation, Jesus implied his own pre-existence. The chief opponent of such an interpretation is H. E. Tödt. He

[1] Brownlee, 'Jesus and Qumran', p. 61.
[2] Ibid., p. 62.
[3] Q was probably of Palestinian provenance – Tödt, p. 138.

insists that there is no hint of pre-existence in any of the Synoptic Son of Man sayings, if they are read without reference to the image of the Son of Man prevalent in Judaism. This methodological stricture seems to us to vitiate the contribution of the religio-historical method unwarrantably. It is well-established procedure to elucidate the meaning of New Testament texts by means of the historical background against which they came into being. Therefore, we suggest that when Jesus used the self-designation 'Son of Man', he and his hearers understood it to imply his pre-existence.[1] The initial impulse for the Christology of pre-existence, developed in various ways by the layers of the Synoptic tradition and by the other New Testament witnesses, came, therefore, from the historical Jesus.

We shall now attempt to analyse and classify the evidence we have examined, by means of the categories drawn from early Judaism in our previous discussion: protological and eschatological pre-existence.

The clearest hints of protological pre-existence occur in Matthew, with the identification of Jesus with Wisdom/Torah and the Enochian Son of Man, both entities which, in the Jewish tradition, existed before the world. Matthew does not make this pre-existence explicit; his interest, however, is in the status of Jesus as the new Law and the eschatological judge, and therefore we have no grounds for asserting that the element of protological pre-existence in these traditional images was unimportant to him. He chose these images to express the dignity of Jesus, and we may presume that he chose them because in their total significance – including protological pre-existence – they communicated what he wanted to say about Jesus. In using symbols, Matthew made explicit statements of Christ's pre-existence unnecessary – the symbols expressed it quite adequately.

[1] This is essentially the same position taken by Erik Sjöberg, *Der Verborgene Menschensohn.* Although we cannot accept his attempt to explain the whole Synoptic and Johannine Christology on the basis of a Son of Man 'schema' of hiddenness and revelation, we do endorse his view that the title expresses Jesus' own self-understanding. Of course, a self-understanding which can appropriately be expressed by means of such a myth is extraordinary and mysterious. We cannot probe behind the myth to ask what the awareness of just this personal pre-existence is like. It is precisely unlike anything we know – the consciousness of a relationship to God which is unique.

Eschatological pre-existence was attributed to Jesus by Q. Q received the tradition that Jesus referred to himself as the Son of Man, and he understood it to imply the pre-existence of Jesus. In his own tradition, however, the understanding of Jesus as the final envoy of Wisdom was of determinative importance. He therefore combined the idea of Jesus as the pre-existent Son of Man with the idea of Jesus as Wisdom's eschatological envoy. This enabled him, by using the Son of Man idea, to distinguish Jesus from the other envoys of Wisdom, while not identifying him with Wisdom itself, as Matthew does. Jesus is, for Q, the Son of Man who existed before his manifestation as Wisdom's envoy, and for this reason is superior in status to all the other envoys. He is not, however, protologically pre-existent like Wisdom. Mark also attributes eschatological pre-existence to Jesus, by identifying him, more explicitly than Q does, with the Danielic Son of Man.

The Synoptic tradition also assumes the ideal pre-existence of Christ in its doctrine of the scriptures as prophetic of Christ; one may suppose that this ideal pre-existence was also protological, God's plan having been formed before the world.

In conclusion, we suggest that the Synoptic tradition, in its ideas of pre-existence and the idea of the scriptures as prophesying Christ, sought to express something about the status or nature of Jesus in himself, not simply to say something about his function. Pre-existence is a stable component of these ideas and, therefore, we suggest that the tradition intended to communicate the pre-existence of Jesus Christ. It does not develop this idea explicitly, but then, it may be asked if it develops any idea explicitly or non-symbolically.

CHAPTER 3

PRE-EXISTENCE IN THE PAULINE WRITINGS

We shall deal with the Pauline writings in the chronological order established by modern scholarship. In this way we hope to avoid the distortions which may result from a premature systematization of Paul's thought. Johannes Munck has shown most effectively how the Pauline letters should be read as occasional writings embedded in the historical context of the mission to the Gentiles. While we cannot agree with many of his conclusions, we are convinced that Munck's method is basically the only sound approach to Paul.[1]

We shall deal first with those letters which are generally attributed to the apostle himself: I Thessalonians, Galatians, Corinthians, Romans, Philippians and Philemon; and then with those whose Pauline authorship is disputed: II Thessalonians, Colossians, Ephesians, Timothy and Titus. Most scholars who dispute the Pauline authorship of the latter group nevertheless agree that they originated in circles under the apostle's influence. They provide valuable evidence for the initial development of the theology of Paul in the early Gentile Church.

I. THE LETTERS WRITTEN BY PAUL

A. *I Thessalonians*

If one begins one's reading of Paul's letters with the brief correspondence to the Thessalonians, one is immediately struck by the strong apocalyptic cast of his thought. He concludes his opening passage by describing his readers as those who have 'turned themselves to God from idols, to serve the true and living God and to await his son from heaven, whom he raised from the dead, Jesus who snatches us from the wrath to come' (I Thess. 1: 9b–10).

---

[1] J. Munck, *Paul and the Salvation of Mankind* (Richmond, Virginia, 1959).

Behind this statement lies the common apocalyptic belief that the things to be revealed in the eschaton are prepared in heaven. The exalted Christ exists in heaven before his eschatological manifestation. Dibelius described this passage as an expression of the common faith of the early Church – *Gemeindetheologie*[1] – and G. Friedrich has argued recently that it is part of a Hellenistic Jewish–Christian tradition taken over by Paul.[2]

The incarnation has, however, modified the traditional apocalyptic scheme in two ways. The one whom the Christians await from heaven has already appeared on earth in great humility. The central apocalyptic reality is therefore the resurrected Messiah. In the Jewish scheme the Messiah was not so unequivocally central to the eschatological events. For Christians, the Messiah became the dominant eschatological entity. Secondly, the incarnation became the immediate *terminus a quo* for the existence of the heavenly Messiah. Whereas in Jewish apocalyptic the pre-existent entities exist from the creation or the period before creation, for these Christians the Messiah exists in heaven primarily since the resurrection. He was elevated to heaven by the resurrection, there to await the last day.

It is difficult to decide whether this letter contains any idea of Christ's existence before his birth. On the one hand, the emphasis on the resurrection could indicate that it does not, and that the Christology implied is similar to that in Romans 1: 3ff. and Acts 2: 36, where Jesus became the Christ as a result of the crucifixion and resurrection.[3] On such a basis, the only pre-existence he would have is the existence between his exaltation and (prior to) his second coming. On the other hand, this theology, which also seems to lie behind II Thess. 2: 8, seems to have identified the resurrected one with the Son of Man of IV

[1] M. Dibelius, *An die Thessalonicher I, II; an die Philipper*, H.N.T. 11 (Tübingen, 1925).

[2] G. Friedrich, 'Ein Tauflied hellenistischer Judenchristen (I Thess. 1: 9ff.)' *T.Z.* 21/6 (1965), 502–16. We may here recall E. Kaesemann's arguments to the effect that Jewish apocalyptic thought was the matrix of Christian theology. Cf. Kaesemann, 'The Beginnings of Christian Theology', in *New Testament Questions of Today*. See also the replies of G. Ebeling and E. Fuchs now collected with Kaesemann's article in *Journal for Theology and Church*, vol. 6, ed. R. W. Funk (New York, 1969), pp. 47–68 and 69–98 respectively, and Kaesemann's response to their criticism, on pp. 99–133.

[3] Friedrich, 'Tauflied', compares the Christology to that of the missionary preaching in Acts and contrasts it with Pauline Christology.

Ezra 13: 8ff.[1] In IV Ezra the Son of Man is he 'who has been kept long ages...' If this Son of Man is in mind here, the idea of Christ's pre-existence before his birth is implied; but, in view of the uncertainty about the common Pauline authorship of I and II Thessalonians, it is hazardous to use II Thess. 2: 8 to interpret I Thess. 1: 9b–10.

There is, however, some solid evidence to be gleaned from this letter; namely, that the earliest Christian theology used the Jewish apocalyptic scheme of things existing in heaven before their eschatological manifestation, in order to express their belief that in the period between the resurrection and the parousia Christ exists in heaven.

Although we should not call the idea expressed in I Thess. 1: 9b–10 pre-existence, we have established an important fact, namely, that Paul shared the common apocalyptic theology of the earliest congregations. In subsequent letters it becomes evident that his Christology and his doctrine of the Church were shaped to a large extent, but not solely, by the apocalyptic pattern of thought.

B. *Galatians*

The letter to the Galatians confirms this judgement. Paul's insistence that the gospel which he preached came to him by revelation and not from human tradition (δι' ἀποκαλύψεως Ἰησοῦ Χριστοῦ, 1: 12) shows that he believed himself to be the recipient of divine information in the same way as the great figures to whom the apocalypses are attributed.[2] A full con-

---

[1] S.-B. III, p. 641.

[2] P. Bonnard, *L'Épître de Saint Paul aux Galates*; and C. Masson, *L'Épître de Saint Paul aux Éphésiens* (Neuchâtel/Paris, 1953), Bonnard, *ad loc.*, argues that 1: 12 is to be understood in this way, along with I Cor. 2: 6ff. H. Schlier, *Der Brief an die Galater*, 12 Auflage, Meyer's Kommentar VII (Göttingen, 1962), and A. Oepke, *Der Brief des Paulus an die Galater*, zweite, verbesserte Auflage, *T.H.N.T.* IX (Berlin, 1957), interpret this verse as referring to the experience of the Damascus road recorded in Acts 9, 22 and 26. Against Schlier and Oepke the following considerations are decisive: It is doubtful that the accounts in Acts are based on an actual event; rather they record a legend designed to stress the divine initiative in the mission to the Gentiles; secondly, the reference to revelation in Gal. 1: 15–16 does not give any indication of an experience like that recorded in Acts, although it does refer to his being commissioned to preach to the Gentiles (vs. 16); thirdly, the reference in 2: 2 shows that such revelations were a continuing phenomenon

sideration of this element in the apostle's experience must include discussion of I Cor. 2: 6ff., where Paul deals with the theme of 'revealed wisdom' in some detail, and II Cor. 12: 1–5, where he gives a vivid account of a mystical experience. At this point we may simply note that Paul describes his most intimate relationship with God in the apocalyptic category of revelation.

(i) *Galatians 3: 19–20.* In chapter 3 Paul's argument rests on the claim that Christ was fore-ordained as 'the offspring' included in the promise to Abraham. The Law was introduced to prepare for the coming of Christ, and is therefore essentially ancillary and subordinate to him, for whose sake it was given. This argument implies the pre-existence of Christ in the mind of God.

At 3: 19–20 Paul endeavours to show the subordinate status of the Law by attributing it to angels and not to God. It was given by the angels, through the mediator Moses, and so came only indirectly from God. Christ, however, comes directly from God. The presence of angels at the giving of the Law is well attested in the rabbinic tradition.[1] For our purposes, however, the important passages come from the apocalyptic tradition. In Jubilees 1: 27ff., 2: 1ff., 6: 22, 30, 12: 21–2, 50: 1ff., we are told in various ways that the angel of the presence, who goes before Israel, wrote part of the Law for Moses on the heavenly tablets, and dictated part of it to him directly. We suggest that one might say of the Law in Jubilees what Paul says of it in Galatians, that it is a device of the guardian angel to provide Israel with a 'custodian' (παιδαγωγός, 3: 24), 'because of transgressions' (3: 19). Paul, however, adds the determinative point, that

in the apostle's experience. J. Munck (*Paul and the Salvation of Mankind*, pp. 11–35) shows how similar Paul's recorded experience seems to be to the recorded 'call' experiences of the Old Testament prophets. These prophetic visions, although they perform a different function in the narratives in which they occur, are not essentially different from the apocalyptic visions.

[1] S.-B. III, pp. 554–6. They list six forms of the tradition of the presence of angels at Sinai. The sixth, on p. 556, talks of their mediatorial function: cf. Jos. Ant. 15. 5. 3, Pesiq. R. 21 (103[B]), R. Eleazar, c. 270. Schlier cites a tradition in which Moses is probably regarded as part of the angelic host, and thus Moses and the angels together mediate the Law. Oepke is probably right in seeing that Paul here attributes the giving of the Law to the guardian angels. They, not God, are its source, and those who obey the Law obey angels rather than God.

Christ has ended the custodianship of the Law by bringing justification by faith (3: 24).

Paul then tries to show that Christ's power to displace the Law rests on the fact that he existed before the Law. The promise to Abraham, given four hundred and thirty years before the Law (3: 17), offered justification by faith. Justification by faith was made possible only by Christ. Therefore the promise to Abraham was made on the basis of Christ's pre-existence in the mind of God. Christ's power to displace the Law's authority derives, therefore, from his pre-existence. The Lawgiving angels also acted with reference to the pre-existent Christ, when they gave the Law as a temporary measure until the (future) coming of Christ.

There is some analogy to this pattern of thought in the Wisdom tradition. Wisd. 7: 27 and the Gospel of the Hebrews[1] tell of Wisdom who enters occasionally into men in the course of the history of salvation. The passage in the Gospel of the Hebrews says that such visitations were temporary and essentially preliminary to the coming of Jesus – in whom Wisdom found her 'rest'. In chapter 3 Paul adopts a similar historical perspective to this wisdom tradition. He sees every epoch prior to Christ as preliminary to the incarnation, yet not without Christ's presence. The faith of Abraham in the promise was a manifestation of Christ, and even the Law as part of God's plan for salvation, was given with a view to Christ's coming to help mankind until he came. A comparable idea occurs in the Assumption of Moses (1: 12–14), where it is said that the world was created for the sake of Moses. In Gal. 3, one could say, Paul is arguing that history was made for the sake of Christ, therefore Christ must have been pre-existent in the mind of God.[2]

(ii) *Galatians 4: 3, 8–10.* The idea that the angels gave the Law implies that theirs is the power which sustains the Law.[3] In 4: 3, 8–10, Paul argues that by observing 'days and months and

---

[1] In Jerome, *Commentary on Isaiah IV*, on Is. 11: 2, in H.-S. 1, pp. 163–4. Spirit and Wisdom were synonyms in the tradition, both describing the revealer; cf. Robin Scroggs, 'Paul as ΣΟΦΟΣ and ΠΝΕΥΜΑΤΙΚΟΣ, *N.T.S.* 14 (167–8), 48–9. Cf. Wisd. 1: 6, 7: 22.

[2] See pp. 76–7 above.

[3] For a different view of the angels as lawgivers see W. D. Davies, 'A Note on Josephus, Antiquities 15: 136', *H.T.R.* 47 (1954), 135–40.

years' and other requirements of the Law, the Christians were serving 'the elements of the universe', that is, the angels.[1] According to much apocalyptic thought everything in the universe had its governing angel, and the Law was no exception. To obey its precepts was to obey an angel (3: 19), and to return to the state of subjection under a guardian.[2]

This is yet another example of the extraordinary importance of apocalyptic ideas for Paul. In this very basic exposition of his attitude to the Law, he uses the apocalyptic ideas of the angelic governors, and of the origin of the Law from the guardian angels.

(iii) *Galatians 4: 26.* In 4: 26 Paul uses the widespread apocalyptic idea of the heavenly Jerusalem.[3] 'The Jerusalem above is

---

[1] On στοιχεῖα see Oepke, pp. 93–5. Cf. G. B. Caird, *Principalities and Powers, a Study in Pauline Theology* (Oxford, 1956), pp. 82, 86, 95; Schlier, *An die Galater*, p. 190, n. 2. The *stoicheia*, according to Schlier, are personally active angelic beings. The closest parallels to Paul's use of the term here are the passages about the angelic governors of the wind, rain, etc. in I Enoch 60: 11ff., 69: 20ff. The term στοιχεῖα was not used in the Rabbinic tradition until post-talmudic times and then not in this sense. Cf. S.-B., III, p. 570. See also H. D. Betz, 'Zum Problem des religionsgeschichtliche Verständnisses der Apokalyptik', *Z.T.K.* 63/4 (1966), 391–409; Col. 2: 8ff., and the Excursus by M. Dibelius in *An die Kolosser, Epheser, an Philemon*, 2nd ed., H.N.T. 12 (Tübingen, 1927), pp. 19–21.

[2] Thus Schlier, *An die Galater*, ad loc. It is not necessary to go as far as A. Schweitzer (*Mysticism*, pp. 70ff.) to claim that Paul regarded the Law as inherently opposed to God. This would contradict the clear statements that the Law is holy and good, in Romans 7: 7ff. All that Paul says is that the στοιχεῖα are 'weak and beggarly' by comparison with God (Gal. 4: 9). While we were in their care we too were weak, mere children; now we are God's mature sons and do not need such care. There is no hint in Galatians that these angels are hostile to God. (The phrase 'the curse of the Law' in 3: 13 does not mean that the Law itself is a curse. Rather, as in Deut. 3: 13, the curse is a consequence of disobedience to the Law. The Law itself is good and capable of producing great blessing.) Such an interpretation can only be read into Galatians from Colossians 2: 8ff. The fact that they are actively hostile and must be conquered by Christ, in Colossians, is an argument against the Pauline authorship of that letter and an indication of a development in the direction of Gnosticism. In Galatians, all Paul wants to say is that the Law is passé; God had done a new thing in Christ, a thing which is at the same time older than the world, powerful with the fullness of God's being; and anyone who would turn from this to the younger, weaker dispensation of the Law would lose his strength and freedom and become the servant of mere angels.

[3] For sources see Schlier, *An die Galater*, pp. 221–6; S.-B. III, p. 573, IV/1,

free, which is our mother', he writes. He contrasts the 'Jerusalem above' (ἡ ἄνω 'Ιερουσαλήμ) in verse 26 with 'the present Jerusalem' (ἡ νῦν 'Ιερουσαλήμ) in verse 25, shifting from spatial to temporal terms without hesitation.

This unconscious shift from temporal to spatial categories shows how in Jewish apocalyptic thought the things which were to be revealed in the end were thought of as already existing. The mind could move from the future expectation to the present existence of the expected things without a sense of inconsistency. The shift from expectation to present existence was concomitant with the shift from temporal to spatial categories. Oepke[1] cites Ex. 25: 40, Acts 7: 44 and Wisd. 9: 8 as examples of the spatial terminology, and Is. 2: 2, Mic. 4: 1, Ezek. 40–8 and Is. 54: 10 as examples of temporal terminology. He judges that the spatial terminology developed out of Jewish roots under the influence of Platonism, which led the Jews to posit a heavenly archetype for every valuable earthly entity. The temporal category, he argues, was part of the eschatological hope.[2] This is precisely the context out of which our category of 'eschatological pre-existence' comes. Future things (temporal category) pre-exist in heaven (spatial category) before their manifestation. 'Eschatological pre-existence' comes to expression when the temporal categories are translated into spatial categories. It is a term describing precisely this spatialization of time.

The rabbis also knew of the Jerusalem above (ירושלם של מעלה) and of the Jerusalem to come, which they contrasted with the

p. 812. Cf. A. Causée, 'Le mythe de la nouvelle Jérusalem du Deutero-Ésaïe à la IIIe Sibylle', *R.H.P.R.* (1938), 377–414; A. Causée, 'De la Jérusalem terrestre à la Jérusalem céleste', *ibid.* (1947), 1–2, 12ff. J. H. Hayes, 'The Tradition of Zion's Inviolability', *J.B.L.* LXXXII (1963), 419–26. A. Cole, *The New Temple; a Study in the Origins of the Catechetical 'Form' of the Church in the New Testament* (London, 1950). C. von Korvin-Krasinski, 'Die Heilige Stadt', *Z.R.G.G.*, XVI (1964), 265–71. On the phenomenology of this idea see M. Eliade, *Cosmos and History, the Myth of the Eternal Return* (New York, 1959), and *The Sacred and the Profane, the Nature of Religion* (New York, 1959). For an exhaustive treatment of the place of Jerusalem in the religion of the Old Testament see J. Schreiner, *Zion-Jerusalem*, Studien zur Alten und Neuen Testaments (München, 1964).

[1] Oepke, p. 113.

[2] Cf. H. Wenschkewitz, *Die Spiritualisierung der Kultusbegriffe: Tempel, Priester und Opfer, im Neuen Testament, Angelos*, Archiv für neutestamentliche Zeitgeschichte und Kulturkunde, Beiheft 4 (Leipzig, 1932).

present Jerusalem.[1] The Jerusalem above was not, however, a community as in Galatians, but a city built in heaven, as in Heb. 12: 22, Rev. 3: 12, 21: 2, 10. The pagans also shared this idea of a heavenly archetype of the great city.[2]

Given the general nature of Paul's thought as we have analysed it so far, we might suppose that his access to this tradition was probably through Jewish apocalyptic. He calls the heavenly city 'our mother' (μήτηρ ἡμῶν);[3] she is also described in this way in II Baruch 3: 1ff. and IV Ezr. 10: 7.[4] The only rabbinic parallel is in the Targ. on the Song of Songs (8: 5), which is somewhat later.

The argument in 4: 21ff. which Paul describes as an allegory[5]

[1] E.g. B.B. 75[B]: 'R. Johannan (d. 279) said: Not as the Jerusalem of this age (ירושלם של עולם הזה) is the Jerusalem of the age to come (ירושלם של עולם הבה). To this Jerusalem everyone is drawn up who wills; to that Jerusalem only those who are called' (S.-B., III, p. 22).

[2] Cf. Werner Müller, *Die Heilige Stadt, Roma quadrata, himmlisches Jerusalem, und die Mythe vom Weltnabel* (Stuttgart, 1961).

[3] The idea probably derives ultimately from such texts as Is. 50: 1, Jer. 50: 12, Hos. 4: 5, although the pagan idea of μητρόπολις was surely also influential in the formation of the idea in Jewish apocalyptic thought. The rabbis called the nation (Ber. 35A = Sanh. 102[A], P. Ber. 9, 14[A], 23), the land (p.M.Q. 381[C], 40) and the Torah (Dt. R. 2 (198[A]), Midr. Ruth 1, 2 (124[B])), 'mother'.

[4] The importance of the idea of the heavenly Jerusalem in apocalyptic Judaism is beautifully illustrated by the following quotation from S.-B., IV/2, p. 812. Commenting on IV Ezra 7: 26 and 13: 36 they write: 'Die unsichtbare Stadt, das himmlische Jerusalem senkt sich auf die Erde herab (IV Ezr. 7: 26, 13: 36) und wird, auf gewaltigen Fundamenten (10: 27) in grosser Herrlichkeit (13: 36) vollkommen erbaut, allen offenbar (13: 36) auf dem bis dahin verborgenen Land.' In 9: 26 this hidden land is given a name derived from ארץ הדשה (the new land), variously given as 'Ardaf', 'Ardas', etc. The land was thought to be hidden because no human building may be present where the New Jerusalem should stand (*ibid.*, n. 1).

The unfavourable connotation of χειροποίητος in a text such as Eph. 2: 11 arises out of this type of thought. Cf. G. Schlier, *Der Brief an die Epheser: Ein Kommentar*, 2. durchgesehene Auflage (Düsseldorf, 1958), p. 119. The eschatological temple is emphatically 'not made by human hands'. In the Old Testament idols were described as χειροποίητος (Lev. 26: 1, 30; Is. 2: 18, Dan. 5: 4, 23 (LXX)). In the New Testament the Jewish temple is referred to in this way (Mark 14: 58, Acts 7: 48, 17: 24, Hebr. 9: 11, 24). Cf. O. Cullmann, 'L'opposition contre le temple de Jérusalem, motif commun de la théologie johannique et du monde ambiant', *N.T.S.* 5 (1958–9), 157–73.

[5] Schlier describes the argument as 'allegorical identification' and compares it with I Cor. 10: 4. Robertson and Plummer, however, point out that

is designed to contrast the heavenly with the earthly Jerusalem. The latter stands for the dispensation of the Law (vs. 25) and life according to the flesh (vs. 23a), while the former stands for the dispensation of the promise and the free life of the spirit (vs. 23b). This anthropological application of the two cities could suggest that Paul did not believe in the literal existence of the heavenly Jerusalem; but verse 26 makes such a deduction impossible. Paul believes both in the representative meaning of each Jerusalem, signifying two ways of life, and in their literal reality. He clearly shares the apocalyptic view that the new Jerusalem to be revealed in the future already pre-exists in heaven. His own peculiar emphasis is that those who live by faith in Christ already live the life of the pre-existent new Jerusalem, are now citizens of heaven (cf. Phil. 3: 20ff., Gal. 2: 19–21).[1]

(iv) *Galatians 4: 4, 6*. Finally, in Galatians, E. Schweizer sees in the formula 'God sent forth His Son' used in 4: 4, 6 – which must be considered along with Rom. 8: 3, John 3: 16ff. and I John 4: 9 – a reference to the myth of pre-existent Wisdom in its Hellenistic-Jewish garb, as identified with Logos.[2] The verb ἐξαποστέλλω is used in Wisd. 9: 10 (cf. Gal. 4: 4) and 9: 17 (cf. Gal. 4: 6), to describe the sending of Wisdom into the world;

in I Cor. 10: 4 the imperfect ἦν suggests the literal pre-existence of Christ, and entails an actual identification between the 'Rock' and Christ, whereas the present tenses of Gal. 4: 24 suggest a looser comparison which is better described as a typology rather than as an allegory [A. Robertson and A. Plummer, *A Critical and Exegetical Commentary on the First Epistle of Paul to the Corinthians*, 2nd ed., I.C.C. (Edinburgh, 1914), p. 201]. Their observation agrees with our contention that the cities are understood both literally and typically by Paul.

[1] See E. Schweizer, 'Dying and Rising with Christ', *N.T.S.* 14 (1967–8), 1–14; A. Schweitzer, *Mysticism*, p. 108 *et passim*.

[2] 'Zur Herkunft der Präexistenzvorstellung bei Paulus', in *Neotestamentica: Deutsche und englische Aufsätze, 1951–63* (Zürich/ Stuttgart, 1963), pp. 105–9, p. 108. Schweizer agrees with Robertson and Plummer, *Corinthians*, pp. 201–2, who see the pre-existence of Christ implied here, and in II Cor. 8: 9, and Rom. 8: 3. See also E. Schweizer, 'Zum religionsgeschichtlichen Hintergrund der 'Sendungsformel' Gal. 4: 4ff., Rom. 8: 3ff., Joh. 3: 16ff.', *Z.N.W.* 57 (1966), 199–210, especially pp. 206–8. Cf. Bultmann, *Theology of the New Testament*, II, 11–12, where the idea of 'sending' is interpreted, by inference against the background of Gnosticism. The dating of the Gnostic sources, however, makes this interpretation problematic.

but it is chiefly in Philo's discourses about the Logos that the three elements of the formula, God, sending forth, and Son of God, occur together. We find this interpretation appealing, as our own investigations which follow tend to confirm the great influence of Hellenistic Judaism, like that attested by Philo, on the early Christology which Paul and John inherited. The 'formula' entails that the one sent is a protologically pre-existent being like the Logos.

There are two dominant ideas of pre-existence in Galatians: one teaches the pre-existence of Christ, the other, the pre-existence of the Church. The latter is represented in 4: 21ff., and is the result of applying the apocalyptic idea of the heavenly Jerusalem to the Christian community. The former is represented in chapter 3 and in 4: 4–6.

Thus we are able tentatively to conclude that Paul thinks of the pre-existence of Christ in terms of the myth of pre-existent Wisdom, and of the pre-existence of the Church in terms of the apocalyptic myth of the presently existing future Jerusalem. The pre-existence of Christ is 'ideal' pre-existence in the mind of God. The apocalyptic tradition seems to be much nearer the threshold of his consciousness than the wisdom myth. The latter he assumes, the former he asserts. The pre-existence of Christ was much more a matter to be taken for granted than the pre-existence of the Church.

C. *The Corinthian Correspondence*

(i) *I Corinthians 1–2*.[1] In the Corinthian correspondence, as in Galatians, Paul is in discussion with representatives of rival ver-

[1] Literature consulted: U. Wilckens, *Weisheit und Torheit*, *B.H.T.* 26 (Tübingen, 1959). H. Köster, 'Review of *Weisheit und Torheit*', *Gnomon*, 33 (1961), 590–5. K. Prümm, 'Zur neutestamentlichen Gnosis-Problematik, Gnostischer Hintergrund und Lehreinschlag in den beiden Eingangskapiteln von 1 Kor?', *Z.K.T.* 87 (1965), 399–442, and *Z.K.T.* 88 (1966), 1–50. C. K. Barrett, 'Christianity at Corinth', *B.J.R.L.* 46 (1963–4), 269–97. Harald Hegermann, *Die Vorstellung vom Schöpfungsmittler im hellenistischen Judentum und Urchristentum*, T.U. 82 (Berlin, 1961). W. Schmithals, *Die Gnosis in Korinth*, *F.R.L.A.N.T.* Neue Folge 48 (Göttingen, 1965). H. Conzelmann, 'Paulus und die Weisheit,' *N.T.S.* 12 (1965–6), 231–44. H. Conzelmann, *Der erste Brief an die Korinther*, Meyers Kommentar v (Göttingen, 1969). J. C. Hurd, *The Origins of I Corinthians* (New York, 1965). A. Feuillet, *Le Christ Sagesse de*

sions of the Gospel. Whereas in Galatians this was not an important factor in the particular texts we discussed, here it is necessary to ascertain the doctrines of his various opponents,[1] if we
are to understand Paul's own use of the idea of pre-existence.
The opposing doctrines are also interesting in their own right as
evidence for the non-Pauline development of early Christian
doctrine.

The most obvious symptom of this doctrinal diversity is the
presence of schismatic groups within the Corinthians congregation. Each group identified itself as the followers of one of the
prominent figures in their experience of the new religion – Paul,
Apollos, Cephas and Christ (1: 12). Paul's refutation of such
partisanship enables us to deduce something of its nature.

The false doctrine of these partisans seems to have emphasized
'wisdom'; what this wisdom was remains to be seen. Paul therefore disowns any such wisdom for himself (1: 17 and 2: 1–5) and
expounds the cross of Christ as in contradiction to the 'wisdom
of this world', as a foolishness rather than a display of wisdom
(1: 12–2: 5). Then in 2: 6–16, as if to balance the severity of his
insistence on the cross as foolishness, Paul reveals that there is a
Christian wisdom. It is reserved for the perfect (τελείοις), and is
not the wisdom of this world, or of its rulers, who are passing
away. It is the wisdom of God, contained in a mystery, ordained
by God before the ages for our glory, and unknown to the rulers
of this age. Because they did not know this wisdom, these rulers
crucified the 'Lord of Glory'; but to the Christians has been
given to know its content, namely, the things which God has
prepared for those who love him.

The Spirit of God, which searches everything, even the depths
of the divine nature, brought this knowledge to the believers;

Dieu d'après les épîtres Pauliniennes, Études Bibliques (Paris, 1966). A. Robertson and A. Plummer, *The First Epistle of St. Paul to the Corinthians*. E.-B. Allo,
Première Épître aux Corinthiens, Études Bibliques (Paris, 1956). J. Héring, *La
première Épître de Saint Paul aux Corinthiens*, C.N.T. VII (Neuchâtel and Paris,
1949). H. Lietzmann, *An die Korinther I/II* (Vierte von W. G. Kummel
ergänzte Auflage) *H.N.T.* 9 (Tübingen, 1949). R. Scroggs, 'Paul as Sophos
and Pneumatikos'.

[1] On Paul's opponents in general see D. Georgi, *Die Gegner des Paulus im
2 Korintherbrief; Studien zur religiosen Propaganda in der Spätantike*, *W.M.A.N.T.*
11 (Neukirchen/Vlyn, 1964), esp. pp. 7–16; and the review of this work by
Erhardt Guttgemanns in *Zeitschrift für Kirchengeschichte* XV (Vierte Folge),
LXXVII Band (1966), 126–31.

they received the Spirit of God 'in order that we may know the things which God has given us' (2: 12). This knowledge comes, emphatically, by the Spirit and not by 'words of human wisdom' (οὐκ ἐκ διδακτοῖς ἀνθρωπίνης σοφίας λόγοις, 2: 13). The receipt of the divine spirit has made the believer a spiritual man (πνευματικός) who is beyond human judgement, for he alone knows the mind of the Lord – on which knowledge alone judgement can be based – he only 'has the mind (νοῦς) of Christ' (2: 15–16). Those who do not share this knowledge, namely, the opponents who base their theology on the wisdom of this world, are psychic (ψυχικός) and are not able to receive the Spirit of God which makes the true knowledge possible.

There are some features of this remarkable passage (2: 6–16) which suggest that it was composed under the influence of Jewish apocalypticism.[1] The phrase 'Lord of Glory' (2: 8) is a *hapax legomenon* in the Pauline literature. It occurs only once again in the New Testament in Jas. 2: 1 in a variant form. It is, however, a frequent title for God in the Enochian literature.[2] I Enoch 63 presents the rulers of the world appealing for mercy to the 'Lord of Glory' on the (implied) grounds that they did not know his 'deep and innumerable secrets' (vss. 3–4) and so trusted in their own strength rather than worshipping him. Whereas the title 'Lord of Glory' usually belongs to God in the Enochian literature, in I En. 63 it applies to the Son of Man (I En. 63: 11).

In I Cor. 2: 9c, Paul talks of 'the things which God has prepared for those who love him' (ὅσα ἡτοίμασεν ὁ θεὸς τοῖς ἀγαπῶσιν αὐτόν). The origin of the 'quotation' of which this is part is much debated; we tend to favour a lost Jewish apocalypse as the source.[3] The pattern of thought in verse 9 is precisely that of the apocalyptic literature in general, and of the parables of Enoch in particular – the things to be revealed in the last days are present in heaven.[4] The Parables talk about these things in

---

[1] Conzelmann, 'Weisheit', 236–40, argues that it is formally a 'revelation' which Paul got from the tradition of his 'Wisdom School'.

[2] E.g. I Enoch 22: 14, 25: 3, 27: 3, 36: 4, 40: 3, 75: 3, 83: 8 (81: 3); (Wilckens, p. 73 n. 1).

[3] Wilckens, p. 66; cf. Hipp. v. 24. 1 and v. 26. 16ff. (Wilckens, p. 77). For a full discussion see Wilckens, pp. 75–80; he shows how this text was influential in later gnosticism. Cf. Col. 1: 5, Phil. 3: 20.

[4] Thus T. W. Manson, 'Some Reflections on Apocalyptic', in *Aux*

the following way. They begin by describing themselves as 'The *words of wisdom*' (37: 2, cf. 37: 3–5). The first parable is 'a *revealing of the secrets* of the righteous' (38: 3). Enoch saw the *dwelling places prepared* for the righteous (39: 4–5, cf. 41: 2), and the 'blessing and glory' to which he had been ordained (39: 9). Then he saw the Son of Man (46: 1ff.). The first task of the Son of Man is to humble the rulers of the world (46: 4–6). In 48: 1ff. the Son of Man was named before the creation of the cosmos (48: 2–3) and ordained to be a 'staff of the righteous', 'the light of the Gentiles', and 'the hope of those who are troubled of heart' (48: 4); but this is all in the future, and 'For this reason hath he been chosen and *hidden* before Him, before the creation of the world and for evermore' (48: 6, par. I Cor. 2: 7). He is not hidden from the righteous, however, since the '*wisdom* of the Lord of Spirits hath revealed him to the holy and righteous' (48: 7, cf. 62: 7, cf. I Cor. 2: 10), but the rulers of earth and heaven shall miss the revelation and perish (vss. 8–10, cf. I Cor. 2: 10–16) for it is hidden from them and revealed only to the elect.

The similarity between these passages and I Cor. 2: 6–16 is obvious; they all tell of a secret wisdom, ordained before the creation and hidden, unknown to the rulers of the world, but revealed to the righteous. In Enoch the content of this secret wisdom is the glory prepared for the righteous, the punishment prepared for the wicked, and the redeemer who is to execute the judgement, the Son of Man.

The use of the term 'wisdom' in the passages from Enoch is twofold; it expresses the plan of God as a whole, and its individual contents. We suggest that synecdoche is employed in I Cor. 2: 6–9, to express a similar twofold meaning. By a simple synecdoche, the whole is taken to signify its parts;[1] 'wisdom', which primarily signifies the totality of the revelation of God's plan, also stands for the individual contents of that plan, namely, in the parables of Enoch, the Son of Man and the glory prepared for the righteous.[2] When Paul talks about the 'wisdom'

Sources de la tradition chrétienne: Mélanges offerts à M. M. Goguel (Paris, 1950), pp. 139ff., and W. D. Davies, *Paul*, pp. 306–7.

[1] 'Synecdoche' is 'A figure by which a more comprehensive term is used for a less comprehensive, or *vice versa*; as whole for part or part for whole, genus for species or species for genus, etc.' (Oxford Universal Dictionary).

[2] On 'wisdom' as the contents of revelation in apocalyptic, see Wilckens, pp. 66 n. 5. He cites II Bar. 54: 13, I En. 63: 2ff., 32, 48: 1, 49: 1, 91: 10,

that is 'hidden', 'contained in a mystery' and 'ordained before the world for our glory', he refers both to the revelation of God's plan for salvation as a whole, and to the individual contents of that revelation – 'the things prepared for those who love him'.

The crucial question that arises for us is, what is the precise nature of the entities contained in the apocalyptic plan, 'the secret wisdom'? Wilckens argues that σοφία was a Christological title among Paul's Corinthian opponents and that in 2: 6–16 the term is to be understood as describing the mythological heavenly Christ;[1]

Nämlich als Bezeichnung eines der wesentlichsten Heilsgüter, die für die Gerechten im Blick auf die zukünftige Offenbarung im Himmel bereit liegen und deren dortiges Vorhandensein wenigen apokalyptischen Weisen bereits vor dem Eschaton offenbart wird.[2]

This is a precise description of the apocalyptic entities we have found presented in I Enoch. The basis of Wilckens' identification of Christ with this heavenly Wisdom is 2: 8; until 2: 8a Paul is, according to Wilckens, within the vocabulary of apocalyptic, but in 8b the implied object of εἰ γὰρ ἔγνωσαν is τὴν σοφίαν, which, in turn, is synonymous with κύριον τῆς δόξης. 2: 8b therefore identifies σοφία θεοῦ and κύριος τῆς δόξης, according to Wilckens; the Wisdom of God is Christ, the Lord of Glory. Therefore, since Paul is using the language of his opponents here, the Gnostic myth of the descending redeemer was well known to the opponents, and is pre-supposed in 2: 8b.[3]

So wird hier der apokalyptische Begriff der Weisheit Gottes als eines Heilsgut in gnostischem Sinne zu einem christologischen Titel.[4]

The difficulties in this thesis are, however, insurmountable, as H. Köster has pointed out.[5] In I Cor. 1: 12 Christ is treated on a par with the other apostolic guides; and it is simply impossible to exclude the phrase ἐγὼ δὲ Χριστοῦ as a designation of a group.[6] The Corinthians did, indeed, make Wisdom the centre of their soteriology, but, as Köster says, only as a state to which

37: 1–3, 83: 10, 92: 1, IV Ezra 14: 25, 38–40, II Bar. 54: 5ff., 59: 9, I En' 99: 10, 98: 3. The solution we are proposing is similar in essence to the view taken by R. Scroggs, 'Paul as Sophos and Pneumatikos'.

[1] Wilckens, p. 68.   [2] *Ibid.*, p. 70.
[3] *Ibid.*, pp. 70–1.   [4] *Ibid.*, p. 73.
[5] *Gnomon*, 33 (1961), p. 591.   [6] As Wilckens does, p. 17 n. 2.

Jesus was, like the other apostles, the guide.[1] It cannot, therefore be shown on the basis of these texts that the Corinthian schismatics identified Christ with the heavenly wisdom, understood as a Gnostic hypostasis synonymous with the descending redeemer. This should not, however, be taken as a final judgement on the role of the heavenly man in their religion; there is still more evidence to be considered. As our discussion of I Cor. 15: 45–49 will show, this figure was important to them as a 'metaphysical' correlate of their anthropological doctrine. Our point here is simply that Wilckens has been too hasty in finding the myth of the Gnostic redeemer in I Cor. 2: 6–9.

The only reasonable solution to the problem of the meaning of the Wisdom spoken of in I Cor. 2: 6–9 is the one we have already suggested. Paul is using synecdoche, and, taking the title of the whole plan, namely Wisdom, he speaks of the contents of the plan. The use of the term 'wisdom' in this particular sense, and the use of the title 'Lord of Glory', suggest that Paul, or his source, had a tradition like the parables of Enoch in mind. The secret wisdom reserved for the perfect is that the humiliated one is indeed the apocalyptic redeemer, and that the crucifixion was part of the divine plan, which could also be called the divine 'wisdom'. Christ, as Lord of Glory, is for Paul pre-existent in the same way that the Son of Man is pre-existent in the Parables of Enoch.

One can explain all except one of the vicissitudes of I Cor. 2: 6–9 on the basis of the passages from Enoch. The secret wisdom is the apocalyptic plan of salvation;[3] the 'rulers of this world' are the earthly rulers, viewed from the point of view of apocalyptic, as quasi-spiritual forces opposing the advent of the new aeon;[4] the contents of the divine plan are the things prepared for the righteous, now pre-existent, then to be revealed; among these things is the Son of Man, the heavenly judge and redeemer, with whom Paul compares the pre-existent Christ, the 'Lord of Glory'. The one element that cannot be explained is the use of the term 'the perfect ones' (τέλειοι) in verse 6.

[1] Köster, *Gnomon*, p. 591.

[2] *Ibid.*, p. 592.

[3] For a list of those scholars, the vast majority, who accept this interpretation, see Wilckens, p. 68 n. 1.

[4] Thus G. B. Caird, *Principalities and Powers*, pp. 16–17.

I Cor. 2: 10–16, which speaks of the Spirit as the revealer of the divine plan, and which is an integral part of the exposition begun in 2: 6, also cannot be fully explained on the basis of the Enochian passages. The nearest equivalents to it in Enoch are in I Enoch 48: 7, where it is said that 'the wisdom of the Lord of Spirits' reveals the Son of Man to the righteous, and in 49: 3, where we read:

> And in him [i.e. the Son of Man] dwells the spirit of wisdom,
> And the spirit which gives insight,
> And the spirit of understanding and might...

Neither of these passages, however, can be construed as teaching a doctrine of revelation by the divine Spirit, like that in I Cor. 2: 10–16. We have to look farther afield for the background against which both the term τέλειος and the idea of revelation by the Spirit might be understood.

τέλειος in 2: 6 means the same as πνευματικός,[1] as can be seen from the correspondence between 2: 6, 2: 15 and 3: 1 in referring to those who have received the spirit of God. To be perfect, in this Pauline passage, is to have received the spirit of God and to have learned the 'spiritual things' (2: 13) which it teaches, the 'things prepared for those who love him' (2: 9). The use of τέλειος and πνευματικός, and the teaching of revelation by the spirit, suggest that the apocalyptic idea of wisdom has been presented in the context of a doctrine of revelation drawn from some other religious tradition.

According to Wilckens,[2] the words τέλειος and πνευματικός point to Hellenistic/Gnostic mysticism as the background from which they come. On the basis of the evidence he presents, he claims, 'dass Paulus hier in der Tat plötzlich ganz wie ein Gnostiker spricht'.[3] The generally late dates which must be assigned to most of the texts he cites makes his conclusion less than certain, even if one allows that later texts often contain much earlier material.[4] In view of the current questioning of the

---

[1] Cf. Wilckens, pp. 53–4. We agree with his interpretation of πνευματικοῖς as neuter in 2: 13b (pp. 84–5).

[2] *Ibid.*, pp. 53–60. Cf. H. D. Betz, *Nachfolge und Nachahmung Jesu Christi im Neuen Testament*, *B.H.T.* 37 (Tübingen, 1967), pp. 146–7, n. 4. On ψυχικός as a Gnostic term, see Wilckens, pp. 89–91. Cf. W. D. Davies, *Paul*, pp. 191–4, for a criticism of Reitzenstein's interpretation of this passage.,

[3] Wilckens, *ibid.*, p. 60.   [4] W. D. Davies, *Paul*, pp. 191ff.

thesis that there existed an articulated Gnostic system in New Testament times,[1] we must regard Wilckens' claim that Paul speaks as a 'Gnostic' here as unproven. Nevertheless, one cannot deny that Paul's references to the 'perfect ones' and the 'spiritual' ones recall Hellenistic mystical terminology. What could be the background of this passage if not 'Gnosticism'? An exploration of the religion of Paul's opponents should provide an answer.

In I Cor. 1: 18–25, Paul argues against a 'wisdom of the world' (ἡ σοφία τοῦ κόσμου, 1: 20b), which has caused schisms in the congregation. Its chief characteristic is that it is 'eloquent' (σοφία λόγου, 1: 17b). The usual interpretation of the evidence understands σοφία λόγου to describe '(the cultivation of) expression at the expense of matter...the gift of the mere rhetorician, courting the applause (*vanum et inane* σοφῶς) of the ordinary Greek audience.'[2] According to this view, the wisdom which Paul opposes is possessed by the wise man (σοφός), the scribe (γραμματεύς) and the debater (συν3ητητής) (1: 20), and it is the special objective of the Greeks (1: 22). It is unable to attain the knowledge of God as revealed in Christ (1: 21).

σοφός can mean both a Greek philosopher and a Jewish teacher of Torah; γραμματεύς is a translation of the technical term סופר (scribe) and συν3ητητής probably translates דרשן (expositor).[3] It is not unlikely that Paul is alluding to three titles of a rabbi חכם, סופר and דרשן to exemplify the 'wisdom' which empties the cross of all significance.[4] At first glance, there-

---

[1] C. Colpe, *Die Religionsgeschichtlicheschule* (Göttingen, 1961) *passim*.
[2] Robertson and Plummer, p. 5.   [3] Wilckens, pp. 27–8.
[4] Many rabbis aspired to 'Greek wisdom'. On the wisdom of the Greeks see S.-B. IV. 1, pp. 405–14. E.g. BQ 83ᴬ – R. Simeon b. Gamaliel (140): 'A thousand children belonged to my father's household: 500 of them studied Torah and 500 studied "Greek wisdom" (הכמת יונית).' (R. Marcus, 'The Phrase Hokmat Yewanit', *J.N.E.S.* 13 (1954), 86). The rabbis knew Greek literature and science and did not reject it out of hand. Their enthusiasm for it fluctuated with political circumstances. S.-B. III, p. 325, identify the 'wisdom of the world' as this Greek art and science of scribes and debaters. In S.-B. III, pp. 33–6 on Romans 1: 20, the 'wisdom of the world' is also the natural ability to recognize the existence of God. They cite the Maase Abraham [Horowitz: *Sammlung kleiner Midrashim* (Frankfurt a.M., 1881), p. 43, or Jellinek, *Beth ha Midrash*, 2, 118] in which it is told how Abraham deduced the existence of God from the sun and the moon and the weakness of idols. See also Test. Naphtali 3: 2ff.; W. D. Davies, *Paul*, pp. 28–30. On

fore, it seems that the 'wisdom' of chapter 1 is the rhetoric and dialectic of the scholar,[1] by which, either through unaided reasoning or attention to normal kinds of revelation, i.e. revelation which did not obviously humiliate and ridicule the deity, he believed himself capable of attaining the knowledge of God.

This is, however, only a superficial impression; if we consider the whole passage dealing with the problem, namely chapters 1–4, it is possible to describe the 'wisdom' of the Corinthian heretics much more precisely. The effect of the wisdom on the opponents is that they despise the humiliation of the Cross (I Cor. 1: 18ff.) and boast in a wisdom of their own (I Cor. 1: 29–31, 3: 18–23), which is powerful, and enables them to regard themselves as fulfilled, rich and ruling (I Cor. 4: 8). They refer to themselves by the titles σοφός[2] (1: 19–20, 25, 26, 27, 3: 18–23); τέλειος (2: 6, where Paul adapts one of their titles to his own use), and πνευματικός (2: 15, 3: 1, once again adopted by Paul), and they distinguish themselves from the ψυχικοί (2: 14), σάρκινοι and νήπιοι (3: 1). Essential to an understanding of their position is that their wisdom is their own; they did not receive it from anyone; they are essentially self-taught. 4: 7 shows this clearly; Paul's rhetorical question, τί δὲ ἔχεις ὃ οὐκ ἔλα-βες; εἰ δὲ καὶ ἔλαβες, τί καυχᾶσαι ὡς μὴ λαβών; obviously refutes the claim that they did not receive anything, but were self-taught. Their special apostolic leaders were, on this interpretation, only guides to the realization of their own potentiality. There is a striking parallel to this type of piety in the writings of Philo.

Hellenistic influences in the Rabbinic tradition see W. D. Davies, 'Reflections on tradition: the Aboth revisited', in *Christian History and Interpretation*, pp. 127–59, especially pp. 138–51, and note 1 on pp. 138–40. He compares, for instance, the chain of tradition in the Aboth with the traditions of the Greek philosophic schools. In this he follows the lead of E. Bickermann, in his article, 'La Chaîne de la tradition pharisienne', *R.B.* 59 (1952), 44–54.

[1] This understanding of the wisdom Paul opposes is shared by J. Héring (*Corinthiens*); E.-B. Allo (*Corinthiens*); Plummer and Robinson (*First Epistle to the Corinthians*); R. Scroggs ('Paul as Sophos and Pneumatikos'). Cf. W. Wuellner, 'Haggadic Homily Genre in I Corinthians 1–3', *J.B.L.* 89 (1970), 199–204, suggests that chs. 1–4 have the form of a rabbinic homily and come from a rabbinic 'school' debate in the Corinthian Church. His thesis merits serious consideration, which we were not able to give it here.

[2] Paul adapts this self-designation in 3: 10.

According to Philo the man who has attained salvation is both σοφός[1] and τέλειος.[2] He is also self-taught (αὐτομαθής καὶ αὐτοδίδακτος),[3] and the only true ruler and king.[4] Abraham and Jacob achieve supreme wisdom by effort of some sort, but Moses and Isaac have it by nature (καὶ αὐτομαθεῖ τῇ φύσει, Som. I. 168).[5]

Wisdom is, for Philo, the divine spirit in man, as Exodus 31: 2ff. shows, saying of Bezaleel that God 'filled him with the divine spirit, with wisdom, understanding, and knowledge to devise in every work.'[6] The mind (διάνοια) of the wise man is the dwelling place of God,[7] and his soul is an epiphany of God on earth;[8] there is a consubstantiality between it and God.[9]

The precise status of the various traditions in Philo is a vexed question, on which there is much work still to be done. It is clear that Philo's own point of view sees salvation as the result of moral achievement, and preserves the Biblical discontinuity between the human and the divine; but he has incorporated other, more mystical traditions. Shining through his writings one can see a conception of salvation, based on a consubstantiality between the divine being and the human soul, and taking the form of an ascent of the divine in man to its source in God.[10] The divine in man is a 'natural' endowment, given at creation; indeed, the real 'man' is the divine spirit, or Logos, or Wisdom, in man.[11] This apparently represents a mystical tradition which was present in the Hellenistic synagogue for which Philo writes.

Returning to I Corinthians 1–4, one is immediately struck by

[1] Agr. 99, Quis Her. 21, Quod Deus 3, Mig. 38.

[2] Leg. All. III. 140, where Moses is called ὁ τέλειος σοφός. In Leg. All. III. 207, Philo distinguishes between τῶν ἀτελῶν and τῶν δὲ σοφῶν καὶ τελείων.

[3] Fug. 166, Congr. 111, Op. 148. Cf. I Thess. 4: 9, where the true believers are called θεοδίδακτοι (I owe this reference to W. D. Davies, in private correspondence).

[4] Somn. II. 243–4, Mut. 152; Post. 138.

[5] Somn. I. 166–70.   [6] Gig. 23–4.

[7] Praem. 123, cf. Somn. II. 248–9.   [8] Quis Heres 88, cf. Conf. 81.

[9] Cf. Op. 134–6, Leg. All. III. 161, Quis Her. 55–7, Quod Det. 80–90, where this is said to be the case with all men, and is the anthropological possibility of salvation. See below, pp. 132–44.

[10] See the recent attempt to recover a 'Wisdom mystery' from the Philonic texts by H. Hegermann, *Die Vorstellung vom Schöpfungsmittler*, pp. 9–87. See also E. R. Goodenough, *By Light, Light*.

[11] Quod Det. 83.

the similarity between the religion of the opponents and this mystical tradition behind Philo. The only terms used by the opponents, which are not in Philo, are πνευματικός, ψυχικός, σάρκινος, and νήπιος, well known in the mysteries. This may be explained by the fact that Philo was seeking to counteract the full-blown mysteries, as Hegermann points out, and purposely avoided using these terms. The central term, σοφός, however, he simply could not avoid if he was to remain in conversation with them. There is, however, evidence to suggest that, although precisely these terms were not used by Philo, the ideas which they communicate, and, at times, close variations of the terms, are present in Philo.[1]

Against this Philonic background I Cor. 2: 10–16 makes good sense. The mystics say that there is a consubstantiality between their own spirit (wisdom, mind) and the divine; Paul emphatically denies this (2: 10–12); the divine spirit performs in God the same function as the human spirit in man; but each in his own sphere. The Christian received (ἐλάβομεν, 2: 12) the divine spirit from without; the heretics believed they had always had it and denied receiving anything (4: 7). The Christian has (received) the mind of Christ (νοῦν Χριστοῦ ἔχομεν, 2: 16); the heretic has always had the divine mind, as his true self within him.[2] Having once received the divine spirit the Christian community has the same spiritual capabilities as the mystics claimed to have, and so Paul can use their terminology in verses 13–16; but because theirs is really 'the Spirit of the world' (τὸ πνεῦμα τοῦ κόσμου, 2: 12) they miss the true revelation of the things prepared for the righteous (2: 9), and the true manifestation of God's wisdom in the Cross, while the Christian who has the spirit of God sees these things. A mystic, who believed that he

[1] See: B. A. Pearson, 'The pneumatikos–psychikos Terminology in I Corinthians: A Study in the Theology of the Corinthian Opponents of Paul and its Relation to Gnosticism', Abstract in *H.T.R.* 61 (1968), 646–7; U. Früchtel, *Die kosmologischen Vorstellungen bei Philo von Alexandrien*, Arb. *L.G.H.J.* 2 (Leiden, 1968), pp. 105 (Mig. 46) and 139–40 (Mut. 201–63). E. Brandenburger, *Fleisch und Geist, Paulus und die dualistische Weisheit*, *W.M.A.N.T.* 29 (Neukirchen, 1968).

[2] W. D. Davies points out, in a private conversation, that the plural may be significant in these verbs. The Christians receive these spiritual endowments not as individuals, like the mystics, but as a community, and individually as participants in the life of the community.

had discovered his true divine self, would need nothing more; he would be 'filled, enriched and a ruler' (4: 8); there is no place for the future resurrection or the eschatological 'not yet' in his religion; and so the stage is set for the great debate in I Cor. 15.

The point at issue between Paul and his opponents is the question of the ontological continuity or discontinuity between man and God. The opponents preach that man's spirit is consubstantial with the divine, and that their various apostolic leaders made them aware of this and showed them how to realize their divine potential. Paul, rooted in Judaism,[1] denies any consubstantiality. In systematic terms, the opponents deny the ontological gap between man and God, whether it is expressed in an existential category such as 'received', or in eschatological (temporal) categories such as 'now' and 'then'. Here Paul counters them with the existential category; in chapter 15 he uses the eschatological. One can, however, discern, even here, the eschatological mode, in the use of apocalyptic language, and the reference to traditions similar to the parables of Enoch in 2: 6–9. Those who really understand the 'secret wisdom' know that the 'things prepared' – which include the heavenly man – are reserved for the end of time.

At last we can ask the question, Do either Paul or his opponents conceive of Christ as pre-existent? The opponents regard him as one manifestation of eternal Wisdom which is the divine in man and in the universe. Paul understands Christ to be pre-existent in the way that the things promised in the parables of Enoch are pre-existent. He presents Christ as a figure like the Son of Man, who was, according to the Parables of Enoch, created before the world. The resurrection of Jesus enables Paul or his tradition to regard Christ as a heavenly being. If we are right in seeing a tradition like that in I Enoch as the influence behind this passage, we may say that for Paul Christ is pre-existent before the world, and pre-existent with reference to the end, and that his pre-existence is actual rather than ideal. An important feature of this argument of Paul's is that, when faced by Hellenistic mysticism, he resorts to the categories of Jewish apocalyptic.[2]

[1] On the special nature of Jewish mysticism in preserving the distinction see G. Scholem, *Major Trends in Jewish Mysticism*, pp. 1–39.

[2] This judgement should not be understood to exclude the possibility of

(ii) *I Corinthians 3: 5–17*. The discussion of the schisms and the true and false wisdom continues down to 4: 13. It is followed by a transitional passage, 4: 14–21, which leads into the ethical injunctions in 5: 1ff. Paul continues to base his argument with the heretics on apocalyptic ideas; in chapters 1–2 he applied these ideas to Christ; here he applies them to the Church.

The metaphor of planting and watering in 3: 5–9 ends with the summary, 'You are God's planting (γεώργιον), God's building (οἰκοδομή)' (3: 9b).[1] Thus the horticultural metaphor is brought to an end, and an architectural metaphor is introduced.

In Jer. 18: 9, 24: 6 and Ezekiel 36: 9–10, the metaphors of planting and building are found together. They are applied to the Israel of the future. In several apocalyptic works Israel, or the community of the righteous, is called the 'planting' or 'plant'. In C.D. 1. 5, the community understands itself to be something God 'made to spring forth from Israel and Aaron, a root of His planting to inherit His land.' In I En. 62: 8, imme-

Hellenistic elements being present in Jewish apocalyptic. See on this, H. D. Betz, 'On the Problem of the Religio-Historical Understanding of Apocalypticism', in *Journal for Theology and Church*, VI, 134–56.

[1] The images of building and planting are often found together in the contemporary literature as symbols of all life, in the town and in the country respectively. Cf. A. Friedrichsen in *Th. Stud. u. Krit.* (1922), pp. 185ff.; 1930, pp. 298ff., etc., cited in Hans Lietzmann, *An die Korinther I, II*, vierte von W. G. Kümmel ergänzte Aufl. (Tübingen, 1949), p. 171. Ph. Vielhauer, in *Oikodome* (Karlsruhe, 1940), has shown that the Pauline idea of οἰκοδομεῖν from which οἰκοδομή derives here, refers primarily to the building up of the community and only secondarily to the building up of the individual, through the community. The image derives from Jer. 24: 6 and was transferred from the Jewish nation to the Church. In 3: 10ff. Paul has, according to Vielhauer, combined this with a Stoic image of founding and building as a description of spiritual activity. Cf. J. Pfammatter, *Die Kirche als Bau, Eine exegetisch-theologische Studie zur Ekklesiologie der Paulusbriefe*, Anal. Gregor., 110 (Rome, 1961). Lietzmann says that in verse 9b–10 the building symbolized teaching, not the community, but since Paul wants to combine the image with the test of fire he awkwardly slips into another, more literal, reference for 'building'. This heavy-handed attempt to distinguish between 'teaching', 'community' and literal 'building' does violence to the imagery in the name of tidiness, and reduces poetry to logical absurdity. Had Paul wished to make a simple denotative statement he would probably have avoided metaphor. In the New Testament the image of building is found chiefly in Corinthians, Romans and Ephesians, and in Acts 9: 31, 20: 32, Jude 20, I Pet. 2: 5. In Matt. 7: 24–7 the image portrays sound moral conduct and its opposite.

diately following a statement that the Son of Man was hidden from the beginning and revealed to the elect (verse 7), the text runs, 'And the congregation of the elect and holy shall be sown'. In I Enoch 93, part of a revelation of the saving history which describes itself as 'this complete doctrine of wisdom' (92: 1), Israel is referred to as 'the elect of the world...the plant of uprightness' (verse 2); Abraham is called 'the plant of righteous judgement', and his posterity 'the plant of righteousness' (verse 5). As the saving history closes and the last judgement is described, we are told that 'The elect righteous of the eternal plant of righteousness (are chosen), to receive sevenfold instruction concerning all his creation' (verse 10).[1] One of the last acts is that 'a house shall be built for the Great King in glory for evermore' (91: 13, Charles' reconstruction). In Jubilees 1: 16–17, also part of a recital of the consummation of the saving history, we read:

and I will remove them the plant of uprightness...and I will build my sanctuary in their midst, and I will dwell with them, and I will be their God and they shall be My people in truth and righteousness.[2]

This evidence suggests that Paul is still under the influence of the apocalyptic tradition, where 'plant' and 'building' are sometimes associated, and used as metaphors for the people of God. Apocalypticism is the key to an understanding of the metaphor of the building which we must now examine.

Paul compares the Church to a building in order to warn those who labor in the Gospel to be careful what they teach, since teaching, like construction materials, must stand the test of the final judgement. He claims that he alone laid the foundation of the Church at Corinth,[3] and no other foundation

---

[1] Cf. I Enoch 10: 16, 84: 6, and Charles, *A. and P.* II, p. 194 n. 16.

[2] See also the discussion by Dibelius, *An die Kolosser, Epheser, an Philemon* 2, *H.N.T.* 12 (Tübingen, 1927), pp. 53–5. Cf. the mixed metaphors in Eph. 3: 18 and Col. 2: 7.

[3] He calls himself σοφὸς ἀρχιτέκτων. The context of this passage is the discussion of partisanship and true and false wisdom. In 2: 6–16 Paul claimed to possess a secret wisdom. His founding of the Corinthian congregation is the work of a 'wise builder'. There may be some allusion here to Exod. 31: 1–11, 35: 30–36: 1, where the builders of the tabernacle were supernaturally endowed with the necessary building skills, which are, by implication, called 'wisdom'. (The phrase σοφὸς ἀρχιτέκτων is used in Is. 3: 3, LXX, but this

can be laid beside the one already laid by him.[1] This is part of his polemic against the schismatics (verses 10–11). Suddenly, however, he identifies the foundation already laid with Jesus Christ (verse 11b).

It is possible that Paul wishes to identify his initial preaching in Corinth with Jesus Christ, in a similar sense to 1: 23. He compares his preaching to the laying of a foundation and the content of his preaching, 'Christ crucified', to the foundation itself. But this understanding does not facilitate the interpretation of the rest of the passage. If one considers verses 10–17 as a whole it seems more likely that, in identifying Jesus Christ as the foundation of the Church, Paul is thinking in the apocalyptic manner of the heavenly Christ, once revealed to the elect, now hidden in heaven until the final judgement. In the course of claiming to have laid the foundation of the Corinthian church, Paul's mind made one of its characteristic associative leaps to the Church universal and its eternal foundation.[2]

is of no importance for the present passage.) There is an important indication in Ex. R. 48 (102D) (on Ex. 35: 31) that the rabbis believed that the eschatological temple would be built as the world (Pr. 3: 19), the tabernacle (Exod. 35: 31) and the temple of Solomon (I Kings 7: 15) were built, through wisdom, insight and knowledge. 'And so, when in the future God sets out to build, it will be built by these three things, as it is said, "By wisdom is a house built, and by insight it is established, and through knowledge the rooms are filled."' (Prov. 24: 3ff.) Cf. Tanchuma 123^A; *ibid.* B, 6 (61^B). Paul may have thought of himself as endowed, like Bezaleel in Ex. 35: 31, with special wisdom to 'build' the Church. Cf. Philo, Gig. 23–4, where the skill of Bezaleel is attributed to the same Spirit of God, which is perfect Wisdom, which Moses passed on to the seventy elders. On the relations between Paul and Philo see the judicious article by H. Chadwick, 'St. Paul and Philo of Alexandria', *B.J.R.L.* 48 (1965–66), 286–307.

[1] A. Friedrichsen, *Th.Z.* 2 (1946), 316ff., cited in Leitzmann, *An die Korinther I, II*, p. 172) believes he has discovered an inscription which shows that κείμενος is a technical term for the 'already present foundation'.

[2] We agree with E.-B. Allo, *Corinthiens*, p. 59, who writes against an understanding of 'foundation' as 'faith' or 'doctrine' (cf. Lietzmann, *An die Korinther I, II*, p. 16), as follows: 'Mais avec son réalisme mystique, Paul entendait encore autre chose: la personne même du Christ, qu'il a comparé ailleurs à la pierre angulaire, à la tête du corps.' Cf. Robertson and Plummer, I.C.C. p. 61, who distinguish the historical reference of the words in verses 10–11 – Paul's preaching – from the 'metaphysical' meaning – the work of God in Christ. They interpret in the light of Eph. 2: 20 and Acts 4: 11, Paul's preaching simply brings to light the eternal pre-existent foundation of the Church, and if the foundation is eternal, so is the Church.

On this view, the Church is a divine entity manifest in time. Its foundation is in heaven and the building up of the Church on earth is really a spiritual labor whose effects are realized in heaven. Therefore, 'gold, silver and precious stones' stand for labor that is truly spiritual, which produces heavenly effects, while 'wood, hay and stubble' stand for labor that is not (verse 12).

The metaphor of the Church as a heavenly building was drawn from the apocalyptic idea of the heavenly temple.[1] In Tobit 13: 16–17 we read, 'Jerusalem [of the future] will be built with sapphire and smaragd and costly stones, its walls and towers and its bulwarks, with pure gold' (cf. Ex. R. 15 (77[A]); Rev. 21: 11), and in O. Sibyll, 3. 657ff., 'The temple[2] of the great God will be full of glorious wealth, of gold and silver and purple jewelry'. It would be manifested during the last judgement. Lietzmann rather prosaically remarks that Paul's choice of fireproof materials as opposed to the fire-prone 'wood, hay and stubble' was unfortunate, since a building of gold, silver and precious stones would melt in a fire.[3] Such is the absurdity one comes to if one overlooks the apocalyptic influence on Paul's thought at this point. He did not choose precious metals and jewels because he believed them to be fire-proof from a physical point of view. He chose them because they were traditionally the components of the eschatological temple which would be there after the fire of judgement had done its work.

Those who teach and preach in the Church should be building the eschatological heavenly temple, according to Paul, but some are not. Their work is only of this aeon, contrived by the 'wisdom of this aeon', which is perishing. Such a teacher might escape with his soul, but his work would be revealed for the transitory thing it is, and would be destroyed (verse 15).

[1] Cf. S.-B. IV/2, pp. 919ff., pp. 932ff., for the copious references to the new Jerusalem and the heavenly temple in apocalyptic and rabbinic literature. Cf. M. Fraeyman, 'La spiritualisation de l'idée du temple dans les épîtres pauliniennes', *Ephem. Theol. Lov.* XXIII (1947), 378–412; A. M. Denis, 'La Fonction apostolique et la liturgie nouvelle en esprit; Étude thématique des métaphores pauliniennes du culte nouveau', *R.S.P.T.* XLII (1958), 401–36, 617–56. J. Héring, *Corinthiens*, p. 32, states that Paul identifies Christ with the perfect temple of the eschaton, and cites Jub. 1: 17 and I Enoch 91: 13.

[2] Reading ναός with S.-B., Meincke and Geffcken, against Lanchester in Charles, *A. and P.* p. 390 n. 657.

[3] Lietzmann, *An die Korinther I, II*, p. 17.

The apocalyptists and the rabbis would probably have taken the components of the heavenly temple literally. For Paul, 'Gold, silver and precious stones' were metaphors for sound preaching and teaching. Likewise, the literal heavenly temple of the Jewish tradition was for Paul a metaphor for the Christian community.[1] The Christians are related to the Christ in heaven as the walls and roof of the heavenly temple are related to their foundation. The Spirit of Christ is present in their midst as the Spirit of God is present in the eschatological temple. Using this imagery, Paul presents the real heavenly community, which is the Church.

Paul concludes the discussion by calling the Christian congregation 'God's temple' (verses 16–17). The primary basis for this metaphor is the idea that the spirit of God is present in the congregation as the divine presence dwells in the sanctuary (ναός). If the presence of the spirit in the congregation is similar to the presence in the temple, the congregation itself may be compared to the temple building. The temple in question is not the earthly temple, which is possessed by those who rejected Christ, but the heavenly, eschatological temple.[2] Thus the statement in verses 16–17 makes an ontological claim about the church, warning the schismatics that they are destroying not merely an earthly society, but a heavenly entity.

The Church is pre-existent like the heavenly temple. It will be fully revealed in the eschaton; in the mean time it is being revealed to the elect, as they become part of the church on earth. Under the metaphor of the temple, Paul has expressed his belief in the predestined solidarity of the redeemed with the heavenly redeemer. A. Schweitzer argued that this was an essential element in Paul's doctrines of Christ and the Church and that it was the result of apocalyptic influence from texts such as I Enoch

[1] B. Gärtner, *The Temple and the Community in Qumran and the New Testament*, *S.N.T.S.*[1] Monograph Series 1 (Cambridge, 1965), shows that the identification of the community as a temple took place at Qumran. Gärtner argues that the New Testament borrowed this idea from Qumran. There are many good ideas, well proven, in this book, but in general it is so controlled by the desire to prove that Qumran is behind all references to the temple in the New Testament that it turns out to be a *tour de force*. It neglects, for the most part, the whole apocalyptic tradition of the heavenly temple.

[2] Héring, *Corinthiens*.

38: 1–5, 62: 7–8, 14–15, IV Ezra 9: 39 – 10: 57. We may recall Schweitzer's summary:

The Pauline mysticism is therefore nothing else than the doctrine of the making manifest, in consequence of the death and resurrection of Jesus, of the pre-existent church (the community of God).[1]

Such an understanding of the Church conditions the following passages on Church life and conduct.[2] In 4: 8–13 Paul condemns those who have taken the heavenly nature of the Church too seriously; he reminds them of present sufferings. In 5: 9–13 his moral injunctions are clearly based on the doctrine of the Church as a community distinct from this aeon (cf. 6: 11). In 6: 1ff. the Church is to judge the cosmos, including the angels.[3] In 6: 12ff., the idea of the temple is applied to the individual's body in order to dramatize exhortations to chastity. There are parallels to this imagery in Philo and the Stoics,[4] but it is not improbable that it occurred to Paul to use it here because the metaphor of the Church as a temple was in his mind.[5] In 7: 32ff. the eschatological nature of the Church, which is also its heavenly nature, dominates Paul's advice on marriage and family life. In 7: 36 where we read of women who lived with men as 'virgins', there may be a hint of the attempt to live the heavenly life of the church. In Matt. 22: 29–32 there is the tradition that in heaven there is no marriage and hence no sex. It is not unlikely that the Pauline churches knew this tradition,

[1] Cf. above p. 9; A. Schweitzer, *Mysticism*, p. 116. See below for the contribution of the idea of the heavenly 'anthropos' to the idea of the Church.

[2] Cf. W. D. Davies, *Paul*, pp. 130, 232, who quotes with approval P. Carrington's description [*The Primitive Christian Catechism* (Cambridge, 1940), p. 21] of the early Church as a 'neo-levitical community'.

[3] Cf. S.-B. III, pp. 362ff.; Jude 14–15, 6, II Pet. 2: 4, I En. 91: 15, E.-B. Allo, *Corinthiens*, pp. 133–4; Robertson and Plummer, I.C.C., p. 111, suggest that 'judge' means 'rule' in the sense of Judges 3: 10, 10: 2–3, etc.

[4] Cf. Philo Somn. I. 149; Epictetus Diss. II. 8. 13–15: 'wretch, you are carrying God with you, and you know it not. Do you think I mean some god of silver or gold? You are carrying him within yourself, and perceive not that you are polluting him by impure thoughts and dirty deeds' (cited after Robertson and Plummer, p. 128). Cf. John 2: 21, Rom. 8: 11, II Cor. 6: 16ff., II Tim. 1: 14.

[5] Thus Robertson and Plummer, *ibid*.

not necessarily as a saying of Jesus,[1] and tried to live as the angels in heaven, because of their belief that the Church was the heavenly congregation of the end of time. This brief survey of the moral teaching in I Corinthians confirms the thesis that in 3: 9–17 Paul understands the Church as a pre-existent heavenly entity manifested on earth, and that he expresses this belief by means of the metaphor of the heavenly temple.[2]

(iii) *I Corinthians 8: 6.* It is generally agreed that in this passage Paul identifies Christ with hypostatized, pre-existent Wisdom, through whom 'the all' was created.[3] According to this verse 'the all' (τὰ πάντα) came from the one God, and we go to him. He is the source and goal of all things, including ourselves. Christ is he through whose mediation the universe and the Church came into being.[4]

The formula 'from... through... and to...' which is used to describe the respective roles in creation of the Father (from... to) and the Son (through) occurs also in Romans 11: 36. It derives ultimately from ancient Greek physics through Stoicism, with influence from Hellenistic mysticism.[5] The verse as a whole has

---

[1] See S.-B. I, pp. 889ff., for evidence concerning the wide prevalence of this tradition. E.g. Ber. 17A. Cf. A. Isaksson, *Marriage and Ministry in the New Temple, A Study with special reference to Mat. 19: 3–12 and I Cor. 11: 3–16*, Acta Seminarii Neotestamentici Upsaliensis, xxiv (Lund, 1965).

[2] This thesis is argued also by L. Cerfaux, *The Church in the Theology of St. Paul*, pp. 147–8, cf. pp. 345–72. Paul's comparison of this apostolic work to 'temple service' in I Cor. 9: 13–14 and Rom. 15: 16 probably also derives from this understanding of the Church. Cf. A. M. Denis, *R.S.P.T.* XLII; K. Weiss, 'Paulus–Priester der christlichen Kultgemeinde', *T.L.Z.* 79 (1954), 355–64; Cerfaux, *Church*, pp. 42–4.

[3] Cf. E. Schweizer, *Neotestamentica*, pp. 105–9. He cites J. Weiss, *Der erste Korintherbrief* (1910), pp. 226ff. (p. 106 n. 8); A. Feuillet, *Le Christ Sagesse*, pp. 59–85.

[4] The curious change of subject from τὰ πάντα to ἡμεῖς indicates a change from a cosmological to a soteriological interest, Feuillet, p. 66; cf. p. 65, where he says we must understand ἔσμεν after the final ἡμεῖς δι᾿ αὐτοῦ. This brings out the soteriological meaning, i.e. we are *Christians* through him. It also includes the characteristic Pauline understanding of salvation as a 'new creation'.

[5] Cf. M. Aurelius Med. 14: 23; O. Michel, *Der Brief an die Römer*, Meyers Kommentar IV, 12 Auflage (Göttingen, 1963), p. 286. See Feuillet, *Le Christ Sagesse*, p. 73; on the difference between Paul's statement and Stoic pantheism; and *ibid.*, pp. 80–1 on the similar use of these prepositions in the Hermetic literature.

a formulaic ring, and J. N. D. Kelly suggests that it is a brief liturgical formula already familiar to Paul's readers.[1] The reference is introduced so suddenly in this context that we may assume that Paul was merely reminding his readers of what they already took as familiar doctrine.[2] The liturgical cadences are discernible, but this is perhaps too small a sample to identify it positively as a fragment from a liturgy or hymn.

I Cor. 8: 6 introduces the vitally important idea of the pre-existent Christ, mediator of creation. We shall take up the discussion of this theme from time to time, as the idea develops in the Pauline correspondence (e.g. II Cor. 4: 4, Col. 1: 15ff., cf. John 1: 1ff.).

(iv) *I Corinthians 10: 4*.

And all drank the same spiritual drink; for they drank from the spiritual rock which followed them, and the rock was Christ.

Once again Paul refers rather suddenly to the identification of Christ with pre-existent Wisdom, in the midst of a moral allegory. 'The rock which followed the Israelites was Christ.'

The passage, 10: 1–12, is a midrash based on Ex. 13: 21 (clouds), 14: 21–2 (sea), 16: 4, 14–18 (manna) and 17: 6 and Num. 20: 7–13 (water-springs), with strong Hellenistic-Jewish influences present.[3] The idea of the rock following the Israelites is well attested in rabbinic and Hellenistic Jewish sources.[4] The

---

[1] J. N. D. Kelly, *A Commentary on the Pastoral Epistles, I Timothy, II Timothy, Titus*, Harper's New Testament Commentaries (New York, 1963), p. 63. He compares it with I Tim. 2: 5–6. Feuillet, *Le Christ Sagesse*, calls it 'La profession de foi...'

[2] J. Jervell, *Imago Dei, Gen. 1: 26ff. im Spätjudentum, in der Gnosis und in den paulinischen Briefen, F.R.L.A.N.T.* 76 (Göttingen, 1960), p. 171, points out that although Paul does not identify Christ with pre-existent Wisdom very often, this is no indication that the idea was unimportant in his theology. Since his letters were occasional and *ad hoc*, Paul frequently refers, we might assume, to tenets which are well known to his correspondents. Jervell argues that 'the weight of the kerygma rests precisely upon those points which he [Paul] does not find it necessary to illuminate'. This cannot be made a general rule, as Jervell makes it, but it must be kept in mind by the exegete.

[3] Lietzmann, *An die Korinther I, II*, p. 44. See Feuillet, *Le Christ Sagesse*, pp. 87–111.

[4] E.g. Tos. Sukka 3, 11ff. etc. Cf. S.-B. III, pp. 406ff.; W. D. Davies, *Paul*, p. 153.

identification of the moving rock with Wisdom was made by Hellenistic Judaism, as Philo attests.

In Leg. All. II. 86 he writes: ἡ γὰρ ἀκρότομος πέτρα (Dt. 8: 15) ἡ σοφία τοῦ θεοῦ ἐστιν (cf. Quod Det. 115). In the same paragraph the Manna is called λόγος τοῦ θεοῦ. In Quod Det. 118, the rock in Deut. 32: 13 is compared with the Manna and described as λόγος θεῖος (cf. Leg. All. III. 162). Clearly the myth of pre-existent Wisdom acting in the history of salvation, which we recognized in the book of Wisdom and the Gospel of the Hebrews,[1] is present in these statements. Paul identifies Christ with this pre-existent Wisdom.[2]

The use of the imperfect (ἦν) in 10: 4 shows that Paul has the real pre-existence of Christ in mind, and not simply a typological identification between the rock and Christ.[3] Feuillet writes,

Le même Christ, qui soutient actuellement les chrétiens dans leur marche vers la patrie céleste, soutenait déjà leurs 'pères', les Hébreux, dans leur marche vers la Terre Promise.[4]

(v) *I Corinthians 15: 45–9*.[5] Paul is defending the possibility of bodily resurrection (verse 35). He argues that just as there is an appropriate body for every form of life in the natural order, so there is a body for the life of the resurrection; but the rabbi is

---

[1] Cf. Wisd. 7: 27, Ev. Hebrews in H.-S., pp. 163–4; Cf. Feuillet, *Le Christ Sagesse*, p. 105–6, who points out further evidence of this motif in Wisd. 10–12; e.g. Wisdom saved the patriarchs (10: 1–14), she descended into prison with Joseph (10: 14) and she led the people out of Egypt (10: 15–11:4), she punished the Egyptians and the Canaanites (11: 5–12: 25).

[2] The same hermeneutical method is found in C.D. 8: 6, where the springs in Num. 21: 18 are identified with the Torah. I Cor. 10: 11 seems to express the same basic hermeneutical assumption as the Qumran commentaries, namely, that all the prophetic scriptures apply to the community because it is the eschatological community (Lietzmann, *An die Korinther, I, II*, p. 181).

[3] Robertson and Plummer, I.C.C. pp. 201–2; Héring, *Corinthiens*, p. 77.

[4] *Le Christ Sagesse*, p. 105. Cf. Jude 5, John 12: 41, Heb. 3: 1–6, 12: 25.

[5] Literature consulted: C. K. Barrett, *From First Adam to Last* (New York, 1962); E. Brandenburger, *Adam und Christus, W.M.A.N.T.* 7 (Neukirchen, 1962); W. D. Davies, *Paul*; J. Jervell, *Imago Dei*; H. Schlier, *Der Brief an die Epheser* (Düsseldorf, 1958); A. Schweitzer, *The Mysticism of Paul the Apostle*; R. Scroggs, *The Last Adam* (Philadelphia, 1966); Basil A. Stegmann, *Christ, the 'Man from Heaven'*, The Catholic University of America New Testament Studies no. VI (Washington D.C., 1927).

not satisfied with mere logic, he cites scripture to settle the proof.

Genesis 2: 7 in the LXX runs as follows:

καὶ ἔπλασεν ὁ θεὸς τὸν ἄνθρωπον χοῦν ἀπὸ τῆς γῆς
καὶ ἐνεφύσησεν εἰς τὸ πρόσωπον αὐτοῦ πνοὴν ζωῆς,
καὶ ἐγένετο ὁ ἄνθρωπος εἰς ψυχὴν ζῶσαν.

Paul quotes the last member with two additions: ἐγένετο ὁ πρῶτος ἄνθρωπος ᾽Αδὰμ εἰς ψυχὴν ζῶσαν (15: 54a). It is apparently important for his argument that the man who is called 'a living soul' (ψυχὴ ζῶσα) be clearly identified as the *first* man, and that he be named *Adam*. This man, furthermore, bears the 'natural' body (τὸ ψυχικόν, vs. 46a), and originates in the earth (15: 47a). For the last point Paul has in mind the account in Gen. 2: 5ff. of the creation of man from the dust of the earth.

In contrast to the first man Adam, Paul sets the *last* Adam who is 'a life-giving spirit' (ὁ ἔσχατος ᾽Αδὰμ εἰς πνεῦμα ζωοποιοῦν, vs. 45b), whose body is spiritual (τὸ πνευματικόν, vs. 46b) and who comes from heaven (ὁ δεύτερος ἄνθρωπος ἐξ οὐρανοῦ, vs. 47b). The matter that concerns us here is the question of the pre-existence of this second man from heaven.

The fact that he is said to be from heaven implies at least that he existed before his manifestation, possessing eschatological pre-existence; but there is much more that can be learned about the idea of pre-existence implied here, from a study of the religio-historical background of the idea of the heavenly Adam. There can be no denying that we have in this passage an instance of the myth of the heavenly man, so widespread in orientally influenced religions of the Hellenistic period. It would be profitable to review some of the evidence for this myth.

Egon Brandenburger provides a recent account of those examples of the myth which are important for an understanding of verses 45–9. He argues that Paul used the myth here because it was an essential part of the doctrine of those who opposed him in Corinth. Referring to Romans 5: 12–21, as well as to I Cor. 15: 45–9, Brandenburger points out that the antithesis between the two representative men which controls the structure of these passages is regarded by many modern exegetes as having been borrowed by Paul from elsewhere; but the precise source has not been identified.[1] The antithesis can best be seen in I Cor. 15, where it is not as well assimilated to Paul's own thought as in Romans, and where the presence of opponents provides the necessary clue to the origin of the doctrine of the two Adams/Anthropoi.[2]

According to Brandenburger, the heresy which Paul faced was a unified phenomenon; therefore I Cor. 15 as a whole must be viewed as an answer to a religious point of view with some inner consistency. The position Paul opposes is essentially the one expressed in II Timothy 2: 18: ἀνάστασιν ἤδη γεγονέναι. The opponents, therefore, denied both the physicality and the futurity of the resurrection, since, if it had already occurred for those still alive in this world, it could be neither physical nor future. They believed themselves to be the present possessors of a spiritual nature, awareness of which they had achieved through Gnosis.[3]

According to Brandenburger, the immediate context of I Cor. 15: 45-9 begins at 15: 35 with a probably sarcastic question about the nature of the resurrected body.[4] Paul takes it seriously and argues for a spiritual body (σῶμα πνευματικόν, vs. 44). In 15: 45-9 he provides a proof from scripture for this conclusion, from Gen. 2: 7.[5] His exegesis of Gen. 2: 7 rests on two presuppositions which are read into the text: (i) the presupposition of the two corresponding Adams/Anthropoi; and (ii) the presupposition that the two Adams/Anthropoi determine two types of human existence, which enables Paul to give the doctrine a soteriological application in 15: 49.[6] The force of Paul's argument, according to Brandenburger, depends on the fact that these presuppositions were held by his opponents. The second (ii) is well known from Gnosticism, and, more recently, perhaps, from Qumran – namely, the 'Two Spirits' doctrine. The first (i) we shall see, is also known in Gnosticism and Hellenistic Judaism; and so there is no reason to doubt that these doctrines were held by the opponents.[7]

The clearest indication of the presence and doctrine of the

[1] Brandenburger, *Adam*, p. 68.
[2] *Ibid.*, p. 69.
[3] *Ibid.*, pp. 70-1.
[4] *Ibid.*, p. 71.
[5] *Ibid.*, pp. 72-3. Davies, *Paul*, p. 43, argues that Paul is citing Christian rabbinic sources.
[6] Brandenburger, *Adam*, pp. 73-4.
[7] *Ibid.*, p. 74.

opponents is the obviously polemical tone of 15 : 46. Among the opponents (τινές) the spiritual Adam is first both temporally and ontologically, while the psychic Adam (ψυχικός) is second, and the object of denigration. Paul uses their terminology in verses 45–9 in order to change the intent and nature of their doctrine.[1] He reverses the order of the spiritual and earthly Adams.

According to Brandenburger, the main features of the opponents' teaching are, therefore: (i) the antithesis of the first and the second Adams/Anthropoi; (ii) the immediate correlation of the two 'men' with two kinds of human existence; (iii) the denigration of the second Adam by comparison with the first; (iv) the presentation of the antithetical scheme within a cosmology of space, which operates in terms of the contrast between 'above' and 'below'.[2]

What is the religio-historical source of this pattern of thought? Brandenburger presents a rich account of evidence from Hellenistic religious sources.[3] The question of the dating of these sources, however, renders them problematic as evidence for the religion of Paul's opponents. They are certainly appropriate examples of how the idea of the two heavenly men was developed in the later tradition. For the sake of caution, we shall, however, consider only those sources which can with some certainty be dated more or less contemporary with Paul: these are, primarily, the first Hermetic tractate, *Poimandres*, and Philo.[4]

(1) The first tractate of the Corpus Hermeticum, also known

---

[1] *Ibid.*, pp. 74–5.   [2] *Ibid.*, pp. 75–6.

[3] *Ibid.*, pp. 77–134. He discusses (a) A Jewish–Gnostic prayer from the magical papyri, in K. Preisendanz, *Papyri Graecae Magicae* (Leipzig, 1928), Vol. I, pp. 12ff. (I. 195–222) and pp. 112–15 (IV. 1167–227). He follows E. Peterson, 'La Libération d'Adam de l'Ananké', *R.B.* 55 (1948), 199–214; (b) A fragment from Zosimus, published by R. Reitzenstein, *Poimandres, Studien zur griechisch-aegyptischen und frühchristlichen Literatur* (Leipzig, 1904); (c) The beliefs of the Naasenes, set out in Hippolytus, *Elenchos*, V. 6–11; (d) Justin's *Book of Baruch*, as reported by Hippolytus, *ibid.*, V. 26. 7ff.; (e) Three Nag Hammadi tractates: *Apocryphon of John* (34: 19, 47: 20, 49: 6), *Hypostasis of the Archons* (135: 12ff.), *On the Origin of the World* (155: 25); (f) Mandaic material.

[4] Brandenburger also discusses these sources. Our interpretation, however, is independent of his. On the date of *Poimandres* see C. H. Dodd, *The Bible and the Greeks* (London, 1935), pp. 201–9. He dates it late in the first or early in the second century; E. Haenchen, 'Aufbau und Theologie des "Poimandres"' in *Gott und Mensch, Gesammelte Aufsätze* (Tübingen, 1965), pp. 335–77.

as the 'Poimandres', is chiefly an account of a soteriology. It reaches a climax in paragraphs 24–6, which tell how the redemption takes the form of an ascent, which begins when the believer leaves behind the dissolving mortal body and rises through the seven spheres of the 'harmony'. At each sphere the self strips off one of the encumbering vices until,

stripped naked of the energies of the harmony, he is changed into the nature of the Ogdoad [the eighth region], having the appropriate power, and hymns the father with the existent ones. Those who are present rejoice together at his presence, and having become like the beings with him, he hears a certain sweet voice of certain powers above the ogdoadic nature singing hymns to God.[1] And then, in order, they go up to God and they give themselves over to the powers and becoming powers they pass into God. This is the good end for those who have knowledge, to be deified (τοῦτό ἐστι τὸ ἀγαθὸν τέλος τοῖς γνῶσιν ἐσχηκόσι, θεωθῆναι, 26).

Poimandres, the heavenly revealer as well as the true self of the believer, reveals the state of man prior to salvation and the way of salvation. He is the redeemer, and without the knowledge that he brings salvation is impossible.

Poimandres reveals who this true self is which needs to be redeemed, and the revelation takes the form of a cosmology, whose chief aim is to explain how man came to be the tragic mixture of spirit and matter that he is. The climax of this first part, which is similar in function to chapter 1: 18 – 3: 20 of the letter to the Romans, is at paragraph 18:

let the mind remember that it is immortal, and that the cause of death is desire, and all things that are. (καὶ ἀναγνωρισάτω ⟨ὁ⟩ ἔννους ἑαυτὸν ὄντα ἀθάνατον, καὶ τὸν αἴτιον τοῦ θανάτου ἔρωτα, καὶ πάντα τὰ ὄντα.)

The paragraphs 19–23, which intervene between this climax of the hamartialogy, and the beginning of the account of the ascent in 24, tell how there are two kinds of men; one made essentially of light and life, like the father from whom came the Man (φῶς καὶ ζωή ἐστιν ὁ θεὸς καὶ πατήρ. ἐξ οὗ ἐγένετο ὁ Ἄνθρωπος. ἐὰν οὖν μάθῃς αὐτὸν ἐκ ζωῆς καὶ φωτὸς ὄντα καὶ ὅτι ἐκ τούτων τυγχάνεις, εἰς ζωὴν πάλιν χωρήσεις, 21). All that the candidate for redemption needs to know is that he is of the same

---

[1] Cf. Philo, Somn. II. 253ff.; Hegermann, Vorstellung, pp. 33–4.

substance as the Father and the Anthropos (21). The motto of this salvation is: ὁ νοήσας ἑαυτὸν εἰς αὐτὸν χωρεῖ (21).

The other kind of man is dominated by the body made of the moist substance produced by the gloomy cosmic darkness, totally part of the sensual world (ὅτι προσκατάρχεται τοῦ οἰκείου σώματος τὸ στυγνὸν σκότος. ἐξ οὗ ἡ ὑγρὰ φύσις, ἐξ ἧς τὸ σῶμα συνέστηκεν ἐν τῷ αἰσθητῷ κόσμῳ, 20).

We cannot pause here to disentangle the threads which make up the cosmogony of pars. 1–18. There is some reason to suspect that there may be at least two originally independent traditions present; a cosmogony based on a mythification of Stoic elements of earth, water, air and fire, on the one hand, and in pars. 12–15, on the other, an anthropogony based on the myth of the heavenly man and the Narcissus motif.[1] We shall concentrate on the latter.

Then the Nous, father of all, being life and light, gave birth to Man, identical with himself, whom he loved as his own child; for he was very beautiful, bearing the image of his father. Since the father loved his own form truly, he handed over to him all his works of creation. (12)

(ὁ δὲ πάντων πατήρ ὁ Νοῦς, ὢν ϛωὴ καὶ φῶς, ἀπεκύησεν Ἄνθρωπον αὐτῷ ἴσον, οὗ ἠράσθη ὡς ἰδίου τόκου· περικαλλὴς γάρ, τὴν τοῦ πατρὸς εἰκόνα ἔχων· ὄντως γὰρ καὶ ὁ θεὸς ἠράσθη τῆς ἰδίας μορφῆς, παρέδωκε τὰ ἑαυτοῦ πάντα δημιουργήματα.)

This Anthropos desired to create and was given leave to do so by the father; the seven governors of the spheres gave him of their power. He peeped down through a breach in the seven spheres – the Harmony – and saw his own reflection (τὸ εἶδος τῆς καλλίστης μορφῆς τοῦ 'Ανθρωπου... τὴν ὁμοίαν αὐτῷ μορφὴν, 14) in the lowest waters. He fell in love with his image, and with the will was the deed; he fell into the lowest matter, and was swallowed up in a frenzy of sexual passion.

And on this account, amongst all the living things on earth, man [alone] is of a dual nature; mortal on account of the body, but immortal on account of the essential man.

(καὶ διὰ τοῦτο παρὰ πάντα τὰ ἐπὶ γῆς ϛῷα διπλοῦς ἐστιν ὁ ἄνθρωπος, θνητὸς μὲν διὰ τὸ σῶμα, ἀθάνατος δὲ διὰ τὸν οὐσιώδη ἄνθρωπον, 15.)

---

[1] On the Narcissus motif see W. L. Knox, *St. Paul and the Church of the Gentiles* (Cambridge, 1969), p. 225.

As a result of the fall the heavenly man became a slave to the powers of the harmony (ὑπεράνω οὖν ὢν τῆς ἁρμονίας ἐναρμόνιος γέγονε δοῦλος, 15). 'This is the mystery which has been hidden until this day' (τοῦτό ἐστι τὸ κεκρυμμένον μυστήριον μέχρι τῆσδε τῆς ἡμέρας, 16).

The essential man is the heavenly Anthropos, who is the image (εἰκών) and substance (μορφή) of God (12), in each mortal man. Salvation consists in being told of this divine essence in each man, and of being enabled to rise out of the bondage of the material body and the governors of the seven spheres, and to return to God. The revealer is the Anthropos himself, called 'the essential man', and 'Nous', 'θεός', and, in his capacity as redeemer, 'Poimandres'.

(2) Philo's exegesis of Gen. 2: 7 in the first tractate of Leg. All. is perhaps the most important indication of the thought of Paul's opponents here. The exegesis is clearly mythological and dualistic. We have already seen how Philo includes soteriological traditions which assume a consubstantiality between man and the divine. Leg. All. I. 31[1] begins with the general pronouncement: 'There are two kinds of men; the one a heavenly man, the other earthly (διττὰ ἀνθρώπων γένη· ὁ μὲν γάρ ἐστιν οὐράνιος ἄνθρωπος, ὁ δὲ γήϊνος). Philo goes on to say that the heavenly man is made after God's image, and is without any part in corruptible matter, while the earthly man is compacted of clay. The heavenly man is God's offspring (as is implied by the denial that the earthly man is God's offspring) while the earthly man is merely the work of an artificer.

Philo then rather surprisingly speaks of an 'earthly mind' (νοῦς γεώδης, 32), which was in need of the divine breath to bring it to life, and which received that breath to become a truly living soul (32). There follows a startling question, which shows that we have before us a different kind of tradition from the normal Philonic traditions about the nature of man. Philo asks: Why God deemed the earthly and body-loving mind worthy of divine breath at all, but not the mind which had been created after the original, and after His own image? (33)

---

[1] Cf. Leg. All. I. 53-4, where the same clear distinction is made between the two men as in this text; but there we are back with the usual Philonic tradition where the heavenly man is the spiritual aspect of empirical man, and the earthly man, the bodily. Cf. O. Cullmann, Christology, pp. 148-50, who also points to Philo's influence on Paul here.

The 'earthly and body-loving' mind which receives the divine breath is the mind of the man we have been considering all along – the twofold soul which has its baser part, corresponding to the blood in the exegesis of Lev. 17: 11, and its higher, ruling part, which is the divine breath in it. The mind created after the image seems to be a being totally independent of the earthly mind. It is not the divine breath which is given the earthly mind, since it could also receive that breath. In this new tradition, therefore, we have three entities: the earthly mind (that is, of the man of clay), the divine breath (which is given to the earthly mind but not to the mind 'according to the image'), and the mind created according to the image (which does not need and so did not receive the divine breath). Against this we may set the other, more normal, Philonic tradition in which there are only two entities, the earthly mind and the divine breath, who is the Logos, and the man according to the image, and which is 'breathed into' the 'earthly mind'.

The only explanation of this phenomenon that one can offer is that in Leg. All. I. 31–3 we have a 'gnosticizing' tradition, which is generally parallel to the tradition given in Op. 134ff., but different in significant details; and that Philo has assimilated it imperfectly. The tradition, one may conjecture, told of a paradigmatic heavenly man and a paradigmatic earthly man and of two kinds of empirical men, each corresponding to one of the paradigms. Those who correspond to the heavenly man have the 'mind according to the image' and those who correspond to the earthly man have the earthly mind. In this dualism the former group are bound to be saved if indeed they even need salvation, while the latter are inevitably, that is, ontologically, doomed. Philo sought to assimilate this tradition by attaching it to Gen. 2: 7, where the account of God's 'breathing in' a soul gave him a chance to overcome the ontological dualism by allowing the 'inbreathing' to bestow on the earthly mind the same possibility of salvation as the heavenly mind possessed (cf. 38), in accordance with the normal Philonic tradition.

The only reason which could have prompted Philo to attempt such a re-interpretation of this 'gnosticizing' tradition was that it was influential in the Hellenistic synagogue. This, we would aver, is the same tradition that Paul's opponents in I Corinthians

15 used in denying the resurrection, and teaching the doctrine of the two paradigmatic men; 'the mind according to the image' needs no resurrection; the earthly mind is ontologically doomed. The 'mind according to the image' ascends to reunion with its paradigmatic heavenly man at bodily death; the earthly returns to dust.

By the portrayal of the divine breath as something distinct from the heavenly man Philo tried to respect the gnosticizing insistence that the heavenly man has no contact whatsoever with anything earthly, while at the same time trying to overcome the ontological dualism in salvation. All he succeeded in doing was to confuse the issue. The essential difference between Philo and this gnosticizing tradition was that for Philo the possibility of salvation was a divine gift to all men, breathed in at creation by the divine breath; for the proto-gnostics it was an ontological fate for some, while not for others.

In the conception of salvation as the re-ascent of the divine in man to its origin in the divinity, Philo and this gnosticizing tradition are at one. One may assume that only ignorance could prevent the realization of the proto-gnostic salvation, and that only temporarily; for Philo moral turpitude could hinder and finally extinguish the divine effulgence in man; salvation was morally conditioned for Philo, while for his 'gnosticizing' tradition it was ontologically conditioned.

In none of the pertinent Philonic texts is the heavenly man called Adam. Indeed, in Leg. All. I. 90ff., Philo expressly forbids that he be called Adam:

Call him earth, he says, for that is the meaning of Adam, so that when you hear the word Adam, you must make up your mind that it is the earthly and perishable mind; for the mind that was made after the image is not earthly but heavenly.

(κάλει δή, φησίν, αὐτὸν γῆν· τοῦτο γὰρ 'Αδὰμ ἑρμηνεύεται, ὥστε ὅταν ἀκούῃς 'Αδὰμ γήινον καὶ φθαρτὸν νοῦν εἶναι νόμιζε, ὁ γὰρ κατ' εἰκόνα οὐ γήινος, ἀλλ' οὐράνιος, 90.)

This means that we have to explain why Paul, in adapting some such tradition as this, called the 'men' Adam. It could be, as Brandenburger argues, that they were in fact called Adam in the tradition. That would suggest that Philo is deliberately correcting the tradition here, and that Paul represents it more accurately. It could, however, also mean that Paul supplied the name Adam out of his own Jewish background.

If we assume that Paul is using terminology drawn from the tradition represented in Leg. All. I. 31–3 in particular, and by Philo in general, we are able to explain the dark points of I Corinthians 15: 45–9. The proof text Paul uses is the same as in Philo: Gen. 2: 7;[1] but Paul adds πρῶτος and Ἀδάμ to it to make it clear that he understands it to refer to the first earthly man, whom Philo calls ὁ πρῶτος ἄνθρωπος (Opif. 136), and to whom the name Adam is alone appropriate (Leg. All. I. 90ff.). In this way he indicates that he has the same tradition of exegesis in mind that Philo represents (15: 45a). Then Paul inserts his own interpretation: the last Adam became a life-giving spirit (ὁ ἔσχατος Ἀδάμ εἰς πνεῦμα ζωοποιοῦν, 15: 45b). This statement is patterned on the citation from Gen. 2: 7; the phrase ὁ ἔσχατος Ἀδάμ corresponds antithetically to ὁ πρῶτος ἄνθρωπος Ἀδάμ, and the phrase πνεῦμα ζωοποιοῦν to ψυχὴν ζῶσαν.

The changes Paul makes are the keys to his own point of view. He changes πρῶτος to ἔσχατος, thereby showing that for him eschatology outweighs protology; the Christ who has come at the end of time takes precedence over Adam who stands at the beginning (vss. 46–7). He leaves out ἄνθρωπος: this may be because he wishes to temper the identification of Jesus with the heavenly Anthropos,[2] for fear that too enthusiastic an identification would imperil the full realization of the incarnation (the fact that he goes on to identify Christ in this way as Anthropos in verse 47 suggests that there he is citing an independent tradition). Thirdly, he calls both men by the name Adam.

The spiritual man comes at the end of time, as Jewish apocalyptic states, not at the beginning, as Philo and the mystics would have it. Thus we see that Paul has set the mystical doctrine of the two men in which the spiritual man precedes the earthly, in which protology predominates, into an apocalyptic framework in which eschatology predominates, and in which the spiritual man follows the earthly. This has the effect of destroying the mystical basis of salvation in the divine spark

[1] W. D. Davies, *Paul*, p. 44. Gen. 2: 7 was not a favourite text for discussion among the Rabbis and the New Testament makes use of it only at this point.

[2] Davies, *ibid.*, p. 52.

present in the human soul, since if the spiritual man is not manifest until the end, he cannot be present in the believer living before the end.

In verses 47 and 48, we suggest that Paul is adapting the same tradition as Philo is in Leg. All. I. 31. This can be seen if one sets the opening lines of the Philonic passage, which, we believe, comes from Philo's gnosticizing tradition, alongside Paul's statement in verse 47: διττὰ ἀνθρώπων γένη· ὁ μὲν γάρ ἐστιν οὐράνιος ἄνθρωπος, ὁ δὲ γήϊνος (Leg. All. I. 31); cf. ὁ πρῶτος ἄνθρωπος ἐκ γῆς χοϊκός, ὁ δεύτερος ἄνθρωπος ἐξ οὐρανοῦ (I Cor. 15: 47).

These are both interpretations of Gen. 2: 7. Paul has not merely copied Philo's gnosticizing tradition, but has interpreted Gen. 2: 7 himself (as the difference between γήϊνος and χοϊκός shows) with it in mind. The presence of the tradition in Paul's mind can be seen, furthermore, from verse 48, where there are two kinds of men mentioned, each corresponding to its paradigm: the two 'types' of Philo's tradition.[1] Pauls' opponents in I Corinthians came, therefore, from the Hellenistic synagogue.

In verse 49, Paul overcomes the ontological dualism by placing it within the framework of eschatology. Whereas Philo tried to overcome it mystically, by seeing the breath of God in every man, Paul overcomes it eschatologically by extending to every man the possibility of union with the last, heavenly man, by faith, which is focused on the future, and whose essence is hope. 'And as we have borne the image of the earthly man, we shall also bear the image of the heavenly man' (15: 49).

The presence of the eschatology of Jewish apocalyptic in this passage raises the question of the relationship between the Anthropos and the Son of Man. Cullmann argues that 'the second man' is merely a variation of the Son of Man concept,[2] itself only a single manifestation of a widespread oriental myth. Brandenburger[3] rejects this view as too facile, but his restatement of the situation is not really different from Cullmann's position, which seems to be essentially correct.

---

[1] Cf. Bultmann, *Theology* I, 174; I Cor. 15: 44–9 is based on Gnostic anthropology; it derives the plight of Adamitic man from his inborn quality of 'Adamness'; he is, without any reference to a fall, both ψυχικός and χοϊκός.

[2] *Christology*, pp. 141–2.   [3] *Adam*, pp. 131–5.

The Son of Man in the similitudes of Enoch, Brandenburger argues, is one manifestation of the myth of the Anthropos which can best be discerned in Philo. I Enoch 70–1 is a fragment of tradition which tells of the ascent of Enoch and his transformation into the Son of Man; this shows that the same soteriological understanding of the anthropos was present in the Enochian circles as in the Philonic. The redeemed ascend to union with the Anthropos in heaven. This early version of the myth can still be seen in I En. 49: 3, 62: 14ff., and 71: 14ff., where the Son of Man and his own people are identified.

The soteriological interpretation of the myth, in which men ascended to unite with the Anthropos in heaven, was modified in Enoch by the apocalyptic eschatology and the idea of the Messiah. Thus the Similitudes of Enoch and I Cor. 15: 45–9 represent the same process of interpretation of the myth of the heavenly man, in terms of apocalyptic eschatology and Jewish Messianism. No longer does the Anthropos remain in heaven and men ascend to him; now he descends to earth at the eschatological moment. The 'man from heaven' in the Pauline text, therefore, if it does not depend on the Enochian Son of Man, is at least a parallel development of the same Anthropos tradition. The similarity between the Pauline layer of tradition in I Cor. 15: 45–9 and the apocalyptic layer in the Similitudes is clear; both have re-interpreted the myth of the Anthropos as the heavenly image to which man ascends; both look forward to the descent of the Anthropos at the end of time, to do the work of the Messiah.

All of this argument leads to the conclusion that Jesus had been understood in terms of the myth of the heavenly man, by the opponents of Paul. Jesus was, for them, the pre-existent, heavenly Anthropos, on earth. Paul does not reject the identification of Jesus with the Anthropos; rather he emphasizes eschatology; as Jervell says, Paul makes Jesus the Anthropos of the end of time.[1] He used the idea of the pre-existent Anthropos because it was part of the religion of those he sought to refute; but this does not mean that he did not regard the pre-existence of the Anthropos as an appropriate attribute of the Christ. As the anthropos of the end of time, Christ is still thought of as pre-existent – before the creation and before his eschatological

---

[1] Jervell, *Imago Dei*, p. 268: 'Christus ist der Anthropos der Endzeit.'

manifestation. His soteriological significance, however, rests not on his pre-creational existence but on his eschatological coming; hence, the emphasis is on Christ as the Anthropos of the end of time. Men are not saved by returning to a prior state of existence, but by receiving a new existence from the coming, future one. Nevertheless, this new existence has always been there, not as man's true self, the 'first Adam', but as Christ's self, the 'last Adam'.

(vi) *II Corinthians 4: 4b*.

...lest they see the enlightenment of the gospel of the glory of Christ, who is the image of God.

In this section the meaning of the word 'image' is our central concern. The term is closely connected with the Adamic motif in Paul's Christology, and is clearly important for his presentation of the nature of Christ.[1]

The present text is probably a fragment from a pre-Pauline confession or hymn, which indicates that the identification of Christ as the image of God took place in the Gentile church prior to the advent of Paul.[2] According to Jervell, this hymnic fragment belongs to the same context of thought as Phil. 2: 6ff. and Col. 1: 15ff. Although II Cor. 4: 4 cannot be understood without some reference to these hymns, we shall reserve a full discussion of them for later.

4: 4 should be read as part of the exposition that includes 3: 18.[3] The theme of 3: 18 is that by beholding the glory ($\delta\delta\xi\alpha$) of Christ, as in a mirror ($\kappa\alpha\tau\sigma\pi\tau\rho\iota\zeta\delta\mu\epsilon\nu\sigma\iota$), the Christians are being changed ($\mu\epsilon\tau\alpha\mu\sigma\rho\phi\sigma\acute{\upsilon}\mu\epsilon\theta\alpha$) into his image ($\tau\grave{\eta}\nu$ $\alpha\acute{\upsilon}\tau\grave{\eta}\nu$ $\epsilon\grave{\iota}\kappa\acute{\sigma}\nu\alpha$); and this transformation is achieved by the Lord who is the Spirit ($\grave{\alpha}\pi\grave{\sigma}$ $\kappa\upsilon\rho\acute{\iota}\sigma\upsilon$ $\pi\nu\epsilon\acute{\upsilon}\mu\alpha\tau\sigma\varsigma$). The theme of 4: 4 is that the

---

[1] Cf. Jervell, *ibid.*, p. 214: 'In der Vorstellung von Christus als εἰκὼν τοῦ θεοῦ finden wir den centralsten Satz der paulinischen Theologie.' Jervell's book shows that Gen. 1: 26–7 had a wide influence on the Jewish Hellenistic religious world. See also F.-W. Eltester, *Eikon im Neuen Testament*, Beihefte zur *Z.N.W.* 23 (Berlin, 1958); H. Hegermann, *Die Vorstellung vom Schöpfungsmittler*; H.-F. Weiss, *Untersuchungen zur Kosmologie des hellenistischen und palästinischen Judentums*, T.U. 97 (Berlin, 1966); W. D. Davies, *Paul*, pp. 147–76, especially pp. 154 and 159ff.; E. Lohse, 'Imago Dei bei Paulus', *Libertas Christiana, Frederick Delekat zum 65 Geburtstag*, W. Matthias ed. (München, 1957), pp. 122–35. [2] Jervell, *Imago Dei*, p. 214.

[3] Jervell, *ibid.*, p. 173, believes that 3: 18 – 4: 4 is an exposition of Gen. 1: 27.

gospel is the 'light' (φωτισμός) of the glory (δόξα) of Christ, who is the image of God (εἰκὼν θεοῦ).

The two probable sources for this conception of Christ and salvation are (a) the Wisdom tradition and (b) Philo.

In Wisd. 7: 25-7, Wisdom is called 'an effluence of the glory of the creator' (ἀπόρροια τῆς...δόξης), 'an effulgence of eternal light' (ἀπαύγασμα φωτὸς αἰδίου), a 'mirror' (ἔσοπτρον) and 'the image of his goodness' (εἰκὼν τῆς ἀγαθότητος). In 7: 27 it is said that she enters 'holy souls' and makes them friends of God and prophets. In verse 22 she is said to be a 'spirit'. There is obviously a close similarity between II Cor. 3: 18 and 4: 4 and Wisdom 7: 22-30.[1] Wisdom as the 'image' of God is the mediator between God and man. But the similarity is not close enough to permit the judgement that Paul has precisely this passage in mind.

The figure of Wisdom as we find it in the Wisdom of Solomon underwent development in the writings of Philo. He identified it with the Logos,[2] and added significantly to its anthropological and soteriological aspects. Jervell believes that this development in the idea of σοφία/λόγος took place as a result of influence from 'gnostic' interpretations of Gen. 1: 26.[3] The Logos became the archetypal anthropos, image of God,[4] as well as the true man within each human being.[5] Both the divine mediator and the inner man bear the same name, 'Logos'. The presence of the logos, or 'image', in man, makes it possible for him to know

[1] Cf. F.-W. Eltester, *Eikon*, p. 134, who paraphrases H. Windisch, 'Die Weisheit und die paulinische Christologie', in *Neutestamentliche Studien für G. Heinrici* (Leipzig, 1914), pp. 220-34, as follows: 'dass der präexistente Christus bei Paulus und die göttliche Weisheit der Juden eine und dieselbe Gestalt sind'. Cf. Jervell, *Imago Dei*, p. 49.

[2] Somn. II. 242, Sac. 64ff., Fug. 108ff., Quis Her. 199ff., Ebr. 30ff., Leg. All. II. 49. In Somn. II. 42, Wisdom is the source of the 'logos' in the virtuous soul. 'Wisdom' is, *mutatis mutandis*, the heavenly eikon, and logos the eikon in man.

[3] Jervell, *Imago Dei*, pp. 57-8. See our discussion of I Cor. 15: 45-9, pp. 132-44.

[4] Leg. All. III. 96, Op. 24-5, Conf. 62-3, 146 (where the logos is called ὁ κατ' εἰκόνα ἄνθρωπος), 147, Fug. 101, cf. C.H. I. 12 for a gnostic expression of this idea; Jervell, *ibid.*, pp. 52-70.

[5] Quis Her. 230-2, Plant. 18-20, Quaes. Gen. II. 62, Fug. 71, Somn. I. 215, Det. 22-3, 84, Gig. 33, Agr. 9, Op. 69, Plant. 42, Quis Her. 56; Jervell, *Imago Dei*, pp. 56ff.

God.[1] The 'image' within man is 'Spirit', having been 'breathed into' him by God, according to Gen. 2:7.[2] This makes possible the mystic–intellectual ascent to God of one's 'true man' or 'spirit' on the 'royal road' to God.[3]

One may see this idea in a more developed form in later Gnosticism. There, the divine image is the first emanation of the supreme god, which performs many functions similar to those of the Logos in Philo. It mediates between God and the world, and is the foundation for the understanding of man and salvation. The major difference between the gnostic eikon and the Philonic logos is that the former, unlike the latter, plays no positive role in the creation of the cosmos, given the generally negative attitude towards creation on the part of the gnostics. There are several synonyms for εἰκών in the gnostic sources at our disposal, which help considerably to illuminate its function.[4] εἰκών is also μορφή in the sense of essence, rather than form.[5] It is the heavenly robe that the soul puts on at the end of its ascent.[6] It is also the seal (σφραγίς)[7] or the face (πρόσωπον)[8] of

[1] Leg. All. I. 38, Det. 86ff., Op. 69ff. Cf. C.H. XI. 20: τὸ γὰρ ὅμοιον τῷ ὁμοίῳ νοητόν, cf. Apocry. Joh. 26: 11–17, where the gnostic principle that only God can know God is expressed. Since that is the case, the 'inner man', 'God's image in man', is the foundation of the possibility of salvation, which is 'to know God'. Jervell, Imago Dei, pp. 130–6.

[2] Leg. All. I. 38, Plant. 18 ff., Som. I. 34, Spec. Leg. IV. 123.

[3] Op. 69ff.; Jervell, Imago Dei, pp. 61–2.

[4] Jervell, ibid., pp. 167–9. On eikon in Gnosticism see the whole section, pp. 122–70.

[5] μορφή can be translated as πνεῦμα in the gnostic milieu (Jervell, ibid., p. 167). Cf. E. Kaesemann, 'Kritische Analyse von Phil. 2: 5–11', Exegetische Versuche etc. I. 51–95; cf. C.H. I. 12–14, Hipp. Ref. VI. 14. 1–6; V. 19. 14; Exc. e. Theod. 31: 3ff., Apocr. Joh. 21: 8–22: 1; Epiphan. Panarion 23.1.4.

[6] Acts of Thomas 112 (H.-S. II, pp. 502–3). For the purpose of understanding II Cor. 3: 18 it should be noticed that in l. 76, Acts of Thomas 112, the psalmist says:
'But suddenly when I saw it over against me,
The ⟨splendid robe⟩ became like me, as my reflection in a mirror.'
The robe is the image of the high god, which the central figure in the Hymn of the Pearl (Acts Thm. 108–13) took off before he set out on his journey to earth, and puts on again when he returns. Cf. Hipp. Ref. V. 19. 21; Od. Sol. 11. 11; 17. 4. Cf. I Enoch 62: 15c.

[7] Hipp. Ref. V. 26. 8ff., 19. 8–12, Acts of Thomas 112, Od. Sol. 4: 7, Pis. Soph. 98. 154. 3, 103; 170. 12; 108. 178. 40. In Philo the logos is a 'seal', functioning cosmogonically.

[8] Od. Sol. 17. 4, Exec. e. Theod. 10. 6.

God, and the head of the universe, or of the individual, symbolizing the spiritual part of his existence.[1]

In calling Christ the 'image of God' Paul seems to have the same tradition in mind as that which gave birth to Philo's Logos. Since he refers to the title 'image' so abruptly, we may assume that his readers knew it well and understood its ramifications. The soteriology implied throughout 3: 18 – 4: 18 is based on the idea of Christ as the pre-existent image of God, the anthropos/logos/eikon/sophia, who is also the spirit within the believer.

The 'image' also has a cosmogonic function for Paul, as can be seen in 4: 6, where there is a remarkable soteriological use of the category of creation (cf. 5: 17). Just as the eikon/logos mediated the creation, so also, as the Christ, he mediates salvation, which is the 'new creation' (cf. 5: 17).

By identifying Christ with the 'image' of God, the pre-Pauline tradition present here proclaimed his pre-existence before the world. It also proclaimed a continuity between the divine activity in creation and in redemption, thereby making it impossible that Christian redemption should be understood as salvation from an alien world.[2]

We may take this opportunity to notice a feature of chapter 4, not closely connected with the idea of 'image' but nevertheless pertinent to the idea of pre-existence. In 4: 16–18 the 'inner man' and the 'eternal, invisible things' belong to the same class of objects. The endurance of persecution 'lays up an eternal weight of glory'. What are these 'eternal things', this 'weight of glory'? The 'unseen things' to which the Christian looks are, in the first place, the heavenly Christ, the celestial archetype of his true humanity, as in 3: 18. Athwart this Philonic conception falls the apocalyptic notion, explored in I Cor. 3: 9–17, that what one does on earth as a Christian produces spiritual goods – glory – in heaven; the Christian is, by his sufferings, 'laying up an eternal weight of glory'. There is, therefore, a hint of the doctrine of the heavenly Church in these chapters.

The same myth of the anthropos which Paul uses in I Cor. 15: 45–9 seems to be present in these chapters also; the only

---

[1] The synonymity of *eikon* and *kephale* in the Jewish tradition is shown by I Cor. 11: 3 and 7. Cf. C.H. X. 11; Apoc. Joh. 26. 9.

[2] F. Craddock, *The Pre-existence of Christ in the New Testament*, pp. 89–92, makes much of this.

difference is that here the word used to describe the heavenly one is 'image', not 'anthropos'. The transcendent image is primarily the resurrected Christ; but the pre-Pauline Church identified the risen Christ with the pre-existent Logos/Wisdom/Anthropos, and themselves with Christ. Soon we shall hear the logical outcome of this: 'even as he chose us in him before the foundation of the world' (Eph. 1: 4). 'Meanwhile, we look not to things seen, but to things unseen, for the things that are seen are temporary, but the unseen things are eternal' (I Cor. 4: 18).

The identification of the Christians with Christ is effected by the presence of the Spirit in the believer; but once again, as in I Cor. 1–4 and 15: 45–9, Paul makes it clear that the Spirit is the Spirit of God given to the Christian from without (3: 5–6, 4: 1) and not a 'natural' human endowment. He compares its advent in the heart to the act of creation (4: 6, cf. 5: 17).

Paul's own interest in this passage, as in I Cor. 15: 45–9, is not primarily in the pre-existence of Christ, but in his work as the eschatological redeemer. However, the language which he uses suggests an interest in pre-existence; it probably comes from the pre-Pauline tradition.

(vii) *II Corinthians 5: 1–10*. Paul develops the soteriology of the inner and outer man (cf. 4: 16) by means of a blend of Philonic and apocalyptic terminology, harnessed in the service of the Christian idea of resurrection. In 3: 18 – 4: 6, he expounded a theology of glory for the individual, drawing on a Jewish–Hellenistic mystical tradition. In 4: 7–15 he balances the glory by introducing the theology of the cross and the eschatological reservation. In 4: 16–18 he amalgamates the two emphases by means of the doctrine of the inner and outer man, and the idea of the future glory, presently being stored up.

5: 1–10 is a presentation of the unseen things – the glory in store for the believer – from the point of view of membership in the heavenly Church. It is based on the apocalyptic and rabbinic notion of 'the Age to come that always is', into which the righteous enter at death.[1]

[1] Davies, *Paul*, pp. 314–17. Lietzmann, *An die Korinther ad loc.* interprets this passage much as we do, on the basis of the apocalyptic paradox of the simultaneity of the two ages, and not on the basis of the Hellenistic dichotomy between flesh and spirit (cf. *ibid.*, p. 202 note on II Cor. 5: 1). Héring,

The earthly body is a temporary dwelling, and when it is destroyed we have 'a house from God, not made with hands, eternal in the heavens' (οἰκοδομὴν ἐκ θεοῦ...οἰκίαν ἀχειρο-ποίητον αἰώνιον ἐν τοῖς οὐρανοῖς, verse 1). In verse 2 Paul speaks of 'putting on' (ἐπενδύσασθαι) this heavenly house 'over' the earthly, that he may not be found naked, that life may swallow up death (verse 3). God has prepared us for this, and the Spirit is evidence of its reality (verse 5). In verse 7 he emphasizes that these realities are unseen, that we walk by faith and not by sight, and he closes in verse 10 with the assurance that we shall all have to face the judgement of Christ.

The 'house not made with hands, eternal in the heavens' is the same thing as the pre-existent image, the anthropos, and as the heavenly temple.[1] The temple imagery of I Cor. 3: 9ff. portrayed the Church as a heavenly community, to be manifested at the end, but presently existing and in the process of being built, as people join the community. The heavenly eikon is also a community, of which the redeemed become a part when they 'put it on' (ἐνδύσασθαι) like a robe (cf. verse 2).[2]

The closest parallel to this pattern of thought occurs in the letter to the Ephesians; in Eph. 2: 15–22 the Church is presented as both a building and the body of Christ. We shall discuss these texts later.

The relationship between this passage and I Cor. 15 has often been discussed. W. D. Davies argues[3] that Paul regarded the resurrection of Christ as an indication that the powers of the Age to Come – which always is – were already at work. Already the resurrection body, for the individual, was being formed.

La Seconde Épître de Saint Paul aux Corinthiens (Neuchâtel and Paris, 1958), p. 47, compares 5: 1 to John 14: 2 and II Enoch 61: 1 and sees an apocalyptic background.

[1] On this mixture of imagery see Schlier, *Epheserbrief*, pp. 141–4, where he discusses the 'Church as Body and Building' at some length. See also W. L. Knox, *Church of the Gentiles*, pp. 136–9, on the background meaning of the imagery of the heavenly house and the heavenly garment.

[2] Cf. Philo, Migr. 28–30, 46, cf. Plutarch, De Iside 53, 56; Quis Heres 101ff., 313, 314–16, Praem. 115–17, Agr. 65, on Wisdom as a heavenly house or place. C. F. D. Moule, 'St. Paul and Dualism: The Pauline Conception of Resurrection', *N.T.S.* 13 (1965–6), 106–23, argues that, while in I Cor. 15 Paul implies that the new body is added to the old, in II Cor. 5 the new is received in exchange for the old.

[3] *Paul*, pp. 285–98, 317.

Paul had died and risen with Christ and was already being transformed. In I Cor. 15 he is thinking about the end of all things
and the consummation of the resurrection now in progress, i.e.
he thinks of the destiny of the race. In II Cor. 5: 1–10 he thinks
of his personal destiny, now aware that he may not live to see
the end of all things. As a Pharisee he would have seen the age
to come as both a realm entered by the individual at death and
as something to come at the end of history. As a Pharisee he
would have had to enter the age to come 'naked' and await the
general resurrection for his spiritual body and full participation.
As a Christian this body was in the process of growing in the
present (p. 317).

Davies is certainly correct about the idea of two 'overlapping
ages', but our investigation suggests that in II Cor. 5: 1–10 Paul
is thinking of the believers – those in whom the powers of the
resurrection are already at work – not only as individuals in
isolation, but as members of the heavenly temple, the transcendent body of Christ. In I Cor. 15, on the other hand, he is
dealing with both the believers – who experience the first resurrection – and all men, who must wait until the end. The believers, as members of the heavenly Church, can expect a
'house not made with hands' at their death. The rest of mankind must wait until the end for resurrection.

The idea of the 'house not made with hands' in heaven
suggests, therefore, the pre-existent Church.

(viii) *II Corinthians 8: 9, 12: 1–5*. We close our discussion of the
Corinthian correspondence by noting two brief texts pertinent
to the idea of pre-existence.

(a) For you know the grace of our Lord Jesus, that although he was
rich, he became poor on your account, so that by his poverty you
might become rich.

In 8: 9 there is a sudden reference to the coming of the redeemer in the midst of a passage of ethical parenesis. There is
broad agreement that the 'riches' of Christ are his pre-existence,[1]
as in Phil. 2: 6 and Rom. 15: 3. The abruptness of the reference

[1] Lietzmann, *An die Korinther I, II*, p. 134. Héring, *II Corinthiens*, p. 69;
A. Plummer, *Second Epistle to Corinth* (I.C.C.), p. 241. F. Craddock, *Pre-
existence*, pp. 99–106.

indicates that the image was well known to Paul's readers. The background is obviously the myth of the heavenly man, modified by the belief in the incarnation.[1] Phil. 2: 6–11 is the closest parallel to this statement and we shall discuss the possible background under that text.

(b) In 12: 1–5, Paul tells of a mystical experience which he describes as 'being snatched up to the third heaven'. There is an abundance of evidence to illuminate the idea of the ascent of the soul, or the whole person, in apocalyptic, rabbinic, Philonic and Hellenistic sources.[2] It is not possible to say precisely which tradition stands behind the experience which Paul recounts here, nor is it important to do so. Paul claims that he had an experience such as he describes. The background of the description is experiential, the form is the widespread and indiscriminate mysticism of the eastern Mediterranean.

The important element to notice is that Paul minimizes, and even denigrates, this mystical experience (vs. 11). The context in which it occurs is the most eloquent exposition of the theology of the Cross in the Pauline writings. The vision is placed for contrast, to bring into sharper focus Paul's real point, that the Christian lives by faith in the grace of the incarnate God, not by knowledge of the exalted God through visions and ecstasies.[3] And it is precisely at this point that the problem of the relationship between the theology of the Cross and the theology of glory, between the emphasis on the futurity of salvation and the conviction that salvation has been achieved already, between the eschatological reservation and the mystical ascent, becomes acute.

[1] E. Schweizer, *Neotestamentica*, p. 108, says that it is the only Pauline passage on pre-existence which cannot be shown to have the Wisdom tradition as a background. This is obviously an exaggeration, but correct as far as II Cor. 8: 9 is concerned.

[2] E.g. Lietzmann, *An die Korinther*, pp. 153–4; Excursus on 'Die Himmelsreise', cf. p. 212 note; also I Enoch 12: 1 *passim*; Plummer, *II Corinthians*, p. 342; E. R. Goodenough, *By Light, Light*; and G. Scholem, *Mysticism*, pp. 40–79.

[3] Cf. Lietzmann, *An die Korinther*, p. 212, where Kümmel cites Kaesemann (reference not given) to the effect that Paul plays down the importance of the vision because it was a purely private matter which he did not consider to have anything to do with his apostolic status in the community. It seems to us, however, that the opinions expressed in chs. 11 and 12 are relevant to more than the apostle's position in the community. The emphasis on apostolic suffering, for instance, expresses a general Christian truth.

The passages we have examined have shown that Paul believed in two pre-existent entities, Christ and the Church. The forms in which he expressed this belief were taken from Jewish apocalyptic, Jewish wisdom speculation, and a Hellenistic–Jewish mysticism which is present in the writings of Philo. The new element in the Corinthian correspondence, by comparison with Galatians, is the strong influence from this mysticism.

On the basis of the evidence we have seen, one has to acknowledge that Paul believed both in the presence of salvation and in its futurity. Out of this paradox came his mystical pronouncements (e.g. I Cor. 2: 6–16, II Cor. 3: 16–4: 6, 5: 1–10, 12: 1–5) and his rejections of mysticism in favor of a futurist eschatology (e.g. I Cor. 15, II Cor. 4: 7–15).

Paul believed that the eschatological age began with the resurrection of Jesus. He lived in overlapping worlds, and expressed in the Corinthian letters the rich ambiguity of membership in both. Pre-existence was an attribute of everything belonging to the new world, when looked at from the point of view of the old. The new world existed already in its own right, but not yet there where the old world took up time and space as it decayed. Christ and the Church are part of the new world (I Cor. 2: 6–16, 3: 9–17); they are pre-existent within the scheme of eschatology. 'Pre-existent' is, in fact, the one adjective which describes precisely the status of entities in the new world, from the point of view of the old. Although Paul would never have used the term 'pre-existence', the concept which it describes is constitutive of his whole soteriological scheme. We have called this concept 'eschatological pre-existence' because it occurs in the context of eschatology.

The eschatologically pre-existent entities were identified with items that were believed, in the traditions from which they came, to have existed before the world. Christ was identified with Wisdom (I Cor. 8: 6, 10: 4), which, according to Jewish wisdom tradition, existed before the world and participated in creation, and with the primal man who in certain Hellenistic and Hellenistic–Jewish traditions was the first emanation of the high God. We have proposed that this idea according to which something existed before the world be called 'protological pre-existence'. In the Corinthian correspondence, eschatology preponderates over protology. The only obvious passage where the protological aspects of the idea of pre-existence have not been overshadowed by the eschatological is I Cor. 8: 6, where Paul refers to Christ's role as the mediator of creation. The aim of this reference is to establish that idols really are nothing, do not exist, by reminding the reader of the sole creatorship of God, through the sole medium of Christ.

In II Cor. 3: 18 – 4: 6, protological pre-existence is implied in the doctrine of personal salvation. In the mystical systems (e.g. C.H. I), soteriology is dominated by protology; it is the doctrine of how to reverse or escape from the disaster of creation and return to the *status quo ante*. One form of this piety was the mystical assimilation to the primal image through an ascent of the spirit. In II Cor. 3: 18 – 4: 6 and 4: 16 – 5: 10 (cf. I Cor. 15: 45ff.), Paul seems to be expounding precisely this way of salvation, with only one reservation, that the ascent and assimilation was not attainable before the eschatological denouement. If this is so, the salvation envisaged would be essentially the same as the gnostic restitution to an original status, with only the stipulation added that it cannot take place before the end of all things.

Despite superficial similarities between Paul's conception of salvation here, and the mystic scheme, his is quite different in essence. It lacks the ingredient of consubstantiality between man and God essential to mystical soteriology. The Christian is being transformed into the image of Christ, which is different from that of Adam before his fall. Salvation is not therefore a process of rediscovering what man has always possessed and temporarily lost. It is the reception of a new gift, the experience of a new creation; justification is not the restoration of man to the image of God, understood as Adam before the fall, but the transformation of man into the image of Christ.

The protological pre-existence implied in II Cor. 3: 18ff. is the pre-existence of Christ as the image according to which Adam was created. The conception of salvation as a new creation (II Cor. 5: 17) is based on the belief that the same image which produced Adam is producing the new life of the redeemed; but instead of being merely copies of that image as Adam was, the Christians are part of the heavenly image himself.

D. *Romans*

(i) *8: 28–30*

But we know that all things work together for good for those who love God, who are called according to plan. For those whom he fore-knew, he also fore-ordained to be conformed to the image of His Son, in order that he might be the first-born among many brothers; and those whom he fore-ordained he also called; and those whom he called, he also justified; and those whom he justified he also glorified.

There are two items of interest for us in this text: (a) the references to 'calling according to plan' (κατὰ πρόθεσιν), 'foreknowledge' (προέγνω) and 'foreordination' (προώρισεν); and (b) the use of the phrase 'conformed to the image of his Son'.

(a) The language of election and foreordination suggests that the idea of predestination is present. The Christians were chosen by God for salvation sometime before they began to experience it. 'When did this election take place?' one may ask. Was it before the world, at the creation, or at the resurrection? Most commentators believe that it took place in the eternal counsels of God, before the creation of the world.[1] This conclusion is based on the order of the verbs in verse 30, where the resurrection seems to correspond to the 'calling', and is, therefore, preceded by the foreordaining. The Church is thought of here as having been foreordained in the mind of God.

There is some reason, however, to believe that something more 'concrete' than 'foreordination' is in mind here. Sanday and Headlam[2] suggest that προγινώσκω ('I know beforehand') is being used in a sense similar to the one it has in Hos. 13: 5, Amos 3: 2 and Matt. 7: 23, where it means 'to take note of', 'to fix regard upon' something, preliminary to selecting it for some special purpose. Such a meaning would entail that the believers existed in some form more substantive than an idea; or that an idea in God's mind is thought of as having existence and reality. This conception is aptly called 'ideal pre-existence'. In Rom. 8:

---

[1] E.g. W. Sanday and A. C. Headlam, *The Epistle to the Romans*, I.C.C. (Edinburgh, 1902), p. 217; O. Michel, *Der Brief an die Römer*, Meyer IV (Göttingen, 1963), p. 211; C. K. Barrett, *The Epistle to the Romans*, Harper's New Testament Commentary (New York, 1957), p. 169.

[2] *Romans*, p. 217.

28–30, therefore, the Church pre-exists the world, in the mind of God.

(b) The phrase 'conformed to the image of his Son' recalls our discussion of I Cor. 15: 45–9 and II Cor. 4: 4. Jesus as the Son is the 'Image' of God, the pre-existent mediator and the true humanity of each man.[1]

Here we can see more clearly than in II Cor. 4: 4 how Paul modifies the soteriology connected with the idea of the image. In the original Wisdom myth, the pre-existence of the image as a collective entity including all who belong to him, and the presence of that image in a man, was the ontological ground of the possibility of salvation. Only those who shared the same substance as the redeemer would be saved. Paul seems to transpose these categories of substance into idealistic and volitional categories. The ontological possibility of salvation is not the real pre-existence of the individual in the redeemer, but his pre-existence as an idea in God's mind and as the object of God's will.

If, however, the commentators are correct in saying that προγινώσκω should be understood as it is in the Old Testament and not as a designation for abstract intellection,[2] then the apparent transposition of categories is not complete. If the verb means 'to take note of', 'to fix regard upon', the objects of this knowing must have been sufficiently existent to fulfil their proper function as objects of such activity. The verb, therefore, faintly implies that the elect (8: 33), really existed when the choice was made.[3] We have called this idea 'ideal pre-existence'.

---

[1] O. Michel, *Der Brief an die Römer*, p. 212, confirms this impression. He compares the use of εἰκών and πρωτότοκος here with Col. 1: 15 and 18, and concludes that Paul is using a tradition of the pre-Pauline church. His suggestion that the root of the tradition is the apocalyptic concept of the appearance of the Messiah with the redeemed, represented in IV Ezra 7: 28, is sound.

[2] E.g. Sanday and Headlam, p. 217.

[3] We may notice here the rabbinic belief that Adam was shown all the future generations and their acts. This idea probably goes back to the second generation Tanna, R. Eleazar b. Azariah. Thus R. Scroggs, *The Last Adam*, p. 41 n. 34; see also pp. 38–42. Notice too that in I Enoch 37–71, 'the elect' is a frequent title for those who are to be saved, e.g. 38: 3, 4; in 48: 2, where the Son of Man is named before the creation of the world, verse 1 could be interpreted to mean that the elect were present at his naming. Cf. IV Ezra 7: 28: 'For my son the Messiah shall be revealed,

This text, therefore, teaches the 'ideal' protological pre-existence of the Church, and the protological pre-existence of Christ as the 'image' of God.

The evidence of Romans serves to confirm that the idea of pre-existence is one of the assumptions made by Paul. He talks quite naturally about the ideal pre-existence of the Church, and assumes the idea of Christ as the pre-existent image of God. He also uses the apocalyptic pattern of the plan of God in which future things pre-exist, in developing his conception of the relationship between Christ and Israel (Chs. 9–11).

One is impressed by the ease with which the idea of pre-existence is assumed as the background for certain aspects of Paul's theology, especially for his doctrines of Christ and the Church.

E. *Philippians*

(*i*) *Phil. 2: 5–11 and 3: 20–1.* The famous hymn in 2: 5–11 is the centre of our concern in this epistle.[1] The reason for discussing it in the same section as 3: 20–1 will become apparent in the course of exposition. An understanding of the hymn depends on the solution of two related problems, the structure of 2: 5–11,

together with those who are with him.' Cf. Michel, *Der Brief an die Römer*, p. 212.

[1] From a large amount of literature on the subject, we have chosen the following as guides: F. W. Beare, *A Commentary on the Epistle to the Philippians*, Harper's New Testament Commentaries (New York, 1959). G. Bornkamm, 'Zum Verständnis des Christus-Hymnus Phil. 2: 6–11', *Studien zu Antike und Urchristentum – Gesammelte Aufsätze* II (München, 1959), pp. 177–87. Fred B. Craddock, *The Pre-existence of Christ*, pp. 99–112. Dieter Georgi, 'Der vorpaulinische Hymnus Phil. 2: 6–11', *Zeit und Geschichte*, pp. 263–93. J. Jeremias, 'Zu Phil. 2: 7: "EAYTON EKENωΣEN"', *Nov. Test.* 6 (1963), 182–8. J. Jervell, *Imago Dei*, pp. 203–8. E. Kaesemann, 'Kritische Analyse von Phil. 2: 5–11', *Exegetische Versuche* I, pp. 51–95. E. Lohmeyer, *Der Brief an die Philipper*[10], Meyers Kommentar 9 (Göttingen, 1929 and 1956). His analysis of the hymn was first set out in *Kyrios Jesus: Eine Untersuchung zu Phil. 2: 5–11*, Sitzb. Heidelb. Akad. d. Wiss. phil.-hist. Kl. (1927/8), which we have not seen. (Cited by Kaesemann, 'Analyse', p. 52 n. 2.) R. P. Martin, *Carmen Christi, Philippians 2: 5–11 in Recent Interpretation and in the Setting of Early Christian Worship*, S.N.T.S. Monograph Series 4 (Cambridge, 1967). J. A. Sanders, 'Dissenting Deities and Philippians 2: 1–11', *J.B.L.* 88 (1969), 279–90. G. Strecker, 'Redaktion und Tradition im Christus-hymnus Phil. 2: 6–11', *Z.N.W.* 55 (1964), 63–78. C. H. Talbert, 'The Problem of Pre-existence in Phil. 2: 6–11', *J.B.L.* 86 (1967), 141–53.

and its background in the history of religions. Any adequate interpretation has to explain both problems. It is a basic weakness of all the interpretations we have consulted that they neglect one of these two problems. Charles Talbert[1] presents a persuasive solution to the problem of the structure of the hymn. Taking as his criteria the inner parallelisms of the passage and the principle that strophes should express complete thoughts, he proposes the following pattern:

(1) ὃς ἐν μορφῇ θεοῦ ὑπάρχων
οὐχ ἁρπαγμὸν ἡγήσατο τὸ εἶναι ἴσα θεῷ ἀλλὰ ἑαυτὸν ἐκένωσεν
μορφὴν δούλου λαβών.

(2) ἐν ὁμοιώματι ἀνθρώπων γενόμενος
καὶ σχήματι εὑρεθεὶς ὡς ἄνθρωπος ἐταπείνωσεν ἑαυτὸν
γενόμενος ὑπήκοος μέχρι θανάτου.

(3) διὸ καὶ ὁ θεὸς αὐτὸν ὑπερύψωσεν
καὶ ἐχαρίσατο αὐτῷ τὸ ὄνομα
τὸ ὑπὲρ πᾶν ὄνομα

(4) ἵνα ἐν τῷ ὀνόματι Ἰησοῦ
πᾶν γόνυ κάμψῃ ἐπουρανίων καὶ ἐπιγείων καὶ καταχθονίων
καὶ πᾶσα γλῶσσα ἐξομολογήσηται ὅτι κύριος Ἰησοῦς Χριστὸς
εἰς δόξαν θεοῦ πατρός.

The theological interpretation of this analysis is, unfortunately, less convincing than the literary work. The premise on which Talbert's method of interpretation rests is, 'a proper delineation of *form* leads to a correct interpretation of *meaning*'.[1] One cannot quarrel with this statement as long as one takes 'leads to' in a general sense, implying some such qualification as 'all else being equal'; but Talbert takes it in the sense 'amounts to', or 'necessarily determines', and this brings him to the con-

---

[1] 'Pre-existence', pp. 144–7. For a review of the proposals of Lohmeyer and Jeremias, see pp. 142–4; for Strecker's proposal, see Strecker, 'Redaktion', pp. 71–2. Kaesemann, 'Analyse', p. 52, and Bornkamm, 'Verständnis', p. 179, accept Lohmeyer's analysis; Martin's proposal is very similar to Lohmeyer's (*Carmen Christi*, pp. 36–41); and Georgi and Beare do not discuss the literary problems. For an exhaustive review of proposed analyses, see Martin, *ibid.*, pp. 24–35. The excision of θανάτου δὲ σταυροῦ from the end of verse 8 is accepted by all these commentators. Dibelius and Michaelis would retain it (according to Kaesemann, 'Analyse', p. 82).

[2] 'Pre-existence', p. 141.

clusion that there is no idea of pre-existence in the Philippian hymn.[1]

Talbert argues that since stanzas 3 and 4 are carefully linked by a type of chiasmus (a a, b b, c c) and the clearly indicative conjunctions διό and ἵνα, stanzas 1 and 2 must also have been deliberately connected. The absence of any such indications in stanzas 1 and 2, like the ones he finds in 3 and 4, becomes for Talbert the positive evidence of connection – a doubtful argument from silence! Since the writer carefully links 3 and 4, and omits such connecting signs in 1 and 2, a link between 1 and 2 may be assumed? Not at all!

Nevertheless, a formal parallelism between 1 and 2 can be shown (1a 2a, 1b 2b, 1c 2c). Talbert claims that this is a synthetic parallelism, because 'the language does not clearly and explicitly reveal a contrast in the meanings of strophes 1 and 2'. He turns to the history of religion in order to substantiate the point, and argues that stanzas 1 and 2 speak of Christ as the second Adam and the Son of Adam, on the basis of Gen. 5: 1–3 in the LXX, and as the Servant of Yahweh, on the basis of M.T. Isa. 53: 12. On this evidence there is no reference to the pre-existence of Christ in stanzas 1 and 2.

We must, however, judge this part of Talbert's work to be a failure, for the following reasons: (a) Gen. 5: 1–3 does not really explain the crucial terms μορφὴ θεοῦ and ἴσα θεῷ;[2] (b) the parallelism between 1 and 2 cannot be so strict that it breaks up the coherence of thought in each stanza – for example, Talbert's argument that ἴσα θεῷ cannot be interpreted by μορφὴ θεοῦ, since 1b can be interpreted only by its parallel 2b, contradicts his own criterion that each stanza should express a complete idea; (c) when each stanza is taken both as a whole and as a series of parallel members, it becomes clear that, in themselves and on the evidence from the history of religions, stanzas 1 and 2 are antithetical to each other and not synonymous. Talbert has not, therefore, succeeded in showing that there is no idea of the pre-existence of Christ expressed in the Philippian hymn.

---

[1] J. A. Sanders, 'Dissenting Deities', p. 281 n. 12, also makes this objection to Talbert's thesis.

[2] *Ibid.*, p. 151. The argument here is particularly weak. He cites not one parallel to μορφὴ θεοῦ. He refers to Gen. 3: 4 as the origin of the οὐχ ἁρπαγμὸν κτλ. but 1b cannot be understood apart from 1a.

Strophe 1 seems to speak of his pre-existence, and strophe 2, in turn, of his incarnation.

Perhaps the weakest point in Talbert's argument is his reconstruction of the religio-historical background of the hymn. There has been a long debate on this matter, whose dominant moments we shall now summarize: on the one hand, the Palestinian Jewish interpretation represented by E. Lohmeyer,[1] and, on the other, the Hellenistic interpretation represented by E. Kaesemann.[2]

Lohmeyer argued that the style and structure of the hymn were Semitic, and that its fundamental rhythm of humiliation and exaltation expressed a central characteristic of Biblical faith.[3] The paradoxical insight that election by God meant both humiliation and exaltation came out of the tension between the historical experience of Israel and the glorious expectations which were part of the belief in election. The figure of the Servant of Yahweh in Isaiah 53 expresses this paradox succinctly, and, according to Lohmeyer, the composer of the hymn had the Servant in mind. J. Jeremias, taking Lohmeyer's argument further, claims that ἑαυτὸν ἐκένωσεν (verse 7) is a direct translation of the Hebrew הערה...נפשו in Is. 53: 7.[4]

According to Lohmeyer, verses 6, 7 and 8 outline the stages of the Servant's humiliation from divine status (verse 6) to incarnation as a servant (7) and death (8).[5] The phrase εὑρεθεὶς ὡς ἄνθρωπος (8) is impossible in Greek; ὡς ἄνθρωπος, therefore, probably translates the Aramaic Kᵉbarnasch, which, in turn, refers to the Son of Man in Daniel 7: 13. The idea of the Servant has, therefore, according to Lohmeyer, been blended with the idea of the Son of Man, to give this essentially Jewish-Christian interpretation of the transcendent Christ.[6]

---

[1] Lohmeyer, *Philipperbrief*, pp. 90–9.

[2] Kaesemann, 'Phil. 2: 5–11'.   [3] Lohmeyer, *Philipperbrief*, p. 93.

[4] Jeremias, 'Phil. 2: 5–11'; in our opinion he defends this thesis, first put forward in *T.W.N.T.* v, 708, 24ff., successfully in this recent article.

[5] Lohmeyer, p. 91.

[6] *Ibid.*, p. 95. Kaesemann (*Versuche* I, p. 75) calls this interpretation of ὡς ἄνθρωπος 'too adventurous', which is hardly a convincing argument against it. Strecker ('Redaktion', p. 74) argues that since after verse 7 the human Jesus is spoken of, the phrase cannot be a reference to the Son of Man. This argument presupposes that the human Jesus is not, and could not have been, referred to as, the Son of Man; a presupposition which has itself to be proven.

At verse 9 the direction is reversed and the exaltation begins, in obedience to the basic pattern of humiliation and exaltation. This Christology of exaltation cannot be attributed to Paul; for him the resurrection was the turning point, while here it is the ascension. The climax for the hymn comes when Christ is enthroned as Lord of the world.[1]

Lohmeyer suggests that the phrase ἐν μορφῇ θεοῦ indicates that Christ is essentially divine, that equality with God (τὸ εἶναι ἴσα θεῷ) is a present possession of his (*res rapta*), but the 'name' and power of the Kyrios, as distinct from the divine nature, could be his only by the 'normal' Biblical process of humiliation and exaltation, which was God's plan for all his elect. By the incarnation and death, Christ achieved the 'name', which is tantamount to achieving lordship over the cosmos, and so from this point of view τὸ εἶναι ἴσα θεῷ is also *res rapienda*. Finally, Lohmeyer affirms that the hymn is not intended to provide an ethical example; but his statements on this matter are not clear.[2]

Lohmeyer, therefore, sees the Christ of this hymn as the Son of Man and the Servant of the Lord, who is of the divine nature *ab origine*, but who must endure humiliation before he can be endowed with the divine power.

At the extreme from this Jewish interpretation is Kaesemann's attempt to place the hymn in the context of Hellenistic religion.[3] After a review of previous work, showing how the passage has generally been understood as a piece of ethical parenesis – the act of renunciation of the pre-existent Christ being interpreted as an example – Kaesemann analyses the hymn in order to show that the ethical interpretation is mistaken, and that the Jewish background is not as appropriate as that of Hellenistic religion. Scholars have misunderstood the meaning of μορφή, he argues, because they have interpreted the word on the basis of classical rather than Hellenistic usage. In classical Greek the word meant the 'form' of an entity as distinct from its substance; but since the distinction between form and substance

---

[1] Lohmeyer, *Philipperbrief*, pp. 97–8.

[2] Cf. the apparent contradiction on p. 98, where he regards the pattern of humiliation and exaltation as a universal norm, applicable especially in a situation of martyrdom. Cf. Kaesemann, 'Analyse', pp. 56–7.

[3] Kaesemann, 'Analyse'.

had lost its power in Hellenistic times, the word had either to lose its meaning or acquire a new one. It took on the meaning of 'a way of being under particular circumstances', a *Daseinsweise*. The use of ἐν with μορφή, similar to Paul's use of ἐν with Χριστῷ, is a technical usage which conveys the idea of being in a field of determining forces. The Hellenistic individual understood the shape and substance of his existence to be the result of a constellation of forces. There were several such constellations, each of which signified a distinct ontological realm. Divine power implied divine nature; therefore ἐν μορφῇ θεοῦ and τὸ εἶναι ἴσα θεῷ were synonyms.[1]

The idea of equality with God, Kaesemann continues, was foreign to Judaism,[2] but at home in Hellenistic culture. Ever since Homer ἰσόθεος and ἰσοδαίμων had been frequently used of the heroes. Divinity was sometimes bestowed on men, as the consummation of their humanity, and as divine men they exhibited an ideal to which every human being could aspire.

In our passage, however, equality with God is not a universal ideal, according to Kaesemann, but the specific and unique endowment of a single being. C.H. I. 12–14 provides a passage so similar to Phil. 2: 6 that one can only conclude that the two texts come from a common tradition. In C.H. I. 12 the primal man is ἰσόθεος, and in 14, ἔδειξε...τὴν καλὴν τοῦ θεοῦ μορφήν. His endowment is also specific and unique. The terminology of verse 6 suggests therefore, Kaesemann affirms, that the Philippian hymn draws on the myth of the heavenly primal man, present also in C.H. I, who is Logos and Wisdom in Philonic Judaism.[3]

Equality with God, Kaesemann continues, is to be understood as Christ's present possession (*res rapta*) in the sentence, οὐχ ἁρπαγμὸν ἡγήσατο τὸ εἶναι ἴσα θεῷ because that interpre-

---

[1] *Ibid.*, pp. 67–8; e.g. Orac. Sibyll. VIII. 458, βροτεὴν ἐνεδύσατο μορφήν and II. 230, καὶ πάσας μορφὰς πολυπενθέας εἰς κρίσιν ἄξει.

[2] Cf. Philo, Aet. Mundi, 43; Leg. All. I. 49.

[3] 'Analyse', pp. 68–9. The important phrases from C.H. I. 12–14 are: ὁ Νοῦς, ὢν ζωὴ καὶ φῶς, ἀπεκύησεν Ἄνθρωπον αὐτῷ ἴσον...τὴν τοῦ πατρὸς εἰκόνα ἔχων (Par. 12, Nock and Festugière, p. 10, lines 15–18); καὶ ἔδειξε...τὴν καλὴν τοῦ θεοῦ μορφήν (par 14, *ibid.*, p. 11, lines 8–12). Philo describes the logos, which he identifies with Wisdom, in similar terms: e.g. Conf. 146: ...καὶ γὰρ ἀρχὴ καὶ ὄνομα θεοῦ καὶ λόγος καὶ ὁ κατ' εἰκόνα ἄνθρωπος καὶ ὁ ὁρῶν Ἰσραήλ...

tation corresponds to the sense of C.H. I. 12–14, and because of the antithesis between verses 6 and 7. Col. 1: 15, where Christ is called 'eikon', says the same thing, according to Kaesemann. This evidence points to the 'Redeemer myth' as the pattern for the pre-existent Christ.[1] The phrase 'he thought it not robbery...' shows that the glory of the pre-existent one is not treated for its own sake but only as the background against which the incarnation as the paradox of 'God-become-man' takes place.

Accordingly, ἐκένωσεν (2: 7a) refers not to the renunciation of the divinity which had yet to be attained (res rapienda) by the pre-existent one, but rather to his becoming man. This, according to Kaesemann, excludes interpretations that see in the verb a description of a pre-mundane ethical decision. It also means that the incarnate one begins to be spoken about at ἐκένωσεν and not later in the piece. Kaesemann does not believe that the hymn is intended to be an ethical example. It is, rather, a soteriological myth which describes objectively the saving act of a divine being.

The verb ἐκένωσεν is qualified immediately by μορφὴν δούλου λαβών. According to Kaesemann, this means that the savior moves from one 'field of forces' to another, from divine nature to human nature. 'Ihm geht es einfach um den Übergang εἰς ἄλλο γένος'. The main focus of attention in the drama is not on his nature and its persistence through each of the stages of his existence, but on his acts. II Cor. 8: 9 puts the point succinctly: 'Although he was rich, for your sakes he became poor, so that from his poverty you might become rich.' The idea of pre-existence was introduced only to put the act of salvation in the proper light, not to introduce a concern about his nature.

ἀλλά (verse 7) indicates the contrast between his pre-existence and his humanity. The transition from divinity to manhood is stated as in the myths; divinity is put aside and humanity is assumed. This is simply presented as a miracle; no attempt is made to explain it. δοῦλος does not refer to the servant of Yahweh; rather, it expresses an understanding of human existence which was characteristic of the Graeco-Roman period. In Hellenistic religions, humanness is a state of bondage (δουλεία) to the cosmic powers – the stars, matter, εἰμαρμένη – (cf. Gal. 4:

---

[1] 'Analyse', pp. 69–71.

3ff., C.H. I. 15). In this way, according to Kaesemann, the hymn places Christ's pre-existence and his incarnation in sharp antithesis to each other.[1]

Kaesemann believes that the myth of the Gnostic redeemer – which portrays the humiliation of the divine image and its epiphany on earth as the eschatological event – lies behind the Philippian hymn. It has been modified in the light of the myth of Adam's disobedience, so as to present the obedience of a new Adam as the eschatological event (cf. Rom. 5: 12–21). The hymn writer identified the disobedient Adam with the fallen anthropos. The redeemer reversed the effect of that disobedience by his obedience. The effect of disobedience was slavery to the powers, whose epitome is death. By *freely* submitting to death the redeemer broke the power of death and set the anthropos free.

The 'third act' of the drama, according to Kaesemann, presents the triumph of the redeemer (2: 9–11).[2] His victory takes the form of the ascension, rather than the resurrection, and the result is that Christ is installed as 'kosmokrator'.[3] The scheme of the heavenly enthronement, present in I Tim. 3: 16 and Heb. 1: 3ff. as a Christian variation on the 'Redeemer myth', has been introduced here into the idea of the ascension. The climax of the 'third act' is the giving of the Name. The action belongs to the context of ideas of enthronement (cf. Heb. 1: 5ff.). The 'name' is a revelation of the dignity and essence of its bearer. Christ achieves not a new power or a new nature, but a new status; formerly his dignity and essence were hidden, now they are revealed. His triumph over the powers[4] is not the result of a struggle, like the struggle of Baal in Canaanite mythology, but the consequence of revealing what is and has always been

[1] *Ibid.*, p. 73. Cf. C.H. I. 15 (Nock and Festugière, pp. 11–12, lines 22 and 1): ὑπεράνω οὖν ὢν τῆς ἁρμονίας ἐναρμόνιος γέγονε δοῦλος.

[2] ὑπερύψωσεν has superlative force – 'most highly exalted' (Kaesemann, 'Analyse', pp. 82–3).

[3] Cf. verse 10; that Jesus is first Lord (*kyrios*) of the world, and not of the community, is a variation from normal Pauline ideas, as is the emphasis on the ascension at the expense of the resurrection (*ibid.*, pp. 85–6 and 82).

[4] Cf. verses 10–11, which speak of a cosmic worship of Christ – the heavenly, earthly and chthonic powers pay homage (cf. Ign., Trall. 9: 1). The 'earthly' powers include both human and spiritual beings. The 'confession of Lordship' is a requirement of the laws governing enthronement in ancient Israel (cf. pp. 85–6).

the case: that Christ is the pre-existent image of God, equal in divinity with the Father, and Lord[1] of the Cosmos. By obedience – the complete unity of purpose between the Father and the Son – Christ revealed his true nature and claimed his proper status in relation to the cosmos. All this has already taken place, and its results are in effect now.

Kaesemann's Hellenistic interpretation has been refined by the work of J. Jervell[2] and D. Georgi.[3] Jervell focuses on the fact that in C.H. I. 12–14 μορφή has the same meaning, in that passage, as εἰκών. He argues that Christ is understood to be the 'image of God' in Phil. 2: 6, and that the same idea is present here as we have encountered in II Cor. 4: 4, and will encounter in Col. 1: 15. There is, however, a difference between Phil. 2: 6ff. and the other passages, in the use to which the idea of Christ as the image of God is put. In II Cor. 4: 4 and Col. 1: 15, it expresses the presence of God in Christ for the sake of the world, while in Phil. 2: 6ff. it expresses the existence of Christ in God, as pre-existence. The exaltation to Lordship (2: 9–11) is a return to the status ἐν μορφῇ θεοῦ, since, according to Jervell, both in Gnostic and Jewish texts, being in the image of God includes being Lord of the cosmos.[4] In verse 10 the divine name is applied to Christ as a synonymous designation for his original pre-existence. Therefore, the exalted Christ is identical with the pre-existent Christ. Jervell believes that the hymn reflects two separate theologies: in 2: 6–8 it contains the 'Gnostic' idea of the pre-existent redeemer as the image of God, while in 2: 9–11 it expresses the traditional belief of the earliest community, that Jesus became Lord and Son of God by virtue of his resurrection and ascension (Acts 2: 36, 5: 31, 10: 42, Rom. 1: 3ff., I Pet. 1: 11, Heb. 2: 6ff., 5: 5–10). According to Jervell, we have before us in this hymn an early example of the combination of Hellenistic and Jewish traditions.[5]

[1] The title 'kyrios' comes from the LXX where it translates the divine name Yahweh. This is shown by the quotation in 2: 10 of Is. 45: 23 in which Yahweh is proclaimed as Kyrios (Kaesemann, 'Analyse', p. 85).

[2] *Imago Dei*, pp. 228–31, cf. 204–13.   [3] 'Phil. 2: 6–11'.

[4] Jervell, *Imago Dei*, pp. 230–1, n. 220; cf. p. 229, where he cites Phil. 2: 11, Col. 1: 13–20, 2: 15, II Cor. 4: 4 (especially in the light of verses 1–3) and Rom. 8: 18ff. to show that 'being in the image of God' entails Lordship over the powers.

[5] *Ibid.*, pp. 212–13.

D. Georgi paid special attention to the presence of influence from Deutero-Isaiah (especially Is. 45: 23) in the hymn. This led him to argue that the precise background of the hymn was Hellenistic Judaism in which the LXX was a sacred text. According to him, Isa. 40ff. was frequently expounded in the Jewish Wisdom tradition, and Wisd. 1–9 is a good example of such exposition.

Hellenistic religion, according to Georgi, typified and even hypostatized certain ways of existing, and in Wisd. 1–9 the life of the wise man is typified as transcendent Wisdom. The types were usually located in another world, as Wisd. 1: 13, 16 and 2: 23, 5: 23 testify. Wisdom's agents in this present world were humiliated, and nameless; thus the unreality of this order of existence, by comparison with transcendent existence, was emphasized. The life of the 'wise' in this world was essentially docetic, while reality lay with hypostatized Wisdom in another dimension of existence (cf. especially Wisd. 7: 27).

In Georgi's view, this, essentially, was the myth used by the composer of our hymn; but he adapted it radically. The hymn identifies a man with the pre-existent Wisdom, in clear contradiction to the myth. In the myth the wise man is distinguished from Wisdom (Wisd. 6: 16, 7: 11–14, 7: 17); Wisdom 'dwells' in him, but this identity of essences is never an identity of person. The divine essence is undifferentiated and unchanging; variety is an illusion. Wisdom merely 'dwells in' the wise.

The Christian composer of the hymn, whom Georgi believes to have come from the circle of Stephen,[1] began the polemical adaptation of the Wisdom myth by identifying Jesus with preexistent Wisdom. The burden of his polemic, however, is in ἑαυτὸν ἐκένωσεν, where the idea of an eternally self-identical Wisdom merely 'dwelling in' human agents is exchanged for the idea of the self-humiliation of the eternal being. Pre-existent Wisdom actually gave up pre-existence to become man; he surrendered his being in the world of spirit for the life of flesh and blood. His life is not typical, but concretely historical. Thus we are prohibited from using the idea of pre-existence to understand the human life of Jesus. It conveys only the contrast between what he was as a man and what he is in the world of Spirit.

Despite some very illuminating analysis of the Wisdom tradi-

---

[1] D. Georgi, *Zeit und Geschichte*, p. 292.

tion, Georgi seems to us to have failed to dislodge C.H. I from its position as the primary source for the background of the first part of the hymn (2: 6–8). The figure in question is not typified Wisdom, but the Ur-anthropos.

Georgi's suggestion that Wisd. 3 and 4, in which the death of the wise man is understood as an exaltation, and Wisd. 18: 13, which contains a doxology similar to Phil. 2: 11, provide hints of the background of the second part of the hymn, is more convincing.[1] Nevertheless, it is difficult to see why one should entertain the possibility of influence from the Wisdom tradition in the second part of the hymn, after one has denied its influence in the first part; especially in view of other possible sources for the idea of exaltation.

All of the evidence we have reviewed so far indicates that it is not possible to separate the Jewish from the Hellenistic elements in the historical background of this hymn. J. A. Sanders is especially aware of this fact, and, after warning against the discredited, but still operative, rigid distinction between Jewish and Hellenistic elements in the background of the New Testament, suggests that the integration of the Semitic and Old Testament features of the hymn with its Hellenistic mythical images and concepts, took place in first-century Palestine.[2] His own solution is to compare the humble deity of the hymn with the proud, dissenting deities of the Jewish apocalyptic tradition, as seen in I Enoch 6: 2, the Secrets of Enoch, the Life of Adam and Eve and 4 Q Ages of Creation.[3] The Philippian hymn uses a form of the anthropos myth which, although different in detail, is essentially the same as that presented in C.H. I. It differs in that the descent of the anthropos is deeper into death than in C.H. I, and his exaltation is not a return to a previous status, but a promotion to one higher.

G. Strecker[4] also suggests that the background of the hymn is Jewish apocalyptic. Following a suggestion originally made by M. Dibelius,[5] he proposes that the hymn comes from the same

---

[1] Ibid., pp. 274–5. G. Strecker, 'Redaktion', p. 72, shows how the 'enthronement tradition' of the Old Testament is behind this text, and also I Tim. 3: 16, Heb. 1: 2ff., Matt. 28: 18–20.

[2] J. A. Sanders, 'Dissenting Deities', pp. 281–2.

[3] Ibid., p. 284.   [4] 'Redaktion', p. 75.

[5] Philipperbrief[2] (1925), p. 72, cited by Strecker, 'Redaktion', p. 75.

matrix as Phil. 3:20–1. Before Paul interpreted the hymn as an ethical parenesis, it was, like 3:20–1, an account of the humiliation and exaltation of the heavenly man, who was expected to come again in the eschatological time.

In summary, the figure in the Philippian hymn is both the heavenly redeemer of Jewish apocalyptic, and the heavenly anthropos of C.H. I. He also has features reminiscent of the Servant of Deutero-Isaiah. C.H. I. 12–14 clearly states that equality with God was a present possession (*res rapta*) of the anthropos. In applying this idea to the apocalyptic heavenly redeemer, the hymn presents a figure very similar to the Son of Man in I Enoch. He pre-exists creation, and receives homage from all things in the end (cf. I Enoch 63). Furthermore, the hint of features drawn from the portrait of the 'Suffering Servant' might recall Wisd. 2–4, where the wise man, as the servant of God, is portrayed as humiliated and exalted. Whatever the actual historical matrix of the hymn might have been, its own testimony indicates a time and place where Jewish apocalyptic and Hellenistic mysticism were blending, in possible conjunction with the Jewish Wisdom tradition.

What role does the idea of pre-existence play in this passage? If, as some argue,[1] the hymn is a piece of ethical parenesis, the pre-existence of the redeemer serves to make the example of his renunciation of equality with God (as *res rapienda*) possible.[2] If, however, his equality with God is a present possession (*res rapta*), the idea of his pre-existence is a foil to the redeemer's humiliation, expressing its intensity, and identifying the humble one as the one who is equal with God.[3] In view of the clear relationship between Phil. 2:6 and C.H. I 12–14, we under-

---

[1] See Kaesemann's reference ('Analyse', p. 53) to all 'von den Reformatoren bis Schlatter' who interpreted the passage in this way.

[2] J. A. Sanders, 'Dissenting Deities', pp. 289–90, understands the equality with God as something to be attained (*res rapienda*), but, by interpreting the hymn in the context of verses 1–11 as a whole, claims that it contains no ethical parenesis. The references in verse 3 to strife, vanity and greed apply to the dissenting deities in the myth and not to the Philippian congregation, according to Sanders. This is an intriguing suggestion, but it is not yet convincing.

[3] Kaesemann, 'Analyse', p. 72, emphasizes the function of pre-existence as a foil to the incarnation. He also suggests that there is no real interest in Christ's nature expressed by the idea (*ibid.*). This we find difficult to accept.

stand equality with God to be a present possession of the Christ (*res rapta*). We see expressed in the hymn a genuine interest in the nature of the redeemer. The incarnation is clearly placed within an understanding of his person as the pre-existent one who is equal with God. It is from this context that the real point of his humiliation derives, and the real basis for his exaltation is provided.

Paul himself seems to have treated the hymn as ethical parenesis. He must, therefore, have understood the equality with God as *res rapienda*. On this view, the idea of pre-existence is eschatological (i.e. prior to the incarnation) in its structure. In the hymn, however, it is protological, since the one who is equal with God might be assumed to have existed before the creation. The hymn demonstrates a Christological interest in affirming the protological pre-existence of Christ. This affirmation secures the divine nature of Christ and provides a foil against which the significance of the humiliation of the Cross becomes fully evident.

II. THE LETTERS WHOSE PAULINE AUTHORSHIP IS UNCERTAIN

A. *Colossians*

(i) *Colossians 1: 15–20*. In this passage the phrase 'image of God' (εἰκὼν τοῦ θεοῦ, 1: 15), which has commanded much attention already, is once again the centre of our interest. Kaesemann claimed that as it is used here it is equivalent to τὸ εἶναι ἴσα θεῷ and ἐν μορφῇ θεοῦ ὑπάρχων in Phil. 2: 6;[1] Jervell treats this passage along with II Cor. 3: 18 – 4: 6 and Phil. 2: 6–11 as an example of a baptismal theology based on a Jewish–Gnostic interpretation of Gen. 1: 27.[2] An understanding of the thought of our passage is closely bound up with the understanding of its literary structure, and so we must begin with some consideration of its form.

In our opinion, J. M. Robinson has provided the most satisfactory analysis of this passage.[3] He believes that 1: 15–20 in-

---

[1] Kaesemann, *ibid.*, pp. 69–71.

[2] *Imago Dei*, pp. 173–256, especially pp. 218–26.

[3] J. M. Robinson, 'A Formal Analysis of Colossians 1: 15–20', *J.B.L.* 76 (1957), 270–87. Other works consulted are: G. Bornkamm, 'Die Häresie des

corporated an existing liturgical piece, within an editorial framework which directs it polemically against the Colossian heresy. Robinson takes the following arrangement by Norden[1] as a point of departure:

ος εστιν εικων του θεου του αορατου, πρωτοτοκος πασης κτισεως	A1
οτι εν αυτω εκτισθη τα παντα εν τοις ουρανοις και επι της γης	A2
τα ορατα και τα αορατα	A3
ειτε θρονοι ειτε κυριοτητες	A4
ειτε αρχαι ειτε εξουσιαι.	A5
τα παντα δι' αυτου και εις αυτον εκτισται	A6
και αυτος εστιν προ παντων	A7
και τα παντα εν αυτω συνεστηκεν	A8
και αυτος εστιν η κεφαλη του σωματος της εκκλησιας	A9
ος εστιν αρχη, πρωτοτοκος εκ των νεκρων	B1
ινα γενηται εν πασιν αυτος πρωτευων	B2
οτι εν αυτω ευδοκησεν παν το πληρωμα κατοικησαι	B3
και δι' αυτου αποκαταλλαξαι τα παντα εις αυτον	B4
ειρηνοποιησας δια του αιματος του σταυρου αυτου	B5
δι' αυτου ειτε τα επι της γης	B6
ειτε τα εν τοις ουρανοις	B7

He focuses attention on the similarity between A1 and B1, A2 and B3, and A6 and B4. Not only do the paired lines contain similar phrases, but they also present them in a similar order.

Kolosserbriefes', *Das Ende des Gesetzes, Paulusstudien, Gesammelte Aufsätze* 1 (München, 1958), pp. 139–56; Fred B. Craddock, *Pre-existence*, pp. 86–99; W. D. Davies, *Paul*; M. Dibelius, *An die Kolosser, Epheser, an Philemon* 2, *H.N.T.* 12 (Tübingen, 1927); F.-W. Eltester, *Eikon im Neuen Testament*; A. Feuillet, *Le Christ Sagesse de Dieu*; H. Hegermann, *Die Vorstellung vom Schöpfungsmittler* (Berlin, 1961); J. Jervell, *Imago Dei*; E. Kaesemann, 'Eine urchristliche Taufliturgie', *Exegetische Versuche* 1, pp. 34–51; C. F. D. Moule, *The Epistles of Paul the Apostle to the Colossians and to Philemon* (Cambridge, 1957); E. Schweizer, 'Die Kirche als Leib Christi in den paulinischen Antilegomena', *Neotestamentica*, pp. 293–316. For a review of scholarship, see H. J. Gabathuler, *Jesus Christus, Haupt der Kirche–Haupt der Welt. Der Christus hymnus Kol. 1: 15–20 in der theologischen Forschung der letzten 130 Jahre*, Abhandlungen zur Theol. des A. and N.T. 45 (1965), pp. 5–186 (cited in *I.Z.B.G.* 14 (1967/8), no. 877). Fred B. Craddock, 'All Things in Him: A Critical Note on Col. 1: 15–20', *N.T.S.* 12 (1965–6), 78–80.

[1] E. Norden, *Agnostos Theos* (1919), pp. 250–4, in Robinson, 'Formal Analysis', pp. 272–3.

Taking this parallelism as a guide Robinson argues further that A7 and A9, A8 and B2 correspond, and were originally part of the unit represented by A1 par. B1, A2 par. B3, A6 par. B4. A9 and B2 belong at the end of strophe B in the original; this can be deduced from the fact that the present position of the couplet is intolerable since it is split by B1, and from a comparison with 2: 9–15, which is an application of our strophe B to a baptismal context. 2: 9–15 uses a form of the strophe in which A9 came later than B3.[1] The original fragment, therefore, looked something like this.

Strophe A = A1, A2, A6, A7, A8; Strophe B = B1, B3, B4, A9, B2. The rest of 1: 15–20 (A3–5, B5–7) are editorial contributions reflecting the presence of the Colossian heresy (A3–5) and the additional Pauline concern to root the event of salvation in the death of Christ (B5–7).

As Robinson recognizes, some of this reconstruction is conjectural; his treatment of A7–9 and B2, for instance, is less than convincing. Nevertheless, the parallelism between A1, 2 and 6 and B1, 3 and 4 is, as he avers,

quite visible without resort to conjectural reconstruction...so carefully constructed in detail as to betray the hand of an exacting composer, and thus provide the critical norm for subsequent discussion.

Be this as it may, we prefer to take A7–9 and B2 as another distinct fragment. There is a parallelism between A7 and A9, but Robinson's arguments for the relationship between A8 and B2 seem forced.[2] Furthermore, the grounds for shifting A9 from strophe A to strophe B – because of the analogy in 2: 9–15 – are rather flimsy, as Robinson seems to sense. It is much more likely that the author of the present Colossian hymn included a fragment of a different hymn in A7–9 under the influence of the liturgical style of A1 par. B1 etc., judging that it repeats the substance of A1, 2 and 6.[3] He felt such repetition to be appropriate at the end of strophe A, after including A3–5. His own

[1] See Robinson, p. 285, for the full argument.

[2] The initial conjunctions are different and the periphrastic verb in B2 destroys all real parallelism.

[3] E. Schweizer, 'Antilegomena', pp. 293–4, regards these lines as a self-contained three-lined strophe, linking A and B, and emphasizing that the creator and the redeemer are the same person. For the rest, he analyses the form of the hymn in generally the same way as Robinson.

contribution was to add τῆς ἐκκλησίας at the end of A9, and in strophe B to include B2 as an underlining of the content of B1.

Strophe A

A1 (vs. 15)	ος εστιν εικων του θεου του
	αορατου,
	πρωτοτοκος πασης κτισεως
A2 (vs. 16a)	οτι εν αυτω εκτισθη
	τα παντα εν τοις ουρανοις
	και επι της γης
	τα παντα δι' αυτου και εις
A6 (vs. 16c)	αυτον εκτισται

Strophe I (Intermediate)

I1 (A7) (vs. 17a)	και αυτος εστιν προ παντων
I2 (A8) (vs. 17b)	και τα παντα εν αυτω συνεστηκεν
I3 (A9) (vs. 18a)	και αυτος εστιν η κεφαλη του σωματος

Strophe B

B1 (vs. 18b)	ος εστιν αρχη,
	πρωτοτοκος εκ των νεκρων
B3 (vs. 19a)	οτι εν αυτω ευδοκησεν
	παν το πληρωμα κατοικησαι
B4 (vs. 20a)	και δι' αυτου αποκαταλλαξαι
	τα παντα εις αυτον

Editorial additions:

vs. 16b: τὰ ὁρατὰ καὶ τὰ ἀόρατα...ἐξουσίαι
vs. 18a: τῆς ἐκκλησίας
vs. 18c: ἵνα γένηται...πρωτεύων
vs. 20b-c: εἰρηνοποιήσας διὰ τοῦ αἵματος τοῦ σταυροῦ... οὐρανοῖς

On the basis of this analysis we are once again in a position to distinguish the pre-Pauline kerygma, contained in A1, 2 and 6 par. B1, 3 and 4, and in A7-9, from the understanding of that kerygma by the author of Colossians; under the special circumstances in which he wrote. We shall consider the pre-Pauline material first and then the Colossian interpretation. We begin our discussion with strophe A (A1, 2 and 6).

Strophe A places Christ within the context of creation while strophe B (B1, 3 and 4) describes his role in the redemption.

The opening phrases of strophe A: εἰκὼν τοῦ θεοῦ and πρωτότοκος πάσης κτίσεως, point one directly to the Hellenistic synagogue, where the Jewish tradition of pre-existent Wisdom, who is also called 'image',[1] the 'gnostic' tradition of the heavenly man, and the Philonic 'Logos' concept[2] flowed together to portray the pre-existent mediator. Like Wisdom in Prov. 8: 22ff. (cf. Sir. 24: 1ff., and Wisd. 7: 25ff.), like Logos in Leg. All. III. 96,[3] and like the heavenly man in C.H. I. 12–15, Christ is the medium through whom the creation took place.

The next phrases (A2, 6) are held together by the formula ἐν αὐτῷ, δι' αὐτοῦ and εἰς αὐτόν. Davies believes that these prepositions express the various meanings of *be*, in a rabbinic exposi-

---

[1] E. Schweizer, 'Antilegomena', pp. 295–6, says that everything attributed to Christ in strophe A is said of Wisdom in the Jewish tradition; but he does allow that Logos and Anthropos are interchangeable with Wisdom in this connection. H. Hegermann, *Vorstellung*, argues that the hymn is based on a Wisdom mystery whose presence can be discerned behind the Philonic text; especially behind the text of Quaes. Exod. II. 27ff. and Dec. 33ff. (pp. 29–46). On Wisdom as 'image' see also W. L. Knox, *Church of the Gentiles*, pp. 159–60. A. Feuillet, *Christ Sagesse*, pp. 166–273, argues that a sufficient explanation of these terms can be based solely on those passages on Wisdom which happen to be part of the canon of the Roman Catholic church, such as Prov. 8: 22ff., Sir. 24: 1ff., Wisd. 7: 25.

W. D. Davies, *Paul*, pp. 151–3 and 172, accepts the argument of C. F. Burney that the phrases refer to Prov. 8: 22 and the word *reshith* (beginning) used there: 'The Lord created me as the beginning (*reshith*) of his works.' The rabbis interpreted the bereshith of Gen. 1: 1 in terms of Prov. 8: 22, so that bereshith could mean 'by Wisdom', as well as 'in the beginning'. Col. 1: 15ff. is a rabbinic exposition of bereshith = 'by means of Wisdom', giving three meanings to *be* and four to *reshith*. The identification of Wisdom with Torah, in passages such as Sir. 24: 23, suggest that Paul identified Christ as the new Torah with pre-existent Wisdom. This kind of rabbinic speculation was obviously part of the general speculation on Wisdom in Judaism. It does not seem likely, however, that this rabbinic form, rather than the Hellenistic Jewish form of the speculation, was in the mind of the hymn writer.

[2] Robinson, 'Formal Analysis', pp. 277–80, cites Conf. 41, Leg. All. I. 65, Spec. Leg. I. 81, Conf. 146, Op. 25, Agr. 51, Theophilus ad Autol. 2. 22, Hippolytus, Ref. VIII. 12, Wisd. 7: 26–27a, par. Heb. 1: 3, Aesclepius 34 par. John 1: 3a–b, C.H. I. 2 par. Phil. 2: 6a–b; when we add this to the evidence cited by Feuillet and Davies we get some idea of the widespread dissemination of the idea of the pre-existent mediator in the Jewish–Hellenistic milieu in which Paul moved. Cf. Conf. 147.

[3] Cf. Jervell, *Imago Dei*, pp. 53–5.

tion of *bereshith* (Gen. 1 : 1); but that seems unlikely in view of
the repetition of this sequence as a formula elsewhere in the New
Testament[1] and in pagan philosophic and gnostic texts.[2] It is,
more likely, a reflection of the Stoic formula for omnipotence,
transferred to the cosmic Adam, the macro-anthropos. Kaesemann believes that the idea of creation 'in Christ', expressed by
the formula, is derived from a Hellenistic-Jewish form of the
gnostic idea of the 'Aion-body' of the primal man, an entity
which includes all existing things within itself and is co-exten-
sive and, in fact, identical with the cosmos.[3] Eltester seeks to
define the background more specifically; he argues that the
concept of creation 'in Christ' is based on the Philonic idea of
the Logos, who is the first-born son of God and the container of
the noetic world.[4] He is able to show strikingly precise parallels

---

[1] Rom. 11 : 36, I Cor. 8 : 6 (both 'wisdom' contexts, however), Eph. 4 :
5ff. and Heb. 2 : 10.

[2] Robinson, 'Formal Analysis', pp. 276 n. 11, points out that we have
here a mythological form of the idea, as found in Ev. Ver. 18: 45ff., Barn.
12 : 7, C.H. 5. 10, and Asclepius 34, rather than the Stoic philosophical form
found in M. Aurel. 4 : 23 and Seneca Ep. 65. 8. Cf. Jervell. *Imago Dei*,
pp. 225–6. M. Dibelius, *H.N.T.* p. 8, argues that the meaning of this formula
is different from the meaning it bears in M. Aurelius and Seneca; there it
goes back to the distinction of five causes introduced by Plato; here it is used
to present the idea of a mediator of creation, rather than a cause.

[3] Kaesemann, 'Taufliturgie', pp. 40–2. His discussion of the religio-
historical background is judicious; according to him the myth of the
'Urmensch-Erlöser' occurs here in the form it took in Hellenistic Judaism.
Sophia, Logos and Anthropos are identified; he cites Conf. 146, Wisd. 7: 21,
8: 6, 9: 4, 9. ἀρχή is applied to Logos in Conf. 146, and to Wisdom in Prov.
8: 22ff. (see also Leg. All. I. 43), and to Torah (S.-B. II, pp. 353ff.). On the
cosmos as a 'macroanthropos' see Schlier, *Epheserbrief*, pp. 92–3, Dibelius,
H.N.T. pp. 9–12, 'Excursus on Christ as World Soul and Creator'; E.
Schweizer, art. 'soma' in *T.W.N.T.*; 'Antilegomena', pp. 296–7; W. L.
Knox, *Church of the Gentiles*, pp. 35–6, cf. p. 53.

[4] *Eikon*, pp. 140–2; on pp. 142–3 he sets out in tabular form a comparison
between Christ in Col. 1 : 15ff., the Logos of Philo, the Aion in C.H. XI and
the Cosmos in C.H. XII. He is able to show, thereby, that all four entites are
called εἰκὼν τοῦ θεοῦ and the cosmos exists, or came into existence, in each
one. One may add Conf. 62–3 and Spec. Leg. I. 81, in which the Logos is
called *eikon* with reference to its work in creation; Conf. 62–3 and 146–7,
where it is called πρωτόγονον and θεοῦ γὰρ εἰκὼν λόγος ὁ πρεσβύτατος,
Op. 20, Somn. I. 62, Leg. All. I. 96–9, Cher. 27–8, Fug. 12–14, Quaes. Exod.
II. 18, 30, where Logos is the place of the archetypal ideas and mediator of
creation; cf. especially Leg. All. III. 96, where Logos is *eikon* and *paradeigma*.

between the Christ of Col. 1: 15ff., the Philonic Logos, the Aion in C.H. XI, and the Cosmos in C.H. XII. On this evidence, the pre-existent mediator of creation, with whom Christ is identified, is, more precisely, the Alexandrian form of the myth of the primal man, whose body is the Aion.

In strophe B, the fragment describes Christ's redeeming work in words and phrases which are parallel to strophe A. The idea that salvation is a new creation (II Cor. 5: 17) controls the presentation in strophe B. The old and the new creations are held together by the pre-existent Christ who spans both orders. As ἀρχή is a title of the Logos/Wisdom/Anthropos in its role as creator, so it is a title of the Christ whose resurrection inaugurates the new creation; and the same is the case with πρωτότοκος. As the fullness of creative power in him brought creation into being, so the presence of the Godhead in him reconciles the world, manifesting the power of the new creation.

The importance of this entire passage for the doctrine of the Church has been expounded very well by E. Schweizer.[1] He divides the text generally in the way that we have suggested, treating A7, 8 and 9 as a self-contained strophe, linking strophes A and B, and emphasizing that the creator and the redeemer are the same person. In strophe A the idea of Wisdom (Logos) as creator predominates. In strophe I, according to Schweizer, the Hellenistic idea that the cosmos is a body is introduced; the cosmos-body was created through Christ, is sustained by him, destined for him – and he is its head,[2] who reconciles it to God. Christ is that which holds everything together.

Schweizer believes that, for men in Hellenistic times, to find the unifier was to find salvation. The greatest anxiety for Hellenistic man arose from the notion that the unity of the cosmos has been fractured, that heaven and earth, God and man, were estranged.[3] In strophe B the Creator, who is himself the cosmos, restores the cosmos to God. The saving act is the

[1] 'Antilegomena'.

[2] W. L. Knox, *Church of the Gentiles*, p. 161, says that the idea of the cosmos as a body, and the idea of a ruler as 'head' of the cosmos was 'a commonplace of popular theology' in the Hellenistic world, probably derived from Stoicism.

[3] Schweizer, 'Das hellenistische Weltbild als Produkt der Weltangst', *Neotestamentica*, pp. 15–27; *Erniedrigung und Erhöhung* 2 (1962), sec. 12A.

ascension, which is interpreted in physical and metaphysical categories.[1]

Schweizer maintains that the editorial additions transform the meaning of the hymn radically. In 18b the reference to the cosmos (σώματος) is transferred to the church by the addition of τῆς ἐκκλησίας. In 18e, the addition of ἵνα γένηται ἐν πᾶσιν αὐτὸς πρωτεύων shows that for the editor the cosmic powers were not reconciled as in the hymn (verse 20a) but conquered, as in I Cor. 15: 24–7 and Col. 2: 15. The 'All' (τὰ πάντα) is, therefore, the Church and not the cosmos, and verse 20b shows that, for the editor, the Church and not the cosmos is reconciled to God. This means that instead of an 'automatic' salvation which takes place as a transformation of the external, physical and metaphysical world, the editor introduces the necessity of faith and response. This transformation, according to Schweizer, entails that the penetration of the cosmos by the power of reconciliation take place as an historical rather than a physical–metaphysical activity, that metamorphosis becomes mission.[2]

For Christology, Schweizer continues, this means that, whereas in the hymn the line of identifications runs Anthropos (Adam) = Christ = Cosmos, in the editor's view the identification is Anthropos (Adam) = Christ = (the union of Jew and Gentile in) the Church.[3] The editor gives an 'historical' interpretation to cosmic events; the same type of interpretation can be seen in I Tim. 3: 16.

One should not, however, read the latter identification of Christ with the Church in a one-sided way, as Schweizer seems to do. The application of cosmic terms to the Church does not only signify that cosmology is being historicized; it also signifies that history is being mythologized; the Church is being understood as a cosmic, metaphysical entity. The missionary penetration of the world is the penetration of the cosmos by the reconciling power.

One element that may cause confusion is the identification of the one who existed before the cosmos, as creator, with the cosmos itself, in strophe I. Does this mean that the cosmos pre-

---

[1] Schweizer, 'Antilegomena', pp. 305–6.

[2] Ibid., pp. 301–3, 306–9; Rom. 15: 16.

[3] Ibid., p. 305. We have changed Schweizer's scheme by putting Anthropos rather than Adam as the first term.

exists itself? This text may, perhaps, be understood if one thinks of the pre-existence of the creator-cosmos, not temporally but ontologically; the pre-existent creator is related to the cosmos as the source to the stream; but this explanation is not entirely satisfactory. Probably one should simply recognize an aporia here in the logic; the introduction of the Hellenistic idea of the world as the body of the anthropos conflicts with the Jewish Wisdom tradition of a pre-existent agent of creation, not part of creation itself. The identification of the Church as the body of which Christ is head would mean, in terms of the hymn, that the Church is the cosmos; but in terms of the editor's thought it probably means that the Church existed before and exists above the cosmos, as the body of the pre-existent Christ. This means that the missionary preaching which establishes and extends the historical Church is the expression in history of a meta-historical, pre-existent Church. Schweizer is dimly aware of this fact when, rather counter to the main thrust of his argument, he says that 'Christ has already penetrated the cosmos, but only as the Church actually exists and preaches does this metaphysical fact become an historical fact.'[1]

Schweizer believes that the same process of translation, from a cosmic to an historical mode, of the events of salvation, takes place in Ephesians and in I Timothy. We shall, therefore, use our findings in Colossians as a starting point for consideration of the rest of the Deutero-Pauline literature.

We may conclude this section with a quotation from W. L. Knox:

The divine Wisdom, the pattern and agent of creation and the divine mind permeating the cosmos, was identified with Jesus not as a matter of midrashic exposition which could be used and thrown aside, but as an eternal truth in the realm of metaphysics; for only so could the supremacy of Jesus be asserted as against such potent beings as the rulers of the stars in their courses. It is probable that Paul was entirely unaware that his letter would produce this effect: whether he realized it or not, he had committed the Church to the theology of Nicaea.[2]

On the basis of this discussion we may draw the following conclusions about the idea of pre-existence: In the hymn Christ

---

[1] *Ibid.*, p. 314.
[2] W. L. Knox, *Church of the Gentiles*, p. 178.

is the protologically pre-existent mediator of creation in strophe A, and the agent of redemption in strophe B. Strophe I re-emphasizes the protological pre-existence in strophe A. The idea of protological pre-existence serves here to unite creation and redemption; the creation and the redemption have the same transcendent source. This point is also made by the striking verbal and formal parallelism between strophes A and B.[1] The redemption of the cosmos by Christ, as a restoration of its unity, probably reflects the Hellenistic belief that the unity of the cosmos had been fractured and needed to be restored.

By making the pre-existent Christ the head of the Church, rather than of the cosmos, the editor implies that the Church, as the body of Christ, is pre-existent also. This implication is not entirely clear, however.

(ii) *The rest of Colossians*. The apocalyptic idea of heavenly realities hidden in a mystery until the day of revelation, is prominent in Colossians (1: 5, 1: 26ff., 2: 2–3). True knowledge is referred to as 'wisdom' (1: 9–10, 3: 16); it is knowledge of God's mystery, which is Christ, in whom all the treasures of Wisdom and knowledge are hid (2: 2–4); it is contrasted with 'philosophy and empty deceit' (2: 8). As the content of God's mystery, Christ is the bearer of Wisdom. All this is reminiscent of I Cor. 1–4. In both epistles, Christ is the content of the apocalyptic mystery and is implicitly thought of as pre-existent. True Wisdom is insight into the pre-existent status of Christ, and not a 'world-view' based on clever speculation (cf. 2: 23).

The heavenly realities in store for believers are referred to as 'the inheritance' (κληρονομία, κλῆρος, 1: 12, 3: 24). The clearest testimony to this apocalyptic idea is in 3: 1–4.[2] The believer, as one who has been raised with Christ, is exhorted to seek the things which are above (τὰ ἄνω)[3] where Christ himself is, at the right hand of God (cf. Ps. 110: 1). He has died with Christ (cf. Rom. 6: 2) and his new life is a heavenly life, 'hid

---

[1] Craddock, *Pre-existence*, pp. 86–98, suggests that the hymn was formulated initially to exclude the possibility of a negative attitude towards creation, such as was shown by Hellenistic mystics in Corinth.

[2] Moule, *Epistles to Colossians and Philemon, ad loc.*, sees this passage as 'a positive counterpart to 2: 20–3'.

[3] The contrast between 'things above' and 'things below' is frequent in John's gospel. Cf. also Phil. 3: 19–20, Gal. 4: 26.

with Christ in God'.[1] 'When Christ who is our life appears, then you also will be revealed with him in glory'. In this mixture of realized and futurist eschatology[2] the characteristic eschatological mysticism of Paul comes to expression; the Christians lead a heavenly life already, but it is not yet revealed as such. The individual, therefore, enjoys eschatological pre-existence. The main thrust, however, of this idea in Colossians is directed towards establishing the heavenly pre-existence of the Church rather than the individual. As in Gal. 4: 21–31 and I Cor. 3: 10–17, the Church is a heavenly pre-existent entity present in concealment on earth (1: 12–13, 2: 20–3, 3: 10, 3: 15–16). The drama of redemption was played out, to a large extent, in the heavenly realms (1: 15–20, 2: 15, 2: 20). As a result of Christ's work the old religion, based on law and ceremony, is shown to be a mere 'shadow of things to come' (σκιὰ τῶν μελλόντων) while the 'substance' (σῶμα) belongs to Christ (2: 17, cf. Heb. 8: 5, 10); and the Church is precisely that σῶμα τοῦ Χριστοῦ.

B. *Ephesians*

Chapters 1: 3 to 3: 21 in Ephesians form a unit, whose chief concern is to present the mystery of the union of Jew and Gentile in the Church.[3] This unit is hymnic in style.[4] The other major unit in Ephesians, 4: 1 – 6: 22, sets out the morality which those who hold doctrine such as that set out in 1: 3 – 3: 21 should observe.[5] We shall devote our attention to the former unit.

(i) *Ephesians 1: 3–14.* This benediction begins the hymnic section which extends to 3: 21. The reference to God's blessing (εὐλο-γήσας) is explicated in a passage introduced in verse 4 by καθώς and constructed around three verbs: ἐξελέξατο (he chose, 1: 4–6a), ἐχαρίτωσεν (he graciously gave, 1: 6b–7), and ἐπερίσσευ-σεν (he lavishly gave, 1: 8–10). The three verbs express the

---

[1] Moule, *ibid.*, endorses C. H. Dodd's suggestion that this phrase recalls the pagan idea that death means that a man is 'hidden' in the earth.

[2] Moule, *ibid.*, pp. 110–13.

[3] H. Schlier, *Der Brief an die Epheser* 2 (Dusseldorf, 1958) pp. 37–8. Other works consulted: M. Dibelius, *An die Kolosser, Epheser, an Philemon*; H. Odeberg, *The View of the Universe in the Epistle to the Ephesians* (Lund, 1934); E. Percy, *Die Probleme der Kolosser und Epheserbriefe* (Lund, 1946); L. Cerfaux, *Church*, pp. 289–383.

[4] Schlier, *Epheserbrief*, p. 41.   [5] *Ibid.*, pp. 177ff.

election and predestination, the forgiveness of sins, and the initiation into the mystery, respectively, and this scheme corresponds, in turn, to the traditional understanding of the threefold activity of the Father, the Son and the Holy Spirit in the Trinity. 1: 11–14 are an 'addendum' which emphasizes that the 'blessing' introduced in 1: 3 and expounded in 4–10 takes place only 'in Christ' (ἐν αὐτῷ).[1] In the Biblical tradition such an outburst of praise is usually the response to an epiphany or a saving act of God.[2]

We shall discuss only those phrases which are important for the idea of pre-existence:

(a) with every spiritual blessing in the heavenly places in Christ (1: 3).

The 'spiritual blessing' (εὐλογία πνευματική) is experienced ἐν τοῖς ἐπουρανίοις and ἐν Χριστῷ.[3] To be 'in heavenly places' is to be 'in Christ'. Both locative phrases indicate the dimension of transcendence which, to paraphrase Schlier, 'precedes and exceeds earthly Dasein, deepens and challenges it, and puts it in a situation of conflict'.[4] As a member of the Church one lives out of the dimension of transcendence, in the strength of its succour and demand. The 'spiritual blessing' is, therefore, the life conditioned by transcendence, life in the Church.

According to Schlier, the phrase ἐν τοῖς ἐπουρανίοις occurs like a formula in Ephesians, and, except for 1: 3, always with some mention of the spiritual 'powers' (1: 3, 20, 2: 6, 3: 10, 6: 12).[5] It always designates a place; more precisely, the several

---

[1] *Ibid.*, pp. 39–40.

[2] *Ibid.*, pp. 41–2; cf. Ps. 27: 6, Dan. 3: 51, 2: 19ff., I Macc. 4: 24ff., 30ff., etc.

[3] This interpretation differs from that of Schlier (*ibid.*, p. 44), who understands the 'spiritual blessings' to be the Holy Spirit as bestowing the benefits of Christ. It agrees with Dibelius in regarding the blessings as 'concrete' entities, but differs in interpreting ἐν Χριστῷ as in apposition to ἐν τοῖς ἐπουρανίοις instead of as modifying εὐλογήσας. This interpretation of ἐν Χριστῷ follows Schlier, who says of the two phrases, 'Beides zeigt den "Ort" an, wo wir gesegnet würden und – das is nicht davon zu trennen – nun als Gesegnete weilen.'

[4] Schlier, p. 48.

[5] In the rest of the New Testament it designates a place (John 3: 12, Phil. 2: 10); the eschatological phenomena (I Cor. 15: 44ff.) or the eschatological

heavens which Christ filled at his Ascension (1: 10c, 4: 10, cf. Col. 1: 16) or the place where the ascended Christ now is (1: 20). In the 'heavenly places' are: (1) Christ, at the right hand of God, over all the powers, as head of the Church, which is his body (1: 20ff., 4: 13, 15, 5: 23); (2) the Church (1: 3), as God's building (2: 22), God's workmanship (2: 10, 4: 16), Christ's bride (5: 23ff.), and the medium through which God's plan is revealed to the hostile spiritual powers (3: 9–10); and (3) the opposing Aeons (2: 6ff., 2: 2, 6: 12, 16). The Church, therefore, as the body of Christ, is a heavenly entity, eschatologically pre-existent.

(b) he chose us in him, before the foundation of the world (1: 4).

The act of election took place before the creation of the world; it took place in Christ, and it was directed towards the Christians; both Christ, and, in him, the Christians, must have enjoyed 'ideal pre-existence' before the world, therefore (cf. Rom. 8: 28–30). Schlier writes as follows:

Es ist vielmehr gemeint, dass wir auch schon in unserer Erwählung in Christus waren. Sofern wir Erwählte sind und als Erwählte prä-existieren, prä-existierten wir schon in Christus. Das ist eine christliche Umbildung des jüdischen Theologumenon von der Prä-existenz nicht nur des Messias, sondern auch des Heilsvolkes und der Heilsgüter[1]

(cf. John 17: 5, 24; I Pet. 1: 2, 20, I Cor. 2: 7, II Tim. 1: 9). Schlier is right to interpret this pre-mundane election in Christ on the basis of the apocalyptic tradition of the solidarity of the redeemed with the pre-existent redeemer, as, for instance, it occurs in I Enoch. This raises the question, however, of how we are to understand the pre-existence of the individual 'in Christ'.

In terms of what ideas in the religious background might we understand the phrase 'in Christ'? On the one hand, the Israelite idea of corporate personality, of the solidarity of the

phenomena already present (Heb. 3: 1, 6: 4, 8: 5 etc.). Schlier, *Epheserbrief*, p. 45. On the 'heavenly places' see Schlier, *ibid.*, pp. 45–8. Dibelius, *An die Kolosser, Epheser, an Philemon*, pp. 44–5, suggests that it is a formula taken from Iranian sources.

[1] Schlier, *Epheserbrief*, p. 49. See especially note 4 on pp. 49–50; cf. Percy, *Probleme*, p. 270, and Schlier's comment in n. 3, p. 49.

race in a primal ancestor, has been advocated,[1] while on the other hand, the Hellenistic and Diaspora Jewish myth of the macroanthropos, who includes all men and all the cosmos within himself, has been suggested.[2] Both Schweizer and Schlier recognize that these alternatives are not mutually exclusive, and that both traditions probably contributed to the Pauline idea. The real point at issue is whether the Hellenistic macroanthropos in itself symbolizes the physical cosmos, as well as a community of men, as Schlier claims,[3] or whether the understanding of the macroanthropos as a communal being is the result of influence from Jewish speculation on Adam as a representative person, as Schweizer argues.[4] Even these alternatives, however, are not mutually exclusive. It seems that the Adam/Anthropos myth of I Cor. 15: 21-2, 45-9, and Rom. 5: 12-21, which symbolizes the solidarity of all men in Adam, and the macroanthropos myth of the Colossian hymn, which identifies the anthropos with the physical universe, have been blended in Ephesians (e.g. 1: 22-3). By means of the Church, his body, Christ is therefore Lord of the universe; and the Christians exist and pre-exist in that body as parts of the macroanthropos.

The pre-existence of the Christian in Christ works itself out as 'adoption' in his historical life (1: 5), and salvation in the eschatological age (εἰς αὐτόν 1: 5b; εἰς ἔπαινον δόξης τῆς χάριτος αὐτοῦ 1: 6a). Both blessings are present for those who are in the Church.[5] In verse 9 the technical apocalyptic term μυστήριον is used to describe God's activity with reference to the Church,[6] and in verse 10 the eschatological aim of God's plan is presented as 'a plan to sum up the universe in Christ' (οἰκονομίαν…ἀνακεφαλαιώσασθαι τὰ πάντα ἐν Χριστῷ). 1: 11 re-states the eschatological aim of the pre-mundane election, and in verse 14 the Spirit is described as the present guarantee (ἀρραβών)[7] of the future consummation.

---

[1] E.g. Schweizer, 'Homologumena', pp. 273ff.; W. D. Davies, *Paul*, pp. 55-7.

[2] E.g. Schlier, *Epheserbrief*, pp. 92-3.   [3] *Ibid.*, p. 91.

[4] 'Homologumena', pp. 273ff.; W. D. Davies, *Paul*, pp. 55-7.

[5] Cf. Rom. 8: 29ff.

[6] Schweizer, 'Antilegomena', pp. 301ff., argues that the content of the mystery in Ephesians is the mission to the Gentiles; it is explained in 2: 1-22.

[7] On ἀρραβών see S.-B. III, p. 494; it is a Semitic word introduced into Greek by the Phoenicians. The LXX translates ערבון in Gen. 38: 17, 18, 20,

The pre-mundane election of the Christians in Christ is presented, therefore, by means of the myth of Christ as the macro-anthropos, who contains in himself all the believers as well as all the (redeemed) universe. This Christ – who, as a communal entity, is also the Church and the redeemed universe – pre-existed in the mind (election) of God before the actual creation. We have, therefore, the idea of ideal protological pre-existence here, like the idea expressed in Rom. 8: 28–30.

(ii) *Ephesians 1: 15–23*. Schlier describes this section as a 'prayer for knowledge of the hope'. It asks that God may give to the readers a 'Spirit of wisdom and revelation' (πνεῦμα σοφίας καὶ ἀποκαλύψεως, 1: 18)[1] so that they may know the inheritance,[2] that is, the pre-existent 'goods' – stored up for them until that day; in which they presently participate through their membership in the Church; and that they may know the power of God, demonstrated in the resurrection and exaltation of Christ, which secures that inheritance (1: 18–20).

At verse 20 the passage shifts its attention from the believer to his Lord. Christ has been raised from death and exalted above all spiritual powers,[3] in both aeons;[4] he is seated at the right

as ἀρραβών; cf. Pes. 118B, Midr. Esther 3: 10 (97A). On the evidence from the papyri see Dibelius, p. 47. Cf. II Cor. 1: 22, 5: 5, Rom. 8: 16, 23.

[1] Cf. I En. 48: 1, 49: 3, I Cor. 2: 5, 2: 6–16, 12: 7, 14: 6, 26, 30, and our discussion on pp. 118–123 above. Cf. Col. 1: 9. Schlier, *Epheserbrief*, pp. 77–9, especially p. 78 n. 1; he calls it 'the Messianic spirit of inspiration that penetrates the secrets of God'.

[2] Cf. Eph. 5: 5. The nature of this inheritance (1: 18b) is not clear; it seems to designate a personal status – full sonship – rather than objects to which the believer will fall heir. The reference to Christ's resurrection and exaltation suggests that the resurrection and exaltation of the believer is meant; but one cannot really separate this from ideas of place and objects; ἐν τοῖς ἁγίοις means 'in God's heavenly place, where he is with his angels' (Schlier, *ibid.*, pp. 82–4).

[3] On the four ranks of spiritual powers named here see S.-B. III, pp. 581–4. Test. Levi 2: 1ff. is a good example of the Jewish apocalyptic interest in the ranks of angels. Cf. I En. 61: 10. The New Testament as a whole knows five classes of angels (cf. Eph. 3: 10, Rom. 8: 38, Col. 1: 16, I Pet. 3: 22). The θρόνοι of Col. 1: 16 is the extra class; cf. Phil. 2: 9–11, Col. 1: 18.

[4] 1: 21b: 'this age and the age to come' are reminiscent of rabbinic eschatological terms. They seem to have a spatial rather than a temporal meaning here. In rabbinic circles they also had a double spatial and/or temporal meaning. Cf. W. D. Davies, *Paul*, pp. 314–17; Schlier, *Epheserbrief*, p. 88.

hand of God and all things have been subjected to him.[1] He has been made 'head of the universe' (κεφαλὴν ὑπὲρ πάντα) and, as such, has given to the Church (τῇ ἐκκλησίᾳ) which is his body, the fullness (πλήρωμα) of him who fills the universe in every part (τοῦ τὰ πάντα ἐν πᾶσιν πληρουμένου, 1: 20–3). This raises again the question of the relationship between Christ, the Church and the Universe, which we encountered in the Colossian hymn and in the previous section of Ephesians.

E. Schweizer[2] argues that precisely the same process of re-interpretation was at work in Ephesians as in Colossians. Behind this passage lies a Christology which identified Christ with the cosmos and saw the ascension as the reunification of heaven and earth. Ephesians has identified this act of reconciliation with the mission of the Church and the union of Jew and Gentile within its congregations (2: 11–22). Schweizer regards this interpretation as the historicization of metaphysics; our present passage, however, seems to attest the opposite process; the Church is regarded as a metaphysical entity.

The Church is the 'body' of the exalted one,[3] and his fullness,[4] with which he fills the universe. Both terms are pre-supposed by the writer as well known to his readers. The meaning of 'body of Christ' has already been discussed; the phrase identifies Christ with the representative anthropos who includes all men in himself, and the macroanthropos whose body is the physical universe. The term pleroma stands for the totality of the divine presence (Col. 2: 9ff.), in Colossians and Ephesians. Although it became a technical term for the Valentinian divine world, in these letters it probably derives from the tradition which is also deposited in the Odes of Solomon (e.g. 26: 7, 17: 7, 19: 5, 36: 6, 7: 11, 41: 13, 7: 3, cf. Ign. ad Trall. 1: 1ff.), and not from the fully 'gnostic' tradition.

Eph. 1: 22b–23 says, therefore, that Christ became head of

---

[1] Ps. 110: 1, 8: 7. This recalls the well known tradition in the New Testament based on Ps. 110: 1 – cf. Rom. 8: 34, Col. 3: 1, Heb. 1: 3, 8: 1, 10: 12, 12: 2, I Pet. 3: 22, Acts 2: 33ff., 5: 31, 7: 55ff.; Schlier, Epheserbrief, pp. 86–7. On Ps. 8: 7 see I Cor. 15: 27, where it is used in an eschatological context.
[2] 'Antilegomena', pp. 303–4.
[3] See Schlier, *Epheserbrief*, pp. 90–5, for a full discussion of the Church as the body of Christ in the New Testament in general and Ephesians in particular.
[4] Schlier, *ibid.*, pp. 96–8, for a discussion of the meaning of *pleroma*.

the cosmos by his exaltation; this means that the cosmos is identified with the Church, since in the myth the cosmos is a body, and in the tradition the Church is a body, and Christ is the head of both. How can the Church be identified with the cosmos? It is the full presence of him who, as head of the cosmos, fills its every part with his presence; the Church is the real presence of the new head of the cosmos in his body, the cosmos. Christ is Logos/Wisdom, creator and sustainer of the cosmos, and the Church is his body.

The Church is not identical with the cosmos, however. It is identical with Christ first of all, and only when he became head of the cosmos was the Church related to the cosmos. As the body of Christ the Church pre-exists creation; only subsequently is it related to creation. The end of creation is to be summed up in the Church (1: 10).

This passage serves our purpose by confirming the heavenly nature of the Church; as the body of Christ it is united to its head, who is above all aeons in the heavenly places.

(iii) *Ephesians 2: 10.* The 'works which God has prepared beforehand' seem to suggest a strong predestination; but we favour Schlier's alternative explanation.[1] The new structure of existence given the believer in baptism inevitably issues in good works. The προ- of προητοίμασεν refers to the moment of baptism, when God's structure of existence is given to the believer. The willing realization of this new existence issues in the good works which God has prepared beforehand. The pre-existing entity here is not individual 'good works' but the plan for our new existence, in God.

(iv) *Ephesians 2: 19–22 and 4: 16 (cf. Col. 2: 19).*[2] By juxtaposing these two texts, one can see that both the apocalyptic image of the heavenly temple and the Hellenistic Jewish image of the heavenly man have been used by the author of Ephesians to symbolize the Church. We have already discussed both images at some length; nevertheless it seems worthwhile to add to that discussion here.

The first text, 2: 19–22, expresses the idea of the heavenly temple in a straightforward way. We may emphasize again that

---

[1] Schlier, *ibid.*, pp. 117–18.
[2] On this subject see Cerfaux, *Church*, pp. 345–7.

the earthly phenomenon of the union of Jew and Gentile is considered to be a heavenly phenomenon at the same time. The entry of the Gentiles into the Church makes them members of the heavenly city or household (2: 19). In verse 20 the members of the Church are regarded as the fabric of the heavenly temple; they are founded on the apostles and prophets, with Christ as the capstone,[1] and together they grow as a holy temple in which God dwells. There could be no clearer confirmation of our argument on I Cor. 3; the Church is the heavenly temple of apocalyptic thought, present on earth; the one advance over apocalyptic is that the fabric of the eschatological temple is redeemed human lives, the community, and not some supernatural substance.[2] The image of a completed building (verses 19–20) is transferred to the community.

The second text, 4: 16, describes the Church as a body, knit together by joints and operating in harmony, which grows (αὔξησιν) and builds itself up (εἰς οἰκοδομήν). The use of οἰκοδομήν in the context of an image of the body shows how deeply rooted in the Pauline consciousness of the Church is the image of the 'building' or 'temple'; its influence is responsible for the mixed metaphor.

These two texts confirm our thesis that the Church as a heavenly entity – firstly the apocalyptic temple, and later the body of the exalted Christ – is central to Pauline theology. In Eph. 4: 16, there is a hint of influence from the one image upon the other, resulting in the mixed metaphor of the 'building up' of the 'body'.

(v) *Ephesians 3: 1–13.* This passage provides a striking example of the apocalyptic idea of 'mystery',[3] which the privileged man

---

[1] Bauer, *L.N.T.*, suggests either 'cornerstone' or 'capstone' for ἀκρογωνιαῖος. We suggest 'capstone' here since it corresponds to the idea of Christ as head, and provides a contrast with the apostles and prophets as foundation. In the garbled image in 4: 15–16, there is talk of 'growing up into Christ', who is the head. There the metaphor of body and building is mixed in such a way as to suggest that 'head' would correspond with 'capstone' in any careful comparison of images. Cf. Ps. 117: 22, Jeremias in *Angelos*, 19 (1925), 65ff.

[2] On the heavenly building see further: M. Dibelius, *H.N.T.* pp. 53–5; Schlier, *Epheserbrief*, pp. 141–4; cf. Gärtner, *Temple and Community*, p. 65, who believes that the identification of the temple with the community originated in Qumran.

[3] Cerfaux, *Church*, pp. 320–56; Bornkamm, *T.D.N.T.* IV, pp. 802–27.

learns by revelation (3: 3). The new element which this passage contributes is that the content of the mystery of Christ is that the Gentiles are to share in the blessing of Christ's work (3: 6). The mission of the apostle is to make this previously hidden mystery known to all creation (3: 9). Suddenly, the historical work of the apostle in making this mystery known (3: 8–9) is paralleled by the supra-historical work of the church, which reveals to the spiritual powers the 'many-faceted' wisdom of God (3: 10);[1] and all this is according to God's pre-mundane plan (3: 11).

The historical mission of the apostle and the cosmic mission of the Church are essentially the same activity – the making known to all creation that God's eternal wisdom, his long-hidden mystery, is this: that Jews and Gentiles be one race in the Church. One may assume, however, that the reconciliation of Jew and Gentile is the expression of God's plan only on the historical level; amongst the aeons the reconciliation is the re-uniting of the fractured universe. What a bold doctrine! The mission to the Gentiles is an essential part of the restitution of cosmic unity; reconciliation amongst men, and reconciliation in the cosmos at large, is one activity.

The Church is therefore pre-existent in the plan of God. It is also a heavenly entity, pre-existent in the apocalyptic sense; its apostolic mission on earth and its cosmic labor as a heavenly hypostasis – one and the same work – express its nature as a heavenly entity.

(vi) *Ephesians 4: 8–10.* In 4: 8–10 the Christian myth of the heavenly redeemer is present;[2] it describes his victorious progress through the cosmos, which is described as 'filling all things' (ἵνα πληρώσῃ τὰ πάντα, 4: 11). One should compare this with 1: 23, where the church is the pleroma of Christ, his 'full presence' in the cosmos.

---

[1] See Schlier's excellent excursus on 'Wisdom' on pp. 159–66, especially pp. 158–9.

[2] Schlier, *Epheserbrief*, pp. 192–3, cf. Heb. 7: 26, Eph. 1: 10, II Cor. 5: 1, 12: 2, Heb. 4: 14. He correctly treats τῆς γῆς in 9c as an appositive genitive. The descent is to earth, therefore, and not to regions under the earth. This redeemer is not the same as the 'Gnostic redeemer' of Reitzenstein and Bultmann, but the result of a Christian adaptation of apocalyptic imagery.

In Ephesians the temporal aspect of eschatology has been transmuted almost entirely into spatial imagery. For the rest, the ideas of Christ as pre-existent Wisdom/Anthropos, and the Church as the body of the anthropos and the heavenly temple, persist, and are developed. The notion of the pre-existence of the elect in the purpose of God, which we met in Romans 8, is repeated here with greater clarity. The Church, therefore, is both protologically pre-existent in the plan of God, and eschatologically pre-existent as a heavenly entity.

C. *The Pastoral Epistles*

The Christology of the Pastorals is controlled by the idea of 'epiphany'.[1] Christ 'appeared' in this world in the incarnation, and he will 'appear' again at the end of time (I Tim. 6: 14, II Tim. 1: 10, 4: 1, Tit. 2: 13). Obviously, this type of thought presupposes the idea of the pre-existence of Christ before his epiphanies. We have called this type of idea 'eschatological pre-existence'.

(i) *The 'Epiphany' Texts.* There are three general kinds of epiphany texts:

(a) *I Tim. 3: 16, II Tim. 1: 9–10, Tit. 1: 2–3 (cf. 3: 4–8) The Epiphany of the pre-existent Christ has already occurred or is occurring in the present*

Each of these passages refers to the incarnation as the epiphany of Christ. They are liturgical or semi-liturgical in form, and represent what Dibelius calls 'the realized eschatology' so

---

[1] ἐπιφάνεια is a technical term in Hellenistic religion for the self-manifestation of a god or semi-divine being, such as a king. It applies to occasions such as the birthday of the god, the anniversary of the king's coronation, or the return of the king from a long journey (Kelly, *The Pastoral Epistles, ad loc.*). R. H. Fuller, *Foundations*, pp. 217, 226–9, points out the difference between the understanding of the incarnation as an epiphany, especially in I Tim. 3: 16 and John 1: 1–18, and as a *kenosis*, especially in Phil. 2: 5–11. He believes that the epiphany Christology was developed 'to express another [other than his humanity and humility] element in the Church's assessment of Jesus which was present right from the start, namely his *exousia* and his conveyance of a direct confrontation with the revelatory presence and saving action of God himself' (pp. 228–9). The Hellenistic idea of the 'divine man' was used to make this point.

characteristic of liturgical pieces that come from the school of Paul.[1]

I Tim. 3: 16 is a hymn, arranged in three couplets, each of which expresses an antithesis – flesh/spirit, angels/nations, world/glory.[2] The antitheses are arranged in a chiasmus, ab, ba, ab. The hymn is introduced as 'the mystery of godliness' (cf. 3: 9), a phrase which recalls the apocalyptic mystery so central to the idea of pre-existence. The content of the mystery is the manifestation of Christ in three stages, each stage being twofold, encompassing the worlds of flesh and spirit.

(i)	'He appeared in[3] flesh	a
	He entered the divine sphere[4] in spirit	b
(ii)	He was seen by angels	b
	He was proclaimed to peoples	a
(iii)	He was believed in the world	a
	He was taken up in glory'	b

'Mystery' therefore has the meaning of 'the plan of God for the salvation of men', as in I Cor. 2: 6–16 (cf. Rom. 16: 28, Col. 1:

[1] M. Dibelius, *Die Pastoralbriefe*, 3, neu bearbeitet von Hans Conzelmann, *H.N.T.* 13 (Tübingen, 1955), on II Tim. 1: 9–10. Other works consulted: C. K. Barrett, *The Pastoral Epistles in the New English Bible*, New Clarendon Bible (Oxford, 1963); J. N. D. Kelly, *A Commentary on the Pastoral Epistles*; E. Schweizer, 'Two New Testament Creeds Compared', *Neotestamentica*, pp. 122–35; 'Antilegomena'; E. F. Scott, *The Pastoral Epistles*, Moffatt New Testament Commentary (New York and London, undated).

[2] Kelly, *ad loc.* Schweizer, *Two Creeds*, p. 125. Dibelius/Conzelmann, *Pastoralbriefe*; C. K. Barrett, *Pastoral Epistles*, sees a temporal progression through the six successive lines rather than antithetical couplets; we are not convinced. Jeremias (*N.T.D.*, 1953, *ad loc.*, reported by Kelly and Dibelius/Conzelmann), suggests that the threefold structure reflects the enthronement ritual of Egypt and the Ancient Near East, which contains the same three moments of exaltation, presentation and enthronement as the hymn. The moments of the hymn do not, however, correspond with the three 'enthronement' stages.

[3] The ἐν here and in the next line is instrumental; the phrases designate 'ways of being' (Dibelius/Conzelmann).

[4] This paraphrase of ἐδικαιώθη follows suggestions of Dibelius/Conzelmann. They cite C.H. XIII. 9, Ign. Phld. 8: 2, cf. Od. Sol. 31: 5; Phil. 2: 9ff., Col. 2: 15, to show that δικαιοῦσθαι frequently means, in contexts such as this, 'to enter the sphere of δικαιοσύνη', the divine sphere. This is merely a more specific statement of the essential meaning of the usual translation, 'vindicated'.

26, Eph. 1: 9, 3: 9ff.). The 'itinerary' of Christ, from heaven to earth and back, is present in the hymn.[1]

II Tim. 1: 9–10 is also vaguely 'hymnic' in style. Kelly suggests that it is a freely moulded piece of 'semi-stereotyped catechetical material' – if that means anything! We cannot determine any fixed structure in this brief passage, although it is reminiscent of passages such as Eph. 3: 4ff., 9–11, Rom. 16: 25ff., I Pet. 1: 20, which Dibelius/Conzelmann describe as 'kerygmatic'.

The passage stresses the determining power of God's purpose (cf. Rom. 8: 28, 9: 11, Eph. 1: 11, 3: 11). The thought of verse 9 is very similar to that in Eph. 1: 3–14, and much of what we said about that passage is applicable here too. The 'grace' was given us 'in Christ Jesus before the eternal ages' (πρὸ χρόνων αἰωνίων); we must therefore have existed before the ages – that is, enjoyed a pre-temporal existence – in Christ. The emphasis is on the pre-existence of Christ, however, and the pre-existence of the Christian can be introduced only by a deduction which the author probably did not intend us to make. The plan of God for our salvation, focused in the pre-existent Christ, was certain of fulfilment then; and now it has been fulfilled, so that one can speak as if the beneficiaries of the plan were present at its pre-temporal formulation. The benefits of the pre-temporal grace have been made available in the manifestation of Christ, its pre-existent bearer.

Titus 1: 2–3 says largely the same thing, with one difference: the eternal life, which God promised before the world (πρὸ χρόνων αἰωνίων) is being manifested at the appropriate time – the present – in the apostolic preaching. The epiphany is present and continuous.

There can be no doubt that the pre-existence of Christ is implied in this 'epiphany-Christology'. To say, with Dibelius/Conzelmann,[2] that there is no speculation of a metaphysical nature in this Christology is to state the obvious – we are never dealing with mere speculation in the New Testament. The fact

---

[1] Cf. Dibelius/Conzelmann, ad loc., and on 2: 5; cf. Od. Sol. 41: 9ff.

[2] Ibid., p. 9: 'Da aber nicht metaphysisch über Wesen und Naturen nachgedacht wird, tritt ein anderer Gesichtspunkt hervor: unter dem Gesichtspunkt des Heilshandelns rücken Gott und Christus Seite an Seite...Es stimmt zu dieser unspekulativen Art, dass an der Entfaltung des Präexistenzgedankens kein Interesse besteht.'

that the idea of pre-existence is not 'developed' may indicate a lack of interest in speculation, but that does not mean that the idea of pre-existence was unimportant in the Christological scheme to which they subscribed. It is vitally important that Christ come from God's side of reality, which is what the idea of pre-existence entailed by the 'Epiphany-scheme' implies.

In these texts the epiphany of the pre-existent Christ occurred in the past, in the incarnation, and occurs in the present, in the apostolic preaching. The Christ who appears, it is said explicitly, existed before the creation.

(b) *I Tim. 6: 14, II Tim. 4: 1*
The epiphany of the pre-existent Christ will occur in the future

These texts need simply to be pointed out. They assume the same 'epiphany-Christology' as those examined in the previous section; but whereas the others look to a past or present epiphany, these look to a future coming of Christ to judge.

(c) *Titus 2: 11–13*
The epiphany of the pre-existent Christ is both past and future

Each of these three kinds of epiphany texts probably represents the partial expression of a unified threefold view which understood the epiphany of the pre-existent Christ to be a past event, a present reality, and a future possibility.

(ii) *Christ the Mediator, I Tim. 2: 5.* 'There is one mediator between God and man' suggests the myth of the heavenly mediator through whom God deals with creation – Wisdom, Anthropos, or Logos, in the various Jewish and Hellenistic traditions which we have already discussed. Kelly believes we have here the same idea of the second Adam as occurs in Rom. 5: 12–21 and I Cor. 15: 21–2, 45–9, while Dibelius/Conzelmann after citing a wide range of possibilities[1] conclude that one cannot exclude the presence of the myth of the cosmic redeemer, although only the idea of atonement has been developed in this passage.

Once again this important Christological statement occurs in a fragment of a catechetical or liturgical formula. It is a bi-

---

[1] Cf. Vit. Mos. II. 166, Quis Her. 206, Plutarch, Is. and Os. 46, Gal. 3: 19–20, Heb. 8: 6, Test. Dan. 6: 2, Od. Sol. 41: 9.

membered fragment like I Cor. 8: 6, and was probably known to the readers of the epistle. It may also be compared with Eph. 4: 5–6. On the basis of this comparison Dibelius/Conzelmann suggest that there is a 'one God' formula being employed, although this remains a conjecture.

(iii) *The Heavenly Church, I Tim. 6: 18–19, II Tim. 4: 8, 18.* In our commentary on I Cor. 3: 9ff. we argued that the apocalyptic idea of the heavenly temple or city influenced Paul's idea of the Church. According to him the Church is the earthly manifestation of a heavenly entity, and work in the Church on earth has its effect in the heavenly Church. The same idea is present here.

I Tim. 6: 18–19 is, on first examination, a mixed metaphor; it talks of 'treasuring up a foundation' (ἀποθησαυρίζοντας ἑαυτοῖς θεμέλιον καλὸν εἰς τὸ μέλλον). However, θεμέλιον can have the meaning 'treasure' or 'reserve' in certain cases,[1] and that may be the sense in which it is used here. Whatever the meaning, the phrase teaches that the good works of the Christian contribute to a heavenly reality which is stored up for him until the last day, when he shall come into possession of it.[2] If the word θεμέλιον has any of its primary meaning in this passage, we are reminded of I Cor. 3: 10–11 (cf. II Tim. 2: 19–20) where the heavenly Church is said to be built on the 'foundation' of the exalted Christ; but this connection of ideas cannot be more than conjecture.

II Tim. 4: 8 expresses the same idea of things stored up for future revelation; 'the crown of righteousness is laid up for me, which the Lord will give me in that day' – while II Tim. 4: 18 refers to the kingdom of God as 'heavenly' (ἐπουράνιος; cf. Eph. 1: 3ff.).

In these texts eschatological pre-existence is attested; things exist in heaven before their manifestation in the 'last day'.

[1] Bauer, *L.N.T.*, *ad loc.*, cites Philo, Sacr. 81, Leg. All. III. 113 and K. L. Schmidt in *T.D.N.T.* III, pp. 63–4. Schmidt mentions a conjecture suggested by Nestle: κειμήλιον (treasure) for θεμέλιον.

[2] Cf. Matt. 6: 19–21 ‖ Luke 12: 33–4 ‖ Mark 10: 21; Luke 12: 21, Matt. 19: 21, Jas. 5: 1–3.

III. SUMMARY AND CONCLUSION: THE IDEA OF PRE-EXISTENCE IN THE PAULINE WRITINGS

A. *The Religio-Historical Background*

We have attempted to read the Pauline texts without presupposing one particular and consistent background. Rather, we have followed the directions indicated by the specific texts themselves. The result is an untidy, but, we hope, honestly established congeries of religio-historical influences. They may be generally classified as: Jewish Apocalyptic, Hellenistic–Jewish mysticism, Apocalyptic and Hellenistic–Jewish ideas of the Anthropos, Hellenistic–Jewish Wisdom speculation with special emphasis on the mediator, who is called Wisdom, Logos, Image or Anthropos, and Old Testament ideas of God's foreknowledge and foreordination.

Such a variety of ideas and influences is what one should expect if one takes seriously the situation in which the Pauline epistles were written. The Apostle and his disciples were involved in interpreting the Gospel for a diverse world in which various Jewish and Hellenistic religious influences were at work. Many of the passages we have examined contain hymns or fragments which existed before the letters in which they occur and were taken over. Other passages are determined by the debate or conversation with opponents, whose religion influenced the formulation of the passages. In order to reconstruct the history of the idea of pre-existence in the Pauline writings one must attempt to deal with the idea in terms of the layers of tradition in which it occurs.

B. *The History of the Idea of Pre-existence in the Pauline Writings*

(i) *Pre-Pauline Hymns and Fragments.* The following passages are probably, more or less, pre-Pauline: I Cor. 8: 6, 10: 4, 15: 45–9, II Cor. 4: 4b, 8: 9, Phil. 2: 5–11, Col. 1: 15–20, and I Tim. 3: 16. Some, like I Cor. 8: 6, 10: 4 and II Cor. 8: 9, are not fragments of a hymn or text as such, but rather references which by their tone suggest that the concepts they present are well known to those addressed. Others, like I Cor. 15: 45–9, II Cor. 4: 4b, Phil. 2: 5–11, Col. 1: 15–20 and I Tim. 3: 16, seem to be fragments or larger sections of previously existing pieces.

There is some consistency among these texts in their conception of the idea of pre-existence. I Cor. 8: 6 and 10: 4 identify Christ with pre-existent Wisdom; I Cor. 15: 45–9, II Cor. 8: 9, Phil. 2: 5–11 and I Tim. 3: 16 identify him chiefly with the pre-existent heavenly anthropos; and II Cor. 4: 4b and Col. 1: 15–20 identify him with the pre-existent 'image' of God. We have seen, however, that Wisdom, Anthropos and Image were all alternative designations of the mediator of creation and salvation in Hellenistic Judaism. We suggest, therefore, that one stage of the history of the idea of pre-existence is constituted by the idea of Christ as the pre-existent mediator, an idea formulated in the Pauline Churches under the influence of Hellenistic Judaism.

(ii) *Paul's own understanding of Pre-existence.* Paul generally accepts this Hellenistic–Jewish–Christian idea of Christ, but he does modify it. The chief influence in terms of which he makes changes is Jewish apocalyptic. We shall first consider his presentation of apocalyptic ideas of pre-existence in his own right, and then his modification of the tradition which he takes over.

Paul assumes the apocalyptic idea of things 'stored up', pre-existent in heaven, before the end (I Cor. 1–2, II Cor. 4: 16–18, Rom. 11: 33–6, 16: 25–7, cf. I Thess. 1: 9b–10, Gal. 4: 4, 8–10, II Cor. 12: 1–5, Gal. 1: 12). The main pre-existent entity, however, as far as Paul is concerned, is the Church. It is the heavenly city or heavenly temple, to be revealed at the end but pre-existent now in heaven. The Christians, although they live on earth, belong essentially to this heavenly community (Gal. 4: 26, I Cor. 3: 5–17). For Paul, membership in that Church depends on the foreordination of God, and so, using an alternative pattern of thought to the apocalyptic mythology, drawn from the Old Testament tradition of promise and fulfilment, Paul could also attribute ideal pre-existence in the mind of God to the Church (Rom. 8: 28–30).

Paul's re-interpretation of the Hellenistic–Jewish–Christian idea of Christ as the pre-existent mediator focuses chiefly on its soteriological implications. It was interpreted by some (I Cor. 1–4, 15: 45–9) to mean that Christ was the original principle of Wisdom in the universe and in man, and that salvation was a return to or rediscovery of this origin. Paul accepts the idea that

Christ is the original mediator of creation (I Cor. 8: 6), but distinguishes him from the original man, and from the true humanity potentially present in men. He does this by means of eschatology. Jesus Christ, who pre-existed the world and mediated the creation, will, nevertheless, be fully manifested only at the end of time. Then only will the full experience of salvation be realized (I Cor. 1–4, 15: 45–9). However, the fact that Paul takes over the scheme of thought in which Christ is the pre-existent mediator shows that it is important for him that the one who appears at the end be the one who has existed from the beginning.

In the pre-Pauline tradition one might assume that one of the reasons for the idea of the pre-existent Christ as creation's mediator was to bind creation and redemption together. Salvation was not to be salvation from a hostile creation, but the salvation of creation as a whole. Paul's development of this same theme in II Cor. 4–5 shows that he accepted this aspect of the tradition whole-heartedly.

There is some indication, as we have seen, that the term 'image' had soteriological significance in Hellenistic Judaism. It stood for that divine element in man by virtue of which he could achieve union with God. Paul removes all possibility that the consubstantiality of man and God is the basis for salvation; he makes the 'bearing of the image' a future experience (I Cor. 15: 49), and grounds the hope of salvation in the will of God rather than the nature of man (Rom. 8: 28–30).

Paul's adaptation of the 'anthropos' idea, by placing it in an eschatological context, suggests that the idea of the Son of Man, as it occurs, for instance, in the Parables of Enoch, was at least present in his mind, even though he never refers to the title explicitly (I Cor. 15: 45–9, cf. 1–4). The fact that he does not use the phrase 'Son of Man' could have been the result of its being a 'barbarism' which would have been unintelligible to most of his readers.

The most explicit treatment of the pre-existence of Christ with reference to God, is the Philippian hymn (2: 5–11). Christ's pre-existence is a foil to his incarnation. Paul uses the pre-existence of Christ as an ethical example in this case. One should not, however, take this to indicate that Paul was interested, in general, in soteriology rather than Christology. The fact that he uses a Christological concept for moral exhortation shows that the concept was a common assumption of his and of his readers.

Paul's main contribution to the idea of pre-existence, therefore, is to re-affirm the protological pre-existence of Christ, but to place it within the framework of apocalyptic eschatology. This framework included the idea of the Church as the eschatologically pre-existent heavenly temple.

(iii) *The Deutero-Pauline understanding of Pre-existence.* Paul leaves us with two pre-existent entities – Christ and the Church – more or less unrelated. There are some hints, however, in the references to the Church as the body of Christ (Rom. 12: 4–5, I Cor. 12: 12–27), which are merely metaphorical here, of the way in which these two entities might be integrated. The Deutero-Pauline writers develop this line of thought.

Col. 1: 15–20 takes over a hymn in which Christ is identified with the cosmos. He transforms the idea of the cosmos into the Church (18b), thereby making the Church the mythological body of the pre-existent Christ. The idea of the Church as the heavenly temple does not appear in this reformulation.

In Ephesians, however, the attempt is made to maintain both the image of the heavenly temple and the body of the heavenly Christ. This results in a curious mixed metaphor of a 'building growing' (Eph. 2: 19–22 and 4: 16, cf. Col. 2: 19). Ephesians also develops another aspect of Paul's thought on pre-existence, namely, the idea of pre-existence in the mind of God (Rom. 8: 28–30). In 1: 3–14 and 1: 15–23, the idea of being 'chosen in Christ before the creation' (1: 4) is elaborated in spatial terms by means of the idea of Christ as a macroanthropos, and by transforming the idea of pre-mundane election (temporal category) into the idea of a heavenly life (spatial category).

Other elements from the pre-Pauline and Pauline traditions persist in the Deutero-Pauline literature. The apocalyptic idea of heavenly entities is present (e.g. Col. 1: 5, 1: 26ff., 2: 2–3, 3: 1–4, Eph. 3: 1–13); the idea of the church as an apocalyptic heavenly entity (I Tim. 6: 18, II Tim. 4: 8, 18); and the idea of the heavenly anthropos/redeemer (Eph. 4: 8–10, I Tim. 2: 5). The latter idea receives further development in the 'epiphany' texts in the Pastorals (I Tim. 3: 16, II Tim. 1: 9–10, Tit. 1: 2–3 etc.).

(iv) *Pauline ideas of pre-existence and the Synoptic tradition.* We have seen how the Synoptic tradition develops the concepts of Wisdom and the Son of Man. Q provides the starting point for Matthew's explicit identification of Jesus with pre-existent Wisdom, while all layers of the tradition, right back to the teaching of Jesus himself, identify him as Son of Man. It is not unlikely, therefore, that the pre-Pauline identification of Jesus with Wisdom/Anthropos etc. is part of the same development which took place in the Synoptic tradition. Paul takes over this Christological tradition from the Hellenistic–Jewish–Christian churches.

Paul's unique contribution, therefore, to early Christian thought about pre-existence is not in the realm of Christology, but in the doctrine of the Church. He makes the Church a pre-existent entity like Christ, and provides the basis, in his metaphor of the Church as the body of Christ, for the Deutero-Pauline doctrine of the Church as the body of the mythological heavenly Christ.

CHAPTER 4

PRE-EXISTENCE IN THE GOSPEL
OF JOHN

The Prologue to the Fourth Gospel introduces one to a world of thought in which the idea of pre-existence seems especially at home. Most scholars have recognized the presence of the idea in the gospel of John, but recently Ernst Kaesemann has made pre-existence the key which unlocks the entire Johannine Christology.[1]

He has argued that the climax to the gospel is the prayer of Jesus in chapter 17, presented as a conscious counterpart to the Prologue. In the Prologue the Logos is portrayed as coming from eternity into time while in the prayer his return to eternity takes place.[2] The Johannine Christology therefore takes the form of a 'journey' of the pre-existent Christ, from pre-existence through time back to eternity.

Kaesemann characterizes the Christology of John as a 'naive docetism' in which Christ never is really incarnated, but remains a divine being in human disguise.[3] Furthermore, he sees no real place for the passion narrative in the gospel.[4] The climax of the presentation is reached in chapter 17, with the return of the Logos to eternity, and the passion narrative (chapters 18–20) is merely an appendage for the sake of convention.

We have certain serious reservations about Kaesemann's characterization of John's Christology as a 'docetism', as we

---

[1] E. Kaesemann, *Jesu Letzter Wille nach Johannes 17* (Tübingen, 1967), E.T. *The Testament of Jesus*, trans. G. Krodel (Philadelphia, 1968). (All references are to the German text.)

[2] Cf. R. Bultmann, *Das Evangelium des Johannes* (Göttingen, 1962) (with supplement), p. 1. He writes: 'Only when the circle has been closed and the Son has returned to the "glory" which the love of the Father prepared for him before the world was created (17: 24), only when the reader has been led back from the sphere of time into the sphere of eternity, is it possible finally to understand the sense in which the Prologue leads one from eternity into time.'

[3] Kaesemann, *Letzter Wille*, p. 52.

[4] *Ibid.*, p. 19.

shall show in the course of the discussion. At this point it seems appropriate to state our views on the place of the Passion narrative in the gospel.

We agree with Gunther Bornkamm[1] that the Passion narrative is an integral part of the whole gospel. There are in the body of the gospel too many references to the Passion to regard the narrative as of peripheral importance only. The cross, rather, is the climax of Jesus' work (19: 30). The confession of the Baptist (1: 26, 29), the references to his 'hour' (2: 3, 7: 30, 8: 20, 12: 23ff., 13: 1, 17: 1), the interpretation of the cleansing of the temple (2: 13ff.), the discourses on 'coming and going' (3: 12–15, 6: 63ff., 12: 32ff.), the raising of Lazarus (11: 45ff.), the anointing of Jesus (12: 1ff.) and the discourse on the grain of wheat (12: 24ff.) all testify to the centrality of the Passion in John's Christology. (See also 1: 51, 6: 61ff., 8: 28, 10: 11.)[2] Hence, the cross is the historical way by which the Son returned to the Father.

In the Fourth Gospel, the relation between the trans-historical and the historical dimensions of Christ's being is a very complex matter. We cannot enter into the discussion here. Nevertheless, we may confidently assert, in the light of a great weight of scholarship, that John is not a docetist. True, he emphasizes the trans-historical dimension and significance of Christ's being; but this being and its significance are revealed in history – in the life, death and resurrection of Jesus.[3]

Despite these criticisms, we must recognize that Kaesemann's attempt to read John from the point of view of chapter 17 does focus our attention on the distinctive feature of the Fourth Gospel, which sets it off from the Synoptics – namely, its explicit presentation of the divine glory of Christ, in the words and works of Jesus. The relationship between chapter 17 and the Passion narrative need not be construed as Kaesemann suggests, in such a way as to render the Passion unnecessary to the unfolding of the Christ event. On the contrary, chapter 17 may be viewed as the climax of those discourses (chs. 13–17) in which –

[1] G. Bornkamm, 'Zur Interpretation des Johannesevangeliums, Eine Auseinandersetzung mit Ernst Kaesemanns Schrift *Jesu Letzter Wille nach Johannes 17*', in *Evangelische Theologie* 28 (1968), 8–25.

[2] *Ibid.*, p. 18.

[3] C. H. Dodd, *The Interpretation of the Fourth Gospel* (Cambridge, 1960), p. 444.

as is John's custom[1] – the significance of an event is set out; in this case the Passion as the event by which the Redeemer re-ascends into his full power. This interpretation seems to be true to John's intention: to hold together, in a mighty paradox, the pre-existent Word of God, and the man who was among us in great humility, whose finest hour was the hour of his death.

With the proper reservations, we shall follow Kaesemann's suggestion, and focus our study on the Prologue and chapter 17, in that order. They seem in fact to represent the two termini of John's Christology: the coming of the Logos from eternity and his return thither, expressed in the form of discourses.

However, before we can begin our study, some consideration of the state of the source criticism of the Fourth Gospel is in order. Unlike the Synoptic gospels, the source criticism of John is still at an early stage. Bultmann set the pattern for recent discussion when he proposed three major sources behind the gospel: the 'Revelatory Discourses Source', the 'Signs or Miracle Source', and the 'Passion Source'. In addition he envisages an evangelist who moulded these sources into a gospel; and an 'ecclesiastical redactor' who added certain passages in order to make the gospel palatable to nascent orthodoxy.[2] These proposals have been severely tested by subsequent scholarship, and the most durable source seems to be the 'Signs or Miracle' source.[3]

---

[1] John presents, throughout his gospel, events and discourses which unfold the significance of those events for the Christian faith; cf. Dodd, *Interpretation*, pp. 289–91. Chapters 13–20 are a special case of this procedure, in which the discourses, contrary to precedent, precede rather than follow the narrative. Nevertheless, the same intention is in view.

[2] Bultmann's views are set out in the course of his commentary, already referred to. A handy summary and analysis of his theories is presented by D. M. Smith, in *The Composition and Order of the Fourth Gospel* (New Haven and London, 1965). S. Schulz, *Untersuchungen zur Menschensohn-Christologie im Johannesevangelium* (Göttingen, 1957), proposes a different approach to the sources from Bultmann's. He calls his method the 'history of themes'. He isolates 'themes' such as 'the Son of Man', instead of written sources. J. M. Robinson, 'Recent Research in the Fourth Gospel', *J.B.L.* 78 (1959), 247–52, has criticized Schulz's approach convincingly. E. Ruckstuhl, *Die literarische Einheit des Johannesevangelium* (Freiburg in der Schweiz [Fribourg], 1951), rejects any literary sources at all. See H. M. Teeple, 'Methodology in the Source Analysis of the Fourth Gospel', *J.B.L.* 81 (1962), 279–86.

[3] D. M. Smith, *Composition*, pp. 85–115; R. Fortna, *The Gospel of Signs*, *S.N.T.S.* Monograph 11 (Cambridge, 1969).

We cannot adopt Bultmann's solution to the problem of the sources of the Fourth Gospel; nevertheless we must be aware of the possibility in any specific passage that the evangelist is using and adapting a source that he received in the tradition. This awareness is essential to an understanding of the Prologue. The gospel we approach is therefore a composite – and probably unfinished[1] – piece of literature.

I. THE PROLOGUE

There is some disagreement whether the Prologue is a literary unity, or whether it is based on a source. The weight of opinion, however, seems to favor the view that it is based on a hymn, which the evangelist adapted and edited.[2] We follow this weight of opinion, and so the first task is to separate the underlying hymn from the Johannine editorial work.

The Prologue has strong traces of Aramaic style in it; but there is not sufficient evidence for Bultmann's thesis that the hymn on which it is based was in Aramaic.[3] It is also doubtful that the hypothetical hymn was pre-Christian – in praise of John the Baptist, for instance – as Bultmann argues.[4]

The following steps seem to bring the underlying hymn to light: (i) Remove verses 6–8, which are probably the opening lines of the 'Signs' source, with a Johannine editorial transition

---

[1] Smith, *Composition*, p. 239, suggests that the gospel is unfinished in its present form, and that Bultmann has not 'restored an original' gospel but carried through an editing which the primitive editor did not complete.

[2] Dodd, *Interpretation*, and C. K. Barrett, *The Gospel according to St. John* (London, 1958), believe it to be a unity, not dependent on sources. Bultmann, *Evang.*; E. Kaesemann, 'Aufbau und Anliegen des johanneischen Prologs', *Exegetische Versuche*, II, 155–80, E.T. *New Testament Questions of Today*, trans. W. J. Montague (Philadelphia, 1969), pp. 138–67 (references are to the German edition); E. Haenchen, 'Probleme des johanneischen Prologs', *Z.T.K.* 6 (1963), 305–34; R. Schnackenburg, 'Logos-Hymnus und johanneischen Prolog', *B.Z.* 1 (1957), 69–109. All these scholars recognize it to be based on a hymnic source. R. E. Brown, *The Gospel according to John* (i–xii), The Anchor Bible (New York, 1966), pp. 21–3, provides a good review of the various literary theories about the Prologue.

[3] Kaesemann, 'Aufbau', pp. 157–9.

[4] Schnackenburg, 'Logos-Hymnus', pp. 90–6. Kaesemann, 'Aufbau', p. 166.

in verse 8.[1] (ii) Assign verse 2, as a repetition,[2] and verse 5, on grounds of content and style, to the Johannine editor.[3] (iii) Recognize, on various grounds, that verses 10b,[4] 12,[5] 13,[6] 14b–c,[7] 15,[8] 17 and 18[9] also come from the editor. The hymn that emerges, as reconstructed by Schnackenburg, looks like this:

I. (V. 1) Ἐν ἀρχῇ ἦν ὁ λόγος
καὶ ὁ λόγος ἦν πρὸς τὸν θεόν,
καὶ θεὸς ἦν ὁ λόγος.
(V. 3) Πάντα δι' αὐτοῦ ἐγένετο,
καὶ χωρὶς αὐτοῦ ἐγένετο
οὐδὲ ἕν, ὃ γέγονεν.

II. (V. 4) Ἐν αὐτῷ ζωὴ ἦν,
καὶ ἡ ζωὴ ἦν τὸ φῶς τῶν ἀνθρώπων.
(V. 9) Ἦν τὸ φῶς τὸ ἀληθινόν,
ὃ φωτίζει πάντα ἄνθρωπον.

[1] Fortna, *Gospel of Signs*, pp. 161–6. One must include the μαρτυρεῖν περί of verse 7 in the Johannine editing (Schnackenburg, 'Logos-Hymnus', p. 78, Fortna, *ibid.*, p. 164).

[2] Schnackenburg, 'Logos-Hymnus', p. 79.

[3] *Ibid.* Schnackenburg applies the style-critical method of Schweizer and Ruckstuhl (cf. E. Schweizer, *Ego Eimi* (Göttingen, 1939); E. Ruckstuhl, *Literarische Einheit*) to the verses which, on other grounds, he attributes to the Johannine editor. The sample is so small and the stylistic marks frequently so minute that we cannot accept the arguments based on style unless they are confirmed by other kinds of evidence. In verse 5 the use of σκοτία rather than σκότος which is usual in the New Testament (stylistic mark of John number 22, according to Ruckstuhl) gains force from the use of καταλαβεῖν in the same way as John uses it in 12: 35. On grounds of style and content, therefore, we assign 1: 5 to the Johannine editor (Schnackenburg, 'Logos-Hymnus', p. 79).

[4] Schnackenburg, *ibid.*, p. 87: because the idea of 'cosmos' in 10a and c is 'world-denying' as in 'gnosticism' and 10b counteracts this by asserting yet once more that the cosmos is a creation of the Logos.

[5] *Ibid.*, p. 79, on the same grounds as verse 5: ἔλαβον takes up the παρέλαβον of verse 11 (Johannine stylistic mark number 7, Ruckstuhl). To 'receive someone' is the same as 'to believe in him' (cf. 13: 20a–b, cf. 4: 53a–b) in Johannine thought.

[6] *Ibid.*, p. 75. It is an explanatory gloss.

[7] *Ibid.*, p. 79. Typical Johannine statements; cf. 11: 40, 12: 41, 17: 24, 1: 18, 3: 16, 18.

[8] *Ibid.*, pp. 72–4; it breaks the progress of thought.

[9] *Ibid.*, pp. 74; the ideas are incongruous with the rest of the Prologue, and there are stylistic reasons.

III. (V. 10) Ἐν τῷ κόσμῳ ἦν,
καὶ ὁ κόσμος αὐτὸν οὐκ ἔγνω.
(V. 11) Εἰς τὰ ἴδια ἦλθεν,
καὶ οἱ ἴδιοι αὐτὸν οὐ παρέλαβον.

IV. (V. 14) Καὶ ὁ λόγος σὰρξ ἐγένετο
καὶ ἐσκήνωσεν ἐν ἡμῖν,
πλήρης χάριτος καὶ ἀληθείας.
(V. 16) Ὅτι (Καὶ) ἐκ τοῦ πληρώματος αὐτοῦ
ἡμεῖς πάντες ἐλάβομεν,
καὶ χάριν ἀντὶ χάριτος.

Having separated the hymn from the Johannine editorial
work, we are in a position to interrogate each layer of tradition
about pre-existence. We shall first consider the idea of pre-
existence in the hymn, and then in the additions. We follow
Schnackenburg's reconstruction of the hymn and shall deal with
it according to his strophic divisions.

Strophe 1 (verses 1 and 3) begins with an allusion to the
opening phrase of the creation narrative in Genesis 1;[1] but –
unlike Genesis 1: 1 – the first concern of the passage is not
creation, but the eternal being of the Logos. The word 'Logos'
is used without explanation; and therefore seems to be well
known to the readers. The imperfect tense ἦν in verse 1 indicates continuous existence, so that ἀρχή cannot be construed as
the first event in a series; rather it refers to that 'realm' which
'was' before the 'series' of events which began with creation.[2]

The first line, therefore, is not an answer to the philosophic
and gnostic question about the origin of the world – what is the
ἀρχή or 'first-principle' of the world? Verse 1, as we have said,
does not say anything about the world; rather it is concerned to
establish the pre-existence before the world of the divine
Logos.[3]

From the absolute pre-existence of the Logos in line 1, the

[1] Haenchen, 'Probleme', p. 311. [2] Haenchen, *ibid.*

[3] Bultmann interprets the idea of pre-existence in passing, as follows:
The assertion of pre-existence is made with reference to the incarnation;
it is the pre-existence of the revealer. 'Dass heisst: in der Gestalt und im
Worte Jesu begegnet nichts, was in Welt und Zeit entsprungen ist, sondern
begegnet die Wirklichkeit, die jenseits von Welt und Zeit liegt' (*Evang.*,
p. 16). Jesus the Logos stands over against the world critically, and can set
men free from the world (*ibid.*).

strophe moves, in lines 2 and 3, to the relationship between the Logos and God. He was πρὸς τὸν θεόν and he was θεός. The phrase πρὸς τὸν θεόν states that there always were two divine beings. In 'mythological language' it excludes any idea that the Logos was an emanation or offspring of a primal being, who preceded him.[1] The phrase θεὸς ἦν ὁ λόγος excludes any idea of polytheism; the Logos and Theos are one and the same, even though they are distinct.[2]

We cannot anticipate the philosophical attempts to explain this unity in separation which constitute the history of Trinitarian doctrine. It is sufficient to recognize, with Bultmann, the intention of this paradoxical statement – to establish that in dealing with Jesus, the Logos, one has to do with God. Barrett summarizes aptly:

John intends that the whole of his gospel shall be read in the light of this verse. The deeds and words of Jesus are the deeds and words of God; if this be not true the book is blasphemous.[3]

The next step in strophe 1 establishes the relationship between the Logos and the created world. The punctiliar aorist ἐγένετο (in verse 3) contrasts with the linear ἦν of 1 : 1,[4] bringing out the difference between the timeless existence of the Logos in himself, and the temporal existence of the created order, which has

---

[1] Bultmann, *Evang.*, pp. 16–17.

[2] The absence of the article before θεός could be merely a stylistic variation. E. C. Colwell ('A Definite Rule for the Use of the Article in the Greek New Testament', *J.B.L.* 52 (1933), 12ff.) shows that definite predicate nouns which precede the verb usually lack the article – an exception to the rule that such nouns take the article. C. F. D. Moule, however (*An Idiom Book of New Testament Greek* (Cambridge, 1960), p. 116), points out that in John 1 : 1 the word order seems to have been deliberately chosen in order to make a theological point: that θεός describes the nature of the Word and does not identify his person. In that case, therefore, the idiom of New Testament Greek is made to serve theology. C. H. Dodd (*Interpretation*, p. 280), in the course of his judicious discussion of the background of the term Logos, identifies the usage θεός – as distinct from θεῖος or θεοῦ on the one hand, and ὁ θεός on the other – as Philonic. θεός is the proper description of the Logos in Philo, while ὁ θεός is reserved for 'the Fons deitatis (πηγὴ τοῦ λόγου)'. Dodd, however, does not accept that θεός is a description of the nature of the Word. He demands θεῖος or θεοῦ for that meaning. θεός, if we understand Dodd correctly, merely names the Logos, as Philo names the Logos.

[3] Barrett, *Gospel*, p. 130. [4] Moule, *Idiom Book*, pp. 5ff.

a fixed point of origin.[1] In this context πάντα meaning the 'universe', must be distinguished from κόσμος (1:10), meaning the 'world of men'.[2] The totality of the created universe, including mankind, came into being through him.[3]

The opening strophe, therefore, tells of the pre-existence, full divinity, and creative activity of the Logos.[4]

In strophe 2 (verses 4 and 9)[5] man is singled out from the whole of creation, and the relationship between him and the Logos is set forth, in principle, as part of the ontological definition of man, prior to any consideration of man in history. Logos is the life of every man, which is the same thing as the true light which enlightens every man. Life is Light; to live is to see. What man 'sees' may be deduced from the context: he sees that he is a creature,[6] but more especially that he is part of a creation which is itself the revelation of God's nature. Not to 'see' this is to be dead. Such a view comes close to the gnostic idea of the pneumatic man who needs only to be reminded of his essential divinity in order to be saved; but there is a difference between the gnostic view and the idea of the hymn. According to the hymn the knowledge of God and of oneself as His creature be-

---

[1] Barrett, *Gospel*, p. 127.

[2] Haenchen, 'Probleme', p. 316; Barrett, *Gospel*, p. 135.

[3] Haenchen, 'Probleme', pp. 317–21, has shown that ὁ γέγονεν is part of verse 3, not of verse 4. The shift in punctuation which transfers it to verse 4 is gnostic in origin and purpose. The later gnostics tried to see in John 1:1ff. the origin of the Ogdoad out of the primal God, e.g. *Excerpta e Theodoto* 6:1ff. This made it necessary, in order to preserve the scheme of male and female pairs of emanations, for verse 4 to read: 'That which came into being in him (the Logos) was ζωή'. This punctuation is also found in Heracleon (in Origen: Commentary on John, II, 21, who identifies the αὐτῷ with the pneumatic, who is also identical with the Logos), among the Naassenes (Hippol. V. 8. 4) and the Perates (Hippol. V. 16). The Naassenes were also able, on this punctuation, to read καὶ χωρὶς αὐτοῦ ἐγένετο οὐδὲ ἕν as 'the nothing which came into being without him is the (material) world' (Hippol. V. 8. 4).

[4] Cf. Schnackenburg, 'Logos-Hymnus', p. 85.

[5] This arrangement of the strophe contradicts Kaesemann ('Aufbau', p. 159–60) and Bultmann (*Evang.*, p. 4). Both believe that the first 'section' of the hymn ends with 1:4 and that 1:5 begins a new section, followed by verse 9ff.

[6] Bultmann, *Evang.*, p. 379 (cf. p. 25): 'Im Präexistenten war die Offenbarung die der schöpferische Macht, die für die Menschen Licht gewesen wäre, wenn sie sich als Geschöpfe verstanden hätten.'

stows life; it does not remind one of a divine life which one had all along as a 'natural' endowment; it bestows something new.

Although we postpone the discussion of the historical background, it is important to recognize the similarity between the teaching of this strophe, and the Philonic teaching that the Logos is the image of God in man and his capacity for knowing God.[1]

The Logos in strophe 2, therefore, is the 'natural' knowledge of God (and/or capacity for such knowledge) given to man as part of his created being. This knowledge consists, essentially, in the recognition of God as creator and man as creature.

The understanding of the third strophe (verses 10 and 11) depends on the meaning of τὰ ἴδια and οἱ ἴδιοι in verse 11. Barrett suggests that 'his own home' or 'his property' (τὰ ἴδια) and 'his own people' (οἱ ἴδιοι) are Israel, the chosen people; but he allows that similar statements could be made in the Platonic sense of the Logos coming to the world as its natural counterpart, or the Stoic sense of the Logos coming to the rational man.[2] Bultmann rejects any suggestion of Israel in these references, pointing out that in Ex. 19: 5, Deut. 7: 6, 14: 2, 26: 18 and Ps. 135: 4, the LXX translates the Hebrew for 'his own people' (עַם סְגֻלָּה) as λαὸς ἐπιούσιος and not λαὸς ἴδιος. According to Bultmann, verses 10 and 11 each have essentially the same meaning, the second merely explicating the meaning of the first. Hence, τὰ ἴδια refers to the world of men – the κόσμος of the first line of verse 10 – which should have recognized the Logos as its creator; and οἱ ἴδιοι refers to the men who make up that world.[3] C. H. Dodd takes these verses to be a reference to the coming of the Word of God to the people of Israel through Moses and the prophets.[4] Much of his argument rests, however, on verse 12, which our analysis attributes to the Johannine editor and not to the hymn.

We therefore follow Bultmann in interpreting the third strophe of the hymn; it speaks within the context of the whole creation, established by strophe 1, of the coming of the Logos to the world of men – all men – and of his rejection.

---

[1] See pp. 144–8 above. Cf. Schnackenburg, 'Logos-Hymnus', p. 86, who interprets the strophe in the light of the Wisdom myth.

[2] Barrett, *Gospel*, p. 136.   [3] Bultmann, *Evang.*, pp. 34–5, n. 7.

[4] C. H. Dodd, *Interpretation*, pp. 270–1.

The religio-historical background of this strophe is probably the Jewish Wisdom myth,[1] in the form in which it occurs in Sir. 24 and I Enoch 42. Wisdom comes from heaven to the world of men, seeking a dwelling place, and is rejected. We shall return to this discussion of the historical background.

Finally, in strophe 4 (verses 14 and 16), the Logos becomes incarnate; he enters history in a new and decisive way. The precise meaning of ἐγένετο in the phrase καὶ ὁ λόγος σὰρξ ἐγένετο (verse 14) is difficult to ascertain. ἐσκήνωσεν occurs parallel to it, and this suggests a certain reservation in the meaning of ἐγένετο. ἐσκήνωσεν, to dwell in a tent, implies a temporary presence.[2] Bultmann denies any reservation in the meaning of ἐγένετο. The Logos 'became flesh' fully and unreservedly. According to Bultmann, 1: 14 presents the incarnate Logos as 'nothing but a man' ('nichts als ein Mensch').[3] Kaesemann[4] is justified, however, in his criticism of this view as too much under the influence of later dogmatics; more precisely, as we see it, under the Kierkegaardian influence of dialectic theology.[5] For Kaesemann the emphasis in this section of the Prologue falls on 'we beheld his glory' (verse 15). Although, on our analysis, this phrase is not part of the hymn, the statements that he was 'full of grace and truth' and that 'we all received of his fullness', which are part of the hymn, support Kaesemann's interpretation rather than Bultmann's. However, Kaesemann errs in the opposite direction in presenting John's Christology as docetic. Although our analysis of the hymn differs from that of Kaesemann, the general point that he makes about 1: 14 is compelling. He writes: 'Der kosmologische Aspekt characterisiert eben nicht bloss die Einleitungsverse, sondern den gesamten Prolog, der sich darin wieder mit dem Evangelium in völliger Übereinstimmung befindet...[6] Mit Nachdruck ist daran festzuhalten,

---

[1] Schnackenburg, 'Logos-Hymnus', pp. 87–8; Haenchen, 'Probleme', p. 321; Dodd, *Interpretation*, pp. 274–5; Bultmann, *Evang.*, pp. 34–5, n. 7.

[2] As in Sir. 24: 8, but cf. I Enoch 42: 2; Barrett, *Gospel*, p. 138.

[3] Bultmann, *Evang.*, p. 40. [4] 'Aufbau', pp. 170–4.

[5] Cf. Bultmann's insistence that all knowledge of God 'previous' to the incarnation is 'negative' (*Evang.*, p. 39); which may be compared with Barth's exegesis of Rom. 1: 18ff., in the *Römerbrief*; and Bultmann, *Evang.*, pp. 46–7, where Kierkegaard is quoted to dismiss the 'half-liberal, half-pietistic' understanding of ἐθεασάμεθα by Zahn.

[6] 'Aufbau', p. 161.

dass nach dem vierten Evangelium wie übrigens auch nach den Synoptikern der Fleischgewordene nicht aufhört Himmelswesen zu bleiben, dass er keiner "Transformation" unterliegt, und dass Johannes, wie Schlatter es ausdrückt, das Wirken des Wortes in der Fleischwerdung nicht als Erniedrigung empfunden hat.'[1] Barrett is near the mark when he understands ἐγένετο to mean 'came upon the human scene', as in 1:6. This translation is about as near as one can get to expressing the delicate balance of ἐγένετο and ἐσκήνωσεν used together.

In verse 14, therefore, we have the climax of the historical presence of the Logos, as he takes up temporary residence in the world, in his own person. There is no concern in this text about the relationship between 'the divinity and the humanity' of the Logos, as is expressed in the later debates that culminated in the creed of Chalcedon. Our hymn tells of the self-revelation of the Logos, through which man receives grace and truth, the essence of the being of the Logos. He comes not to impart a teaching, but to give himself.[2] In his incarnation he does not cease to be a divine being, at the same time as he really becomes flesh.

The four strophes of the hymn, therefore, tell of the preexistent Logos, who is of the same substance but not the same identity as God; who is the natural knowledge of God in man, given as part of man's created being; who was ignored and rejected in his approaches to man; and who finally and decisively came in the flesh to dwell among us.

The old question, where in the hymn the pre-incarnate Logos is spoken of, and where the incarnate, may be answered as follows: in strophes 1 through 3 the pre-incarnate Logos is the subject, in strophe 4 the incarnate Logos. There is, however, a false antithesis implied in this whole question. The subtle qualification of ἐγένετο by ἐσκήνωσεν in verse 14 suggests, we have argued, that the incarnation is not understood as a negation of the pre-existent dignity of the Logos. The incarnate one remains the pre-existent one; this paradox must be maintained.[3]

There seems to be an agreement amongst scholars that the Hellenistic–Jewish Wisdom myth lies behind the Johannine Prologue.[4] Disagreements arise when the details of the myth

---

[1] *Ibid.*, p. 175.   [2] Bultmann, *Evang.*, p. 42.

[3] Kaesemann, 'Aufbau', pp. 161, 175.

[4] E.g. Bultmann, *Evang.*, pp. 8–11, cf. 'Der religionsgeschichtliche Hinter-

itself, and the way in which it influenced the Prologue, are discussed.

Bultmann sees the Wisdom-myth and the Logos-hymn as two different expressions of the same redeemer-myth, which is more primitive than either. They are derived from this common ancestor, and not the one from the other.[1]

The chief difficulty with this view is that there is no certain evidence for the prior existence of this redeemer myth, apart from the Wisdom-myth, the Logos-hymn, and other similar pieces, namely, sources which the prior myth is supposed to explain. This is a circular argument which may indeed be vicious, but not necessarily. Carsten Colpe has recently shown the precariousness of this situation.[2] It is not certain that such a myth existed; nevertheless one could safely use the term 'redeemer myth' to refer at least to a phenomenon which these sources have in common. But this is not the sense in which Bultmann intends it, and so we shall avoid the term.

C. H. Dodd discusses at length the possibility that the Logos may owe something to the Old Testament conception of the 'Word of God', which was hypostatized from time to time (Is. 55: 10–11, cf. Wisd. 18: 15–16). However, he concludes that the major influence behind the Johannine Logos is the Philonic Logos, chiefly in its function as the expressed thought of God (λόγος προφορικός) and the mediator between God and the creation.[3]

J. Jeremias accepts the Alexandrian-Jewish background and argues that the Prologue represents a relatively advanced stage of the Logos idea. Rev. 19: 11–16 is a more 'primitive' form of

grund des Prologs zum Johannesevangelium' in *Eucharisterion* II, pp. 3–26; C. H. Dodd, *Interpretation*, pp. 273–85; J. Jeremias, 'Zum Logos-Problem', *Z.N.W.* 59 (1968), 82–5.

[1] A convenient summary of the redeemer-myth, as Bultmann reconstructs it, occurs in his *Primitive Christianity in its Contemporary Setting* (New York, 1956), pp. 162–71.

[2] Carsten Colpe, *Die Religionsgeschichtlicheschule: Darstellung und Kritik ihres Bildes vom gnostischen Erlösermythus* (Göttingen, 1961). Wayne A. Meeks, *The Prophet-King, Moses Traditions and the Johannine Christology*, Supplements to Novum Testamentum XIV (Leiden, 1967), pp. 2–16, gives a judicious summary of the representative theories concerning the Johannine background, in the course of which (pp. 12–17) he shows how Bultmann's 'synthesis' has begun to 'dissolve' under critical examination.

[3] Dodd, *Interpretation*, pp. 263–85.

the Christian idea of the Logos, and when this primitive form is compared with Wisd. 18: 14–16, the Alexandrian-Jewish provenance of the idea becomes apparent. According to Jeremias, the earliest Christian usage attributed the title Logos to the Lord returning in the eschaton. The Prologue and I John 1, by using it to designate the Christ as pre-existent, show that they represent a relatively advanced form of the idea,[1] a stage at which eschatology had begun to be balanced by protology.

We have already presented the Alexandrian-Jewish evidence relevant to our concern. We may, at this point, simply remind ourselves of the Wisdom/Logos tradition. Wisdom is the pre-existent mediator of creation, and Philo interprets her status in middle-Platonic terms, changing the name from Wisdom to Logos. Wisdom is also the agent of salvation and revelation who comes to men in general – in the myth – and is rejected (Sir. 24, I Enoch 42), or comes in wise men and prophets to the people of Israel (Wisd. 2–7, 10–11, Gosp. of Hebrews, in Jerome, *Commentary on Isaiah* IV, on Is. 11: 2, Philo) and suffers the same fate. Logos is also the 'image of God' in man, understood as the capacity for the knowledge of God. C. H. Dodd presents two useful tables comparing phrases in the Prologue with the Wisdom literature in general (Prov., Sir., and Wisd.) on the one hand, and Philo in particular on the other.[2] They seem to establish beyond reasonable doubt the relationship between the Prologue and the Wisdom/Logos tradition of the Hellenistic synagogue of Alexandria.

The Logos-hymn seems to be a version of the myth.[3] The Logos is the pre-existent mediator through which God created the world (strophe 1). He is also the 'natural' capacity in man for the knowledge of God (strophe 2). He came to the world of men and was rejected (strophe 3). He became present in the world of men as a man – he became flesh. All of these elements in the Logos doctrine have parallels in the Wisdom myth, excepting the incarnation.

There are two modifications of the myth in the hymn. The first results from the biblical affirmation of the goodness of crea-

---

[1] Jeremias, 'Zum Logos Problem'.

[2] Dodd, *Interpretation*, pp. 274–7.

[3] At this point, we refer the reader to the evidence set out in pp. 144–8 above.

tion; there is no necessity to remove God from direct contact with the world, as Philo's Platonism demands, and so the Logos is not an intermediary being but truly God, in that aspect of his being which is turned towards and involved in the world. The second modification arises out of the Christian confession that Jesus is 'God amongst us' – the Creator with the creation. Whereas, in the Wisdom of Solomon, and in Philo, the Logos is present within the world in certain men, as a 'spiritual' presence, in the Logos-hymn he becomes present in his own flesh, thus revealing himself fully, as never before. The hymn, therefore, is not pre-Christian in origin, but fully Christian.

When we turn our attention to the editorial work of the evangelist, by means of which he incorporated the hymn into his gospel, we find that in general he agrees with the doctrine of his source. Verses 2, 5, 6–8, 9c, 10b, 12–13, 14b–c, 15, 17–18, are the verses in question, and we shall discuss them in order.

Verse 2 is a repetition of the point that the Logos is co-eternal with the primal God – in the absolute 'beginning' he was in the presence of the Father. He is not a 'subsequent' emanation or off-spring. This emphasis could be construed as a polemic against the view that the Logos was an emanation of the primal God. If that conjecture were correct, it would suggest the presence of a 'gnostic' doctrine of aeons in the Johannine milieu.[1]

1 : 5 was written by the evangelist to introduce 1 : 6–7, which are the opening lines of the 'Signs Source'; verse 8 was written by him to provide the transition to verse 9. 1 : 5 shows that he understands strophe 2 of the hymn to be concerned to set out the relationship between the Logos and man; but, whereas the thought of the hymn is ontological, the thought of the evangelist is historical.

The hymn interprets the Logos in strophe 2 as the 'natural' capacity of man to know God, given in creation; the evangelist understands him as the historical presence of 'wisdom' in the great men – the 'friends of God and prophets' (Wisd. 7: 27) – of the history of God's self-revelation. John the Baptist (verses 6–7) is precisely one of these bearers of the Logos/Wisdom, in

---

[1] On the classification of the various forms of Gnosticism, pre-, proto- and Gnosticism proper, see Ugo Bianci, *Le Origini dello Gnosticismo/The Origins of Gnosticism, Colloquium of Messina*, 13–18 April, 1966 (Leiden, 1967), pp. xxvi–xxix.

whom the 'light shines on in the darkness' (verse 5) and through whom 'the real light which enlightens every man was even then coming into the world' (verse 9). The tradition represented in Luke 7: 35, par. Matt. 11: 19c, shows that in the tradition behind Q this view concerning John was also present. This means in effect that the evangelist eliminates the second stage of the career of the Logos, as the natural light in man, and moves the Logos from absolute pre-existence directly into the history of salvation. The 'light' in verse 5 is the word of the prophets and wise men, and the darkness which does not overcome the light is the darkness of historical opposition to the bearers of the Logos – the 'killing of the prophets and the stoning of those sent' (Matt. 23: 37, par. Luke 13: 34, Q).[1] The evangelist underlines this by adding 1: 9c, ἐρχόμενον εἰς τὸν κόσμον, as a modifier for φῶς.[2] This links strophes 2 and 3 inseparably, so that there is a continuous movement of thought from 1: 5, where the Logos appears in history and suffers the opposition of the 'darkness', which does not overcome him, through the concrete example of the type of historical presence he had, in John the Baptist, to the explicit rejection of the pre-incarnate Logos (1: 10–11), probably exemplified in the minds of the readers by the fate of John.[3]

In 1: 12–13 the evangelist adds a reference to the 'remnant' of sacred history. He understood that it was possible to be 'saved' by a proper response to the pre-incarnate Logos present in the prophets. In the hymn 'his own' to whom he came, are *all* men, not only Israel, but according to the evangelist they are the people of Israel, the recipients of the pre-incarnate, historical

[1] Cf. Matt. 8: 20, par. Luke 9: 58 (Q); Matt. 11: 19c par. Luke 7: 35 (Q), Haenchen, 'Probleme', p. 321; M. Jack Suggs, *Wisdom, Christology and Law in Matthew's Gospel*, p. 43, makes precisely the same point.

[2] Barrett, *Gospel*, p. 134. We read it as a neuter nominative agreeing with φῶς rather than a masculine accusative agreeing with ἄνθρωπον, following the internal evidence of our argument and the opinion of Barrett. We do not agree with Barrett, however, that this entails a reference to the incarnation.

[3] It is significant that the rejection is expressed in terms of 'not knowing' him: ὁ κόσμος αὐτὸν οὐκ ἔγνω. This confirms our interpretation of 'the light of men' as the capacity to know God. Knowledge is a central category in the Wisdom tradition. See Barrett, *Gospel*, pp. 419–20; and pp. 135–6: 'John's characteristic use, however, concerns knowledge of the divine persons, of the relation between them and especially of the mission of Jesus to the world' (p. 135).

self-revelations of the Logos, through the prophets. The evangelist has changed the context of operation of the pre-incarnate Logos from creation to sacred history.

In strophe 4 the evangelist interprets the event of the incarnation by adding 1: 14b–c, thereby making of it a revelation and a final opportunity to see clearly and without distortion the being of the Logos. 'We beheld his glory' is, indeed, as Kaesemann claims, the central affirmation of the whole gospel. The abused, rejected Logos of the history of salvation became present literally – and he received from the sacred people the same treatment as he had received in his pre-incarnate presence. Some, however, saw him for what he is, and theirs is the reward set out in chapter 17 – to be with him where he is, in glory.[1]

1: 15 emphasizes the historical point of view of the evangelist, over against the cosmic view of the hymn. It is a precise expression of the myth of self-revealing Wisdom. John the Baptist confesses his own dependence on the pre-existent Logos, who now has become flesh, 'after him'. There is a strange distortion of normal time in this verse, which can be understood only from the myth – the one who comes after John is the pre-existent Wisdom who is before him, and before all things; the final statement – ὅτι πρῶτός μου ἦν – introduces the notion of ontological superiority in addition to that of temporal priority, showing how the one is tantamount to the other in a historically oriented pattern of thought.

1: 17–18 continue the historical interpretation: the final revelation of the incarnate Logos is compared with the Law, which was also believed to be a manifestation of pre-existent Wisdom.[2] The evangelist is concerned in these verses to emphasize the finality and superiority of the revelation by incarnation; he continues the argument of 1: 15. Just as John, a bearer of the Logos, takes second place to the incarnate Logos, so does the Law. 1: 18 sums up the argument for the priority of the incarnation: in all the previous revelations the Logos was present indirectly – no one can claim on the basis of them to have seen God – but now, 'we have seen his glory'.

The modification of the wisdom myth in the hymn, in terms of the Biblical doctrine of creation and the Christian experience

---

[1] Dodd, *Interpretation*, p. 402; cf. John 12: 37–42.
[2] See the evidence in S.-B. II, pp. 353–8.

of the man Jesus, has been carried further by the evangelist. Beginning from the fact of Jesus, the Logos present in history, he has placed the incarnation in the context of the Biblical history of revelation. Man is not mankind in general endowed with a natural capacity for God – as in the hymn – but the people of Israel, endowed with the presence of the Logos in their prophets and wise men, but rejecting him. In the evangelist we find a view of history that is authentically 'Heilsgeschichte' – a history motivated from beyond this world, not explicable in terms of itself, but only in terms of a pre-existent agent.[1]

Finally, we must ask where, in the evangelist's interpretation, the Prologue begins to speak about the incarnate Logos. Bultmann says that, whereas for the hymn 1 : 14 is the first reference to the incarnate Logos, for the evangelist it occurs at 1 : 5.[2] According to him, 1 : 14 is, in the scheme of the evangelist, a climax to which every statement about the incarnate Logos since verse 5 is anticipatory. For the hymn, however, every statement prior to verse 14 concerns the pre-incarnate Logos, manifested only in creation; and so verse 14 is even more of a climax in the hymn.[3] In both strata, however, the dominant note is the incarnation of the Logos, in verse 14a.

For Kaesemann, the hymn ends at verse 12; verse 14 cannot, therefore, be its climax.[4] The dominant note sounded is in verse 5: καὶ τὸ φῶς ἐν τῇ σκοτίᾳ φαίνει. For him, therefore, it is a hymn to the epiphany of the Logos, rather than to his incarnation. The evangelist understood and accepted this view, adding verses 14–18.[5] He wrote 14a, ὁ λόγος σάρξ ἐγένετο, as a transitional sentence to the important statement in 14: b–c: καὶ ἐθεασάμεθα τὴν δόξαν αὐτοῦ, δόξαν ὡς μονογενοῦς πάρα πατρός.[6] Since the prologue speaks of manifestation, rather than incarnation, the 'incarnate' Logos comes on the scene in verse 5, according to Kaesemann.[7] This view can be maintained only if his estimate of verse 14a is correct.

---

[1] See Kaesemann's illuminating remarks on the idea of 'history' in this gospel, in *Letzter Wille*, pp. 63–8, e.g., 'Geschichtlichkeit ist nicht wirklich ein Attribut der Welt als solcher. Sie gibt es nur, sofern der Schöpfer handelnd auf den Plan tritt' (p. 65).

[2] Bultmann, *Evang.*, p. 4.   [3] *Ibid.*, p. 38.

[4] Kaesemann, 'Aufbau', pp. 166–7 and p. 170.

[5] *Ibid.*, p. 168.   [6] *Ibid.*, pp. 170–1.

[7] *Ibid.*, p. 162.

On this interpretation, neither the hymn nor the evangelist expresses any ontological contrast between the Logos in his pre-incarnate and in his incarnate state. There is no μετάβασις εἰς ἄλλο γένος involved in the incarnation.[1] The real contrast is that between the creator and the creatures, 'Seine Fleischwerdung ist Epiphanie des Schöpfers auf Erden...'[2] 'Flesh' is the possibility of the communication of the Logos, as creator and revealer, with men. This theme is expressed in 1:14c: 'We beheld his glory.' 'Dieses Thema ist zugleich das des gesamten Evangeliums, in welchem es durchweg und allein um die *praesentia dei* in Christus geht.'[3] This is a compelling interpretation, but it cannot be accepted as it stands; if Bultmann has made too much of the incarnation of the Logos, Kaesemann has made too little.

The way to an accurate understanding of the importance of the incarnation for the evangelist, and for the hymn, begins with a re-consideration of the literary evidence. We have seen good reasons for including 1:14 and 1:16 in the hymn. That means that in the hymn the incarnation is the climax of the revelation of the Logos, whose career is traced from his absolute pre-existence, through his pre-incarnate presence in creation, and in history – as the 'natural light' which constitutes in man the possibility of knowing God,[4] and the divine 'wisdom' who has from time to time entered history to save men – to his final self-revelation in his own flesh. The hymn uses the Jewish myth of Wisdom, together with the Philonic idea of the Logos as the

---

[1] *Ibid.*, pp. 172–3.

[2] *Ibid.*, p. 174. Cf. Kaesemann, *Letzter Wille*, p. 28: 'In Wahrheit ändert er nicht sich selbst, sondern nur seinen jeweiligen Ort, und wird er an menschliches Schicksal dahingegeben, um es auf göttliche Weise zu bestehen und zu überwinden.'

[3] 'Aufbau', p. 174. Cf. *Letzter Wille*, pp. 22–3.

[4] It is unfortunate that Kaesemann uses labels like 'Idealism' to refute Ruckstuhl's attempt to do justice to this element in the passage. True, Ruckstuhl is too much an 'Idealist' when he describes this 'natural light' as the natural endowment of will and understanding; but the answer to this is surely not to say that 'evangelical theology does not accept this kind of interpretation.' Rather one should show how, according to the text, this 'natural light' is the possibility of knowing God – a religious, not an anthropological, category (Kaesemann, 'Aufbau', p. 160). Bultmann approaches our understanding when he says apropos of 1:9, 'Es ist dabei vorausgesetzt, dass menschliches Dasein nach dem Lichte fragt, d.h. nach dem Verständnis seiner selbst sucht, und dass es sich gerade im solchem Suchen verirren kann... (*Evang.* p. 32).

image of God in man, to express the career of the Logos. 1 : 14a is not merely a transitional passage by the evangelist, as Kaesemann claims, but the culmination of the hymn, in the sense that the attempts of the Logos to reveal himself in human nature and in the prophets reach their term here. This means, on the one hand, that there is a real continuity between the previous revelations of the Logos and his new incarnate presence, as Kaesemann insists; but it also signifies a decisively new stage in the career of the Logos, as Bultmann emphasizes.

This means that for both the hymn and the evangelist the incarnate Logos begins to be spoken about only in verse 14. Nevertheless, the Logos was present in the world from 1 : 5 on, in his pre-incarnate state. The main change that the evangelist makes in the hymn is to portray the presence of the pre-incarnate Logos in the world in historical rather than in ontological or mythological terms. The pre-incarnate Logos is present as the words of the prophets and wise men of sacred history, not as a 'natural light' in man, nor as a mythological figure who comes from heaven and finds no acceptance on earth (Sir. 24, I Enoch 42).

Nevertheless, for the evangelist, the Logos who spoke by the prophets remains a pre-existent, heavenly being, co-eternal with God. In this respect he is at one with the hymn in presenting the idea of the pre-existent Christ, in the tradition of Hellenistic Judaism. There is something here reminiscent of the 'word of God' of Old Testament prophecy, but it is only a very faint hint. Hellenistic Judaism has transformed the idea of the 'word of God' into the Logos – a pre-existent mediator of creation and revelation.

II. CHAPTER 17

As we have already indicated, chapter 17 is, within the gospel, a counterpart to the prologue and a summary of Johannine Christology.[1] It tells of the return of the Logos to pre-existence. It is the climax of the 'farewell discourses' (chs. 13–17), and immediately thereafter the passion narrative begins.

[1] Dodd, *Interpretation*, p. 420: 'the climax of the thought of the whole gospel'; Barrett, *Gospel*, p. 417, 'The present prayer is a summary of Johannine theology relative to the work of Christ'. Bultmann, *Evang.*, p. 1; Kaesemann, *Letzter Wille*, pp. 12–13.

Before we begin to consider the ideas contained in this chapter we must take note of certain literary problems. The 'farewell discourses' are notoriously unsatisfactory in their present arrangement. The extent of the problem can be appreciated from a brief glance at Bultmann's attempt to arrange them in some rational order. According to him they are to be read in the following order: 13: 1a (omit 1bff.), 13: 2–30, 13: 31, 1b, 4a; 17: 1b–26 (omit 1a), 13: 31–5, 15: 1 – 16: 33, 13: 36 – 14: 31. The opening of chapter 17 would, on this plan, comprise 13: 31a, 1b, 4a, and 17: 1b.[1] However ingenious this reconstruction might be, it involves too many tiny modifications, such as the splitting up of 13: 1–4, 13: 31 and 17: 1, to be convincing.[2] There is no theory that could account for such an atomizing of the original text. Furthermore, the prayer in chapter 17 is so climactic in tone that it is more likely to be in its original place at the end of the 'farewell discourses' than in the place suggested by Bultmann; any discourse which followed it would be an anticlimax. To say that we are not convinced by Bultmann is not to imply that we are satisfied that the present order of the 'farewell discourses' is original; it is rather to recognize that the problem remains to be solved. One thing is clear; that the interpretation of chapter 17 must take passages such as 13: 1–4, 31–5 and 12: 20–33 into account; but we do not at present have sufficient grounds for changing their place in the Johannine order so as to bring out the interconnections more clearly.

The form of the 'farewell discourses' as a whole is that of a Hellenistic, mystical, revelatory discourse, such as those found in C.H. I and XIII. In each of these the revealer, in a discourse, tells his 'son' the way of salvation, and it ends with a prayer or hymn, the recital of which by the recipient of revelation constitutes his salvation or union with the divinity.[3]

---

[1] Bultmann, *Evang.*, p. 351.

[2] See the criticism of Bultmann's theory in D. M. Smith, *Composition and Order*; Bultmann's' revelatory discourses' source, to which he attributes the 'farewell discourses', has not been generally accepted. It is more likely that we have the work of the evangelist in these discourses.

[3] C.H. I. 31–2, XIII. 17–20, cf. v. 10b–11, Asclepius (Latin) 41, cited by Dodd, *Interpretation*, pp. 420–3 (p. 420 n. 1); Barrett, *Gospel*, pp. 417–18, who also (p. 324) cites the following remarkable parallel to 17: 1 from a miracle worker's prayer to Isis: Ἴσις...δόξασόν μοι ὡς ἐδόξασα τὸ ὄνομα τοῦ υἱοῦ σου Ὥρος (Pap. Lond. 121. 503ff.).

That is to say, they are a dialogue on initiation into eternal life through the knowledge of God, ending with a prayer or hymn which is itself the final stage of initiation.[1]

If this judgement is correct, and we see no reason to doubt it, two consequences follow: chapter 17 cannot occur at any other place in the discourses than its present final one; and, wherever else we may look for aid in understanding it, we must pay serious attention to the religion of the Hermetica.

Barrett divides the chapter into four sections, as follows: (i) 17: 1–5, Jesus addresses the Father; (ii) 17: 6–19, Jesus prays for the disciples gathered around him; (iii) 17: 22–4, the scope of the prayer is extended to include those who will believe because of the witness of the disciples; and (iv) 17: 25–6, Jesus reviews the results of his ministry. Bultmann divides it as follows: (i) 13: 31a, 1bff., introduction, Jesus is the complete Gnostic, knowing where he comes from, whither he is going, who are those who belong to him, and the hour of his departure; (ii) 17: 1–5, the request for glorification, in which, using the language of the Gnostic redeemer myth, Jesus expresses that he has become 'the eschatological event beyond which history cannot go'; (iii) 17: 6–26, the intercession for the community, which firstly states the grounds for the intercession (6–8) – by their faith they have shown that they are not of this world; secondly prays for the protection and sanctification of the community (9–19); thirdly prays for the unity of the community (20–3) and fourthly prays for the fulfilment of the believers, in heavenly union with the exalted Christ. Neither of these analyses is entirely satisfactory, but they do provide a point of departure. We cannot accept Bultmann's introduction, on literary grounds; but it does direct us to passages in the gospel which form the background against which the chapter must be interpreted.

In 13: 1–4, where the 'farewell discourses' begin, Jesus is introduced as one who knows that the hour has come for him to leave the world of men, who knows that he has power over the all, given him by the Father, and 'that he came forth from the Father, and returns to him' (ὅτι ἀπὸ θεοῦ ἐξῆλθεν καὶ πρὸς τὸν θεὸν ὑπάγει, verse 4). He is also intimately bound up with 'his own who are in the world' (13: 1). In a new departure the work

---

[1] Dodd, *Interpretation*, p. 422.

of the revealer is described as love (13: 1).[1] Only from the perspective of the end of his work could it be characterized in this way.[2] Thus the gospel expresses the eternal bond between Christ and the Church.

One has, however, to go back even further than 13: 1–4 in order to put chapter 17 in perspective. As Bultmann points out, 12: 20–33 raises the question how the believers are related to Christ after he has 'gone away', the question which the 'farewell discourses' seek to answer. The gentiles who ask to 'see Jesus' (12: 21) are symbolic of the believers beyond the circle of those who saw his earthly glory. In answer to their request, the evangelist presents the death of Jesus as the exaltation which makes access to Jesus universally possible. This is dramatically stated when, instead of the expected response to the request of the 'Greeks', Jesus solemnly pronounces, 'The hour has come for the Son of Man to be glorified' (12: 23) and, after some elaboration, 'I, if I be lifted up from the earth will draw all men to myself' (κἀγὼ ἐὰν ὑψωθῶ ἐκ τῆς γῆς, πάντας ἑλκύσω πρὸς ἐμαυτόν, 12: 32). The usual dramatic irony is present, and the crowd asks, 'Who is this Son of Man?' (12: 35), a very important hint of the interpretative background of the subsequent discourses.

There follows in 12: 37ff.[3] a sort of editorial summary of the gospel up to this point: despite the miracles he had performed they did not believe in him. This fulfils the prophecies of Isaiah (53: 1 in verse 38; 6: 9 in verse 40). 'Isaiah said this because he saw his glory and spoke about him' (ταῦτα εἶπεν Ἡσαίας ὅτι εἶδεν τὴν δόξαν αὐτοῦ, καὶ ἐλάλησεν περὶ αὐτοῦ, 12: 41). The myth of pre-existent Wisdom which we discovered in the Prologue is present here. Isaiah's vision (Is. 6: 1ff.) was a vision of

---

[1] Bultmann, *Evang.*, p. 372; Dodd, *Interpretation*, p. 398, presents a table which demonstrates how ἀγάπη is a 'new key-word' in the farewell discourses. Prior to the discourses the words ἀγάπη and ἀγαπᾶν are used only 6 times to describe the work of Christ: ζωή, φῶς and related words are used 82 times to describe his work. In the discourses, the latter class of words is used only 6 times, while ἀγαπᾶν and its derivatives are used 31 times.

[2] Bultmann, *Evang.*

[3] Bultmann transposes 12: 34–6 to 8: 29, and 8: 30–40 to 12: 33; after 8: 40 he reads 6: 60–71 and concludes the section with 12: 37–43. 12: 44–50 he transposes to 9: 29, where it is read after 8: 12 and before 8: 21–9 and 12: 34–6.

the pre-existent Logos; his message was a form of the pre-incarnate presence of the Logos; the fate of Isaiah's message – its rejection – is the paradigmatic fate of the Logos in the world of men. The incarnate Logos is about to play out the perpetual drama of the sacred history, once again, and once for all time.

The next section, 12: 44–50, may be out of place. Bultmann makes it part of the discourse on light in chapter 9; but if we read the present order, it is another reminder of the heavenly origin and nature of the revealer.

The immediate background of the 'farewell discourses', therefore, is the presentation of the crucifixion as the 'glorification-by-exaltation' of the pre-existent Logos, the return to heavenly glory which makes universal access to the Logos possible. Thus ends 'the revelation of the Glory to the World' – which is Bultmann's description of chapters 1–12 – and 'the revelation of the Glory to the Community' (chs. 13–20) is about to begin.

Against this background the reader can understand the shattering significance of the 'foot-washing'; and he follows with heightened awe the last words of the pre-existent Logos as he prepares to depart. These solemn words reach their climax in the prayer of chapter 17. The 'farewell discourses' begin with an act, 'the foot washing', move through dialogue to monologue (chapters 14–16) and culminate when the revealer speaks no longer to his disciples, but to his Father.[1]

Kaesemann has called chapter 17 'The Last Will of Jesus'. This applies to all the farewell discourses, however. Chapter 17 is, more precisely, the 'last words' of Jesus – traditionally the weightiest that a man will ever speak.[2] It is not a prayer in the sense of a request for divine aid; rather, it is a conversation between equals. As Kaesemann says, 'the disciples are witnesses to a conversation between the Father and the Son...they penetrate the depths of a heavenly event'.[3] This is a revelation of the

---

[1] Dodd, *Interpretation*, p. 400; W. D. Davies, *Invitation to the New Testament* (New York, 1966), p. 467, and *Paul*, p. 110 n. 1, suggests that the Jewish rite of the Passover meal is the *Sitz im Leben* of the farewell discourses. The questions asked by the disciples reflect the questions asked by the children in the Passover rite. We find this less convincing than Dodd's view of a 'Hermetic' background, which we have followed.

[2] Kaesemann, *Letzter Wille*, pp. 14–15.

[3] *Ibid.*, p. 16.

'Eternal Gospel', of Rev. 14: 6, a secret revelation to the disciples:[1] that Jesus is the eternal Logos, in the beginning with God (παρὰ σεαυτῷ and παρὰ σοί, 17: 5, cf. πρὸς τὸν θεόν, 1: 1).

There is no need for us to give a detailed exegesis of the whole chapter. It is clearly the work of the evangelist and full of Johannine phrases.[2] Rather, we shall concentrate on those verses which are important for the idea of pre-existence. Verse 1 introduces the prayer: Jesus addresses his Father, saying that the 'hour' so often referred to in the gospel has come – the hour of his death, which is also the hour of his glorification. Jesus repeats as a prayer precisely what he says in an address to the people in 12: 23. The first phrase which calls for close attention is in 17: 2. With the full force of its double meaning, the evangelist has Jesus use the word 'glorify': 'Glorify me [i.e. exalt me through the Cross] in order that I may glorify thee [i.e. draw all men unto you] [cf. 12: 32] even as you have given me authority over all flesh [cf. 5: 27] to give eternal life to everyone whom you have given me.'

C. H. Dodd[3] suggests that 17: 2 might reflect the influence of the common early Christian tradition concerning the Son of Man. The phrase ἔδωκας αὐτῷ ἐξουσίαν πάσης σαρκός recalls Matt. 28: 18, ἐδόθη μοι πᾶσα ἐξουσία ἐν οὐρανῷ καὶ ἐπὶ τῆς γῆς. The phrase πᾶσα σάρξ is a Semiticism, used frequently in the LXX to translate כל בשר. It is, however, uncommon in the New Testament. The phrase ἐξουσία πάσης σαρκὸς does not occur in the LXX, but in Bel and the Dragon 5, the phrase πάσης σαρκὸς κυρείαν occurs, in which the word κυρεία is a synonym for ἐξουσία. The phrase ἐδόθη ἐξουσία occurs in LXX Dan. 7: 14, where it is part of the description of the enthronement of the Son of Man, as Lord over the four 'beasts', a vision which partakes of the traditional creation-imagery, part of the story in Gen. 1: 28 (cf. Ps. 8: 7–8) concerning the Lordship of man over the beasts.

Dodd concludes that the sentence 'you have given him authority over all flesh' is an 'epitome, entirely in Biblical lan-

---

[1] *Ibid.*, p. 17.

[2] Dodd, *Historical Tradition in the Fourth Gospel* (Cambridge, 1963), p. 361. He cites the following examples (n. 2): ἐλήλυθεν ἡ ὥρα, δοξάζειν, ζωὴ αἰώνιος, γινώσκειν θεόν, ἀληθινός, ἔργον τελειοῦν, ὁ δέδωκας αὐτῷ.

[3] Dodd, *Historical Tradition*, pp. 361–3.

guage, of the vision of the enthronement of the Son of Man in Daniel 7'. We are persuaded by Dodd's argument, and would point out further that in John 5: 27 the following sentence occurs: καὶ ἐξουσίαν ἔδωκεν αὐτῷ κρίσιν ποιεῖν, ὅτι υἱὸς ἀνθρώπου ἐστίν.[1] Here the phrase ἐξουσίαν ἔδωκεν αὐτῷ is explicitly connected with the Son of Man. This seems to suggest that either John or his tradition associated the phrase concerning authority with the idea of the Son of Man, and to provide support for Dodd's thesis that 17: 2 reflects the influence of Dan. 7. John 17 tells about the 'enthronement' of Jesus as the Son of Man.

In 12: 34c, which we believe to be part of the setting of the 'farewell discourses', the people ask, 'Who is this Son of Man?' In the light of Dodd's interpretation of 17: 2, one might see chapter 17 as part of the answer to that question. The Son of Man is Jesus, now returning to 'glory'.

Jesus Christ – the Son of Man – is the one sent from God (17: 3), and to know this is eternal life. He has finished the work which he was sent to perform (17: 4) – of judging and life-giving[2] – and prays, 'Now glorify me, Father, in thy presence, with the glory which I had in thy presence before the world was' (καὶ νῦν δόξασόν με σύ, πάτερ, παρὰ σεαυτῷ τῇ δόξῃ ᾗ εἶχον πρὸ τοῦ τὸν κόσμον εἶναι παρὰ σοί, 17: 5). This language recalls the language of the Prologue and suggests that the content of the 'glory' for which he prays might be seen by reading 1: 1–4 again. It is pre-existence πρὸς τὸν θεὸν (1: 1, cf. παρὰ σεαυτῷ and παρὰ σοί in 17: 5). The images of the 'Son of Man' and the 'Logos' are, therefore, blended in this passage.

At this point, the attention of the prayer shifts to the disciples; to those whom (the Father) 'gave me out of the world.' They were always the Father's, and he gave them to the Son. Their election is confirmed by their obedience to God's word (17: 6).

---

[1] The absence of the articles does not mean that John does not have the Son of Man in mind. See Barrett, *Gospel*, p. 218, who suggests that he may even be returning to the precise words of Dan. 7: 13 (ὡς) υἱὸς ἀνθρώπου; thus also S. Schulz, *Untersuchungen*, pp. 111–13. A. J. B. Higgins, *Jesus and the Son of Man* (London, 1964), pp. 165–7, believes that the rule that 'definite predicate nouns preceding a verb usually lack the article' (Moule, *Idiom Book*, pp. 115ff.) explains the grammatical case; he also believes that the form of the title is determined by its Semitic origin.

[2] Bultmann, *Evang.* pp. 378–9.

The basis of the Christian community, therefore, is the 'election' of God; only those who always have 'belonged to' God receive the revelation of his name.[1] The real origin of the Church is in God; not in the world. The idea of the divine origin of those 'spiritual ones' who accept the message of the revealer, is a characteristic part of the redeemer-myth, as Bultmann presents it, especially in its gnostic expression.[2] In the apocalyptic myth of the Son of Man, as it occurs, for instance, in the Parables of Enoch, the idea of the solidarity of the redeemer with his own is expressed as the pre-existence of the community of the righteous with the Son of Man.[3] There is, therefore, a transcendent ground of unity between Christ and the Church, namely, the eternal will of God by which He acknowledged those who belonged to Him, and then gave them to Christ.

Receiving the revelation of God's name (17: 6) is tantamount to recognizing the words and deeds of Jesus as the words and deeds of God, that is, recognizing 'that I came out from you and...that you sent me' (ὅτι παρὰ σοῦ ἐξῆλθον, καὶ...ὅτι σύ με ἀπέστειλας, 17: 8). Recognition that the earthly Jesus is the pre-existent Logos is of the essence of Johannine faith.

The prayer continues in 17: 9–10 to emphasize the community of activity between the Father and the Son, and begins to focus particularly on the distinction between the Christian community and the world. He prays for his own, not for the world (17: 9), because they are His and the Father's, and through them the Father and the Son will continue to be 'glorified', that is, continue to be present in the world even after the departure of Jesus (17: 11).

At the end of verse 11 we hear that the real concern of Jesus is that the community be united. He kept them together[4] while he was with them, but after his departure they will experience the

---

[1] *Ibid.*, pp. 380–1. It is not the 'name' in the sense of a magical word endowed with power to effect the ascent of the soul, as in Hellenistic mysticism or magic. Cf. 12: 28, 17: 11, 26. The meaning of the revelation of the 'name' is explained in 17: 8ff.; it is the 'words' which God gave the Son to reveal.

[2] *Ibid.*, p. 395 n. 4.

[3] A. Schweitzer, *Mysticism*, pp. 102–3; I En. 38: 1–5, 62: 7–8, 14–15. We have discussed this in the chapter on Paul, pp. 103–92 above.

[4] The primary reference of this statement is to the twelve disciples only, as the mentioning of Judas, the exception, indicates, and this is in accordance with the dramatic setting. The 'twelve' symbolize all the Church.

hatred of the world, 'because they do not have their origin in the world even as I do not have my origin in the world' (ὅτι οὐκ εἰσὶν ἐκ τοῦ κόσμου καθὼς ἐγὼ οὐκ εἰμὶ ἐκ τοῦ κόσμου, 17: 14, cf. verse 16). In a striking way the solidarity of the revealer and his community as heavenly entities is set forth in these verses. This unity is underlined in 17: 18, when the mission of the Church in the world is compared with that of Christ to the world. The foundation of the Church's mission is Christ's completed work; therefore he offers himself in consecration as a sacrifice (17: 19).[1]

In verses 20ff. the main emphasis is also on the unity of the Church; Jesus prays that they may be preserved in unity in order that men may believe that Jesus is the one sent from God (17: 20–1). Belief in Jesus can arise only if the Church remains united; the reason for this is expressed in 17: 22. Verse 22 is the climax of the series of statements which have identified Christ and the Church-in-the-world. The revelation of the name of God is now described as the giving to the community by Jesus of the 'glory' which he received from the Father, and the object of this endowment is that 'they may be one as we are one'. The 'glory' of Jesus is his work as revealer, his being the one sent from the Father who brings life to the world. To give his glory to the community is to make it a participant in his work of revelation – as is said in verses 18, 21 and 23b.

'Indeed', Bultmann writes,

that he gives them his glory means that they represent him in the world after he has gone away that, his 'history' never becomes a piece of the past, but rather, that as the eschatological event, it remains always present in the world, in the eschatological community.[2]

In verse 23 the relationship between Christ, God and the Church is expressed by ἀγαπᾶν.

The next verse of the prayer (17: 24) is well described by Bultmann as a prayer for the fulfilment of the believers in heavenly union with the exalted Logos.

Father, I desire that those also whom thou hast given me may be with me where I am, to see my glory, which you have given me because you loved me before the foundation of the world.

[1] Barrett, *Gospel*, p. 426–7.   [2] Bultmann, *Evang.*, p. 395.

(Πατήρ, ὃ δέδωκάς μοι, θέλω ἵνα ὅπου εἰμὶ ἐγὼ κἀκεῖνοι ὦσιν μετ' ἐμοῦ, ἵνα θεωρῶσιν τὴν δόξαν τὴν ἐμήν, ἣν δέδωκάς μοι ὅτι ἠγάπησάς με πρὸ καταβολῆς κόσμου, 17: 24.)

The destiny of the believers is to be with Christ in glory – the glory which the Father gives him at the Resurrection and Ascension, which can be spoken of in the Perfect tense as if already given, because of the love He had for the Logos before the world began. Verses 25–6 summarize the prayer and bring it to a conclusion.

The prayer in chapter 17 tells of the pre-existent Christ, who came forth from God and is about to return to him, but who already speaks as if the return had been accomplished. It also tells of a pre-existent community, whose origins are not in this world, and whose destiny is the same as Christ's. While it is on earth, the community is the presence of Christ in the world. Christ returning to glory is portrayed, by implication, as the Son of Man – he who in 12: 23 and 32–4 must be 'lifted up to glory' on the Cross, in order to draw all men to himself.

III. THE SON OF MAN, A PRE-EXISTENT HEAVENLY BEING ON EARTH

There have been hints so far – 17: 2, 12: 34c, 5: 27 – that the figure of the Son of Man played some part in the Johannine presentation of Christ as a pre-existent heavenly being; here we shall follow them up.[1]

The phrase 'Son of Man' is used thirteen times in the gospel, compared to fourteen times in Mark; the evangelist must have been indebted for it to the common tradition of early Christianity.[2] Schulz has tried to show that the sayings about the Son of Man constitute relatively stable units of tradition, a series of

[1] Dodd, *Interpretation*, pp. 241–9, gives a judicious discussion of the theme 'Son of Man' in the gospel. Cf. p. 279, where he argues that 'Son of Man' is one of the ways in which John refers to the Logos, since in Philo the Logos is, amongst other things, ὁ ἀληθινὸς ἄνθρωπος. Other recent treatments include Stephen S. Smalley, 'The Johannine Son of Man Sayings', *N.T.S.* 15 (1968–9), 278–301; E. D. Freed, 'The Son of Man in the Fourth Gospel', *J.B.L.* 86 (1967), 402–9, and the important work by J. Louis Martyn, *History and Theology in the Fourth Gospel* (New York, 1968), pp. 91–142.

[2] Dodd, *Interpretation*, p. 241; R. Schnackenburg, 'Der Menschensohn im Johannesevangelium', *N.T.S.* 11 (1964–5), 123–37.

which he calls a 'theme', but he has not succeeded in showing that they represent more than a motif.[1] He believed he could demonstrate that the 'theme' of the Son of Man originated in Jewish apocalyptic circles and went through two editings, modifying it in the direction of the Gnostic idea of the heavenly Anthropos; but without success.[2] We cannot delineate the clear profile of a theme which begins in an apocalyptic matrix and grows towards Gnosticism. The problem of different sources for the various Son of Man sayings is best considered, to the extent that it is necessary and, at this point in time, possible, during our consideration of the texts.

The passages in question may be classified under four headings: (A) Coming and Going, 1: 51, 3: 13, 6: 62; (B) Exalted and Glorified (= Crucified), 3: 14, 8: 28, 12: 23, 12: 34 (occurs twice), 13: 31; (C) Judge, 5: 27; (D) Salvation-bringer, 6: 27, 53, 9: 35.

(A. 1) *Coming and Going*

(*i*) *1: 51.* Truly, truly, I say to you, you will see heaven opened and the angels of God ascending and descending upon the Son of Man.

This verse concludes the section on the call of Nathanael which begins at verse 45. It is set off from the foregoing by the

---

[1] Schulz, *Untersuchungen*; J. M. Robinson, 'Recent Research in the Fourth Gospel', *J.B.L.* 78 (1959), 242–52. Robinson summarizes the description of a 'theme' thus: 'A certain term (or pair of terms such as "Son of Man") forms the center (a) around which motifs cluster, some of which are expressed (b) with a constant terminology and some (c) with merely a constant meaning; and of course any individual saying reflecting a 'theme' may have (d) motifs peculiar to itself and not shared with other sayings of the same "theme"' (p. 248, Schulz, *Untersuchungen*, p. 87). Robinson points out that, in the case of the 'Son of Man' passages, (b) the constant terminology, is missing, and concludes, correctly we believe, that without this there can be no 'theme' in Schulz's sense, only a motif (p. 249). 1: 51, 3: 13–15, 5: 27–9, 6: 27, 53, 13: 31ff. are the sayings which Schulz regards as relatively complete, and on which he bases the argument for a theme. In 6: 62, 8: 28, 12: 23 and 34, 'splinters' of the Son of Man theme occur. The absence of common terminology in the former groups is evident; and if that group cannot be identified, the 'splinters' certainly cannot be either.

[2] Robinson, 'Recent Research', pp. 250–1. Cf. Smalley, 'Johannine Son of Man', for an attempt to locate the background of these sayings in Jewish apocalyptic and in the teaching of Jesus. We find his conclusions less acceptable than those of Schulz, although there is much of value in his article.

solemn introduction, ἀμὴν ἀμὴν, so that Bultmann believes it to be the work of the evangelist, appended to a source.[1] Schulz, on the other hand, holds that a tradition is represented here. His analysis is most convincing, even though his theory about a 'theme' does not satisfy.

According to Schulz, there are two strata of ideas in the saying: (a) The Jacob–Bethel motif and (b) the Son of Man motif. The former is expressed by ἄγγελοι τοῦ θεοῦ ἀναβαίνειν καὶ καταβαίνειν ἐπὶ (LXX, Gen. 28: 12), and the latter by ὄψεσθε τὸν οὐρανὸν ἀνεῳγότα καὶ τὸν υἱὸν τοῦ ἀνθρώπου.[2] In Schulz's view the latter stratum predominates, because Jesus is identified with the Son of Man; the Bethel motif serves only to express the content of this identification.[3]

The Jacob–Bethel motif obviously comes from Gen. 28: 12.[4] In the LXX the angels ascend and descend ἐπ' αὐτῆς, which presumably refers to the ladder, κλῖμαξ (= ladder) being feminine like αὐτῆς. There are indications in a later Rabbinic Midrash that in some circles Gen. 28: 12 was interpreted to say that the angels were ascending and descending on Jacob (Bereshith Rabbah, 68: 12, 69: 3).[5] According to the Midrash the interpretation 'upon the ladder' occasions no difficulty; but 'upon Jacob' needs some explanation. Freedman (Soncino edition) translates the explanation in Ber. Rab. 68: 12 as follows:

The statement that they were ascending and descending on Jacob we must take to mean that some were exalting him and others degrading him, dancing, leaping and maligning him. Thus it says, 'Israel in whom I will be glorified' [Is. 49: 3]; it is it thou said the angels whose features [εἰκών – אקין] are engraved on high; they ascended on high and saw his features [εἰκόνιον – אקונין] and they descended below and found him sleeping.[6]

---

[1] Bultmann, *Evang.*, pp. 74–6; R. E. Brown, *John*, pp. 88–9, confirms the view that it is relatively independent of its context.

[2] Schulz, *Untersuchungen*, p. 98.   [3] *Ibid.*, pp. 102–3.

[4] See R. E. Brown, *John*, pp. 88–92, for a judicious discussion of this subject, and a good bibliography.

[5] English text in *Midrash Rabbah*, *Genesis*, Vol. II, trans. H. Freedman (Soncino, London, 1939), pp. 626 and 631. For a discussion see Brown, *John*, pp. 90–1; Dodd, *Interpretation*, pp. 245–6; Bultmann, *Evang.*, p. 74 n. 4.

[6] Freedman, *Midrash Rabbah*, p. 626. Cf. Dodd, *Interpretation*, p. 245, who follows Burney's translation of Odeberg's Hebrew text, which differs somewhat from Freedman's. The Greek and Hebrew in the translation were added from Burney's version as quoted by Dodd.

This seems like an attempt to 'demythologize' the view of Jacob as a figure who joins heaven and earth like a ladder.[1] Instead, the passage suggests that Jacob on earth is related to Jacob in heaven as a copy is to its archetype. A myth in which Jacob was a great figure uniting heaven and earth has been translated into Platonic categories.[2]

John seems to have known and accepted the interpretation of Gen. 28: 12 which understood it to say that the angels ascended and descended on Jacob. For Jacob he substituted the 'Son of Man', whom he also probably understood as a representative figure, as Jacob was the representative of the people of Israel.[3] Bultmann accepts, in its general outline, this view of the background of 1: 51,[4] while Barrett accepts it with caution,[5] and Brown finds the argument unconvincing.[6] It is dangerous to use a midrash from the third century to elucidate the New Testament; nevertheless, with due caution, we follow Dodd in allowing it to illuminate, to whatever extent it can, the plain statement in 1: 51 that the angels ascended and descended upon the Son of Man. The Son of Man is the place where eternity is present in time, where the 'gates of heaven' are.

The other layer of interpretation isolated by Schulz says that the heavens will open and the believers will see the Son of Man. I Enoch 46: 4, 55: 4 and 62: 1 speak of 'seeing' the Son of Man in his final self-revelation, and I Enoch 38: 1–5, 62: 7–8, 14–15, 49: 3 and 71: 14ff., tell of the solidarity of the righteous in a community with the Son of Man. Higgins, following Matthew Black, would have the revelation of the Son of Man as the sole important content of 1: 51.[7] By translating the ἐπί in question

---

[1] The same process occurs in Ber. Rabb. 69: 3. If the text intends 'on him' (i.e. Jacob) by עליו it should be read 'over him', in the sense that God 'stood protectingly over him' (Freedman, *Midrash*, p. 631).

[2] Cf. L. Wächter, 'Der Einfluss platonischen Denkens auf rabbinische Schöpfungsspekulationen', in *Z.R.G.G.* 14 (1962), 36–56.

[3] C. H. Dodd, *Interpretation*, pp. 245–6. Dodd also makes much of the reference to Is. 49: 3 in Ber. Rabb. 68: 12, and shows how throughout the gospel there seems to be an element in the presentation of Jesus drawn from the 'Servant passages' (e.g. Is. 49: 3 and John 13: 31, 12: 23, Is. 49: 5, John 11: 52, Is. 49: 6, John 12: 46, 8: 12) (*ibid.*, pp. 246–7).

[4] Bultmann, *Evang.*, pp. 74–5. He does not share Dodd's view of the Son of Man as a 'collective' figure.

[5] Barrett, *Gospel*, p. 156.   [6] R. E. Brown, *John*, pp. 90–1.

[7] Higgins, *Jesus and the Son of Man*, pp. 158–9. M. Black in his *Aramaic*

as 'towards' rather than 'upon', he interprets the verse to be describing the heavens opening to reveal the Son of Man, with the angels converging upon him, and moving away from him. The argument is difficult to decide; however, we see enough reason cautiously to follow Dodd, Bultmann and Schulz in seeing two elements in the verse: the Son of Man as the ladder between heaven and earth, and the Son of Man revealed in heaven and on earth as this glorious bridge.

It is interesting to note that in Ber. Rabb. 68: 12 the explanation of the interpretation 'upon Jacob' draws upon the idea of the heavenly archetype and earthly copy of Jacob. Presumably, the theme of the revealing of the Son of Man in its original form, before it was blended with the interpretation of Gen. 28: 12 to make 1: 51, referred to the revealing of the heavenly Son of Man. If Ber. Rabb. 68: 12 and John 1: 51 belong to the same tradition, and if Schulz is right that 1:51 is made up of a 'ladder' theme and a 'revelation of the Son of Man' theme, the interesting fact emerges that what 1: 51 combines, Ber. Rabb. 68: 12 uses antithetically. It uses a 'modified' form of the 'revelation theme' to explain away the 'theme' of Jacob as the ladder.

Whatever the truth of these speculations may be, John 1: 51 states clearly that the Son of Man is an entity who exists both in heaven and on earth, and thus links the two realms. We see in this a mythological version of the Middle Platonic Logos we know from Philo. Perhaps the best parallel to this text is the Poimandres. C. H. Dodd's summary of the background of all the 'Son of Man' sayings in John may aptly be considered here. He writes:

At any rate, the statements about the Son of Man which are actually made in the Fourth Gospel recall the figure of the heavenly Ἄνθρωπος as we have met it in Hellenistic documents. Whatever may have been the remoter origins of this conception, it meets us in a common and characteristic form in the Hermetic literature, in Hellenistic Judaism as represented by Philo, and in early, semi-Christian or near-Christian 'Gnosticism' – that is to say, in an area of religious thought which, though exposed to various influences, shows most markedly the influence of Platonism and of the more speculative Judaism.[1]

Approach to the Gospels and Acts, p. 85, argues that the Aramaic *al* translated ἐπί in John 1: 51 means 'towards'.

[1] Dodd, *Interpretation*, pp. 243–4.

The best explanation, therefore, of the heavenly archetype whose presence in 1: 51 is implied, is the evidence from Philo and the Hermetica which we have already set out. The archetype is like the Logos, the ἀληθινὸς ἄνθρωπος, or like the first man of Poimandres. There is no precise analogy in these texts to the image of the Son of Man as the ladder between heaven and earth; nevertheless, it is not difficult to imagine how exegesis of the kind we find in Philo could have produced this image out of Gen. 28: 12. It seems also to have produced such an image in the rabbinic tradition.

A striking feature of John 1: 51 is the way in which it combines Hellenistic-Jewish images with apocalyptic terminology. The milieu out of which the saying came was one in which Jewish Platonism and Jewish apocalypticism were blending. R. E. Brown points out an important feature of this process of blending in John 1: 51. The presence of angels with the Son of Man seems, in the apocalyptic traditions behind the New Testament in general, to signify most often the parousia or the resurrection; that is, angels are a sign of eschatological thinking. For example, in Matt. 26: 64 (par. Mk. 14: 62), Jesus replies to Caiaphas' question, whether he is 'the Christ, the Son of God':

The words are yours. But I tell you this: from now on, you will see the Son of Man seated at the right hand of God and coming on the clouds of heaven. (N.E.B.)

This saying is similar in form, content and setting to John 1: 51, which is a comment on Nathanael's statements about Jesus as the Messiah. Its placing on the eve of Jesus' death, resurrection and ascension, probably indicates the earliest place of such 'Son of Man' sayings in the tradition. Matt. 16: 27–8 (par. Mk. 8: 38b), 'For the Son of Man is to come in the glory of his Father with his angels...' also testifies to the original eschatological force of such sayings. Brown concludes:

We may also suspect that the original meaning of the saying [1: 51] was a reference to the resurrection or to the parousia, where the presence of the angels about the glorified Son of Man would be appropriate. There are no angelophanies in the Johannine account of the public ministry; but angels are associated in all the gospel accounts with the empty tomb and often with the final judgement.[1]

[1] Brown, *John*, p. 89.

If Brown is right, and we see no reason to doubt that he is, John 1: 51 is a good example of the translation of eschatology into protology, by means of Platonic-mythological categories drawn from Hellenistic Judaism. Since all the Johannine 'Son of Man' sayings seem to have been 'de-eschatologized' in similar fashion, this observation might serve as a comment on all the texts we have yet to discuss.

(*ii*) *3: 13*.[1] And no one has ascended to heaven save he who came down from heaven, namely, the Son of Man.

The revealer insists that he alone can tell men of 'the heavenly things' (τὰ ἐπουράνια, 12b) because he alone is the one who has come down from heaven (ὁ ἐκ τοῦ οὐρανοῦ καταβάς); he alone is the Son of Man. These words are reminiscent of 1: 18;[2] like the conclusion to the prologue they insist that the revealer is the only one who can tell men about the Father. There could be no more direct statement: the Son of Man is the pre-existent revealer on earth.

It is as Son of Man that Jesus forms the link between heaven and earth; his earthly existence is the place where heavenly things become visible, and also the place where heavenly things are rejected by mankind.[3]

We may note that the ascent is spoken of in the perfect tense (ἀναβέβηκεν) as if it had already taken place. The one who descended is the one who has already ascended. Here we see, once again, how John has translated an eschatological idea into protological terms. The ascension, already achieved, is presented in terms of pre-existence. This leads to the awkwardness

---

[1] Bultmann, *Evang.*, p. 107 n. 4, is uncertain whether this comes from the evangelist or from a source.

[2] Higgins, *Son of Man*, pp. 171–3, points to Eph. 4: 8–10 and Rom. 10: 6 as evidence of the same tradition of ascent/descent in the Pauline school; he considers Acts 2: 34ff. as 'positive proof that ἀναβαίνειν, the word used in John, was used in the early preaching in connection with the ascent of Jesus to heavenly glory' (p. 172). He takes this to indicate that 'like ὑψοῦν another term in kerygmatic use, ἀναβαίνειν was coupled with the Son of Man in a tradition used only by the fourth evangelist'.

[3] Barrett, *Gospel*, p. 177. Cf. I Enoch 70: 2, 71: 1, with the exception that there is no prior ascent to heavenly glory in John, because of the pre-existence of Christ.

of the statement: 'no one has ascended into heaven, excepting him who descended.' The fact that he ascended into heaven was possible only because Christ was the one who had *previously* descended.

(*iii*) *6: 62* Does this scandalize you? What, therefore, if you were to see the Son of Man ascending to where he was before?[1]

The previous saying is part of a reply to Nicodemus, who fails to understand the discourse on the 'birth from above'. It tells of the coming to earth of the Son of Man. The present saying is a response to those who fail to understand the sayings about the necessity to eat the flesh and drink the blood of the revealer (6: 52ff.). It tells of the going of the Son of Man to heaven. In both cases the conclusive evidence offered in support of the authority of a discourse or injunction is a reference to the origin or destination of the speaker; his authority rests on the fact that he came from heaven and returns thither. True, the method of departure, by way of the Cross, would increase the 'scandal' of his teaching and person, for those who were 'not his own', but for the elect the argument is decisive.

B. *Exalted and Glorified* (= *Crucified*)

(*i*) *3: 14* And as Moses lifted up the serpent in the wilderness, so must the Son of Man be lifted up, so that whosoever believes in him might have eternal life. (Cf. 8: 28, 12: 32 and 34.)

3: 14 belongs together with 3: 13[2] yet it does express a new and separate idea; that the return of the Son of Man to pre-existence is by way of the Cross, and that the Cross has saving power for those who believe. Verse 13, although it does not neglect the ascent – speaking about it, in fact, in the past tense (ἀναβέβηκεν)

---

[1] Bultmann, *Evang.*, p. 340 n. 1, assigns this to the evangelist. He reads it after 8: 37–40, as part of a section on the 'affront' which the revealer was.

[2] Higgins, *Son of Man*, p. 161, classifies the former as 'non-Synoptic', within his 'Synoptic' and 'non-Synoptic' arrangement It is controlled by the καταβαίνειν–ἀναβαίνειν scheme which is thoroughly Johannine. In 3: 14, however, δεῖ shows that the saying about the Son of Man derives from tradition similar to that in the Synoptics; the parallel phrases in Mark 8: 31, Luke 17: 25, 24: 7 and Matt. 26: 54, testify to the existence of this tradition. Schulz, *Untersuchungen*, pp. 108–9, says, quite plausibly, that it comes from an apocalyptic tradition.

as if the exaltation had already taken place – emphasizes the descent of the Son of Man. Verse 14, and the parallel verses in 8: 28 and 12: 34, emphasize the ascent. In chapter 3, verses 13–15 form a unit, and so the emphasis on the ascent must be seen within the context of the Johannine pattern of 'coming and going'.

The central statement in 3: 14 is ὑψωθῆναι δεῖ τὸν υἱὸν τοῦ ἀνθρώπου. The same phrase occurs in 12: 34, with a minor variation: δεῖ ὑψωθῆναι τὸν υἱὸν τοῦ ἀνθρώπου. The necessity of the Cross is being emphasized. In 8: 28 the element of necessity is not expressed; the phrase is simply ὅταν ὑψώσητε τὸν υἱὸν τοῦ ἀνθρώπου. The expression of necessity is probably part of common early Christian tradition (cf. Mark 8: 31, Luke 17: 25 and Matt. 26: 54).

The primary motif in 3: 14 is the exaltation of the Son of Man. The motif of the bronze serpent, taken from Num. 21: 8–9, is an interpretative device used to express the soteriological significance of the exaltation. It is a way of saying that he who believes in the exalted one gains life (3: 15). The fact that ὑψοῦν is not used in the passage in Numbers, contrasted with the three-fold occurrence of this term in the gospel, shows that the two motifs – of exaltation by the Cross, and the lifting up of the serpent – were originally separate.[1] The evangelist has interpreted the motif of the exalted Son of Man in terms of a text from the Old Testament, formally the same procedure as in 1: 51, where the motif of the revelation of the Son of Man is interpreted by means of the Jacob–Bethel story.

The motif of exaltation is a constant feature of early Christian tradition. In Acts 2: 33 and 5: 31, Christ is 'exalted to the right hand of God'; in Phil. 2: 9 he is 'highly exalted'.[2] The frequent use of Ps. 110 in the New Testament is evidence of this tradition.[3] The Johannine use of the tradition is unique in identifying the exaltation with the crucifixion (John 12: 32–3).[4] In 3: 14

---

[1] T. W. Manson, 'The Argument from Prophecy', *J.T.S.* 46 (1945), 129–36, especially pp. 130–1, provides a good discussion of these texts.

[2] Higgins, *Son of Man*, pp. 162–3.

[3] Matt. 22: 44, 26: 64, Mark 12: 36, 14: 62, 16: 19, Luke 20: 42–3, 22: 69, Acts 2: 34, I Cor. 15: 25, Eph. 1: 20, Col. 3: 1, Heb. 1: 3, 1: 13, 8: 1, 10: 12, 13, 12: 2, 5: 6–10, 6: 20, 7: 3, 11, 15, 17, 21, 24, 28.

[4] Higgins, *Son of Man*, pp. 168–9. The active voice in 8: 28 (ὑψώσητε) shows that the primary meaning is 'crucify', since the agents are the enemies

the evangelist has, therefore, taken over a tradition about the exaltation of the Son of Man, re-cast it by identifying the exaltation with the crucifixion, and expressed its soteriological significance by means of the image of the serpent in Num. 21 : 8–9, and by adding the explicit soteriological application in verse 15. The nailing of Christ to the Cross – although this element is played down[1] – and the lifting up, are like the attaching of the serpent to the standard; in that way Christ is glorified and all who look to him are saved from death.

In the other texts, 8: 24 and 12: 32, cf. 34, fragments of the same tradition are present.[2] Most of these sayings express the soteriological meaning of the ascent: in 3: 15 ἵνα πᾶς ὁ πιστεύων ἐν αὐτῷ ἔχῃ ζωὴν αἰώνιον; in 8: 28 τότε γνώσεσθε ὅτι ἐγώ εἰμι; and in 12: 32 πάντας ἑλκύσω πρὸς ἐμαυτόν.

The tenses of these sayings (3: 14, 8: 28, 12: 32 and 34) are interesting. In 3: 14–15 and 12: 32 and 34, when they refer to the crucifixion, they seem to be timeless, expressing only its necessity (ὑψωθῆναι δεῖ, 3: 14; ἐὰν ὑψωθῶ, 12: 32; δεῖ ὑψωθῆναι, 12: 34). When they refer to the 'drawing of all men to Christ' they are, however, future (ἔχῃ ζωὴν αἰώνιον, 3: 15, which is somewhat ambiguous, however, and could be timeless or 'gnomic'; πάντας ἑλκύσω πρὸς ἐμαυτόν, 12: 32). 8: 28 is clearly future in both references: Ὅταν ὑψώσητε τὸν υἱὸν τοῦ ἀνθρώπου, τότε γνώσεσθε ὅτι ἐγώ εἰμι. The presence of ἐγώ εἰμι, however, could provide an overarching sense of the present, so that the verse really says that the future act of the Cross will merely reveal an eternal situation.

of Jesus. The conjecture that ὑφόω is a translation of the Aramaic 'izdᵉ keph, which has the double meaning (ibid., pp. 163–4), is interesting, but not necessary to establish the Johannine meaning, in the light of the clear statement in 12: 32–3.

[1] Schulz, *Untersuchungen*, pp. 107–8, follows Odeberg in interpreting the omission of σημεῖον (= standard) from the text taken from Num. 21: 8ff. as an indication that the emphasis in our text is on the exaltation to heaven, and not on the crucifixion – i.e. the reference to the fastening of the serpent to the pole is played down and so there is no primary allusion to the nailing of Jesus to the Cross. He takes 12: 33 as a Johannine explanatory gloss, deliberately interpreting what was an emphasis solely on the exaltation as a reference to the crucifixion. These are convincing arguments for the interpretation of the exaltation in terms of Num. 21: 8ff. being a pre-Johannine tradition. Cf. T. W. Manson, 'Argument', pp. 130–1.

[2] Schulz, *Untersuchungen*, pp. 119–20.

We tend to see the references in 3: 14, 12: 32 and 34 as time-less expressions of the necessity of the Cross, and 8: 28 to be dominated by the present ἐγώ εἰμι, so that its future reference to the Cross is not a real, historical future, but merely an attempt to state that the Cross will reveal what has always been the case. The future 'drawing of men' in 12: 32 refers to the future building of the Church, as the outworking of the exaltation on the cross, which, from the point of view of the evangelist, is now taking place.

The realized eschatology of the evangelist is not really com-promised in these sayings: with reference to the work of Christ all is already accomplished (19: 30); the building of the Church, however, is still in process, and looks to the future.

(ii) 12: 23 and 13: 31. The hour has come for the Son of Man to be glorified (12: 23)
Now the Son of Man has been glorified (ἐδοξάσθη) (13: 31)

These verses are parallel to the foregoing sayings insofar as they treat the exaltation of the Son of Man. If the previous sayings on exaltation are concerned to express the soteriological significance of the ascent, these verses emphasize that it is a return to pre-existence. They refer to the ascent as a glorification – δοξάζειν.[1] We have already seen that 'glory' is the quality of the pre-existent Logos, and that 12: 23 is part of the background to chapter 17, where the return of Christ to 'glory' is presented at length. There is no need to discuss 12: 23 further here; 13: 31, however, calls for some comment.

Schulz[2] argues that 13: 31–2 comprise a pre-Johannine hymnic fragment. This is a plausible suggestion, especially because of the repetition of δοξάζειν, although he goes too far when he suggests that, as a hymn to the Logos opens the first part of the book, so a hymn to the Son of Man prefaces the

[1] Higgins, *Son of Man*, pp. 177–8, shows how 'throughly Johannine' the word 'glorify' is. E.g. 14: 13, 15: 8, 8: 54, 16: 14, 11: 4, 7: 39, 12: 16, 17: 11, 21: 19; in 12: 23 and 13: 31ff. it has the same double meaning as ὑψοῦν. It also occurs in Acts 3: 13, Luke 24: 26, and Heb. 5: 5ff., which Higgins interprets as showing that it was in general use in the early Christian preaching. John, however, gives it his own, rather fuller, significance. See G. B. Caird, 'The Glory of God in the Fourth Gospel: An Exercise in Biblical Semantics', *N.T.S.* 15 (1968–9), 265–77.

[2] *Untersuchungen*, pp. 120–2.

second.[1] The opening line, νῦν ἐδοξάσθη ὁ υἱὸς τοῦ ἀνθρώπου, looks *back* to the glorification of the Son of Man as something already achieved. Schulz believes that it refers to the enthronement of the Son of Man, understood in the way it is presented in I En. 51: 3, but there is no real ground in this text for defining the idea of 'glorification' as precisely as this. Rather, it refers in general to the return of Christ to the pre-existent unity with God.

The pre-existence of the Son of Man is the assumption on which this hymn rests. The νῦν ἐδοξάσθη shows how the traditional futurist eschatology has been transformed into a fully realized one; the future tenses describe the situation from the human point of view; from the divine point of view all is accomplished.[2] 'What is said of the Son in chapter 17, therefore, is said of the Son of Man in our passage.'[3]

C. *The Judge*

5: 27 And He has given him the authority to pass judgement, because he is the son of Man.

The theme of judgement is associated with the Son of Man in Daniel. In I Enoch that figure is expressly said to be the judge.[4] Judgement is also an important function of the revealer in the gospel of John.[5] In this text judgement is the function of the Son of Man, 'because he is the Son of Man'.[6] Judgement is part of the definition of the person of the Son of Man.

Bultmann, Schulz and Higgins regard verse 27 as a fragment from a source other than that from which the rest of the discourse comes. Bultmann conjectures that it comes from the

---

[1] *Ibid.*, p. 120 n. 9.   [2] Bultmann, *Evang.*, p. 402.

[3] Higgins, *Son of Man*, pp. 180–1.

[4] E.g. Dan. 7: 10, 14, 26; I Enoch 69: 27: 'And he sat on the throne of his glory and the sum of judgement was given unto the Son of Man, and he caused the sinners to pass away and be destroyed from off the face of the earth, and those who have led the world astray.' Cf. J. L. Martyn, *History and Theology*, pp. 130–1: 'In some respects John 5: 27 appears to be the most "traditional" Son of Man saying in the whole of the New Testament'.

[5] John 3: 17, 19, 5: 22–30, 7: 24, 51, 8: 15–16, 26, 50; 12: 31, 48, 16: 8, 11.

[6] We cannot accept the suggestion that this means he is judge because he is a man. See Higgins, *Son of Man*, p. 167 n. 1, for the supporters of this view and pp. 166–7 for some reasons why one should reject it.

evangelist, or perhaps the redactor, who added 5: 28–9 as part of his attempt to reconcile the eschatology of the gospel with that of early 'orthodoxy'.[1] Schulz sees the section from 5: 27 to 29 as a piece of pre-Johannine apocalyptic tradition based on Dan. 7: 3–14 in 5: 27 and Dan. 12: 2 in 5: 28.[2] Higgins regards it as an 'isolated' saying from a pre-Johannine tradition.[3]

We have already noticed the similarity between 5: 27a καὶ ἐξουσίαν ἔδωκεν αὐτῷ and Dan. 7: 14, καὶ ἐδόθη αὐτῷ ἐξουσία in connection with the discussion of John 17: 2. There is more evidence for this similarity. Both in 5: 27b and in Dan. 7: 13 the title 'Son of Man' occurs, without the article. It would seem that the Daniel passage is in mind here, as it was in 17: 2. Schulz believes that this is demonstrated by the absence of the article with 'Son of Man'. This feature also shows, according to Schulz, that the title has not yet become a technical term as it has in I Enoch, and therefore comes straight from Daniel 7. The phrase κρίσιν ποιεῖν is also an apocalyptic term, as I Enoch 1: 9 and Jude 14 show. This and other evidence serves Schulz to locate the usage represented in John somewhere between Jewish apocalyptic and the Synoptic tradition – the title Son of Man has not yet been applied to Jesus in the tradition present here, as it has been in the synoptic tradition. 5: 28–9 also are reminiscent of Daniel (12: 2), and serve to underline the apocalyptic nature of the conception of the Son of Man in this text.

Schulz is perhaps too precise in his conclusions about the tradition behind this saying, but it is clearly influenced by Jewish apocalyptic. There is also the same formal procedure – of interpreting an identification of Jesus as Son of Man in terms of texts from the Old Testament (Dan. 7), as in 1: 51 and 3: 14, and this indicates at least a certain, identifiable, tradition of exegesis at work.

D. *The Salvation Bringer*

(*i*) *6: 27* Labor not for the food that perishes, but for the food that endures to eternal life, which the Son of Man will give you.

6: 53 Truly, truly, I say to you, unless you eat the flesh of the Son of Man and drink his blood, you do not have life in yourselves.

[1] Bultmann, *Evang.*, pp. 196–7.
[2] Schulz, *Untersuchungen*, pp. 109–14.
[3] Higgins, *Son of Man*, pp. 165–8.

Both of these texts are part of the discourse on the bread from heaven, which follows the miracle of the 'Feeding of the Five Thousand' in chapter 6. The discourse clearly and unequivocally identifies Jesus with the Manna, 'the bread which came down from heaven' (6: 51). This bread is the 'food that endures to eternal life' given by the Son of Man (6: 27), which is the flesh of the Son of Man himself (6: 53). The sayings cannot be understood apart from their context in the discourse, and so we must consider the discourse as a whole.

The sources and structure of John 6 have been discussed at length in modern scholarship. We shall concentrate on the discourse section which begins at verse 26. Bultmann regards the discourse as disorganized in its present form and reconstructs the original order as follows: verses 27, 34, 35, 30–3, 47–51a, 41–6, 36–40. Verses 51b–58 are an addition by an ecclesiastical redactor, along with the addition 'and I will raise him up on the last day' to verses 39, 40 and 44. Verse 28 is an editorial addition also. Behind the discourse, according to Bultmann, lies the 'Revelatory discourse' source, a section of which the evangelist utilized in composing the present text.[1] Peder Borgen argues that John 6: 31–58 is a homiletic midrash on Exodus 16: 4, 13–15 – ἄρτον ἐκ τοῦ οὐρανοῦ ἔδωκεν αὐτοῖς φαγεῖν (John 6: 31). The midrash is present in Philo (Mut. 253–63 and Leg. All. III. 162–8) and there are parallels to it, both in form and content, in the Palestinian haggadah as well, as may be seen by comparing John 6: 31–3 with *Mekilta* Ex. 16: 15 (cf. Philo, Quod Det. 47–8) and *Mekilta* Ex. 15, 11 (cf. Philo, Migr. 1 and 43). It is essentially an 'exegetical paraphrase' of the Biblical text. This type of homiletic Midrash on the 'bread from heaven' was, therefore, Borgen argues, a common element in Jewish tradition both in Palestine and the Diaspora.[2] It is difficult to assess the validity of Borgen's thesis without an extended discussion, because of the wealth of technical detail involved. We have, however, seen enough reason to accept it with caution. We shall read the discourse in the order in which it stands, and refer to Borgen's thesis when necessary.

[1] Bultmann, *Evang.*, pp. 161–4.

[2] Peder Borgen, *Bread from Heaven, An Exegetical Study of the Concept of Manna in the Gospel of John and the writings of Philo*, Supplements to Novum Testamentum x (Leiden, 1965).

Wayne Meeks draws attention to John 6: 14–15, as a reference to the prophet-king who was, in the tradition of Moses, to come into the world.[1] J. L. Martyn sees Jesus in this chapter as 'the Mosaic Prophet-Messiah' on the basis of 6: 14 and 30–2.[2] Clearly, the figure of Moses casts a shadow over the figure of the Christ in this chapter.

Martyn has shown that one strand of the Christology of the gospel as a whole begins with the idea of the Messiah as the Mosaic prophet-king, moves through a midrashic discussion of that identification, to the identification of Jesus as the Son of Man. The texts in question are:

Jesus as Mosaic prophet-king	Midrashic Discussion	Jesus as Son of Man
3: 2	3: 4 (cf. 3: 9)	3: 13
3: 14a		3: 14b
6: 14	6: 30ff.	6: 35, 38, 53, cf. 6: 27
7: 31, 40	7: 52, cf. 7: 42, 8: 13	8: 12, 28
9: 17	9: 28ff., 34	9: 35ff.[3]

In 6: 14 Jesus is identified as the Mosaic Messiah; in 6: 30–2 a sign of his Mosaic dignity is demanded: the people ask him to provide manna as Moses had done. This demand, according to Martyn, is based on an inherited typology between Moses and the Messiah. Martyn believes that in 3: 14 he has detected a formula expressing a typological correlation between Moses and the Messiah: Just as (καθώς...) Moses lifted up the serpent...so (οὕτως) must the Son of Man be lifted up. In 6: 58 ('This is the bread which came down from heaven, not just as (οὐ καθώς) the fathers ate and died') he finds a negative application of the formula, denying the validity of the typology.[4] In 6: 31 Martyn hears a demand based on the logic of this typology. The assumption behind the demand in verse 31 might be set out thus:

Just as [καθώς] Moses gave them bread from heaven to eat,
So also [οὕτως] will the Messiah give bread in the coming age.[5]

Jesus denies this typology when he says,

Moses did not give you the bread from heaven, but my Father gives you the true bread from heaven. For the bread of God is he who

---

[1] Wayne A. Meeks, *The Prophet-King*, pp. 87–99.
[2] J. L. Martyn, *History and Theology*, pp. 112–19.
[3] Martyn, *ibid.*, pp. 122–5.   [4] *Ibid.*, pp. 108–9.   [5] *Ibid.*, pp. 115–17.

comes down from heaven and gives life to the world...I am the bread of life. (6: 32–3, 35a)

Borgen cites verses 31–3 as an example of the homiletic midrash John is drawing on. It begins with a quotation of scripture (6: 31) which, the midrash implies, has been misunderstood, for it goes on to negate one understanding of the text (6: 32) and to present the 'true' interpretation (6: 33). *Mekilta Ex.* 16: 15, 15: 11, Philo, Quod Det. 47–8 and Migr. 1 and 43 show this form also.[1]

Within the Johannine discourse, therefore, there seems to be a denial of the 'Mosaic Messiah' Christology in favor of the Son of Man. The dispenser of the enduring bread is the Son of Man (6: 27) and not Moses, whose bread did not endure. The 'true bread' which came down from heaven (6: 30–5) is the flesh of the Son of Man (6: 53). Martyn, therefore, characterizes the argument in 6: 26ff., amongst other texts, correctly as a movement 'From the Expectation of the Prophet-Messiah like Moses...to the Presence of the Son of Man'.[2]

The historical background of this Christology is complex. Meeks has shown how rich the background of the Mosaic Messiah is, especially in Hellenistic Judaism. In Philo, for instance, Moses is sometimes portrayed as a heavenly being, and is also a symbol for the Logos.[3] But, since John denies the Mosaic messiah in favor of the Son of Man, this information is not directly relevant to an understanding of John's Christology here.

Borgen believes that the discourse is based on a midrashic tradition common to Hellenistic and Palestinian Judaism. In the larger tradition of which the midrash is part, the bread from heaven was identified with Wisdom and Torah.[4] Furthermore, the homily of John 6: 31–58 presupposes the giving of the Torah at Sinai as a model.[5] C. H. Dodd accepts the presence of this allusion to the Torah, but is well aware that John's chief Christological title is Son of Man.[6] He understands the Son of Man as the 'true man' (ἄνθρωπος ἀληθινός), who is also the

---

[1] P. Borgen, *Bread*, pp. 61ff.
[2] Martyn, *History and Theology*, pp. 91–142.
[3] Meeks, *The Prophet-King*, pp. 100ff., especially pp. 117–25.
[4] Borgen, *Bread*, pp. 148–64.   [5] *Ibid.*, p. 148.
[6] Dodd, *Interpretation*, pp. 336–7.

divine Logos.[1] J. L. Martyn looks to apocalyptic Judaism as the matrix of John's Christology here – especially Dan. 7.[2]

What are we to make of this embarrassing wealth of historical allusion? On the one hand the Wisdom (= Torah) tradition of Hellenistic Judaism seems to have been established by our consideration of the Prologue as part of John's background. On the other hand, the Son of Man sayings point undeniably to Jewish apocalyptic influences. We can only accept this twofold background: John seems indeed to be 'A Gospel for Two Worlds'.[3] If the gospel is, as J. L. Martyn believes, the product of a debate between the Church and the Synagogue, that Church and that Synagogue[4] must have been located ideologically – as well as geographically, perhaps – where Hellenistic and apocalyptic Judaism flowed together. In this milieu the Johannine argument that Jesus as the Son of Man who gives his flesh for the life of the world takes precedence over Moses who gave the Manna (= Torah), would be very apt.

(ii) *9: 35–7*. Jesus heard that they had cast him out, and finding him, said: 'Do you believe in the Son of Man?' He answered and said, 'And who is he, sir? so that I might believe in him'. Jesus said to him, 'You have both seen him, and the one who is speaking to you is he.' And he said, 'I believe, Lord.'

This text is striking because of the demand by Jesus to be recognized as the Son of Man on earth. 'Nowhere else in the gospel tradition does the Jesus who walks among men on the face of the earth require of someone the confession of himself as the Son of Man'.[5] Martyn possibly overlooks Mark 2: 10, or interprets 'Son of Man' in that text as a term signifying 'man in general', in making this statement. We tend to accept Mark 2: 10 as saying the same thing as John 9: 35–7, so that the 'Son-of-Man-on-earth' seems to be a category taken over by John from the tradition.

Nevertheless, one is justified in calling this 'Son-of-Man-on-earth' 'the fundamental and principal Christology' of the

---

[1] *Ibid.*, p. 341.
[2] Martyn, *History and Theology*, pp. 129–35.
[3] W. D. Davies, *Invitation to the New Testament*, pp. 389–408.
[4] Martyn, *History and Theology*, pp. 3–88.
[5] *Ibid.*, p. 131.

gospel, as A. J. Higgins does.[1] Jesus is the pre-existent Son of Man on earth, whose real home is in heaven. The eschatological figure of the Son of Man has been identified with the historical Jesus by a shift in the horizon of transcendence from the future to the present, and – in the Prologue – to the past.

IV. SUMMARY AND CONCLUSION: LOGOS, SON OF MAN AND PRE-EXISTENCE IN JOHN'S GOSPEL

The dominant images by means of which John expresses the pre-existence of Christ are 'Logos' and 'Son of Man'. The Logos is a Hellenistic-Jewish term for pre-existent Wisdom. Son of Man is a Palestinian apocalyptic image for the eschatological judge. Under the image of Logos, Christ's protological pre-existence is affirmed. Son of Man has been identified with Logos so that it too expresses protological pre-existence. In the tradition from which it came it usually, with the exception of I Enoch, expressed only eschatological pre-existence. John has definitely shifted the emphasis from eschatology to protology in the idea of pre-existence.

We have argued that Son of Man in the Synoptic tradition, especially the theme of the Son of Man on earth, derives from the teaching of the historical Jesus, and that in Q and Matthew this initial hint of Christ's pre-existence was interpreted in terms of the Wisdom myth, in one form or another. Paul, we suggested, received a doctrine of the pre-existence of Christ expressed in terms of Wisdom in which a form of the myth of the heavenly man also played a part. Now we see that John also uses the images of Wisdom and Son of Man to express Christ's pre-existence. It seems, therefore, relatively well established that the earliest statements of the pre-existence of Christ were consistently formed by images from Jewish apocalyptic and Jewish Wisdom speculation. The apocalyptic image of the Son of Man probably comes from the lips of Jesus himself; and the impulse to apply the Wisdom myth to him might also have come initially from his style of teaching – in Wisdom forms, like the parables.

John's specific contribution to the Wisdom Christology was to identify Jesus as Wisdom with the Logos of Alexandrian Judaism.

[1] Higgins, *Son of Man*, p. 155. Martyn, *History and Theology*, p. 129, and Bultmann, *Evang.*, p. 76, agree with this view.

This enabled him to make the connection between Jesus, the Logos and the Son of Man, since the Logos was also the true heavenly man. In Matthew Jesus was identified with Wisdom by means of the idea of the Torah; but Jesus as the Son of Man was only incidentally linked with Jesus as Wisdom Torah, by means of the idea of the Son of Man as the eschatological judge – a legal activity associated with the idea of Torah. John welds the two titles together in the term Logos.

By comparison with Paul, John is remarkable for his emphasis on protology. Whereas Paul seems to counteract a mystical understanding of salvation as a return to the pre-existent anthropos by making the revelation of that anthropos an eschatological, future event, John emphasizes the protological pre-existence of Christ, the anthropos. In John 17 there is some awareness of the important Pauline theme of the pre-existence of the Church, but John seems to express the idea entirely in terms of the will or mind of God – the Church pre-exists in God's mind – and does not, with the possible exception of John 2: 19–22, make anything of the idea of the Church as the heavenly temple of Jewish apocalyptic.

CHAPTER 5

PRE-EXISTENCE IN THE REST OF
THE NEW TESTAMENT

I. THE GENERAL EPISTLES: HEBREWS, I AND
II PETER, JUDE

A. *Hebrews*

The religio-historical matrix of the idea of pre-existence in the New Testament has already been set out, and so we can proceed without repetition of the evidence. Hebrews essentially provides confirmation of the structures of the idea proposed so far, and so our discussion will be brief.

It is well known that the opening verses proclaim the pre-existence of Christ in terms of the Wisdom myth (Wisd. 7: 27):[1] the message given by the prophets in the course of the history of salvation comes to final and definitive expression in the Son, in these last days (1: 1–2).[2] He is the one through whom God created the universe and towards whom everything moves for fulfilment.

In verse 3 the same attributes are applied to Christ as are applied to Wisdom in the tradition. The same word, ἀπαύγασμα, is applied to Wisdom in Wisd. 7: 26, and the general description of Wisdom in Wisd. 7: 25 – 8: 1 corresponds closely to Heb. 1–3. The attributes of Philo's Logos are also similar to those of the Christ of Hebrews (Quod Deus 31, Conf. 97, Spec. Leg. I. 81,

---

[1] R. H. Fuller, *Foundations*, pp. 220–1, believes that verse 3 and most of verse 4 contain a hymn of two three-lined stanzas. He ranks this with the other Christological hymns: Phil. 2: 5–11, Col. 1: 15–20, I Tim. 3: 16, I Pet. 3: 18–22 and John 1: 1–14, which he regards as products of the Hellenistic Gentile mission. His strongest point in favour of such a view is the similarity of content between this hypothetical hymn and the other recognized Christological hymns. Nevertheless, the generally rhythmic nature of the whole chapter makes this isolation of a few lines less than convincing. We must, however, recognize, with Fuller, the similarity between the Christology of this chapter and the other hymns.

[2] E.g. C. Spicq, *L'Épître aux Hébreux*, 2 vols. (Paris, 1953), II, 1–13; Hugh Montefiore, *A Commentary on the Epistle to the Hebrews* (New York, 1964), pp. 33–7.

243

Somn. I. 239, Det. 83).[1] In Plant. 8 and Quis Heres 188 the Logos sustains the world, as the Christ does in Heb. 1: 3, although the phrase 'by his word of power' in Hebrews seems to be a reference to the creative activity of God as recorded in Gen. 1, rather than to the Philonic Logos. We have already seen how Logos and Wisdom were identified in Philo (Leg. All. I. 65, II. 86, Quod Det. 116–19, Quaes. Gen. IV. 97). Wisd. 9: 12 shows how they were identified in the work of creation. The verse (3) closes with a fragment from Ps. 110: 1.

Verses 1–3 are followed by a series of seven quotations from the Old Testament designed to prove, by means of pesher exegesis,[2] that the Son is superior to the angels. We have already taken note of the phenomenon of the exegesis of scripture in the construction of Christological doctrine. There is no need to assume the existence of an actual book of testimonies from which these seven quotations were drawn; all that is necessary is to recognize that certain 'blocks' of texts, which were fluid in extent, existed, and were applied to certain fixed Christological themes.[3]

The present series seems to have been selected, in the tradition behind Hebrews, primarily to interpret the resurrection and exaltation of Jesus; then secondarily applied to prove his pre-existence; here it is used in a third way, to demonstrate his superiority to angels. This is a curious application of the catena[4] which can only be explained by assuming that the author found it necessary to combat an 'angel-Christology'.[5] This Christology

---

[1] Cf. Montefiore, p. 36.

[2] S. Kistemaker, *The Psalm Citations in the Epistle to the Hebrews* (Amsterdam, 1961), pp. 88–94, who argues that the epistle uses the 'pesher' method of interpretation, even more clearly than Matthew does. F. F. Bruce, '"To the Hebrews" or "To the Essenes"', *N.T.S.* 9 (1962–3), 221 n. 6, agrees that the epistle employs pesher exegesis but says that Kistemaker exaggerates the resemblance between Hebrews and Qumran in this respect.

[3] Montefiore, p. 43. C. H. Dodd, *According to the Scriptures*, p. 108. The question of the existence of 'Testimonia' lists has been reopened by the discovery of 4 Q Testimonia, which suggests that such lists were compiled at Qumran. See F. M. Cross, *The Ancient Library of Qumran* (New York, 1961), pp. 218–19 and *passim*. Cf. Kistemaker, *Psalm Citations*, pp. 88–94, who denies the use of Testimonia in Hebrews.

[4] Montefiore (p. 44) points out that only one of them in the LXX mentions 'angels'.

[5] Kaesemann, *Das wandernde Gottesvolk*, *F.R.L.A.N.T.* 55 (Göttingen,

was probably a reflection of a tradition, like that in 11 Q. Melch., which identified Melchizedek as an angel.[1] The author of Hebrews wished to use the name of Melchizedek to interpret Christ, and made sure in chapter 1, before he began the argument, that Christ would not be confused with the angel Melchizedek. This opening argument – that Christ is the Son and therefore superior to all angels – is part of the author's creative appropriation of Ps. 110: 4 and the Melchizedek tradition for Christology. A brief consideration of each quotation in the series throws light on how the early exegetical tradition understood the pre-existence of Christ.

Ps. 2: 7 (LXX) (verse 5a) was used at Qumran as a Messianic prophecy (1 Q. Sa 2: 11) and in the early Church. Initially it was applied to the resurrection (Rom. 1: 4, Acts 13: 33ff.), then it was conflated with Is. 42: 1 to form the words spoken from heaven at Jesus' baptism (Mark 1: 11, pars.); at Luke 9: 35 it describes Jesus' dignity in the Transfiguration; and here it conveys his eternal generation.[2] The trajectory traced by this text is paradigmatic of at least one way in which the doctrine of pre-existence developed: from the resurrection through the earthly life to pre-existence.

II Sam. 7: 14 (LXX) (verse 5b) was also known at Qumran (4 Q Testimonia) as a Messianic prophecy.[3] It is originally part of the promise to David. In II Cor. 6: 18 it is used in a modified form linked with Is. 52: 11 as part of an exhortation to separate oneself from the world, and in Rev. 21: 7, linked with Ps. 88: 26 (LXX) to refer to the eschatological reward of those who persevere.[4] Here it describes the eternal status of the Son in a special relationship with the Father, not enjoyed by angels.

Verse 6 comes from the LXX of Deut. 32: 43 (it is not in the

1959), rejects this kind of explanation as too much under the influence of the Tübingen school. He explains the concern with angels as a result of an enthronement pattern behind chapter 1, like that in Phil. 2: 6–11, Col. 1: 15ff. and I Tim. 3: 16 (pp. 58–61). The enthronement pattern is present here and in the other texts mentioned, but we fail to see why it should be directed here against the view that the Son is an angel, unless there is some polemical intent.

[1] Cf. M. de Jonge and A. S. van der Woude, '11 Q Melchizedek and the New Testament', *N.T.S.* 12 (1965–6), 301–26.

[2] Montefiore, *Hebrews*, p. 44.

[3] F. F. Bruce, '"To the Hebrews" or "To the Essenes"', p. 221.

[4] Montefiore, p. 45.

Hebrew text).[1] The introductory clause, 'Again when he brings the first-born into the world' refers to the birth of Jesus, and the whole verse is reminiscent of the Lukan tradition of the angels present at Jesus' birth (Luke 2: 13). 'First-born' refers to the eternal status of the Son (cf. Conf. 146, Rom. 8: 29, Col. 1: 15, 1: 18, Rev. 1: 5), and the citation proves the Son superior to the angels since they worshipped him when he came into the world. In its original context, Deut. 32: 43 refers to God; this is a case, therefore, of a text which initially refers to God, being applied to Jesus.

Verse 7 comes from Ps. 103: 4 (LXX) and originally stood sixth in the catena, Montefiore suggests,[2] as a testimony of the Christian Pentecost (cf. Acts 2: 2ff.). In its present position it stresses that the angels were made (ὁ ποιῶν...) that is, they came into being, whereas the Son's existence is eternal, as the contrast in verse 8 shows.

Verses 8–9 cite Ps. 44: 7–8 (LXX), a royal nuptial psalm, which in the original should probably read 'God is thy throne' since it is addressed to the king. The Christian writer understands ὁ θεός to refer to Jesus, and the opening verse of the citation to prove his eternal existence. Verse 8b (Heb. 1: 9) calls him ὁ θεός also.[3]

In 10–12, Ps. 101: 26–8 (LXX) addresses Jesus as Creator, applying to him a text originally addressed to God,[4] and expressing how he will endure when all else comes to an end. He is in fact the eschatological judge, as well as the creator: 'he will roll all things up like a mantle' (verse 12). The catena comes to an end in the famous Ps. 110: 1 (LXX Ps. 109: 1),[5] which has already been hinted at in verse 3.

The first chapter of Hebrews is a good example of how the

[1] Hebrews changes 'sons of God' in the LXX to 'angels of God' (Montefiore, p. 46).

[2] Montefiore, pp. 46–7.

[3] Thus also, R. E. Brown, 'Does the New Testament call Jesus God?' *Theological Studies*, 26 (1965), 562–3.

[4] κύριε has been added to the Hebrew text by the LXX; Siniaticus and some other mss., however, omit it from the LXX text. Brown, p. 563, says, however, that we have no way of knowing what the phrase 'O God' in the Psalm meant to the writer of Hebrews.

[5] Cf. Rom. 8: 34, Eph. 1: 20, Col. 3: 1, I Pet. 3: 22, Rev. 5: 1, Mark 12: 35–7; N. Perrin, *Rediscovering*, pp. 176ff.

assumption that Jesus is pre-existent, like Wisdom, reflects on the exegetical tradition and transforms what were initially testimonies to his resurrection and exaltation into testimonies to his protological pre-existence.

Christ is also identified with the last Adam or the Anthropos in Hebrews. The polemic against the superiority of angels continues in 2: 5ff., by means of an interpretation of Ps. 8: 5–7. The psalm speaks of 'man' and, in synonymous parallelism, of 'the son of Man' – designating thereby mankind in general. Man is lower than the angels for a little while (βραχύ τι can have both a temporal and a qualitative meaning),[1] crowned with honor, and has all creation subjected to him (2: 5–8). The psalm recalls Adam as described in Gen. 1: 26, being in God's image and having dominion. The *auctor ad Hebraeos*, on the other hand, recalls Jesus, the last Adam, to whom all things likewise have been subjected. Although we do not yet see this Lordship in its full actuality, we do see the humiliated one exalted to God's right hand (cf. 1: 13) and crowned with glory. This is a preview of the future, a vision of the true order of things. All things are subject to him; the present appearance is illusory. 'The world to come, of which we are speaking', was subjected not to angels but to 'the Man'.

There is no need to torture the text, as Zuntz does,[2] in order to find a specific reference to the Son of Man in verse 6. There may be a hint of influence from Dan. 7: 13; but primarily we have an exegesis of Ps. 8, based on Ps. 110: 1. These psalms also occur together in I Cor. 15: 25–7, in a chapter concerned, amongst other things, with Christ as the 'man from heaven' (15: 47) and the last Adam (15: 22, 45). We saw that Paul was influenced there by the doctrine of his opponents, in his explication of the scheme of the two Adams. There is no explicit mention of Adam

[1] Montefiore, p. 57; C. Spicq, II, 32–3.
[2] G. Zuntz, *The Text of the Epistles* (London, 1953), pp. 48ff., cited F. F. Bruce, *The Epistle to the Hebrews, New International Commentary on the New Testament* (Grand Rapids, Mich., 1964), p. 31 n. 12. Zuntz would read in verse 6, τίς ἐστιν ἄνθρωπος with P 46, instead of τί... and a rough breathing on ἄνθρωπος as a result of a putative crasis ὁ and ἄνθρωπος. In the next line he would read ἦ with a circumflex accent, instead of ἤ 'or'. All this jugglery yields the translation:

'Who is the man whom thou mindest?
Truly the Son of Man, for him thou visitest.'

in our present text, but it is clearly assumed that Jesus is the inclusive or representative man. The point of the argument turns precisely on the ambiguity of the references to man – they are both to man in general and to Jesus. In verse 8 the threefold repetition of αὐτῷ shows that it is significant; the reader immediately asks, 'To whom, to man in general, or to Jesus?' The author answers that Jesus is the first manifestation of that triumph, that mankind and Jesus cannot be separated. This is precisely what 2: 10–18 goes on to underline; he calls men his brothers, because he too, like them, has been subjected to the angels for a little while; but now he is free. Having risen, he assures us that all men will be liberated. Jesus is the representative man, the last Adam.

One cannot fail to hear the echoes of the anthropos myth which we analyzed in our consideration of I Cor. 15.[1] The startling statement in verse 11: 'he who sanctifies and those who are sanctified have all one origin' (ἐξ ἑνὸς πάντες) can really be explained only as a fragment of the anthropos myth.[2] Another fragment appears in verse 15, where the redeemer has to come to earth to 'deliver all those who through fear of death were subject to lifelong bondage' (cf. 10: 20, where the veil between heaven and earth is the flesh of Christ, suggesting that his body has, like the anthropos, cosmic dimensions, and is, somehow, identified with the cosmos).[3]

---

[1] Cf. E. Kaesemann, *Das wandernde Gottesvolk*, pp. 61–71. He sets out the evidence for the understanding of 'Son' in Hebrews, especially in chapter 1, in terms of the anthropos myth, in its Hellenistic–Jewish garb.

[2] Cf. C. Spicq, pp. 40–1, who interprets the phrase as meaning 'from God', as the common source of all life. Spicq gives a review of the traditional ways in which this text has been understood: 'from one seed, blood, or race' (taking as neuter), or 'from Adam', or 'from Abraham'.

[3] The interpretation of 'through his flesh' in this verse as meaning 'by means of the sacrifice of his flesh' (e.g. Montefiore, pp. 173–4) is unacceptable because it changes what in the text is considered a barrier ('flesh' being parallel to 'veil') into a way of access (Spicq, p. 316). Spicq's understanding of it as a reference to the 'rending of the veil' in Matt. 27: 5 is also doubtful (*ibid.*). We have more probably a fragment of the myth of the anthropos in a Hellenistic–Jewish form. This text could probably be elucidated by an investigation of the cosmic symbolism of the High Priest's person and robes in Mos. II of Philo. W. Manson, *The Epistle to the Hebrews* (London, 1951), pp. 67–8, calls the identification of the veil, which is itself a metaphor drawn from the architecture of the temple, with the flesh of Christ, 'a mystical allegorical touch'. This is an accurate description of the form of exegesis, but

The myth, excepting for these tell-tale fragments, has been transmuted into priestly imagery, however; the redeemer's descent becomes a priestly identification with his people, and his liberating act an expiation of sin.[1]

The understanding of hope in Hebrews, as the presence of the future, is important for the idea of pre-existence. Christ, the representative man, is Lord of the future; his exaltation shows this. But what precisely is the ontological status of that future? Does it exist already or not? The answer which the *auctor ad Hebraeos* gives to these questions takes the form of a doctrine of hope, founded on the eschatological idea of pre-existence.

The note of hope is introduced in 3: 6, and 3: 14 (cf. 6: 11), along with a strong emphasis on the end, and on perseverance. The object of this hope is the 'rest' of God which has existed since the last day of creation (e.g. 4: 1–5),[2] as Gen. 2: 2 (verse 4) testifies. The pattern of thought is one in which certain things exist – although it is not clear how a 'rest' can be said to exist – which are as yet not manifest but only promised. The argument is again built on citations from scripture, Ps. 95: 7–11 (Heb. 3: 7–11) and Gen. 2: 2 (Heb. 4: 4).[3]

In 6: 4 the experience of salvation is described as 'tasting the heavenly gift' (τῆς δωρεᾶς τῆς ἐπουρανίου) and in verse 5 this is

it does not affect the fact that the allegory draws on the myth of the anthropos in explaining the veil in this way.

[1] Kaesemann, *Das wandernde Gottesvolk*, pp. 125 ff., argues that this high-priestly interpretation of the anthropos/redeemer is not original with the Christian exegetical tradition, but derives from the apocalyptic belief in a heavenly cultus, and the expectation of a messianic high-priest in the Test. XII Patr. for example (Test. Reub. 6, T. Sim. 7, T. Lev. 2, 3, 8, 18, etc.). One might add evidence from 1 Q.S. 9: 10–11, 1 Q.S. 6: 4–6, 1 Q Sa 2: 18ff., of a priestly and a prophetic messiah. (Cf. K. G. Kuhn, 'The Two Messiahs of Aaron and Israel', in *The Scrolls and the New Testament*, ed. K. Stendahl (New York, 1957), pp. 54–64.) This influence is undeniable; but the sources on which Kaesemann bases his further identification of the 'recurring' Adam–Elijah–Melchizedek of Gnosticism are not clear, and not even presented by him.

[2] Bruce, *Hebrews*, pp. 73–4. Philo, Cher. 26, Sacr. 8, cf. Ber. Rabbah 17 (12a), 'The Sabbath is the image of the world to come' (Montefiore, p. 85).

[3] The use of 'rest' in this vague way, as if it were a place prepared for men, arises out of the use of Ps. 95: 7–11 as a proof, that in turn seems to be dictated by a need to warn the readers against apostasy. 'Rest' should probably be thought of as a state in this context; soon other images, like 'temple' and 'city' are used to describe the same reality.

referred to as 'the powers of the age to come' (δυνάμεις τε μέλλοντος αἰῶνος). The parallelism of these two phrases – 'heavenly gift' and 'powers of the age to come' – shows the presence of the idea of eschatological pre-existence; the age to come, whose powers they have tasted, is present in heaven, and can be described as a 'heavenly gift'.

In 6: 13 the whole scheme is said to rest on the promises, so that 'hope' is equivalent to 'faith and patience' in the promises (6: 12). Abraham endured because he had confidence in what God had promised; and God assured the reliability of his word by swearing an oath. The things promised by God are certain to come to pass, so certain in fact that they are thought of as already existing. As soon as this happens the categories of expression change from temporal to spatial, as in 3: 11, 14 and 6: 11. Here 'hope' has reference to the heavens where Christ has gone:

We have this as a sure and steadfast anchor of the soul, a hope that enters into the inner shrine behind the curtain, where Jesus has gone as a fore-runner on our behalf, having become a high priest for ever after the order of Melchizedek.

Things promised for the future are already present in heaven.

Chapter 11 probably comes from a pre-Christian source.[1] In the opening statement faith is tantamount to hope – the making present of future expectation, the making real of things unseen. The whole chapter is based on the theme of the unseen, yet real, city towards which the great figures of the history of salvation were moving (11: 7, 9–10, 13–16, 27). No one of them achieved his goal, for it could not be realized without the believers in Christ (11: 39–40). Now, however, all history has been completed, and the men of old have, with Christ, arrived in the presence of God. In Christ we all stand at the heavenly mount Zion, Jerusalem, the city of God (12: 18–24). We have received an eternal kingdom (12: 28), which is the abiding city to come (13: 14). But it is in heaven, and therefore all this is an expression of the hope which makes real the unseen, pre-existent things.

The best-known feature of Hebrews is the priestly Christology which identifies Christ with Melchizedek, the eternal high priest. In 4: 14 – 5: 10 the central argument of the epistle be-

---

[1] Kaesemann, *Das wandernde Gottesvolk*, pp. 117–18.

gins.[1] It is expressed succinctly in two citations from Ps. 2: 7, 'Thou are my Son, this day have I begotten thee' (5: 5), and Ps. 110: 4, 'Thou art a priest forever, after the order of Melchizedek' (5: 6, cf. 5: 10). This means that 'we have a great high priest who has passed through the heavens' (4: 14), that is, one who has gone through the seven spheres[2] to the right hand of God, who is enthroned beyond the heavens. From now on Christ is presented as the eternal priest, the guide through the veil to the throne. He, being made perfect through suffering, leads many sons to glory, as the pioneer or forerunner (2: 10). There are two possible sources for the imagery employed here. Dibelius[3] sees the influence of the Hellenistic mystery cults. Christ is, according to him, the great mystagogue, and τελειοῦν[4] signifies the completion of initiation into the mystery. Jesus, having been fully initiated by passing through all the spheres, is now ὁ τῆς πίστεως ἀρχηγὸς καὶ τελειωτής (12: 2), where τελειωτής means 'the initiated one', 'the mystagogue'.[5] Dibelius summarizes:

Das zentrale Heilsereignis ist...die Erhöhung Christi, dargestellt als kultische Handlung des Sohnes, die auch den 'vielen Söhnen' (2: 20) den Zutritt zu diesem Heiligtum eröffnet. Die Christen sind die 'Herantretenden', die durch den himmlischen Hohenpriester die vollendende Weihe erhalten.[6]

[1] G. Schille, 'Erwägungen zur Hohepriesterlehre des Hebräerbriefes', *Z.N.W.* 64 (1955), 81–109, and G. Friedrich 'Das Lied vom Hohenpriester in Zusammenhang von Hebr. 4: 4 – 5: 10', *T.Z.* (Basel), 18 (1962), 95–115, believe that an early Christian hymn is behind this section.

[2] Cf. II Cor. 12: 2, Eph. 1: 3, 20, 22, 4: 10, T. Levi 2: 7ff., Asc. Is. 6: 13, 7: 13, Chag. 12B (Cited by Bruce, *Hebrews*, p. 85 n. 61; cf. Montefiore, p. 90). On salvation as ascent see Poimandres 24–6 and A. Dieterich, *Eine Mithrasliturgie* (Darmstadt, 1966).

[3] M. Dibelius, 'Der himmlische Kultus nach dem Hebräerbrief' in *Botschaft und Geschichte* II, Gesammelte Aufsätze, ed. G. Bornkamm and H. Kraft (Tübingen, 1956), pp. 160–76, esp. pp. 170–1.

[4] Used nine times (i) of Christ, 2: 10, 5: 9, 7: 28; (ii) of the believer 10: 14, 11: 40, 12: 23; (iii) negatively of the old cultus, 7: 18, 9: 9, 10: 1 (Dibelius, p. 167).

[5] Dibelius, p. 171; cf. Kaesemann, *Das wandernde Gottesvolk*, pp. 82–90. He accepts this interpretation but extends and modifies it in terms of the anthropos myth. The anthropos is both the guide to heaven and the heavenly home itself. He is both perfecter (τελειωτής) and perfected (τελειωθείς) to the extent that those whom he redeems bring his own 'body' to perfection.   [6] *Ibid.*, p. 172.

Other traces of 'mystery' language are, according to Dibelius, present in 5: 13–14, where, as in I Cor. 3: 1–3, the readers are called 'babes' (νήπιοι) or 'mature' (τέλειοι), terms which are well known as 'ranks' in the process of initiation.[1]

More recently, it has been argued that the references to perfection and the attendant imagery can be explained on the basis of the Qumran texts.[2] Yigael Yadin[3] first pointed out the possible relationship between the Qumran texts and our treatise. He concentrated attention on the teaching about angels and the Messianic expectation in the respective texts. His most telling point, in our opinion, is the suggestion that the *auctor ad Hebraeos* is attempting to show that Jesus, who was not of a recognized priestly tribe (7: 14) is indeed a High Priest of an order superior to the Aaronic priesthood – the order of Melchizedek. This attempt was motivated, according to Yadin, by the desire to commend Jesus as Messiah – both royal and priestly – to a group which expected two Messiahs, one royal and one priestly. Such a group was the Qumran community, and the writer attempts to show that Jesus combined in himself both kinds of Messiah.

For our immediate purpose, however, the argument of B. Rigaux[4] is more important. He maintains that the idea of perfection in Hebrews is similar to the idea of perfection in the Qumran texts. According to him, perfection at Qumran is threefold: fundamentally, it is a practical conception, of life in obedience to the will of God expressed in the Law; secondarily, however, it is the inspiration of the Spirit which purifies man and leads him beyond the normal limits of human knowledge to, thirdly, a special knowledge of the divine Law and the divine

---

[1] Kaesemann, *Das wandernde Gottesvolk*, pp. 119–20. But see B. Pearson, 'Pneumatikos–Psychikos Terminology', for the possible Philonic derivation of these terms.

[2] On the general problem of the relation between Hebrews and Qumran see Y. Yadin, 'The Dead Sea Scrolls and the Epistle to the Hebrews', *Scripta Hierosolymitana*, IV (1958), 36–55; C. Spicq, 'L'Épître aux Hébreux', *Rev. Q.*, I (1959), 365ff.; H. Kosmala, *Hebräer–Essener–Christen, Studien zur Vorgeschichte der frühchristlichen Verkündigung*, S.P.B. I (Leiden, 1959); F. F. Bruce, '"To the Hebrews" or "To the Essenes"?'.

[3] 'Dead Sea Scrolls and the Epistle to the Hebrews', *passim*.

[4] B. Rigaux, 'Révélation des Mystères et Perfection à Qumran et dans le Nouveau Testament', *N.T.S.* 4 (1957–8), 237–62.

plan. Rigaux characterizes these three moments as 'practical', 'mystical' and 'gnostic', respectively.[1]

In Hebrews, according to Rigaux, Jesus and the Christians aim at such perfection. Jesus has achieved it (8: 1–2, 2: 10, 5: 9–10, 7: 25) but the Christians are still far from it (5: 11–14). This teaching on perfection is the basic doctrine of the epistle, and it is established by exegesis of the scriptures[2] (e.g. 2: 10).

Rigaux's argument is compelling but not totally convincing. Heb. 2: 10 tells of Jesus being perfected in suffering in order that he might 'lead many sons to glory' as the 'pioneer'. The High Priest in Jewish ritual does not take anyone with him into the sanctuary, and it does not seem sufficient to this image of the 'pioneer' to remark that the Jewish High Priest was a representative figure. The nearest the Scrolls approach to this idea of the solidarity of the believers with their 'forerunner' and their passage with him into heaven is the idea expressed in 1 Q.S. 11: 8 that the community is united with the angels, and is a heavenly community. However, the image from the mystery cults of the mystagogue leading the initiates to perfection seems to provide a closer analogy.

At this point, pending further work on the background of the epistle, we must recognize a blend of Jewish apocalypticism and Hellenistic mysticism in its matrix. One possible background comes immediately to mind: the Philonic. The Philonism of Hebrews has long been recognized and cannot be ignored.[3] A Hellenistic synagogue, therefore, in which Qumran influence was strongly felt, along with the more familiar middle Platonic syncretism, is the most probable tentative matrix for our treatise; but work has still to be done on this subject. The understanding of perfection as the result of obedience (e.g. 5: 9) is like that at Qumran; the idea of the forerunner leading many sons to glory is like the activity of the Hellenistic mystagogue.

Chapters 7–10 contain an extended discussion of Christ as a priest like Melchizedek and argue that his ministry is superior to everything that has gone before.[4] The argument rests on the

---

[1] *Ibid.*, pp. 239–41.

[2] *Ibid.*, p. 259, 'Perfection de Jésus et perfection de l'église constituent le fond de la doctrine de l'épître aux Hébreux.'

[3] E.g. Spicq, *Hébreux*, I, 39–91; Montefiore, pp. 6–9.

[4] Kaesemann, *Das wandernde Gottesvolk*, p. 110: 'dass mit Kap. 7 nicht

assumption that Ps. 110: 4 applies to Christ (Heb. 5: 6, 6: 20, 7: 11, 15, 17, 21, 28), which is, in turn, a development of the interpretation of the resurrection in terms of Ps. 110: 1, which took place early in the tradition. The writer goes to Gen. 14: 17–20 and uses it to interpret Ps. 110: 4. The point of comparison between Christ and Melchizedek is that they both, according to the scripture, 'continue forever' (7: 24, 28, cf. 7: 16–17). Ps. 110: 4 is cited in 7: 17, after the statement that the new priest has supplanted the Aaronic priesthood 'by the power of an indestructible life' (κατὰ δύναμιν ζωῆς ἀκαταλύτου, 16) and not in virtue of a more prestigious genealogy. The emphasis in the citation falls, therefore, upon 'forever': σὺ ἱερεὺς εἰς τὸν αἰῶνα κατὰ τάξιν Μελχισεδεκ.

The author finds a parallel to this in the fact that the original Melchizedek is presented in Gen. 14 without reference to his parentage. The process of exegesis is as follows: Ps. 110: 4 identifies Jesus as an eternal priest 'after the order of Melchizedek'; that directs attention to Melchizedek in Gen. 14; he must also have been an eternal priest if Ps. 110: 4 is to make sense; since no mention is made of his parentage we may assume that he too is eternal. The results of this exegesis are set out in 7: 3, where Melchizedek is said to be:

> ἀπάτωρ, ἀμήτωρ, ἀγενεαλόγητος,
> μήτε ἀρχὴν ἡμερῶν μήτε ζωῆς τέλος ἔχων,
> ἀφωμοιωμένος δὲ τῷ υἱῷ τοῦ θεοῦ,
> μένει ἱερεὺς εἰς τὸ διηνεκές.[1]

allein das "Kernstück des Hebr. sondern auch Enthüllung von Geheimnissen" einsetzt' (citing Michel, p. 73ff.). In his view 5: 11 – 6: 12 is a 'preparation for a λόγος τέλειος'. In Gnosticism (or the mysteries) those about to receive the revelation are questioned about their worthiness, the testing they have been subjected to, and warned not to divulge the secrets (p. 123). 5: 11 – 6: 12 corresponds to this preliminary examination. 7: 1 – 10: 39 is the λόγος τέλειος itself. The evidence for this practice in Gnosticism is somewhat slender. It is also doubtful that one should speak of Gnosticism in this early period. However, the evidence for the practice in the mysteries is plausible.

[1] As set out by M. de Jonge and A. S. van der Woude in '11 Q Melchizedek and the New Testament', N.T.S. 12 (1965–6), 301–26. Kaesemann, pp. 134–5, says that these predicates are as a whole the same as those which Gnosticism usually attributes to the 'Aeon', but he does not present the evidence.

This interpretation cannot be derived from the story in Gen. 14 without external influence.

The last line is obviously derived from Ps. 110: 4, while the third line is a constructive attempt to relate the figures of Christ and Melchizedek. Bruce calls it a 'typological' exegesis,[1] and this is justified by the fact that ἀφωμοιωμένος is a perfect passive of the verb meaning 'to make like', implying that the person or thing made like another is inferior to its model.[2] The Son is the type and Melchizedek the antitype – a reversal of the usual order of typological exegesis.[3] This reading of 7: 3 amounts to a direct statement of the unconditional pre-existence of the Son, 'without father, mother, or genealogy, having neither beginning of days, nor an end of life'.

The argument proceeds from silence on the rabbinic principle of 'quod non in thora non in mundo';[4] but one may naturally ask whether there is not a positive tradition about Melchizedek from which what the author reads into the silence might be derived.[5] The usual place to look is Philo, where Melchizedek is ἱερεὺς γὰρ...λόγος κλῆρον ἔχων τὸν ὄντα...(Leg. All. III. 82).[6] Melchizedek is identified with the Logos, but so are many others.[7] The decisive argument against a Philonic derivation of Heb. 7: 3 is the fact that for Philo the Logos has both a father and a mother; God is the father and Wisdom the mother (Fug. 108ff.).[8] New evidence from Qumran suggests that the identifi-

---

[1] Hebrews, p. 136.

[2] De Jonge and van der Woude, '11 Q Melchizedek', p. 321 n. 4.

[3] Rigaux, 'Révélation', p. 260.

[4] S.-B. III, p. 694–5; de Jonge and van der Woude, pp. 320–1.

[5] Kaesemann, Das wandernde Gottesvolk, pp. 124–40, gives an excellent, if somewhat diffuse, discussion of the religio-historical problem. He concludes that the anthropos myth influences Hebrews even in the priestly Christology. The discovery of 11 Q Mech. makes his identification of Melchizedek with Michael and Elijah, the recurring manifestations of the primal Adam in gnostic thought for which the evidence is itself slender, at best a secondary element in the background of the Christology of Hebrews. See also, A. J. B. Higgins, 'The Priestly Messiah', N.T.S. 13 (1966–7), 211–39.

[6] Bruce, Hebrews, pp. 135–6, who rejects Philonic influence on the grounds that Philo's allegory differs from our typology. Cf. Kaesemann, Das wandernde Gottesvolk, pp. 124ff., who also rejects Philonic influence. On Logos as High Priest in Philo see Schrenk in T.W.N.T. III, pp. 273ff.

[7] E.g. Moses, Aaron, Phinehas (Leisegang, II, p. 502).

[8] H. Hegermann, Schöpfungsmittler, pp. 54.

cation of Christ with Melchizedek might have occurred as a result of influence from Qumran. Thirteen fragments from Qumran's Cave 11 portray Melchizedek as the angelic leader of the eschatological armies of heaven.[1] Fitzmeyer summarizes as follows: Melchizedek in this text

is associated with the deliverance of the divine judgement, with a day of atonement, with a year of jubilee, and with a role that exalts him high above the assembly of heavenly beings. Such associations make the comparison in Hebrews between Jesus the high priest and Melchizedek all the more intelligible. The tradition is not the same; but what we have in 11 Q Melch. at least furnishes new light on the comparison.[2]

The pre-existence of Melchizedek as the one without genealogy or parents could have been part of the tradition of Melchizedek as the angelic leader of God's hosts. The idea of Melchizedek as a pre-existent heavenly being was known at Qumran, and in view of the use of pesher exegesis in this epistle, it is probable that there was some influence from Qumran at work in its theology. Christ is pre-existent because he is, like Melchizedek, an eternal priest; but he is higher in dignity than Melchizedek; Melchizedek is an angel, but Christ, according to ch. 1, is the Son. As an angel Melchizedek is eschatologically pre-existent; as the Son, Christ is protologically pre-existent, the eternal pre-creational Wisdom of God. Melchizedek was the antitype of the pre-existent Son, even though he occurred before the Son in the course of historical time.

We have seen that the apocalyptic idea of a heavenly temple

---

[1] De Jonge and van der Woude; J. A. Fitzmeyer, 'Further Light on Melchizedek from Qumran Cave 11', *J.B.L.* 86 (1967), 25–41. The fragments were first published by van der Woude in 1965: 'Melchisedek als himmlische Erlösergestalt in den neugefundenen eschatologischen Midraschim aus Qumran Höhle XI', *Oudtestamentische Studien*, 14 (1965), 354–73. Fitzmeyer's reconstruction varies from de Jonge and van der Woude so as to bring out the priestly function of Melchizedek, which the latter think is absent from the fragment.

[2] 'Further Light on Melchizedek', p. 31. Cf. de Jonge and van der Woude, p. 321: 'On the evidence of 11 Q Melch. the most plausible inference is that he [auc. ad Heb.] regarded Melchizedek as an (arch-)angel who appeared to Abraham long ago. The ἀφωμοιωμένος δὲ τῷ υἱῷ τοῦ θεοῦ does not imply a limitation to the description in scripture but seeks to emphasize the subordination of the (arch-)angel Melchizedek to the pre-existent heavenly Son of God.'

or cultus is important for the understanding of the Church in the Pauline writings. In Palestinian Judaism the heavenly temple is one of the principal items which are eschatologically pre-existent. Ezekiel 40–8 and Ex. 25–9 are the major early sources for the idea of the heavenly cultus. Hebrews cites Ex. 25: 40 to confirm its argument about the heavenly cultus (8: 5–6). It sees Christ as the eternal priest officiating in the heavenly sanctuary.[1]

The heavenly temple already exists, and Christ has entered it by his ascension. Nevertheless, the present age still continues, and while it does so, access to the heavenly world is barred for ordinary men (9: 8–9). Here we have the apocalyptic idea of the 'overlapping of the ages'. Christ, by entering heaven – which is also the new age – has inaugurated the new age. From the point of view of the old age, the entities in the new, that is the heavenly cultus, pre-exist 'eschatologically'.

We must, however, recognize that the apocalyptic idea of the heavenly sanctuary has been blended with the middle Platonic conception of a 'true' (ἀληθινός) world of 'types' or 'ideas' and a world of antitypes (e.g. 9: 24) or shadows (e.g. 10: 1), in Hebrews. Rather than attempting to understand Hebrews against one background exclusively, one should welcome as an important phenomenon in the history of early Christianity, this blending of Jewish apocalyptic and middle Platonic traditions, and allow this datum to lead one inductively to a perhaps hitherto unknown religious milieu, in which Jews found the heavenly world of apocalyptic to be consonant with the ideal world of middle Platonism.

Hebrews contains both types of the idea of pre-existence. Protological pre-existence is attributed to Christ by means of the Wisdom myth, and by means of the Midrashic argumentation concerning Melchizedek, in chapter 7. A version of the myth which deals with Adam or the anthropos is also present. Eschatological pre-existence is expressed in the teaching on

---

[1] See A. Cody, *Heavenly Sanctuary and Liturgy in the Epistle to the Hebrews: the Achievement of Salvation in the Epistle's Perspectives* (St Meinrad, Indiana, 1960); F. J. Schierse, *Verheissung und Heilsvollendung, Zur theologischen Grundfrage des Hebräerbriefes*, Münchener Theologische Studien, 1, Historische Abteilung, 9. Band (Munich, 1955). Both of these works include a treatment of the idea of the heavenly cultus in the Biblical tradition.

hope, as the foretaste of already existing future entities, and in the concept of the heavenly cultus.

B. *I Peter*

The texts in question in this work are 1: 3–5, 1: 10–12, 13, 1: 18–21, 2: 4–10, 3: 18–22, 5: 1, 4, 10. All, except those in chapter 5, come from a baptismal liturgy or sermon, contained in the section 1: 3–4: 11.[1] We shall follow Preisker's analysis of the structure of the sermon in our discussion.[2]

The putative baptismal service begins with a 'Prayer-Psalm' similar to the Thanksgiving hymns of Qumran, contained in 1: 3–12. God is blessed, who has 'begotten us to a living hope through the resurrection of Jesus Christ from the dead' (1: 3). The fundamental Christian theologumenon – the resurrection and exaltation of Christ – is thus introduced. Christ is the ground of our hope, and, since he lives, it may be described as a living hope. Its object is located where he is, in heaven, and is described as an 'imperishable, undefiled and unfading inheritance', kept in heaven and ready to be revealed in the last time:

κληρονομίαν[3] ἄφθαρτον καὶ ἀμίαντον καὶ ἀμάραντον, τετηρημένην ἐν οὐρανοῖς εἰς ὑμᾶς τοὺς ἐν δυνάμει θεοῦ φρουρουμένους διὰ πίστεως

[1] For a review of the literary problems and proposed solutions, see A. R. C. Leaney, 'I Peter and the Passover: An Interpretation', *N.T.S.* x (1963–4), 238–51. We accept the position of Windisch as refined by Preisker, except for his theory that 4: 12 – 5: 11 belongs to the liturgy (1: 3 – 4: 11). Cross's theory, extended by Leaney, that 1: 3 – 4: 11 is a homily based on Pascal themes and delivered on the occasion of a baptism-cum-eucharist is intriguing, but not yet established, in our opinion. The arguments for Petrine authorship, which entail a rejection of the view that a liturgy is present, are quite unconvincing. (For instance, R. H. Gundry, 'Verba Christi in I Peter: Their Implications concerning the Authorship of I Peter and the Authenticity of the Gospel Tradition', *N.T.S.* 13 (1966–7), 336–50. Gundry's extraordinary lack of sensitivity to the problems of determining the *verba Christi* in the synoptic tradition, and his uncontrolled use of Johannine material, belong to a pre-critical era.) Cf. also, C. F. D. Moule, *N.T.S.* 3 (1956–7), 4; T. C. G. Thornton, *J.T.S.* XII (1961), 15ff.; W. C. van Unnik, *The Interpreter's Dictionary of the Bible*, III, 760; *N.T.S.* 1 (1954–5), 102; E. Best, 'I Peter and the Gospel Tradition', *N.T.S.* 16 (1969–70), 95–113.

[2] Set out by Leaney, 'I Peter and the Passover', pp. 241–2.

[3] On this word cf. Acts 20: 32, Gal. 3: 18, Eph. 1: 14, 18, 5: 5, Col. 3: 24, Heb. 9: 15, 11: 8. In the Old Testament it regularly refers to the promised land, e.g. Ps. 79: 1, cf. Ps. Sol. 7: 2.

εἰς σωτηρίαν ἑτοίμην ἀποκαλυφθῆναι ἐν καιρῷ ἐσχάτῳ (1: 4–5).

We may draw special attention to the phrases emphasized: (the inheritance) 'prepared in heaven', and the salvation 'ready to be revealed in the last time'. Both express the concept of eschatological pre-existence very clearly. The precise content of the heavenly inheritance is not stated, but it is clear that, in general terms, the life of eternal bliss is being referred to. The adjectives which describe the inheritance all occur in the Wisdom of Solomon. ἄφθαρτος describes the Spirit of God in 12: 1, and the light of the Law in 18: 4; in 4: 2 ἀμίαντος describes the rewards of virtue, and in 6: 12 Wisdom is called ἀμάραντος.[1] If one reads Wisd. 6: 12, where Wisdom is 'radiant and unfading' (λαμπρὰ καὶ ἀμάραντος) together with Wisd. 18: 4, which speaks of the 'incorruptible light of the Law' (τὸ ἄφθαρτον νόμου φῶς) one can hear an allusion to the pre-existent Wisdom/Torah, whose property is unfading and incorruptible light; but this is perhaps too far fetched for our passage. Nevertheless, it is as relevant as the allusion to Luke 12: 22–40, especially verse 33, which both Selwyn[2] and Gundry[3] argue lies behind our passage, in some way. The most that one can say is that all these allusions are part of the traditional Jewish and Christian view that the things to be revealed in the end are laid up in heaven, and that the chief realities there are the eternal Torah and/or the exalted Christ.

In 5: 1ff. the closing section of the treatise reiterates the belief in the 'glory to be revealed' (5: 1) and looks forward to the manifestation (φανερωθέντος) of the 'chief shepherd' and the unfading (ἀμαράντινον) crown of glory (cf. Wisd. 4: 2, 5: 16).

The opening thanksgiving concludes with an apocalyptic description of the history of salvation (1: 10–12). The prophets[4] did not know the plan of God, about which they uncomprehendingly gave testimony. The spirit of Christ predicted the events of his life and passion through them; but full under-

---

[1] E.g. Selwyn, *The First Epistle of St. Peter* (London, 1947), p. 124.
[2] *Ibid.*   [3] 'Verba Christi', p. 337.
[4] These are the prophets of the Old Covenant and not, as Selwyn argues, *ad. loc.*, the Christian prophets, because the pesher exegesis has to do with the old prophets.

standing of these prophecies is given only by the apostolic kerygma. Not even the angels knew this plan of salvation.

We have already discussed the way in which the idea that the scriptures prophesy Christ implies his 'ideal' pre-existence. The view of prophecy expressed here is, once again, that of the pesher exegetes of Qumran and the early – especially the Matthean – Church, as we have already observed.

There is, however, an advance in I Peter 1: 11 on the idea of pre-existence implied in the other examples of pesher exegesis we have considered. In Matthew's use of this exegesis Christ as the fulfilment of the scriptures, who therefore unlocks their true meaning, pre-exists, it is implied, as an idea in the mind of God; in which mind the plan of salvation set forth in the Scriptures was formed. Here, however, his spirit is said to have been 'bearing witness beforehand' (προμαρτυρόμενον) in the prophets. Christ, therefore, must have pre-existed as a πνεῦμα, and not merely as an idea.

Once again we find the nearest analogy to this structure of thought in Wisd. 7: 22–30. Wisdom is the spirit (Wisd. 1: 4–7) that bore witness in the prophets (Wisd. 7: 27 etc.); we suggested that this myth was behind Paul's argument in Gal. 3. There we have 'ideal' pre-existence; here the pre-existent spirit who enters men and makes them prophets.

1: 13 repeats the theme of hope directed towards the end, as it opens an 'instructional address' (13–21) which sets forth the way of holiness for the community and relates it to the work of Christ. Verses 18–20 return to the pre-existence of Christ. The blood of Christ is contrasted with silver and gold – the latter are perishable (φθαρτός)[1] while, by implication, the former is not. This is explained: the blood of Christ is imperishable because it is the blood of one 'destined before the foundation of the world but made manifest at the end of time for your sake.' προεγνωσμένου μὲν πρὸ καταβολῆς κόσμου, φανερωθέντος δὲ ἐπ' ἐσχάτου τῶν χρόνων δι' ὑμᾶς (vs 20). The basis of this statement is, again, the resurrection and exaltation (1: 21).

The two verbs used in parallel tell us something interesting about the idea of pre-existence present here. The former (προεγνωσμένου) has an intellectual force: the object, in normal

---

[1] The use of this term and its negative is infrequent in the Old Testament, but very frequent in Wisd. Sol. (Selwyn, *I Peter*, p. 144). Cf. 1: 23.

use, would be an idea in the mind of the knower. The latter (φανερωθέντος) has, normally, a visual force: its object is something concrete, outside the mind, which can be seen. The contrast expressed in μέν and δέ does not affect the force of the verbs; no change of being is implied in the transition from 'foreknown' to 'manifested'. The sentence suggests that the one foreknown is simply manifested, in the same state. The sentence may also represent liturgical convention (cf. Eph. 1: 4, also a 'hymnic' passage) or traditional usage (cf. I Tim. 3: 16, Col. 1: 26, 3: 4, II Tim. 1: 10, Heb. 9: 26). Be that as it may, the latter verb shows that the pre-existent one was most concretely conceived. This text is a useful confirmation of the thesis proposed, for instance, about Rom. 8: 29–30, where we followed the suggestion that God's fore-knowing those to be called implied the real pre-existence of the Church in the mind of God. The same type of thought occurs in Ephesians (1: 11–12), as we have seen.

At this point, according to Preisker (1: 21), the baptism takes place – a long ceremony involving many persons – as the tenses of the verbs before and after (1: 21 and 1: 22) suggest. There follows a short 'baptismal dedication' (1: 22–5) in which a life of love is suggested instead of the ecstatic utterance which followed many pagan initiations.[1]

2: 1–10 comprises a festal hymn – the usual 'ecstatic utterance' of the pagan mysteries? – into which verses 6–8 have been inserted. The theme of the hymn is familiar to us from the Pauline literature: the spiritual house, comprised of the individual Christians together (cf. I Cor. 3: 9–17, II Cor. 6: 14 – 7: 1, Eph. 2: 19–22, cf. 4: 15–16). The theme is supported by the usual citations from Is. 28: 16 (cf. Rom. 9: 33, 10: 11) and Ps. 118: 22 (cf. Mark 12: 10 par. Acts 4: 11), with concluding allusions to Ex. 23: 22 (verse 9) and Hos. 2: 23 (verse 10). There is no explicit statement that this spiritual house is a heavenly entity, but it may be inferred. It is obviously part of the tradition of the Church as a heavenly entity, and the context, with its strong emphasis on the pre-existence of Christ, suggests such an inference.

The next element in the liturgy (2: 11 – 3: 12) is an exhortation – by another individual – which includes at its climax a

---

[1] Leaney, 'I Peter and the Passover', p. 241.

hymn about Christ (2: 21-4). An apocalyptic discourse follows (3: 13 – 4: 7a) (what Paul in I Cor. 14: 26 would call a 'revelation'), which includes the statement of Christ's descent into hell to preach to 'the spirits in prison, who formerly did not obey, when God's patience waited in the days of Noah' (3: 18-22). The apocalyptic relations of this statement are obvious;[1] once again the drama reaches its climax in the exaltation of Christ (3: 21-2).

Fuller,[2] following Bultmann,[3] argues that a hymn underlies this section. It begins in verse 18 with 'who suffered once for our sins' and, omitting verses 20-1, ends in verse 22 with 'who is on the right hand of God, having gone into heaven, angels and authorities and powers having been made subject to him'. There is much to be said for this thesis, and we are inclined to accept it. However, the suggestion, made by Bultmann, that 1: 20, 'who was destined before the foundation of the world, but was made manifest at the end of the times' is the original opening of the hymn, now out of place, is more difficult to accept. Whether a hymn or not, this passage nevertheless expresses the Hellenistic Christology – rather Jewish than Gentile, as Fuller claims – that we have seen in Phil. 2: 5-11, Col. 1: 15-20 and John 1: 1-18. It lacks explicit reference to Christ's pre-existence. As in I Tim. 3: 16, that is implied.

C. *II Peter and Jude*

There is only one possible hint of pre-existence in II Peter. In 1: 11 it speaks of the 'eternal kingdom' of Christ (τὴν αἰώνιον βασιλείαν) which the Christian shall enter, which suggests something existing perpetually. Jude 6 speaks of the fallen angels kept in eternal chains, which reflects, in general, the apocalyptic view of a heavenly world, probably influenced by later imagery drawn from the experience of chaining in Roman prisons.

F. F. Bruce[4] suggests that the more difficult reading in Jude 5

---

[1] For a full discussion see Selwyn, *I Peter*, pp. 314-62; Bo Reicke, *The Disobedient Spirits and Christian Baptism* (Copenhagen, 1946); cf. I Enoch 90: 20-7, 54, 55; I Tim. 3: 16.

[2] R. H. Fuller, *Foundations*, pp. 218-20.

[3] R. Bultmann, in *Coniectanea Neotestamentica* XI (Festschrift Friedrichsen) (Lund, 1947), pp. 1-14 (as cited by Fuller).

[4] F. F. Bruce, 'Scripture and Tradition in the New Testament', in *Holy*

is preferable. That makes Jesus the one who led the people out of Egypt. Bruce sees this statement then as further testimony to the early Christian belief that Christ was God's agent in the history recorded in the Old Testament. There is good manuscript support for this reading (A, B), and we agree with Bruce, therefore, that Jude 5 is a witness to the belief in the pre-existence of Christ.

II. IDEAS OF PRE-EXISTENCE IN REVELATION

The book of Revelation fits the pattern of apocalyptic thought so well that it may be regarded as a confirmation of the scheme of eschatological pre-existence we have discerned so frequently in the New Testament.[1] It tells of things presently existing in heaven which will be manifested in the final days, being revealed beforehand to the seer. He was shown these things in order that he might inform the believers of 'what must soon take place', and he 'bore witness...to all that he saw' (1: 1–2). He is commanded to 'Write what you see, both the things that are and the things that will be hereafter' (1: 19).[2]

The first thing that he sees is 'one like a Son of Man' whose 'head and hair is white as white wool, white as snow' (1: 12–16). The vision of Daniel in 7: 9–14 is obviously the basis of this reference (cf. 1: 7), but it has been significantly modified. The Son of Man has the white hair of the 'Ancient of Days'; Jesus is identified with God. The foundation of this interpretation of Jesus is the resurrection: 'Jesus Christ the faithful martyr, the first born of the dead, and the ruler of kings on earth' (1: 5, cf.

Book and Holy Tradition, International Colloquium held in the Faculty of Theology, University of Manchester, ed. F. F. Bruce and E. G. Rupp (Grand Rapids, 1968), pp. 84–5.

[1] Because we shall not have occasion to discuss them below, we may mention the apocalyptic idea of the heavenly books; cf. Rev. 3: 5, 5: 1ff., 20: 12ff. Aimo T. Nikolainen, 'Der Kirchenbegriff in der Offenbarung des Johannes', *N.T.S.* 9 (1962–3), 351–61, 360 n. 1, believes that the author is influenced by the composition of the book of Ezekiel.

[2] γράψον οὖν ἃ εἶδες καὶ ἃ εἰσὶν καὶ ἃ μέλλει γενέσθαι μετὰ ταῦτα (cf. Dan. 2: 29). Cf. C.G. II. 1. 2. 16–18 (Apocryphon of John = Cod. Berolinensis 8502, 22. 1–8); W. C. van Unnik, 'A Formula describing Prophecy', *N.T.S.* 9 (1962–3), 86–94. Van Unnik argues that this is a traditional phrase describing prophecy, and shows how it occurs in Jewish apocalyptic, Roman paganism and Gnosticism.

17–18), who is 'the first and the last' (1: 17–18, cf. 2: 8). The pattern of a primitive Christology is again visible: starting with the resurrection and using the Danielic Son of Man myth, it follows Jesus to exaltation and equality with God; this entails the pre-existence of Christ, which, in turn, entails the pre-existence of the Church.

The pre-existence of Christ is explicitly stated by means of the formula, 'I am the Alpha and the Omega'. In 1: 8 God says, 'I am the Alpha and the Omega', and he is described as the one 'who is and who was and who is to come, the Almighty' (cf. 1: 4). In 21: 6 God ('he who sat on the throne', 21: 5) again says, 'I am the Alpha and the Omega, the beginning and the end'. However, in 22: 13 it is Jesus (the one who is 'coming soon', 22: 12) who says, 'I am the Alpha and Omega, the first and the last, the beginning and the end'; and in 1: 17–18 and 2: 8 he is 'the first and the last, who died and came to life', who speaks through the seer to the church at Smyrna.

From this it appears that the writer thinks of the superiority of God over the world in temporal as well as spatial terms. Temporally speaking, he is the 'Almighty' (ὁ παντοκράτωρ, 1: 8, cf. Ex. 3: 14, Is. 41: 4, Am. 3: 13 LXX) because he is the one who is, who was, and who is to come, the beginning and the end. His Godhead as creator of all things consists in his being perpetually – before, during and after the creation. Christ is thought of in the same way. The general direction of thought is towards the end; in a situation of persecution the Christians look forward to the eschatological vindication. The end, however, entails the beginning and he who is to come is the one who already exists, and always has existed.[1] His power to terminate creation derives from his power as creator; he was before the world and will be after it. This represents the ordinary belief of the Old Testament and Judaism in God as the creator and sustainer of the world. The new element is the unequivocal identification of Jesus with God in this capacity.

Together with this temporal statement of the pre-existence of

---

[1] G. B. Caird, *A Commentary on the Revelation of St. John the Divine*, Harper's New Testament Commentaries (New York, 1966), p. 19, writes: 'for he who is Alpha and Omega is also the great I am, in whose presence Christians are perpetually confronted with the Beginning and the End'.

Christ there is the well known spatial scheme of eschatological pre-existence. The tree of life in paradise exists in heaven (2: 7), along with the throne of God (4: 1ff.) and his temple. The throne is the chief heavenly reality and it is in the heavenly temple (7: 15). The theme of the heavenly temple (3: 12), which is virtually the same as the new Jerusalem (cf. 21: 2),[1] occupies the dominant place in the thought of our author. As an address to churches under trial, the book seeks to encourage them not only by reminding them of the imminent eschaton, but also by expounding the transcendental nature of the body to which they belong. It does this by identifying the Church with the heavenly temple or city (21: 2, cf. 3: 12, cf. Eph. 5: 21–33). In this way the idea of eschatological pre-existence provides an ontological ground for existence in the church.

The experience of persecution caused the author to construct the idea of pre-existence in terms of the opposition between good and evil. Paul Minear[2] has brought this out in a discussion of the motif of the temple or city, as it appears in ch. 11. He argues that the chapter may be analysed as a tale of two cities; the city of Satan on the one hand, symbolized as Sodom, Egypt and Jerusalem ('where their Lord was crucified', 11: 8) and elsewhere as Babylon (17: 2), which in turn stands for Rome. All the opposition to God is expressed in the symbol of the 'great city' (11: 8), which has been manifested under various names in the course of history. It is essentially the place where Jesus and his prophets are done to death; where the two witnesses finish their work (11: 7).[3]

On the other hand, the city of God, which 'embraces all the places and times of prophetic vocation',[4] is present where men obey the commands of the living Christ.[5] The letters to the Churches, and the moral exhortations scattered throughout the

---

[1] See G. B. Caird, *Revelation*, pp. 54–5 and 278–9, on the identification between the city and the temple in 3: 12, and the disappearance of the temple, its place being taken by the city, in 21: 22.

[2] 'Ontology and Ecclesiology in the Apocalypse', *N.T.S.* 12 (1965–6), 89–105. See also, P. Minear, *I Saw a New Earth: An Introduction to the Visions of the Apocalypse* (Washington, D.C. 1969).

[3] This is strongly reminiscent of the element of rejection in our 'eschatological wisdom tradition' in Q, represented by sayings such as Matt. 23: 37, Luke 13: 33ff. Cf. Minear, 'Ontology', p. 97.

[4] Minear, 'Ontology', p. 98.   [5] *Ibid.*, pp. 100–3.

book,[1] show that the author saw the presence of the city of God to inhere in the obedience of men to the will of Christ.

The place where these exhortations were heard and obeyed was the place where God dwelt with his people. This was the place where his transcendent city subsisted within the life of the seven churches, the place where the divine and human wills coalesced to form 'one complex reality', the place where residents of the holy city could discern and overcome the parodic claims and wiles of the 'great city'.[2]

The two cities are historical manifestations of the transcendent realities of good and evil. Both forces are given a dimension of 'depth' by means of myth. The dragon (ch. 12) 'that ancient serpent, who is the Devil and Satan' (20: 2) is the reality of cosmic evil which constantly threatens the well-being of man, both in heaven and on earth. God and the Lamb are the perpetual assurance and power of good, whose ultimate triumph is certain. The superiority of God and the Lamb is expressed, on the one hand, by means of the temporal assertion that Satan's power will have an end (20: 10), while God's is eternal.[3] On the other hand, it is expressed by means of the idea of the heavenly temple/city.

Minear's analysis concentrates on showing how a 'symbolism of the center'[4] operates to attract earthly communities to one or another pole. Jerusalem, Egypt, Sodom and Babylon, understood in terms of their content as events rather than their chronology, are manifestations of the 'great city' which opposes God, while the Church is a manifestation of the heavenly city of God, the New Jerusalem.

On the basis of Minear's analysis, the important distinction to be made, for our purposes, is that, in Revelation, the 'great city' is earthly, whereas the city of God is 'heavenly'. The 'symbolism of the centre' makes the earthly communities representatives of transcendent evil, but there is no transcendent community of evil. Nowhere does the author suggest that Satan

[1] E.g. 21: 8, 14: 4, lists of actions by which men are included or excluded; 14: 13, beatitude; 19: 10, direct imperative; see also, 2: 7, 13: 10b, 15: 2 (*ibid.*, p. 101).

[2] *Ibid.*, p. 102.

[3] Cf. the parody of God's title of eternity in 17: 8b, where the 'beast was and is not, and is to come'. See G. B. Caird, *Revelation*, pp. 215–16.

[4] *Op. cit.*, p. 96, quoting M. Eliade, *The Myth of the Eternal Return*, pp. 3–17.

and his hosts have a place of their own in heaven; earth is their place (2: 13, 12: 9), while heaven belongs to God (13: 6). Satan is present in heaven only as an invader (12: 7), and his servants, those marked with his mark, as a defeated army to be executed (19: 20–1). This, to use Minear's language, shows the 'profound antithesis between the ultimate status of the one [city] and the deceptive penultimate status of the other', the detection of which Minear attributes to the author.[1]

Minear's reading of Revelation is mistaken, however, to the extent that he understands it to present a transcendent city of evil.[2] The Devil is a transcendent power; but the only city he has is on earth. The 'great city' is a manifestation in history of the power of Satan; the city of God in history is the earthly manifestation and counterpart of the heavenly temple/city (7: 15, 11: 1, cf. Ezek. 40: 3, Rev. 11: 19, 14: 15–17, 15: 5–8, 21: 1ff.). When the earth is swallowed up in the great judgement, Satan and his city will disappear; but the city of God, the new Jerusalem, will abide forever. This means that the seer took the distinction between the ultimacy of God's kingdom and the penultimacy of Satan's more seriously than Minear recognizes. In essence what the seer is saying is that only the city of God is ontologically rooted; it alone is real. The 'great city' is an illusion, ultimately it is nothing – the abyss is its form and its aim; it is non-being. Those who belong to it are, in principle, with Satan in the lake of fire (20: 10). The city of God is the place of perpetual light and peace, where God's presence constitutes our existence. Its beauty surpasses imagination, for its light is the glory of God (21: 1 – 22: 5). Membership in the church is tantamount to membership in the new Jerusalem; life in the church on earth affects one's status in the heavenly city (3: 12).[3] The city already exists, before the end, as the many visions of it testify (e.g. 4: 1ff.); and it will descend to the new earth, prepared as a bride for her husband (21: 2, cf. Eph. 5: 21–33).

In conclusion we return to the 'prophetic' formula we noted

[1] Minear, 'Ontology', p. 100.

[2] Cf. *ibid.*, p. 99, where he says that the 'great city' inherits its power from the beast of the abyss. This, according to him, means that its power is transcendent but not its substance.

[3] Cf. our discussion of I Cor. 3: 9–17 above. Cf. Aimo T. Nikolainer, 'Der Kirchenbegriff in der Offenbarung des Johannes', pp. 358–9.

at the beginning: 'Write therefore what you see, both the things that are, and the things that shall be hereafter' (ἃ εἶδες καὶ ἃ εἰσὶν καὶ ἃ μέλλει γενέσθαι μετὰ ταῦτα, 1: 19). What does the phrase 'the things that are' mean? It could mean 'the present circumstances', the true state of the churches to which the seer writes; but that is hardly the sort of information that a vision from heaven is necessary to communicate. A clue to the meaning of this phrase occurs in 17: 8 and 11, where the beast is that which 'was but is not' (ἦν καὶ οὐκ ἔστιν). God, on the other hand, is he who 'is, who was, and who is to come' (1: 4, 8, 4: 8, cf. 11: 17, 16: 5, where God is ὁ ὢν καὶ ὁ ἦν). The phrase, 'the things which are', therefore, refers to God in his temporal superiority over the beast; but it speaks of 'things', not of persons. The 'things which are', therefore, must be the divine things which exist perpetually, and which will be revealed in the end. Now, the things shown the seer are both events and entities – the events of the final judgement, and the heavenly temple/city. Events cannot be said to exist before they happen in the mind of one who plans them, only entities can have real pre-existence. The 'things which are' must, therefore, be the heavenly temple/city, the Church.

The idea of the pre-existent Church requires careful consideration. Nikolainen points out that in 8: 1–5 the prayers of the saints on earth participate in the heavenly liturgy; but it is only their prayers, not themselves.[1] In 12: 1ff., where the birth of the Church is symbolized as a cosmic event, which expresses the constant conflict of the history of salvation, only the one child is 'heaven-born' (12: 5) – Christ – and not 'the rest of her offspring' (12: 11) – the Christians. 3: 12 underlines this 'eschatological reservation'; the promise of Christ that the faithful will be pillars in the new temple is strictly for the future. The martyrs are 'under the altar' and must wait until the full number of those predestined to martyrdom has been reached (6: 9–11). In the final battle there are no Christians in the armies of God, only angels (19: 11–21). Nikolainen takes this to indicate that the seer's view of the Church is strictly eschatological, that full membership in the heavenly Church can only follow the final victory of Christ.

[1] Cf. the idea of the Qumran sect that their communities included the angels, e.g. 1 Q.S. 11: 8; Nikolainen, p. 355.

On the other hand, there is an element of 'realized eschato-logy' in Revelation. Nikolainen appreciates this, but emphasizes the 'not yet' rather than the 'already'. For instance, he calls the vision of the redeemed in 7: 9–17 an anticipatory vision of the *ecclesia triumphans*.[1] This is essentially correct, but his distinction between present and future is too sharp. For the apocalyptic mind 'anticipation' is too modern an attitude. It could hold present and future together and preserve the full force of each. One moment the Church is the triumphant heavenly com-munity of the Lamb, enjoying his victorious fellowship (7: 9–17, 12: 10–12); the next, it is the suffering pilgrim people who look for vindication (6: 10–11, 12: 17). In this respect it represents the most constant theme of the New Testament, that the things of our salvation 'are, and are to come hereafter'.

III. CONCLUSION: IDEAS OF PRE-EXISTENCE IN THE GENERAL EPISTLES AND REVELATION

The evidence of these writings serves chiefly to confirm the understanding of pre-existence we have gained so far. To some degree they make more explicit the structures of the idea we have already delineated.

In Hebrews Christ is pre-existent Wisdom, the creator and sustainer of the universe, superior to angels and all previous bearers of God's revelation. There are also fragments of the myth of the pre-existent anthropos present, suggesting that somewhere in the traditions behind Hebrews Christ was identi-fied with that figure. The epistle, therefore, makes most explicit statements about Christ's protological pre-existence.

In its teaching on the already present future, the eternal priest and the heavenly cultus, Hebrews gives perhaps the clearest presentation in the New Testament of the Christian adaptation of Jewish Apocalyptic imagery, in order to express the heavenly pre-existence of Christ and, in principle, since Christ is our forerunner, of the Church. This structure of the idea we have called eschatological pre-existence.

Along with the apocalyptic imagery, however, Hebrews also attests the influence of Jewish middle Platonism. This twofold

[1] Nikolainen, *ibid.*, p. 354.

background raises interesting questions for the history of religion in that period.

I Peter seems to be more in the tradition of Jewish apocalyptic. It knows of the things stored up in heaven, the Church as a heavenly entity, and Christ as the heavenly redeemer or judge of Jewish apocalyptic. It also knows the wisdom tradition, in which Wisdom is a pre-existent spirit which enters the prophets and reveals God's plan to and through them. Finally, it knows the pre-existence of Christ in the mind of God. Jude 5 possibly also attests the tradition of Christ acting in the events of the history of Israel.

Revelation, while it affirms in most explicit terms the eschatological pre-existence of the Church, as the heavenly temple or heavenly city, adds what is perhaps a new form of the idea. In the statements about God and Christ as the ones who 'have been, are and will come' (1: 4, 8, cf. 11: 17, 16: 5, cf. 1: 19, 17: 8, 11), which, as van Unnik has shown,[1] are adaptations of a Hellenistic formula describing prophecy, there is an almost philosophic concern with the concepts of being and time, which is new in the Biblical traditions. God's being is 'defined' with reference to his 'duration'; he is supreme because he is 'before' and 'after', Alpha and Omega. What has been implicit in much of the imagery expressing pre-existence which we have considered, namely, that priority in time entails priority in being or value, here in Revelation approaches explicitness. This idea, however, coheres with the structures we have delineated so far; it may perhaps be regarded as a sub-type of protological pre-existence.

[1] W. C. van Unnik, 'A Formula describing Prophecy'.

CONCLUSION

The idea of pre-existence, in both its forms, is deeply embedded in the Biblical traditions. As protological pre-existence it describes the nature of entities such as Wisdom, Torah and Christ, as especially akin to God. In its eschatological form it is part of the basic pattern of eschatological thought, and, once again, describes the nature of entities like the Son of Man, Christ and the Church, as especially related to the nature of God.

We shall not here recapitulate the history of pre-existence in the Biblical traditions; that has already been presented, in the conclusions to each chapter. Rather, assuming that history, we shall raise certain questions which seem to follow from the discussion, and to be of some interest to the present-day theological endeavor.

The first question is one whose answer has already been anticipated in the previous paragraphs: to what extent does the Bible intend to speak of the *nature* of an entity when it attributes pre-existence to it? This seems a very odd question to pose, but it is necessary in view of the influential arguments of men like Bultmann and Cullmann. Bultmann, as we have seen, understands the pre-existence of Christ to signify only that the proclamation which Christ's presence caused has its origin outside this world.[1] It does not intend to say anything explicit about that realm outside this world in which the proclamation originates. In thus making pre-existence a description of an entity in this world alone – namely the proclamation – Bultmann truncates religious thought, stopping it at the boundaries of time, space and human existence. This is consonant with his view that meaningful religious discourse can only be about human existence in this world. Cullmann also is not too far from this position, in his insistence on the primacy of the function of Christ over his nature in the New Testament understanding.[2]

Do the traditions we have examined provide us with any help in furthering this discussion? First of all we may notice that there

---

[1] *New Testament Theology*, I, p. 305.
[2] *Christology of the New Testament*, p. 247.

is a process of interpretation going on from one tradition to another. The bluntest answer to our question is provided by Philo, John and Hebrews, each of whom interpreted the same interests as are expressed in the apocalyptic and Wisdom mythology of the heavenly world and the heavenly man, in Platonic categories, to a greater or lesser extent. Since the language of 'natures' is more at home in Platonic than in apocalyptic and Wisdom discourse, one could say that these three understood pre-existence to be a statement about the 'natures' of the entities in question.

However, the question which now arises is: What point of contact is there between the apocalyptic and Wisdom traditions on the one hand and Philo, John and Hebrews on the other? In answering this question one has to treat Philo separately. Philo did not, as far as we can tell, reflect on Jewish apocalyptic directly; his point of reference was the Old Testament, and, more specifically, the Pentateuch. We should, therefore, regard his thought as an alternative development to apocalyptic, parallel but independent. The point of contact would, therefore, have to lie further back, in the tradition which the apocalyptists and Philo, respectively, inherited. This was the theology of Promise and Fulfilment, and the Priestly theology of the heavenly world. On this theory, apocalypticism and Jewish Middle Platonism would be alternative developments of the seed of the idea of pre-existence in the religion of Israel. Metaphysical speculation in Hellenistic Judaism, therefore, had its point of contact with the Biblical traditions chiefly in the Pentateuch.

With the Wisdom tradition the matter may be somewhat different. Here, it seems, Philo reflected on the living tradition in the Hellenistic synagogue, which also was alive in Palestine. His interpretation of Wisdom in Middle Platonic terms could, therefore, be a direct reconstruction of the Palestinian tradition, rather than an alternative parallel explanation of a common earlier tradition. In this case, Palestine seems to have preserved the early tradition more or less unchanged, while Hellenistic Judaism re-interpreted it.

It is possible that we have in the metaphysics of Philo, on the one hand, and in the symbolism of apocalyptic and the Wisdom tradition, on the other, different attempts to say the same thing

about the pre-existent entities. There is no metaphysical speculation in the Palestinian traditions, but their myths and symbols
were probably intended, as seriously as Philo's metaphysics, to
say something about the pre-existent entities in themselves. That
they did not use a vocabulary in which a word like 'nature' was
appropriate should not blind us to the force of the mythological
vocabulary they did employ. It expresses in its own way an
interest which in the realm of metaphysical discourse would be
expressed in terms of 'nature'.

In the case of John and Hebrews the Jewish apocalyptic and
Wisdom traditions themselves were drawn upon, and not some
prior common tradition, as in Philo's use of the Pentateuch
rather than the apocalyptic texts. They also, however, drew
upon Hellenistic Judaism. In them, therefore, we see how the
metaphysical intent of the Palestinian traditions was perceived
and given expression in the language of Middle Platonism. But
they are still more under the influence of the Palestinian
mythological vocabulary than that of Middle Platonism, and
so do not make their metaphysical interest explicit in the language of 'nature' and 'idea'. Nevertheless, they do seem to be
aware of that realm of discourse and to regard their native
apocalyptic and Wisdom mythology as an adequate expression
of metaphysical interest.

John and Hebrews are, however, only two sources in the New
Testament. They could, in their metaphysical interest, express
the influence of Hellenistic Judaism, and it could, therefore, be
argued that they do not express the interest of the other Jewish
and New Testament traditions. One must, therefore, consider
those sources themselves. The widespread interest in the
heavenly world and the pre-existent things in the apocalyptic
texts, and the prominence of pre-existent Wisdom, suggest to us
that these Jewish traditions express a real interest in what, in
other language, one might call metaphysical entities. To the
extent that Jesus and Paul shared the imagery by which this
interest is expressed, they might be assumed to have shared the
interest itself.

The assessment of the meaning and force of this imagery depends on the philosophical and cultural presuppositions of the
modern interpreter. Bultmann, for instance, regards mythology
– which is what most of this imagery in fact is – as a primitive,

pre-scientific aberration to be reinterpreted in terms of existentialist philosophy. M. Eliade,[1] however, sees mythology as a primitive form of metaphysics, intending seriously to depict 'the other world'. Insofar as the promulgators of this mythology might be assumed to have taken it literally, it would seem that a modern interpretation which allowed for the existence and knowability of 'another world' would be more adequate than one which, like Bultmann's, seems to allow for its existence but not its knowability. This brings us to the endeavors of modern systematic theology to interpret this Biblical material. We are not competent to discuss them at length, but we cannot forbear to mention some.

Before we turn to the modern systematic theologians, we may notice some representative attempts by historians of dogma to explain the emergence from the New Testament of the patristic concern with pre-existence. We begin with Harnack because, like F. C. Baur, his ghost still haunts modern theology long after his specific theses were thought to have been superseded. Harnack argues,[2] correctly we believe, that in Jewish apocalyptic thought the pre-existent things would be manifested on earth without undergoing any necessary change of nature in the process. However, when Christianity came to express this idea of manifestation in terms of Greek thought, the pre-existent things were made to undergo a change of nature because of a pessimistic Hellenistic dualism in which this world was not able to contain the pre-existent things in their own nature. Thus, according to Harnack, Christianity mistakenly bound itself to the 'refined asceticism of a dying culture',[3] gave a false foundation to its religious perceptions, and started down the cul-de-sac of Christological speculation in terms of natures.

Harnack is correct in his perception of the change in the idea of manifestation, but in judgement of the blending of Greek metaphysics with the Gospel is somewhat harsh. We shall return to this matter; here we wish simply to notice that Harnack considers the movement from Jewish to Hellenistic categories to

[1] *The Myth of the Eternal Return, passim.*

[2] *Dogmengeschichte*, I, pp. 710–11.

[3] *Ibid.*, p. 718: 'So wurde die christliche Religion hineingezogen in die raffinierte Askese einer untergehenden Cultur und ihrer in der Schlichtheit so ernsten Moral ein fremder Unterbau gegeben.'

have been a radical and fundamentally unfortunate event in the history of the Gospel.

F. Hahn shows the continued influence of Harnack when he calls the Christology of pre-existence, first formulated in the Hellenistic church according to him, 'a decisively new stage'[1] in the history of doctrine. Reginald Fuller also locates the origin of the Christology of pre-existence in the Hellenistic Church, and although he does not emphasize its newness he does suggest that it had no importance outside the Hellenistic Church.[2] We have no quarrel with the historical judgement that pre-existence was first treated explicitly in the Hellenistic Church, but we do question whether this was 'decisively new'. The Hellenistic Church gave prominence to the pre-existence of Christ as we have argued, by identifying Christ with Wisdom, but in so doing, we suggest, they were simply giving their own form to an impulse which was expressed in the Palestinian traditions by means of apocalyptic categories, and which derives ultimately from Jesus' own use of the title 'Son of Man'. Furthermore, to make the Christology of pre-existence a 'decisively new' departure in early Christian thought in addition to neglecting the evidence we have presented in the body of this work, seems also to be based, more generally, on the now discredited sharp dichotomy between Palestinian and Hellenistic Judaism. Finally, it betrays the lingering influence of Harnack and Ritschl insofar as it would make it possible to separate a 'pure' or non-Greek form of the Gospel from a later Greek version.

If our understanding of the mythological symbolism of the apocalyptic and wisdom traditions is correct, and our view of the essential continuity of interest in the 'other world' from the Palestinian to the Hellenistic forms of each Christian doctrine is accurate, then modern attempts to appropriate the Gospel cannot ignore metaphysical thought of one kind or another. Paul Tillich insisted on this point with great passion, and provided an impressive example of how ontological thought could be fruitful for an understanding of the Gospel. His attempt to show how the Biblical traditions demand ontological interpretation was, however, not detailed enough and so not entirely

[1] F. Hahn, *The Titles of Jesus in Christology, Their History in Early Christianity*, trans. H. Knight and G. Ogg (New York, 1969), p. 304.

[2] R. Fuller, *Foundations*, pp. 245–6.

successful.[1] Much more successful and, at present, more promising, is the work of the Pannenberg circle.

The Pannenberg school regards Jewish apocalyptic as the dominant conceptual framework of earliest Christianity. We have seen reason in the course of this work to agree with them. Their claim about the horizon of apocalyptic as embracing universal history might be subject to discussion,[2] but their perception of the fruitfulness for modern thought of the apocalyptic emphasis on the future is extremely promising. However, we suggest that, in the light of our findings, Pannenberg's understanding of the relationship between the future and the present might be somewhat modified.

Greek metaphysics, in whose terms God is 'the highest spiritual being', has indeed fallen into disrepute amongst modern men, as Pannenberg claims, and with it that conventional idea of God.[3] The appropriate response to this is not to abandon the metaphysical enterprise altogether, but to conceive an adequate metaphysic. This Pannenberg attempts by means of a genuine sensitivity to the modern world on the one hand, and a searching scrutiny of the Biblical traditions on the other. He finds the Biblical basis for a new metaphysic in the apocalyptic view of the eschaton as the future coming of God. For him, 'God is the power of the future' (p. 63). This is the way in which Pannenberg understands the proclamation by Jesus that the Kingdom of God is imminent. In its imminent

[1] P. Tillich, *Biblical Religion and the Search for Ultimate Reality* (Chicago, 1963). We do, however, find his defence of philosophical eros against the careless condemnation of 'mere speculation' by doctrinaire Biblical scholars apt and telling (*ibid.*, pp. 1–10). E.g., 'It is infuriating to see how biblical theologians, when explaining the concepts of the Old or New Testament writers, use most of the terms created by the toil of philosophers and the ingenuity of the speculative mind and then dismiss, with cheap denunciations, the work from which their language has been immensely enriched.' (*Ibid.*, p. 7.)

[2] See H. D. Betz, 'The Concept of Apocalyptic in the Theology of the Pannenberg Group', in *Journal for Theology and Church*, Vol. 6, 192–207. We do not see how Betz's insistence that apocalyptic is a more varied phenomenon from a religio-historical point of view than the Pannenberg circle suggests, necessarily invalidates their claim that it intends to encompass all history in the eschatological event. This seems to be a clear theme in apocalyptic, whatever other multiple themes it includes.

[3] Wolfhart Pannenberg, *Theology and the Kingdom of God* (Philadelphia, 1969), pp. 55ff.

futurity – not merely a general futurity – the Kingdom defines the nature of the present, and, since it has been imminently future for all prior ages, of the past too.

How is the future at work in constituting the present, for Pannenberg? Pannenberg declares 'that God's being and existence cannot be conceived apart from his rule...the being of the gods is their power' (p. 55). Since God's power or coming rule has not yet been fully realized over this world, 'it is necessary to say that, in a restricted but important sense, God does not yet exist. Since his rule and his being are inseparable, God's being is still in process of coming to be. Considering this, God should not be mistaken for an objectified being presently existing in fullness' (p. 56). However, he writes, 'wherever the message of the imminent Kingdom of God is accepted, God has already come into power and man now has communion with God' (p. 65).

Accepting for the moment Pannenberg's statement that the being of God is His power, we sense a difficulty in his argument. If there is a sense in which God does not yet exist it seems to be in the sense that his sovereignty has not yet been established over all the world. Yet where that sovereignty is established over an individual in the present God is said to exist in the present. Is this a partial existence (whatever that may mean) of God, and if so, how can Pannenberg avoid Whitehead's view – which he explicitly denies – that 'the futurity of God's rule implies a development in God' (p. 62)? Pannenberg seems to suggest that God exists in the present for the believer, but not for the world, and not 'partially' or as a God-in-the-process-of-becoming, but fully: 'He was in the past the same one whom he will manifest himself to be in the future' (p. 63). It seems to us an unfortunately misleading statement, therefore, to say, in however restricted a sense, that God does not yet exist.

The equation of the being of God with his power is another doubtful conception. It is logically very odd; being is one kind of thing, power another. One can say, 'a being has power', and even, 'power has being', but 'a being is power' escapes our understanding.

It seems to us that the primitive conceptuality of apocalyptic is more adequate to Pannenberg's metaphysical proposal than his own structures. Apocalyptic recognizes God as 'the power of the future', whose rule is not yet established over the earth.

It maintains, however, the distinction between God's power and His being. God is present to the world as the power of the future. We find Pannenberg's proposal on this matter of God's presence to the world very illuminating. However, to the individual, to the seers who visit heaven, he is a presently existing being whose dwelling is in heaven. The entities which are the accoutrements of his future coming also exist in heaven. God and salvation are the presently existing final future.

Pannenberg expresses the transcendence of God in a temporal category only – He is future. The apocalyptists use in addition the category of space to express the present existence and accessibility of the future. In this way, by means of spatial categories, they express the real existence of God before the end – the eschatological pre-existence of God and of the 'things of our salvation'. In this way the apocalyptists express that God is the presently existing power of the future. Pannenberg seeks to do without the spatial category because the conception of God in spatial terms is unacceptable to modern man. We ask whether in attempting to use only the temporal category to express transcendence he has not made the idea of God even less accessible to modern man, by making it finally unintelligible. On his scheme why talk of God at all? It is sufficient to talk of the future as the determiner of the present and the past.

At this point in the discussion there seem to be at least two possibilities open to Pannenberg: either to revise his definition of the being of God as His power, or to admit that he is using only one aspect of early apocalyptic thought, namely, its emphasis on the future. If he takes the former way he must, it seems to us, speak of God's being as an objective entity; he could then justly claim to be presenting the view of early apocalyptic. If he takes the second way we suggest that he has omitted from consideration so important a part of apocalyptic thought that he cannot rightly claim to be basing his theology on apocalyptic.

Apocalyptic teaches the real pre-existence of the entities to be revealed in the end. It presents this teaching by means of myth and symbol. It is doubtful that God as a presently existing being who is the power of the future can be spoken of in any other way than symbolically. Therefore, not only in the substance of its thought, but also in its mode of presentation, apocalyptic is a hopeful guide to modern theology.

These criticisms should not, however, minimize the radical importance of Pannenberg's insight that it is the future and not the past that shapes the present. This is generally true to apocalyptic thought. The eschatologically pre-existent entities do not impinge on the present; they are hidden in heaven and kept until the end. In their visions the apocalyptists glimpse them beforehand, but the effect of this is only to kindle and sustain hope in the believers, not to transform the world, nor to inaugurate the end. In Christ the Christians received a similar foretaste and experienced a similar kindling of hope. The Church became the living pledge or foretaste of the end – a special manifestation of the eschatological entities – but still preliminary and provisional. 'Our citizenship is in heaven' (or 'in the future') (Phil. 3: 20).

A metaphysic based on apocalyptic thought cannot, therefore, avoid spatial categories, or the idea of God as a presently existing objective being. However, these are, like the apocalyptic expression itself, symbolic terms, and other symbols more adequate to modern understanding must be found to express the same intention.[1]

Our discussion so far has centred on apocalyptic; what of the Wisdom tradition? Wisdom in early Judaism might be said to be the essence of the creation, its inherent form. It was the blueprint according to which the universe was created. To that extent it could be regarded as a determinant of history from the past rather than the future. In this respect it should be compared with the idea of the plan of God in apocalyptic. The idea of a primordially given plan of which history is simply the outworking is indeed present in the thought of early Judaism and the New Testament.

Does this rob history of its 'newness' and the future of its power?[2] We think not. Wisdom as the essence of the universe and also the true man is chiefly to be revealed in the end. Its

---

[1] Pannenberg's essay, 'Appearance as the Arrival of the Future', in *Theology and the Kingdom of God*, pp. 127–43, is a promising indication of his awareness of this intention and his willingness to deal with it seriously.

[2] Cf. the extravagant arguments of C. Tresmontant for the newness of history in the Bible in *Études de Métaphysique Biblique*, Paris, 1955, and *A Study of Hebrew Thought*, New York, 1960. His views are so much influenced by Bergson that he fails to take account of the Biblical evidence that does not agree with Bergson.

prior manifestation in Christ is preliminary and provisional – it does not impose a pattern on history 'from behind'. (The manifestation in Torah might have been thought of differently, however.) Paul emphasized this especially – true humanity lies in the future and is not a return to a primordial state. There is also in apocalyptic the idea that all history has been arranged from the beginning, and this cannot be minimized. However, from the point of view of man in time, history is still spontaneous and new since the plan is not known to him.

We have tried in these brief and inadequate concluding remarks to show at least one place where the idea of pre-existence in the Biblical traditions impinges on current theological discussions. The chief purpose of our work has, however, been historical and phenomenological.

BIBLIOGRAPHY

Albright, W. F., 'The Oracles of Balaam', *J.B.L.* 63 (1944), 207–33.
Allo, Le P. E.-B., *Saint Paul, Première Épître aux Corinthiens*, Études Bibliques, Deuxième Edition (Paris, 1956).
Saint Paul, Seconde Épître aux Corinthiens, Études Bibliques (Paris, 1956).
Arvedson, T., *Das Mysterium Christi, Eine Studie zu Mtt. 11: 25–30* (Leipzig and Uppsala, 1937).
Baltensweiler, H., *Die Verklärung Jesu* (Zürich, 1959).
Barr, J., *The Semantics of Biblical Literature* (Oxford, 1961).
Biblical Words for Time (London, 1962).
Barrett, C. K., *The Epistle to the Romans*, Harper's New Testament Commentaries (New York, Evanston and London, 1957).
The Holy Spirit and the Gospel Tradition (London, 1958).
The Gospel According to St. John, An Introduction with Commentary and Notes on the Greek Text (London, 1958).
From First Adam to Last: A Study in Pauline Theology (New York, 1962).
The Pastoral Epistles in the New English Bible, with Introduction and Commentary (Oxford, 1963).
'Christianity at Corinth', *B.J.R.L.* 46 (1963–4), 269–97.
Best, E., *The Temptation and the Passion: The Markan Soteriology* (Cambridge, 1965).
Betz, H. D., *Nachfolge und Nachahmung Jesu Christi im Neuen Testament*, *B.H.T.* 37 (Tübingen, 1967).
'Zum Problem des religionsgeschichtliche Veständnisses der Apokalyptik', *Z.T.K.* 63/4 (1966), 391–409.
'The Logion of the Easy Yoke and of Rest (Matt. 11: 28–30)', *J.B.L.* 86 (1967), 10–24.
'Jesus as Divine Man', in *Jesus and the Historian*, written in honour of Ernest Cadman Colwell, ed. F. Thomas Trotter (Philadelphia, 1968), 114–33.
'The Concept of Apocalyptic in the Theology of the Pannenberg Group', *Journal for Theology and Church*, Vol. 6 (New York, 1969), 192–207.
Betz, Otto, *Offenbarung und Schriftforschung in der Qumransekte*, *W.U.N.T.* 6 (Tübingen, 1960).
Bianci, U., *Le Origini dello Gnosticismo/The Origins of Gnosticism, Colloquium of Messina, 13–18 April 1966* (Leiden, 1967).
Bickermann, E., 'La Chaîne de la Tradition Pharisienne', *R.B.* 59 (1952), 44–54.

Black, M., *An Aramaic Approach to the Gospels and Acts; with an Appendix on the Son of Man*, by Geza Vermes, 3rd ed. (Oxford, 1967).

'The Son of Man Problem in Recent Research and Debate', *B.J.R.L.* 45 (1962–3), 305–18.

Blackman, P., *Mishnayoth*, Vol. IV, Order Nezikin (New York, 1965).

Boman, T., *Hebrew Thought Compared with Greek* (Philadelphia, 1960).

Bonnard, P., *L'Épître de Saint Paul aux Galates*, Comm. du N.T. IX (Neuchâtel/Paris, 1953).

Borgen, Peder, *Bread from Heaven: An Exegetical Study of the Concept of Manna in the Gospel of John and the Writings of Philo*, Suppl. to Novum Testamentum X (Leiden, 1965).

Bornkamm, G., *Jesus of Nazareth*, trans. I. and F. McLuskey with J. M. Robinson (London and New York, 1960).

'Die Häresie des Kolosserbriefes', *Das Ende des Gesetzes, Paulusstudien*, Gesammelte Aufsätze I (München, 1958), 139–56.

'Zum Verständnis des Christus-Hymnus Phil. 2: 6–11', *Studien zu Antike und Urchristentum*, Gesammelte Aufsätze II (München, 1959).

'Zur Interpretation des Johannesevangeliums, Eine Auseinandersetzung mit Ernst Kaesemanns Schrift *Jesu Letzter Wille nach Johannes 17*', *Evangelische Theologie* 28 (1962) 8–25.

Article, μυστήριον, *T.D.N.T.* IV, 802–27.

ed. Bornkamm, G. and H. Kraft, *Botschaft und Geschichte* II, M. Dibelius' Gesammelte Aufsätze (Tübingen, 1956).

ed. Bornkamm, G., G. Barth and H. J. Held, *Tradition and Interpretation in Matthew* (Philadelphia, 1963).

Borsch, F. H., *The Son of Man in Myth and History* (Philadelphia, 1967).

Bostrom, G., *Proverbiastudien* (Lund, 1935).

Brandenburger, Egon, *Adam und Christus, Exegetisch-religionsgeschichtliche Untersuchung zu Röm. 5: 12–21 (I Kor. 15)*, *W.M.A.N.T.* 7 (Neukirchen Kreis Moers, 1962).

Fleisch und Geist, Paulus und die dualistiche Weisheit, *W.M.A.N.T.* 29 (Neukirchen, 1968).

Brown, R. E., *The Gospel according to John (i–xii)*, The Anchor Bible (New York, 1966).

'The Pre-Christian Semitic Concept of "Mystery"', *Catholic Biblical Quarterly*, XX (1958), 417–43.

'Does the New Testament call Jesus God?' *Theological Studies* 26 (1965), 562–3.

Brownlee, W. H., 'Biblical Interpretation among the Sectaries of the Dead Sea Scrolls', *B.A.* 14 (1951), 54–76.

'The Servant of the Lord in the Qumran Scrolls', II, *B.A.S.O.R.* 135 (1954), 36–8.

Bruce, F. F., *The Epistle to the Hebrews*, New International Commentary on the New Testament (Grand Rapids, Mich., 1964).

'"To the Hebrews" or "To the Essenes"', *N.T.S.* 9 (1962–3), 221.

ed. Bruce, F. F., *Promise and Fulfilment*, Essays presented to S. H. Hooke in celebration of his ninetieth birthday (Edinburgh, 1963).

ed. Bruce, F. F. and E. G. Rupp, *Holy Book and Holy Tradition*, International Colloquium held in the Faculty of Theology, University of Manchester (Grand Rapids, Mich., 1968).

Bultmann, R., *Theology of the New Testament*, trans. Kendrick Grobel (New York, Vol. I, 1951, Vol. II, 1955).

Primitive Christianity in its Contemporary Setting (New York, 1956).

Die Geschichte der synoptischen Tradition (Göttingen, 1961).

Das Evangelium des Johannes, Meyers Kommentar II, 17th edition (unchanged reprint of 10th edition) (Göttingen, 1962).

'Der religionsgeschichtliche Hintergrund des Prologs zum Johannes-Evangelium', in *Eucharisterion: Studien zur Religion und Literatur des Alten und Neuen Testaments für Hermann Gunkel*, ed. H. Schmidt, *F.R.L.A.N.T.* Neue Folge 19 (2 vols., Göttingen, 1923), II, 3–26.

Burney, C. F., 'Christ as the ΑΡΧΗ of Creation', *J.T.S.* 27 (1925–6), 160–77.

ed. Buttrick, G. A., *The Interpreter's Bible* (New York, 1951–7).

Caird, G. B., *Principalities and Powers, a Study in Pauline Theology* (Oxford, 1956).

A Commentary on the Revelation of St. John the Divine, Harper's New Testament Commentaries (New York, 1966).

'The Glory of God in the Fourth Gospel: An Exercise in Biblical Semantics', *N.T.S.* 15 (1968–9), 265–77.

Causée, A., 'Le mythe de la nouvelle Jérusalem du Deutéro-Ésaïe à la IIIe Sibylle', *R.H.P.R.* (1938), 377–414.

'De la Jérusalem terrestre à la Jérusalem céleste', *R.H.P.R.* (1947), 12ff.

Cerfaux, L., *The Church in the Theology of St. Paul*, trans. G. Webb and A. Walker (New York, 1969).

'La Connaissance des Secrets du Royaume d'après Matt. xiii: 11 et Parallèles', *N.T.S.* 2 (1955–6), 238–49.

Chadwick, H., 'St Paul and Philo of Alexandria', *B.J.R.L.* 48 (1965–6), 286–307.

Cody, A., *Heavenly Sanctuary and Liturgy in the Epistle to the Hebrews: the Achievement of Salvation in the Epistle's Perspectives* (St. Meinrad, Indiana, 1960).

Colwell, E. C., 'A Definite Rule for the Use of the Article in the Greek New Testament', *J.B.L.* 52 (1933), 12ff.

Cole, A., *The New Temple: A Study in the Origins of the Catechetical 'Form' of the Church in the New Testament* (London, 1950).

Colpe, C. *Die Religionsgeschichtlicheschule, F.R.L.A.N.T.*, Neue Folge, 60 (Göttingen, 1961).

Conzelmann, H., 'Die Mutter der Weisheit,' *Zeit und Geschichte*, ed. E. Dinkler and H. Thyen (Tübingen, 1964), 225–34.

The Theology of Luke (New York, 1960).

An Outline of the Theology of the New Testament (New York, 1969).

'Paulus und die Weisheit', *N.T.S.* 12 (1965–6), 231–44.

Craddock, F. B., *The Pre-existence of Christ in the New Testament* (Nashville and New York, 1968).

'All Things in Him: a Critical Note on Col. 1: 15–20', *N.T.S.* 12 (1965–6), 78–80.

Cross, F. M., *The Ancient Library of Qumran* (New York, 1961).

Cullmann, O., *The Christology of the New Testament*, trans. S. C. Guthrie and C. A. M. Hall (Philadelphia, 1959).

Christ and Time: The Primitive Christian Conception of Time and History, rev. ed. with a new introductory chapter (London, 1962).

'L'Opposition contre le temple de Jérusalem: motif commun de la théologie johannique et du monde ambiant', *N.T.S.* 5 (1958–9), 157–73.

'Functional Christology: A Reply', *Theology Digest* x (1962), 216ff.

Davies, W. D., *Paul and Rabbinic Judaism, Some Rabbinic Elements in Pauline Theology*, 2 (London, 1955).

'Reflexions on Tradition: The Aboth Revisited', in *Christian History and Interpretation*, Studies presented to John Knox, ed. W. R. Farmer, C. F. D. Moule, R. R. Niebuhr (Cambridge, 1967).

The Setting of the Sermon on the Mount (Cambridge, 1964).

Invitation to the New Testament (New York, 1966).

Christian Origins and Judaism (Philadelphia, 1962).

'The Jewish State in the Hellenistic World', *Peake's Commentary on the Bible*, ed. M. Black and H. H. Rowley (London and New York, 1962).

'Contemporary Jewish Religion', *Peake's Commentary on the Bible*, ed. M. Black and H. H. Rowley (London and New York, 1962).

'A Note on Josephus, Antiquities 15: 136', *H.T.R.* xlvii (1954), 135–40.

ed. Davies, W. D. and D. Daube, *The Background of the New Testa-*

ment and its Eschatology, In honour of Charles Harold Dodd (Cambridge, 1964).

Delling, G., *Das Zeitverständnis des Neuen Testaments* (Gütersloh, 1940).

Denis, A. M., 'La Fonction apostolique et la liturgie nouvelle en esprit: Étude thématique des métaphores pauliniennes du culte nouveau', *R.S.P.T.* XLII (1958), 401–36, 617–56.

Dibelius, M., *An die Thessalonicher I, II, An die Philipper*, zweite, völlig neu bearbeitete Auflage, *H.N.T.* 11 (Tübingen, 1925).

An die Kolosser, Epheser, an Philemon, zweite, völlig neu bearbeitete Auflage, *H.N.T.* 12 (Tübingen, 1927).

Die Pastoralbriefe, Dritte Auflage neu bearbeitet von Hans Conzelmann, *H.N.T.* 13 (Tübingen, 1955).

Dieterich, A., *Eine Mithrasliturgie* (Darmstadt, 1966).

ed. Dinkler, E., *Zeit und Geschichte, Dankesgabe an Rudolf Bultmann, zum 80 Geburtstag* im Aufträge der Alten Marburger und in Zusammenarbeit mit Hartwig Thyen (Tübingen, 1964).

Dodd, C. H., *The Epistle of Paul to the Romans*, The Moffatt New Testament Commentary (Fontana Books, London, 1959).

The Bible and the Greeks (London, 1935).

According to the Scriptures; the substructure of New Testament Theology (London, 1952).

The Interpretation of the Fourth Gospel (Cambridge, 1960).

Historical Tradition in the Fourth Gospel (Cambridge, 1963).

Eichrodt, W., 'Heilserfahrung und Zeitverständnis im Alten Testament', *T.Z.* XIII (1956), 103–25.

Eliade, M., *The Myth of the Eternal Return*, trans. W. R. Trask (New York, 1954).

Cosmos and History, the Myth of the Eternal Return (New York, 1959).

The Sacred and the Profane, the Nature of Religion (New York, 1959).

Eltester, F. W., *Eikon im Neuen Testament*, Beihefte zur *Z.N.W.* (Berlin, 1958).

ed. W. Eltester and F. H. Kettler, *Apophoreta, Festschrift für E. Haenchen* (Berlin, 1964).

Emerton, J. A., 'The Origin of the Son of Man Imagery', *J.T.S.* N.S. IX (1958), 225–42.

ed. Farmer, W. R., C. F. D. Moule, and R. R. Niebuhr, *Christian History and Interpretation*, Studies presented to John Knox (Cambridge, 1967).

Feuillet, A., *Le Christ Sagesse de Dieu d'après les Épîtres Pauliniennes*, Études Bibliques (Paris, 1966).

Fitzmeyer, J. A., 'Further Light on Melchizedek from Qumran Cave 11', *J.B.L.* 86 (1967), 25–41.

Fortna, R., *The Gospel of Signs, S.N.T.S.* Monograph 11 (Cambridge, 1969).

Fraeyman, M., 'La spiritualisation de l'idée du temple dans les Épîtres pauliniennes', *Ephem. Theol. Lov.* XXIII (1947), 378–412.

Freed, E. D., 'The Son of Man in the Fourth Gospel', *J.B.L.* 86 (1967), 402–9.

Freedman, H., *Genesis in 2 vols, Midrash Rabbah*, London 1939.

Friedrich, G., 'Das Lied vom Hohenpriester in Zusammenhang von Hebr. 4: 4 – 5: 10', *T. Z.* 18 (Basel, 1962), 95–115.

'Ein Tauflied hellenistischer Judenchristen (I Thess. 1: 9ff.)', *T.Z.* 21/6 (1965), 502–16.

Fuller, R. H., *The Foundations of New Testament Christology* (New York, 1965).

Gabathuler, H. J., *Jesus Christus, Haupt der Kirche–Haupt der Welt; Der Christus-Hymnus Kol. 1: 15–20 in der theologischen Forschung der letzten 130 Jahre*, *Ab.T.A.N.T.* 45 (Zürich, 1965).

Gärtner, B., *The Temple and the Community in Qumran and the New Testament*, *S.N.T.S.* Monograph Series 1 (Cambridge, 1965).

Gemser, B., *Spruche Salomonis* (Tübingen, 1963).

Georgi, D., *Die Gegner des Paulus im 2 Korintherbrief: Studien zur religiösen Propaganda in der Spätantike*, *W.M.A.N.T.* 11 (Neukirchen/Vlyn, 1964).

'Der vorpaulinische Hymnus Phil. 2: 6–11', *Zeit und Geschichte, Dankesgabe an Rudolf Bultmann zum 80 Geburtstag*, ed. E. Dinkler (Tübingen, 1964).

Goldberg, A. M., *Untersuchungen über die Vorstellung von der Schekhinah in der frühen rabbinischen Literatur* (Berlin, 1969).

Goldschmidt, L., *Der Babylonische Talmud mit Einschluss der vollstaendigen Mishnah* (Berlin, 1901).

Goodenough, E. R., *By Light, Light; the Mystic Gospel of Hellenistic Judaism* (New Haven, 1935).

Grillmeier, A., 'The Figure of Christ in Catholic Theology Today', in *Theology Today*, Vol. 1, Renewal in Dogma, trans. P. White and R. H. Kelly, ed. J. Feiner et al. (Milwaukee, 1965).

Gundry, R. H., 'Verba Christi in I Peter: their implications concerning the authorship of I Peter and the Authenticity of the Gospel Tradition', *N.T.S.* XIII (1966–7), 336–50.

Guttgemanns, E., Review of *Die Gegner des Paulus im 2 Korintherbrief*, *Zeitschrift für Kirchengeschichte* XV (Vierte Folge), LXXVII. Band (1966), 126–31.

Haenchen, E., *Die Apostelgeschichte*, Meyers Kommentar (Göttingen, 1961).

Gott und Mensch, Gesammelte Aufsätze (Tübingen, 1965).

'Probleme des johanneischen Prologs', *Z.T.K.* 6 (1963), 305–34.

Hahn, F., *The Titles of Jesus in Christology, their History in Early Christianity*, trans. H. Knight, G. Ogg (New York, 1969).

Hamerton-Kelly, R. G., 'A Note on Matt. 12: 28 par. Luke 11: 20', *N.T.S.* 11 (1964–5), 67–9.

'The Temple and the Origins of Jewish Apocalyptic', *V.T.* xx (1970), 1–15.

Haran, Menahem, 'Shiloh and Jerusalem: The Origin of the Priestly Tradition in the Pentateuch', *J.B.L.* 81 (1962), 14–24.

Harnack, A., *Lehrbuch der Dogmengeschichte*, Vol. 1, 2nd ed. (Freiburg i. B., 1888).

Haufe, G., 'Das Menschensohn-Problem in der gegenwärtigen wissenschaftlichen Diskussion', *Ev. T.* 26 (1966), 130–41.

Hegermann, H., *Die Vorstellung vom Schöpfungsmittler im hellenistischen Judentum und Urchristentum*, *T.U.* 82 (Berlin, 1961).

Héring, J., *La Première Épître de saint Paul aux Corinthiens*, *C.N.T.* vii (Neuchâtel and Paris, 1949).

La Seconde Épître de saint Paul aux Corinthiens (Neuchâtel and Paris, 1958).

Higgins, A. J. B., *Jesus and the Son of Man* (London, 1964).

'The Priestly Messiah', *N.T.S.* 13 (1966–7), 211–39.

Hooker, M. D., *The Son of Man in Mark* (Montreal, 1967).

Isaksson, A., *Marriage and Ministry in the New Temple: A Study with special reference to Matt. 19: 3–12 and I Cor. 11: 3–16*, Acta Seminarii Neotestamentici Upsaliensis xxiv (Lund, 1965).

Jansen, H. L., *Die Henochgestalt – eine vergleichende religionsgeschichtliche Untersuchung* (Oslo, 1939).

Jeremias, J., *The Parables of Jesus* (New York, 1963).

Abba, Studien zur neutestamentlichen Theologie und Zeitgeschichte (Göttingen, 1966).

'Zu Phil. 2: 7, "ΕΑΥΤΟΝ ΕΚΕΝѠΣΕΝ"', *Nov. Test.* 6 (1963), 182–8.

'Zum Logos-Problem', *Z.N.W.* 59 (1968), 82–5.

Jervell, J., *Imago Dei, Gen. 1: 26ff. im Spätjudentum, in der Gnosis und in den paulinischen Briefen*, *F.R.L.A.N.T.* 76 (Göttingen, 1960).

Johnson, M. D., *The Purpose of the Biblical Genealogies*, *S.N.T.S.* Monograph Series 8 (Cambridge, 1969).

de Jonge, M. and A. S. van der Woude, '11 Q Melchizedek and the New Testament', *N.T.S.* 12 (1965–6), 301–26.

Jüngel, E., *Paulus und Jesus: Eine Untersuchung zur Präzisierung der Frage nach dem Ursprung der Christologie*, Hermeneutische Untersuchungen zur Theologie 2 (Tübingen, 1964).

Kaesemann, E., *Das wandernde Gottesvolk*, *F.R.L.A.N.T.* 55 (Göttingen, 1959).

Jesu Letzter Wille Nach Johannes 17, trans. G. Krodel, *The Testament of Jesus* (Philadelphia, 1968) (Tübingen, 1967).

Exegetische Versuche und Besinnungen, 2 vols in one (Tübingen, 1964).

New Testament Questions of Today, trans. W. J. Montague (Philadelphia, 1969).

Kayatz, C., *Studien zu Proverbien 1–9, Eine form- und motivgeschichtliche Untersuchung unter Einbeziehung Aegyptischen Vergleichsmaterials, W.M.A.N.T.* 22 (Neukirchen/Vlyn, 1966).

Kelly, J. N. D., *A Commentary on the Pastoral Epistles, I Timothy, II Timothy, Titus*, Harper's New Testament Commentaries (New York, 1963).

Kingsbury, J. D., *The Parables of Jesus in Matt. 13* (Richmond, 1969).

Kistemaker, S., *The Psalm Citations in the Epistle to the Hebrews* (Amsterdam, 1961).

ed. Kittel, G. and G. Friedrich, *Theological Dictionary of the New Testament*, trans. G. W. Bromiley (6 vols., Grand Rapids, 1964–8).

Knox, J., *Christ the Lord; the meaning of Jesus in the Early Church* (Chicago, 1945).

The Death of Christ; the Cross in New Testament History and Faith (New York, 1958).

Knox, W. L., *St. Paul and the Church of the Gentiles* (Cambridge, 1939).

'The Divine Wisdom', *J.T.S.* XXXVIII (1938), 230–7.

von Korvin-Krasinski, C., 'Die heilige Stadt', *Z.R.G.G.* XVI (1964), 265–71.

Kosmala, H., *Hebräer–Essener–Christen, Studien zur Vorgeschichte der frühchristlichen Verkündigung*, S.P.B. 1 (Leiden, 1959).

Köster, H., Review of *Weisheit und Torheit, Gnomon*, 33 (1961), 590–5.

'Hypostasis in the Epistle to the Hebrews', Abstract in *Abstracts of Papers, Society of Biblical Literature, ninety-ninth meeting* (New York, 1963), 12.

'One Jesus and Four Primitive Gospels', *H.T.R.* 61 (1968), 203–47.

Kuhn, H. W., *Enderwartung und gegenwärtiges Heil: Untersuchungen zu der Gemeindeliedern von Qumran*, S.U.N.T. 4 (Göttingen, 1966).

Kuhn, K. G., 'Der Epheserbrief im Lichte der Qumrantexte', *N.T.S.* 7 (1960–1), 334–46.

Kümmel, W. G., *Promise and Fulfilment, the Eschatological Message of Jesus* (Naperville, 1957).

Leaney, A. R. C., 'I Peter and the Passover: An Interpretation', *N.T.S.* x (1963–4), 238–51.

Lebreton, J., *Histoire du Dogme de la Trinité des origines au Concile de Nicée*, Vol. 1 (Paris, 1927).

Leenhardt, F. J., *L'Épître de Saint Paul aux Romains, Comm. du N.T.* VI (Neuchâtel/Paris, 1957).

Le Guillou, M. J., *Christ and the Church, A Theology of the Mystery*, trans. C. E. Schaldenbrand (New York, 1966).

Lichtenstein, E., 'Die älteste christliche Glaubensformel', *Z.K.G.* 63 (1950–1), 1–74.

Lietzmann, H., *An die Korinther I/II*, Vierte von Werner Georg Kümmel ergänzte Auflage, *H.N.T.* 9 (Tübingen, 1949).

Lightfoot, J. B., *Saint Paul's Epistles to the Colossians and to Philemon*, A Revised Text with Introductions, Notes and Dissertations (London, 1916).

Lindars, B., *New Testament Apologetic* (Philadelphia, 1961).

Lohmeyer, E., *Der Brief an die Philipper*, Übersetzt und erklärt von...Nach dem Handexemplar des Verfassers durchgesehene Ausgabe. Meyers Kommentar ix. 1, 11th ed. (Göttingen, 1956).

Das Evangelium des Markus (Göttingen, 1959).

Mack, B. L., 'Logos und Sophia; Untersuchungen zur Weisheitstheologie im hellenistischen Judentum', Unpublished dissertation (Göttingen, 1967).

Malevez, L., 'Functional Christology in the New Testament', *Theology Digest* x (1962), 77–83.

Manson, T. W., 'The Son of Man in Daniel, Enoch and the Gospels', (1949), in *Studies in the Gospels and Epistles by T. W. Manson*, ed. M. Black (Philadelphia, 1962), 123–45.

'Some Reflections on Apocalyptic', in *Aux Sources de la Tradition Chrétienne: Mélanges offerts à M. M. Goguel* (Paris, 1950), 139ff.

'The Argument from Prophecy', *J.T.S.* 46 (1945), 129–36.

Marcus, R., 'The Phrase Hokmat Yewanit', *J.N.E.S.* 13 (1954), 86.

Marlow, R., 'The Son of Man in Recent Journal Literature', *C.B.Q.* 28 (1966), 20–30.

Marsh, J., *The Fulness of Time* (New York, 1962).

Marshall, I. H., 'The Synoptic Son of Man Sayings in Recent Discussion', *N.T.S.* 12 (1965–6), 327–51.

Martin, R. P., *Carmen Christi: Philippians 2: 5–11 in Recent Interpretation and in the Setting of Early Christian Worship*, *S.N.T.S.* Monograph Series 4 (Cambridge, 1967).

Martyn, J. L., *History and Theology in the Fourth Gospel* (New York, 1968).

Masson, C., *L'Épître de Saint Paul aux Éphésiens*, Comm. du N.T. ix (Neuchâtel/Paris, 1953).

Les Deux Épîtres de Saint Paul aux Thessaloniciens, Comm. du N.T. xia (Neuchâtel/Paris, 1957).

ed. Matthias, W., *Libertas Christiana, Frederik Delekat zum 65 Geburtstag* (München, 1957).

Meeks, W. A., *The Prophet-King; Moses traditions and the Johannine Christology*, Supplements to Novum Testamentum xiv (Leiden, 1967).

Michel, O., *Der Brief an die Römer*, Übersetzt und erklärt von...12

neubearbeitete und erweiterte Auflage. Meyers Kommentar IV (Göttingen, 1963).

Minear, P., *I Saw a New Earth: an Introduction to the Visions of the Apocalypse* (Washington, D.C., 1969).

'Ontology and Ecclesiology in the Apocalypse', *N.T.S.* 12 (1965–6), 89–105.

Montefiore, H. M., *A Commentary on the Epistle to the Hebrews* (New York, 1964).

Morgenstern, J., 'The Son of Man of Dan. 7: 13ff.; A New Interpretation', *J.B.L.* 80 (1961), 65–77.

Moule, C. F. D., *The Epistles of Paul the Apostle to the Colossians and to Philemon*, Cambridge Greek Testament Commentary (Cambridge, 1957).

An Idiom Book of New Testament Greek (Cambridge, 1960).

'The Nature and Purpose of I Peter', *N.T.S.* 3, 1 (1956–7), 4.

'St Paul and Dualism: The Pauline Conception of Resurrection', *N.T.S.* 13 (1965–6), 106–23.

Muilenburg, J., 'The Son of Man in Daniel and the Ethiopic Apocalypse of Enoch', *J.B.L.* 79 (1960), 197–209.

Müller, W., *Die Heilige Stadt, Roma quadrata, himmlisches Jerusalem, und die Mythe vom Weltnabel* (Stuttgart, 1961).

Munck, J., *Paul and the Salvation of Mankind* (Richmond, Va., 1959).

Nikolainen, Aimo T., 'Der Kirchenbegriff in der Offenbarung des Johannes', *N.T.S.* XI (1962–3), 351–61.

Norden, E., *Agnostos Theos: Untersuchungen zur Formgeschichte religiöser Rede* (Leipzig and Berlin, 1913).

Noth, M., *Überlieferungsgeschichtliche Studien: Die sammelnden und bearbeitenden Geschichtswerke im Alten Testament*, 1943, 2nd ed. (Tübingen, 1957).

Überlieferungsgeschichte des Pentateuch (Stuttgart, 1948).

Odeberg, H., *III Enoch, or the Hebrew Book of Enoch* (Cambridge, 1928).

The View of the Universe in the Epistle to the Ephesians (Lund, 1934).

Oepke, A., *Der Brief des Paulus an die Galater*, Zweite, verbesserte Auflage, *T.H.N.T.* IX (Berlin, 1957).

Otto, R., *The Kingdom of God and the Son of Man*, trans. Floyd V. Filson and B. Lee-Wolf (London, 1938).

The Idea of the Holy (London, 1959).

Pannenberg, W., *Theology and the Kingdom of God* (Philadelphia, 1969).

Pascher, J., Η ΒΑΣΙΛΙΚΗ ΟΔΟΣ. *Der Königsweg zu Wiedergeburt und Vergottung bei Philon von Alexandreia*, Studien zur Geschichte und Kultur des Altertums, Vol. VII/3–4 (Paderborn, 1931).

Pearson, B., 'The pneumatikos–psychikos Terminology in I Corinthians: A Study in the Theology of the Corinthian Opponents of Paul and its Relation to Gnosticism', Abstract in *H.T.R.* 61 (1968), 646–7.

Percy, E., *Die Probleme der Kolosser- und Epheserbriefe* (Lund, 1946).

Perrin, N., *The Kingdom of God in the Teaching of Jesus* (Philadelphia, 1963).

Rediscovering the Teaching of Jesus (New York, 1967).

Peterson, E., 'La Libération d'Adam de l'Ananké', *R.B.* 55 (1948), 199–214.

Pfammatter, J., *Die Kirche als Bau, Eine exegetisch-theologische Studie zur Ekklesiologie der Paulusbriefe*, Anal. Gregor. 110 (Rome, 1961).

Pittenger, W. N., *The Word Incarnate* (New York, 1959).

Plummer, A., *A Critical and Exegetical Commentary on the Second Epistle of St. Paul to the Corinthians*, International Critical Commentary (New York, 1915).

Preisendanz, K., *Papyri Graecae Magicae* (Leipzig, 1928).

Prümm, K., 'Zur neutestamentlichen Gnosis-problematik, Gnostischer Hintergrund und Lehreinschlag in den beiden Eingangskapiteln von I Kor.?' *Z.K.T.* 87 (1965), 399–442; *Z.T.K.* 88 (1966), 1–50.

Quispel, G., 'The Gospel of Thomas and the Gospel of the Hebrews', *N.T.S.* 12 (1965–6), 371–82.

Reicke, B., *The Disobedient Spirits and Christian Baptism* (Copenhagen, 1946).

Reitzenstein, R., *Die hellenistischen Mysterienreligionen, ihre Grundgedanken und Wirkungen* (Leipzig, 1927).

Rigaux, B., 'Révélation des Mystères et Perfection à Qumran et dans le Nouveau Testament', *N.T.S.* 4 (1957–8), 237–62.

Ringgren, H., *Word and Wisdom: Studies in the Hypostatization of Divine Qualities and Functions in the Ancient Near East* (Lund, 1947).

Robertson, A., and A. Plummer, *A Critical and Exegetical Commentary on the First Epistle of St. Paul to the Corinthians*, 2nd ed., International Critical Commentary (Edinburgh, 1914).

Robinson, J. M., *The Problem of History in Mark* (London, 1957).

The New Quest of the Historical Jesus (Naperville, 1959).

'A Formal Analysis of Colossians 1: 15–20', *J.B.L.* 76 (1957), 270–87.

'Recent Research in the Fourth Gospel', *J.B.L.*, 78 (1959), 242–52.

'Basic Shifts in German Theology', *Interpretation*, 16 (1962), 76–97.

Rost, L., 'Zur Deutung des Menschensohnes in Daniel 7', in *Gott und die Götter, Festgabe für Erich Fascher* (Berlin, 1958).

Ruckstuhl, E., *Die literarische Einheit des Johannesevangelium* (Freiburg in der Schweiz [Fribourg], 1951).

Sanday, W., and A. Headlam, *A Critical and Exegetical Commentary on The Epistle to the Romans*, International Critical Commentary, 5th ed. (Edinburgh, 1902).

Sanders, J. A., 'Dissenting Deities and Philippians 2: 1–11', *J.B.L.* 88 (1969), 279–90.

Schencke, W., *Die Chokma (Sophia) in den jüdischen Hypostasenspekulation* (Kristiania, 1913).

Schierse, F. J., *Verheissung und Heilsvollendung, Zur theologischen Grundfrage des Hebräerbriefes*, Münchener Theologische Studien 1, Historische Abteilung 9. Band (Munich, 1955).

Schille, G., 'Erwägungen zur Hohepriesterlehre des Hebräerbriefes', *Z.N.W.* 64 (1955), 81–109.

Schlier, H., *Der Brief an die Epheser, Ein Kommentar*, 2. durchgesehene Auflage (Düsseldorf, 1958).

Der Brief an die Galater, Übersetzt und erklärt von... 12, neubearbeitete Auflage, Meyers Kommentar VII (Göttingen, 1962).

ed. Schmidt, H., *Eucharisterion: Studien zur Religion und Literatur des Alten und Neuen Testaments für Hermann Gunkel*, *F.R.L.A.N.T.* Neue Folge 19 (2 vols., Göttingen, 1923).

Schmithals, W., *Die Gnosis in Korinth – Eine Untersuchung zu den Korintherbriefen*, 2 neubearbeitete Auflage, *F.R.L.A.N.T.* 66 N.F. 48 (Göttingen, 1965).

Schnackenburg, R., *The Gospel according to St. John*, trans. K. Smyth, Vol. 1 (New York, 1968).

'Der Menschensohn im Johannesevangelium', *N.T.S.* 11 (1964–5), 123–37.

'Logos-Hymnus und johanneischen Prolog', *B.Z.* 1 (1957), 69–109.

ed. Schneemelcher, W., *Edgar Hennecke, New Testament Apocrypha*, English translation ed. by R. McL. Wilson (Philadelphia Vol. 1, 1963, Vol. II, 1965).

Festschrift für Günther Dehn (Neukirchen, 1957).

Scholem, G. G., *Major Trends in Jewish Mysticism* (Jerusalem, 1941).

Schreiner, J., *Zion-Jerusalem*, Studien zur Alten und Neuen Testaments (München, 1964).

Schulz, S., *Untersuchungen zur Menschensohn-Christologie im Johannesevangelium* (Göttingen, 1957).

Schwartz, E., *Aporien im 4. Evangelium* (Göttingen, 1908).

Schweitzer, A., *The Mysticism of Paul the Apostle*, trans. W. Montgomery (London, 1931).

Schweizer, E., *Ego Eimi* (Göttingen, 1939).

Lordship and Discipleship, *S.B.T.* 28 (Naperville and London, 1960).

Erniedrigung und Erhöhung bei Jesu und seinen Nachfolgern, *Ab.T.A.N.T* 28, 2nd ed. (Zürich, 1962).

Neotestamentica, Deutsche und englische Aufsätze 1951–63, German and English Essays, 1951–3 (Zürich/Stuttgart, 1963).

'Der Menschensohn', *Z.N.W.* 50 (1959), 185–209.

'Son of Man', *J.B.L.* 79 (1960), 119–29.

'The Son of Man Again', *N.T.S.* 9 (1962–3), 256–61.

'Zum religionsgeschichtlichen Hintergrund der "Sendungsformel" Gal. iv. 4ff., Röm. viii. 3ff., Joh. iii. 16ff.', *Z.N.W.* LVII (1966), 199–210.

'Dying and Rising with Christ', *N.T.S.* 14 (1967–8), 1–14.

Scott, E. F., *The Pastoral Epistles*, The Moffatt New Testament Commentary (New York and London, undated).

Scroggs, R., *The Last Adam, A Study in Pauline Anthropology* (Philadelphia, 1966).

'Paul, ΣΟΦΟΣ and ΠΝΕΥΜΑΤΙΚΟΣ', *N.T.S.* 14 (1967–8), 33–55.

Selwyn, E., *The First Epistle of St. Peter* (London, 1947).

Sjöberg, E., *Der verborgene Menschensohn in den Evangelien*, Acta Reg. Societatis Humaniorum Litterarum Lundensis, LIII (Lund, 1955).

Smalley, S. S., 'The Johannine Son of Man Sayings', *N.T.S.* 15 (1968–9), 278–301.

Smith, D. M., *The Composition and Order of the Fourth Gospel; Bultmann's Literary Theory* (New Haven and London, 1965).

Spicq, C., 'L'Épître aux Hébreux', *Rev. Q.* 1 (1959), 365ff.

L'Épître aux Hébreux (2 vols., Paris, 1953).

Steck, O. H., *Israel und das gewaltsame Geschick der Propheten*, *W.M.A.N.T.* 23 (Neukirchen, 1967).

Stendahl, K., *The School of St. Matthew and its use of the Old Testament*, with a New Introduction by the Author (Philadelphia, 1969, first published 1954).

Strack, H. L. and P. Billerbeck, *Kommentar zum Neuen Testament aus Talmud und Midrasch* (6 vols., München, 1926–61).

Strecker, G., *Der Weg der Gerechtigkeit, Untersuchung zur Theologie des Matthäus*, *F.R.L.A.N.T.* 82 (Göttingen, 1962).

'Redaktion und Tradition im Christushymnus Phil. 2: 6–11', *Z.N.W.* 55 (1964), 63–78.

Suggs, M. J., *Wisdom, Christology and Law in Matthew's Gospel* (Cambridge, Mass., 1970).

'Wisdom of Solomon 2: 10–5: A Homily Based on the Fourth Servant Song', *J.B.L.* 76 (1957), 26–33.

Talbert, C. H., 'The Problem of Pre-existence in Philippians 2: 6–11', *J.B.L.*, 86 (1967), 141–53.

Taylor, V., *The Gospel According to St. Mark* (London, 1957).

Teeple, H. M., 'Methodology in the Source Analysis of the Fourth Gospel', *J.B.L.* 81 (1962), 279–86.

Thornton, T. C. G., 'I Peter, A Paschal Liturgy?' *J.T.S.* N.S. 12 (1961), 15ff.

Thrall, M., 'Elijah and Moses in Mark's account of the Transfiguration', *N.T.S.* 16 (1969–70), 305–17.

Tillich, P., *Biblical Religion and the Search for Ultimate Reality* (Chicago, 1963).

Tödt, H. E., *The Son of Man in the Synoptic Tradition*, trans. Dorothea Barton (Philadelphia, 1965).

van Unnik, W. C., 'The Teaching of Good Works in I Peter', *N.T.S.* 1 (1954–5), 92–110.

'A Formula describing Prophecy', *N.T.S.* 9 (1962–3), 86–94.

Vermes, G., *Scripture and Tradition in Judaism, Haggadic Studies*, Studia Post-Biblica IV (Leiden, 1961).

Vielhauer, P., 'Ein Weg der neutestamentlichen Theologie? Prüfung der Thesen Ferdinand Hahns', *Ev.T.* 25 (1965), 24–72.

'Jesus und die Menschensohn', *Z.T.K.* 60 (1963), 133–77.

Oikodome (Karlsruhe, 1940).

Wächter, L., 'Der Einfluss platonischen Denkens auf rabbinische Schöpfungsspekulationen' *Z.R.G.G.* XIV (1962), 36–56.

Weiss, K., 'Paulus – Priester der christlichen Kultgemeinde', *T.L.Z.* 79 (1954), 355–64.

Wendland, P., *Hippolytus Werke, III Refutatio Omnium Haeresium*, G.C.S. (Leipzig, 1916).

Wenschkewitz, H., *Die Spiritualisierung der Kultusbegriffe: Tempel, Priester und Opfer, im Neuen Testament* (*Angelos*, Archiv für neutestamentliche Zeitgeschichte und Kulturkunde, Beiheft 4) (Leipzig, 1932).

Wilckens, U., *Weisheit und Torheit; Eine exegetisch-religionsgeschichtliche Untersuchung zu I Kor. 1 und 2, B.H.T.* 26 (Tübingen, 1959).

Wilkens, W., 'Die Redaktion des Gleichniskapitels Mark 4 durch Matth.', *T.Z.* 20 (1964), 305–27.

van der Woude, 'Melchisedek als himmlische Erlösergestalt in der Neugefunden eschatologischen Midraschim aus Qumran-Höhle XI', *Oudtestamentische Studien*, 14 (1965), 354–73.

Wrede, W., *Das Messiasgeheimnis in den Evangelien* (Göttingen, 1963, first published 1901, reprinted unchanged).

Wuellner, W., 'Haggadic Homily Genre in I Corinthians 1–3', *J.B.L.* 89 (1970), 199–204.

Yadin, Y., 'The Dead Sea Scrolls and the Epistle to the Hebrews', *Scripta Hierosolymitana* IV (1958), 36–55.

Zuntz, G., *The Text of the Epistles* (London, 1953).

INDEX OF AUTHORS

INDEX OF PASSAGES CITED

A. OLD TESTAMENT

B. APOCRYPHA AND PSEUDEPIGRAPHA

C. DEAD SEA SCROLLS

D. RABBINIC

E. PHILO

F. OTHERS

G. NEW TESTAMENT